INSIDER TRADING

As long as insider trading has existed, people have been fixated on it. Newspapers give it front-page coverage. Cult movies romanticize it. Politicians make or break careers by pillorying, enforcing, and sometimes engaging in it. But, oddly, no one seems to know what's really wrong with insider trading, or – because Congress has never defined it – exactly what it is. This confluence of vehemence and confusion has led to a dysfunctional enforcement regime in the United States that runs counter to its stated goals of efficiency and fairness. In this illuminating book, John P. Anderson summarizes the current state of insider trading law in the United States and around the globe. After engaging in a thorough analysis of the practice of insider trading from the normative standpoints of economic efficiency, moral right and wrong, and virtue theory, he offers concrete proposals for much-needed reform.

JOHN P. ANDERSON is a professor at the Mississippi College School of Law. He practiced in the areas of securities enforcement and white collar criminal law at the Washington, DC law firms of Eversheds Sutherland and Wilmer Cutler Pickering Hale & Dorr before entering academia. Anderson has won numerous teaching awards and has published several articles in top law reviews and peer review journals on the topics of insider trading, legal and political philosophy, and business ethics. He received a PhD in philosophy and a JD from the University of Virginia, and a BA in philosophy from the University of California, Berkeley.

Insider Trading

LAW, ETHICS, AND REFORM

JOHN P. ANDERSON
Mississippi College School of Law

CAMBRIDGE
UNIVERSITY PRESS

University Printing House, Cambridge CB2 8BS, United Kingdom

One Liberty Plaza, 20th Floor, New York, NY 10006, USA

477 Williamstown Road, Port Melbourne, VIC 3207, Australia

314–321, 3rd Floor, Plot 3, Splendor Forum, Jasola District Centre, New Delhi – 110025, India

79 Anson Road, #06–04/06, Singapore 079906

Cambridge University Press is part of the University of Cambridge.

It furthers the University's mission by disseminating knowledge in the pursuit of education, learning, and research at the highest international levels of excellence.

www.cambridge.org
Information on this title: www.cambridge.org/9781107149199
DOI: 10.1017/9781316568811

© John P. Anderson 2018

First published 2018

Printed in the United States of America by Sheridan Books, Inc.

A catalogue record for this publication is available from the British Library.

Library of Congress Cataloging-in-Publication Data
NAMES: Anderson, John P., 1971– author.
TITLE: Insider trading : law, ethics, and reform / John P. Anderson.
DESCRIPTION: Cambridge [UK] ; New York, NY : Cambridge University Press, 2018.
IDENTIFIERS: LCCN 2018008151| ISBN 9781107149199 (hardback) |
ISBN 9781316603406 (paperback)
SUBJECTS: LCSH: Insider trading in securities–Law and legislation–United States. |
Insider trading in securities–Law and legislation. | Law reform.
CLASSIFICATION: LCC KF1073.15 A95 2018 | DDC 345.73/0268–dc23
LC record available at https://lccn.loc.gov/2018008151

ISBN 978-1-107-14919-9 Hardback
ISBN 978-1-316-60340-6 Paperback

For Jaime, Peyton, Brendan, and Cosette

Contents

Acknowledgments

I earned a PhD in philosophy before I earned a law degree. The philosopher in me was immediately drawn to securities enforcement and especially insider trading cases during my seven years of practice. I was troubled by the lack of statutory or common law guidance for well-meaning traders who wanted to succeed at their difficult and highly competitive jobs while staying on the right side of the law. And, like many others, I also struggled to understand the moral and economic justifications for the prohibition of insider trading. Why were prosecutors seeking such stiff sentences and penalties for conduct that resulted in no obvious harm, and that no one could (or was willing to) define with precision? This problem continued to nag me when I left the practice of law and entered academia. I intended to write just one article on the subject, but one question just seemed to lead to another. Answering these questions led to many more articles and now to this book.

I am grateful for the help and guidance of many people. First and foremost, I thank Professors Ellen Podgor and Joan MacLeod Heminway. Ellen mentored me through the New Scholars program at the Southeastern Association of Law Schools, where I presented my very first scholarly paper on insider trading. Since then, she has continued to provide invaluable advice and guidance. Joan was so kind as to invite me to join a number of panels and discussion groups as I developed the themes of this book. I have learned so much from her, and from those she introduced me to. I am grateful for the friendship and example of these two brilliant women.

I also thank Professors Afra Afsharipour, Christoph Henkel, George Mocsary, Mark Ramseyer, Kelly Strader, Andrew Verstein, and Andrew Vollmer, each of whom took time out of their very busy schedules to read and comment on parts or all of this book. In addition, I thank Professors Miriam Baer, William Carney, Mihailis Diamantis, Kevin Douglas, Celie Edwards, Gregory Gilchrist, Stuart Green, Mike Guttentag, Randall K. Johnson, the late Henry G. Manne, Eric Posner, Jeanne L. Schroeder, William K. S. Wang, and Masa Yamamoto, all of whom read and commented on articles that provided the foundation for this book. I also thank the

x *Acknowledgments*

following panel and discussion group participants who offered helpful comments as I presented on the topic of insider trading over the last few years: Sara Sun Beale, Bradley Bondi, Michael Borden, Mercer Bullard, Mihailis Diamantis, Lisa Fairfax, Joshua Fershee, Jill Fisch, Will Foster, Franklin Gevurtz, Todd Henderson, Peter Henning, Jeremy Kidd, David Kwok, Donald Langevoort, Craig Lerner, Gerry Moohr, Carol Morgan, Haskell Murray, Donna Nagy, Elizabeth Pollman, Veronica Root, Amanda Rose, Kenneth Rosen, David Rosenfeld, Irma Russell, Bernard Sharfman, Lua Yuille, and Todd Zywicki.

These mentors, colleagues, and wise advisors have not always agreed with what I have to say about the problems laid out in this book, nor have they all agreed with the solutions that I propose. They are not responsible for any of the book's flaws, but their support, guidance, and encouragement made the book possible nonetheless.

I would also like to thank my research assistants who have contributed to this book in its various phases: Chelsea Connor, Bethany Gaal, Jhasmine Andrews, Walker Moller, Katie Sanders, Dixie Pond, Thomas Tugwell, Matthew Rich, Laura Barton, and Rita Santibanez. In addition, I thank our librarian, Thomas B. Walter, who worked tirelessly to track down a number of books, articles, and documents in support of this book.

Thanks to the many associations and institutions that hosted presentations in support of this book over the years: the American Association of Law Schools, Southeastern Association of Law Schools, George Mason Antonin Scalia Law School, Houston Law Center, Louisiana State University School of Law, Mercer's Walter F. George School of Law, and Mississippi College School of Law.

Many thanks to my assistant, Brenda Guy, for putting up with me and for putting a smile on my face every day. I am also grateful for the patience and support offered by my wonderful dean, Patricia Bennett, and for my brilliant colleagues not already mentioned, Donald Campbell, Deborah Challener, J. Gordon Christy, Meta Copeland, Lee Hetherington, Judith J. Johnson, Shirley Terry Kennedy, Angela M. Kupenda, J. Larry Lee, Victoria A. Lowery, Phillip L. McIntosh, Richard V. Meyer, Mary Miller, Mark Modak-Truran, Kate Morgan, Alina Ng, David Parker, Mary Largent Purvis, Wendy Scott, Matthew Steffy, Jim Rosenblatt, and Jonathan F. Will.

Thanks to Matt Gallaway and the excellent editorial and marketing staff at Cambridge University Press.

I thank my sister, Kirsten L. Anderson, whom I love very much, who is an excellent lawyer, and who read the entire text of this book and provided very helpful comments and guidance.

Finally, I am so grateful to my beautiful and wonderful wife, Jaime, and to my children, Peyton, Brendan, and Cosette, for supporting me throughout times of doubt, and for doing without a husband and father while I "went up to the office" to work on this book.

Introduction

The "Decade of Greed" was in full swing when Gerald Guterman, a wealthy real estate developer, rented out the entire *Queen Elizabeth II* for his son's bar mitzvah in September 1986. New York City's rich and famous gathered for the event. As the *QE2* pulled into the Hudson River, some guests no doubt gossiped over their champagne about the fact that one of the more celebrated invitees had missed the boat. Then, as James Stewart masterfully described, the guests looked up as a

> helicopter came into view, hovered over the ship, then descended to the sports deck helipad. With the blades still turning, the cockpit door opened, and [Ivan] Boesky, elegantly dressed in a tuxedo and black tie, stepped onto the deck. He flashed a smile and waved as guests laughed and applauded.[1]

The very next day, Boesky – the man who served as the model for Oliver Stone's Gordon Gekko in the iconic Hollywood film *Wall Street*, and who is famous for telling an audience of UC Berkeley Business School students that "greed is healthy" – surrendered to federal agents on charges of insider trading and other financial crimes.

As a former director of enforcement at the Securities and Exchange Commission once noted, "insider trading has a unique hold on the American popular imagination."[2] Newspapers give it front-page coverage. Best-selling books are written about it. Cult movies romanticize and demonize it. Politicians make their careers and fortunes by pillorying, enforcing, and (incidentally) engaging in it. But, oddly, no one seems to have a clear sense of what is wrong with it. As one prominent insider trading scholar once put it, the "short answer to the question of why insider trading is illegal is the one that an exasperated parent is wont to give a misbehaving child:

---

[1] James B. Stewart, *Den of Thieves* (New York: Simon & Schuster Paperbacks, 1991, 2010): 265.
[2] See Laura E. Hughes, "The Impact of Insider Trading on Stock Market Efficiency: A Critique of the Law and Economics Debate and a Cross-Country Comparison," *Temple International & Comparative Law Review* 25 (2009): 488 (quoting Linda Chatman Thomsen).

'Because it is!'"[3] This answer is, however, hardly satisfying to individuals facing more than ten years of prison time for the offense. What is even more perplexing and disturbing is the fact that, since Congress, the SEC, and the courts have failed to define it with specificity, no one seems to have a clear understanding of what insider trading is.

Michael Lewis, the best-selling author of *Liar's Poker*, *The Big Short*, and *Flashboys*, explained in a recent interview that he has "always thought insider trading is a great distraction." According to Lewis, "whenever things go bad on Wall Street, the one thing that prosecutors know how to prosecute is insider trading, so they go looking for insider traders." But, Lewis went on, insider trading "has very little to do with the problems that . . . have led to the [recent] financial crisis."[4] Indeed, in the wake of the 2008 financial crisis, United States Attorney for the Southern District of New York Preet Bharara seemed almost single-minded in his focus on insider trading, achieving a near-perfect conviction rate in more than seventy insider trading cases, with judges in some cases imposing sentences greater than those mandated for violent robbery or rape.[5] This prosecutorial success put Bharara on the cover of *Time* magazine as the man who is "Busting Wall St.,"[6] but it did nothing to address the causes of the financial meltdown that caused so much pain and frustration for "Main Street" America.[7] For some mysterious reason, insider trading regulation has become what Professor Donald Langevoort has termed a "powerful totemic symbol" of the government's championing of the rights of average investors in American securities markets. As such, it has "taken on an expressive value far beyond its economic importance," a value that judges have been "reluctant to undercut."[8] As Professor James Cox once put it, "American jurisprudence abhors insider trading with a fervor reserved for those who scoff at motherhood, apple pie, and baseball."[9]

Given the recent vehemence of insider trading enforcement in the United States, and its symbolic importance for our culture, it is no longer acceptable to leave unanswered the crucial questions of "What is insider trading?," "Why is it wrong?,"

---

[3] Peter Henning, "What's So Bad about Insider Trading?," *The Business Lawyer* 70 (2015): 770–71.

[4] CNBC interview of Michael Lewis, December 6, 2016, https://finance.yahoo.com/video/lewis-insider-trading-great-distraction-183400745.html.

[5] See Charles Gasparino, *Circle of Friends* (New York: Harper Collins, 2013): 155. ("Under the federal guidelines, the maximum sentence for insider trading is nineteen to twenty-four years, while a rapist could get fifteen years to life in prison.")

[6] "This Man Is Busting Wall St.: Prosecutor Preet Bharara Collars the Masters of the Meltdown," *Time* (February 13, 2012), http://content.time.com/time/covers/0,16641,20120213,00.html.

[7] Indeed, "[n]ot a single major financial executive faces jail time for crisis-related crimes. . . . And yet the news of the day is the dramatic rise in cases of insider trading." Gasparino, *Circle of Friends*, 13.

[8] Donald C. Langevoort, "'Fine Distinctions' in the Contemporary Law of Insider Trading," *Columbia Business Law Review* 2013 (2013): 433.

[9] James D. Cox, "Insider Trading and Contracting: A Critical Response to the 'Chicago School'," *Duke Law Journal* 1986 (1986): 628.

and "Whom does it harm?" Uncertainty over these questions has led to a growing consensus that the insider trading enforcement regime in the United States, the oldest in the world, is in need of critical reevaluation and reform.[10]

This book has four principal goals. First, it contextualizes the problems facing insider trading enforcement in the United States by tracing the development of the current law from its historical antecedents, and by comparing it to regulatory regimes in other countries. Second, it argues that the American insider trading enforcement regime is broken. Ambiguity in the law has led to uncertainty for issuers and other market participants. This uncertainty directly impacts shareholder value and unjustly leaves market players at the mercy of prosecutorial caprice. Third, the book sets the stage for intelligent reform by providing a comprehensive answer to the question, "What is wrong with insider trading?" All forms of insider trading currently proscribed by law are tested from the standpoints of economic, moral, and virtue theory. It turns out that while some forms of insider trading are indeed harmful and wrong, one form, issuer-licensed insider trading, is economically beneficial and morally permissible. A key component to fixing the current regime will be to ensure that it proscribes only morally culpable and harmful insider trading. Fourth, the book proposes a concrete path to reform. The final chapter draws upon the historical, empirical, comparative, and normative conclusions reached in previous chapters to shape a comprehensive program for statutory reform that would improve upon the current regime in terms of justice, efficiency, and rationality. The chapter-by-chapter development of these goals proceeds as follows.

Chapter 1 traces the early development of insider trading law from its nineteenth-century state common law origins. These early cases were typically brought as private contract claims concerning face-to-face stock transactions. No uniform approach to insider trading cases had developed by the time of the stock market crash of 1929. A majority of jurisdictions did not recognize a fiduciary or other duty that would preclude senior management from availing themselves of material nonpublic information while trading in their firm's shares. Special facts (such as affirmative misrepresentations or concealment) might give rise to an equitable duty for insiders to disclose information to counterparties in face-to-face transactions, but not over anonymous exchanges. A growing minority of jurisdictions were, however, prepared to recognize a fiduciary duty for senior management to disclose material nonpublic information asymmetries prior to any face-to-face transaction in the firm's shares, but not necessarily when trading over anonymous exchanges. These minority jurisdictions did not, however, recognize trading restrictions for low-level insiders,

---

[10] See J. Kelly Strader, "(Re)Conceptualizing Insider Trading," *Brooklyn Law Review* 80 (2015): 1420–21. ("Recent insider trading enforcement efforts have been unparalleled in their scope and impact, producing the lengthiest insider trading sentences in history and pushing the boundaries of existing law. Largely because of these efforts, insider trading law and policy could well be on the brink of substantial transformation.")

and no jurisdiction imposed civil fines or criminal liability for insider trading prior to the implementation of the federal statutory regime.

Chapter 2 picks up the development of insider trading law in the wake of the market crash of 1929, when the seeds of the modern federal insider trading regulatory regime were planted with the promulgation of the Securities Exchange Act of 1934. The relevant provisions of the Exchange Act failed to reference insider trading (as we understand it today), much less define it as a crime. Congress was simply not concerned about it at the time. The modern insider trading enforcement regime was principally an invention of the Securities and Exchange Commission in the exercise of its authority to implement the general antifraud provisions of the Exchange Act in the early 1960s. The law's subsequent development has been almost entirely a matter of SEC rulemaking and federal common law. It was not until *SEC v. Texas Gulf Sulphur* (1968)[11] that the federal courts recognized insider trading as illegal pursuant to Section 10(b). And the modern insider trading framework was not fully recognized by the US Supreme Court until much later in *United States v. O'Hagan* (1997).[12] The current American insider trading enforcement regime is therefore far from deeply rooted in the nation's history and traditions. The first two chapters paint the picture of an enforcement regime that is very recent in its development and anything but linear in its progression.

Section 10(b) of the Exchange Act is an antifraud provision, and the Supreme Court has made it clear that insider trading liability pursuant to that statute must therefore satisfy the elements of common law fraud. In *O'Hagan*, the Court recognized two theories of Section 10(b) insider trading liability as fraudulent nondisclosure: (1) the classical theory, which covers trading in an issuer's shares by its employees or those closely affiliated with it, and (2) the misappropriation theory, which addresses outsider trading, or trading by persons who are not employees or otherwise affiliated with the issuer (though it can be applied to insiders as well). Liability under either of these theories requires that one seek to benefit from trading on the basis of material nonpublic information in violation of a fiduciary or other similar relation of trust and confidence. Chapter 3, however, identifies an important problem. Neither the SEC nor the courts have offered a clear account of when a "relation of trust and confidence" arises, when information is "material" or "nonpublic," when one has traded "on the basis of" that information, or even the mental state required for Section 10(b) insider trading liability. Worse still, what little guidance the SEC has offered in interpreting these key elements is often at odds with the guidance provided by the federal courts.

Chapter 4 explains how this ambiguity and confusion in the law of insider trading in the United States has yielded a regime that is unjust, incoherent, and irrational. It is unjust because vagueness in the law violates the time-honored "principle of

[11] S.E.C. v. Texas Gulf Sulphur Co., 401 F.2d 833 (1986).
[12] United States v. O'Hagan, 521 U.S. 642 (1997).

legality," which demands that persons be given reasonable notice prior to the imposition of legal sanctions. Uncertainty in the law of insider trading grants regulators and prosecutors vast discretion in defining the scope of liability, leaving even well-meaning market participants with little ex ante certainty concerning the legality of their trading. The insider trading enforcement regime in the United States is incoherent because the SEC and the federal courts continue to explain and justify it by appeal to two irreconcilable theories. The SEC pushes for a parity-of-information or equal-access insider trading regime, while the courts insist that the statutory authority for the regime in Section 10(b) demands that it be based on the fraudulent breach of fiduciary duties. This tension has led to a schizophrenic regime that is both under- and over-inclusive when measured by either model. Finally, the insider trading regime in the United States is irrational because ambiguity and incoherence in the law translate into uncertainty for issuers in the design and implementation of their insider trading compliance programs, which typically leads firms to adopt an overbroad, "play-it-safe" approach. This conservative approach to compliance, however, comes at a heavy price in terms of corporate culture, cost of compensation, and share liquidity. All of these costs have a detrimental effect on shareholder value. Moreover, it will be shown that the broad scope for derivative corporate criminal liability under the current regime sometimes leaves the victims of insider trading liable for the crimes perpetrated against them. For these and other reasons laid out in Chapter 4, the current US insider trading enforcement regime irrationally undermines many of the goals it was intended to promote, and is therefore in need of reform.

Having summarized the current state of insider trading law in the United States and the need for its reform, the book devotes its remaining chapters to outlining a path forward. In anticipation of reform, it is prudent to consider the experiences of other nations in regulating insider trading and to determine what if any lessons might be learned. Chapter 5 therefore offers a survey of insider trading enforcement regimes outside the United States. Prior to the 1980s, most countries left insider trading virtually unregulated. Partly due to US influence, the regulatory tableau has changed dramatically over the last three decades. Today, the vast majority of countries have insider trading laws on the books. These regimes vary significantly in their scope, reach, and enforcement (or lack thereof). The comparative study of these regimes offers ideas and suggests innovations for improving the US regime, but the lack of enforcement and problems of regulatory ritualism in other countries also give grounds for caution against drawing strong conclusions from the global experience. To justify and motivate enforcement, the ethical and economic rationales for the law and its limits must be made explicit – they cannot be assumed. The goal of Part II of this book is to give clear expression to the normative stakes of insider trading and its regulation.

The question of when, if ever, persons should be permitted to profit from information advantages in exchanges is not limited to insider trading. The problem has vexed philosophers, economists, and jurists for more than two thousand years. Chapter 6 prefaces the critical ethical and economic analysis of insider trading specifically by surveying the history of ideas pertaining to information asymmetries in commercial exchanges generally. Throughout history scholars and jurists have advocated rules ranging along the spectrum from the requirement of strict parity of information in all commercial exchanges (Cicero, some Scholastics, Pothier, and others) to the laissez-faire rule of caveat emptor (Chief Justice John Marshall in his opinion in *Laidlaw v. Organ*).[13] All sides of this debate have made regular appeals to the commonsense ethical values of good faith, equality, justice, fairness, autonomy, social welfare, the virtue of generosity, and the vice of greed. These ethical values have then been balanced against the need for economic efficiency and the practical necessities of trade. No single approach to the problem of information asymmetries in trade has won a consensus, leaving normative ambivalence to persist on the issue.

The strategy of this book is not to settle the debate over information asymmetries in commerce by presenting a unified ethical or economic theory as dispositive of the question. Chapter 7 argues that any such strategy would be futile. Rather, this book is pragmatic in its approach to the justification of legal reform. It considers the problem of insider trading from *all* of the evaluative standpoints identified in Chapter 6 (economics, morality, and virtue ethics) and looks to determine what reforms to the current insider trading regime in the United States will represent the proper balance among these important values. To this end, Chapter 7 offers critical introductions to the evaluative theories employed in subsequent chapters: economic and rational choice theory, the critical moral theories of consequentialism and deontology, and virtue ethics. In introducing these theories, the chapter also exposes some of their inherent limits as tools for legal reform.

Chapter 8 considers the economic impact of insider trading by summarizing some of the principal theoretical arguments and empirical data. The chapter considers potential economic harms such as insider trading's impact on counterparties, the problem of adverse selection, its effect on investor confidence and market liquidity, and potential perverse incentives such trading might create. The chapter also considers potential economic benefits, such as increased price accuracy, real-time information, decreased volatility, and its potential as an efficient form of corporate compensation. The theoretical results are mixed, and weak empirical evidence makes it difficult to ultimately quantify the net economic impact of insider trading with any certainty. Nevertheless, at a minimum, Chapter 8's study helps to identify the relevant stakeholders in the insider trading debate – those likely to be economically harmed, and those likely to benefit – even if the relative magnitude of the harms and benefits cannot be determined with certainty.

Even if it were proven with certainty that the practice of insider trading results in a net economic benefit to society, many would argue that it should nevertheless be

---

[13] Laidlaw v. Organ, 15 U.S. 178 (1817).

legally proscribed because "it is just not right!" Chapter 9 analyzes the problem of insider trading from the critical standpoints of consequentialism and deontology, the principal other-regarding moral theories undergirding Western liberal jurisprudence. While it turns out that most forms of insider trading currently proscribed by law in the United States are indeed morally impermissible from the standpoints of both consequentialism and deontology, one such form of insider trading, "issuer-licensed insider trading," is morally permissible and should not therefore be the subject of civil or criminal sanctions.

Anticipating that the conclusion that there are no moral grounds for legally proscribing issuer-licensed insider trading will be controversial, Chapter 10 considers whether there may be an alternative ethical justification for its regulation in virtue theory. Moral conceptions of rights and duties do not exhaust the ethical landscape. The law is sometimes concerned with the type of people its institutions will create and foster. Many scholars and jurists have criticized the practice of insider trading as demonstrative of the vice of greed. But while it is true that some insider traders are greedy, it is argued that the criminalization of the practice would be drastically over- and under-inclusive as a prophylactic against that vice. Moreover, since issuer-licensed insider trading does not harm others, regulating it simply to prevent the character flaw of greed would violate one of the core presuppositions of Western liberal jurisprudence, John Stuart Mill's "Harm Principle." Any such justification for the criminalization of issuer-licensed insider trading would therefore be moralistic, placing it in the same class as the now-discredited legal proscriptions of sodomy, adultery, and same-sex marriage. But if the legal proscription of issuer-licensed insider trading cannot be justified on economic or ethical grounds, how can it be explained? Chapter 10 closes by offering some possible sociopsychological explanations of how the practice of criminalizing even issuer-licensed insider trading may have come about.

Chapter 11 draws upon the lessons and conclusions of previous chapters to outline a concrete plan for reform. It suggests the most promising tack is the adoption of an insider trading statute that improves upon the current common law regime in terms of scope and clarity. Incoherence in the current regime (between the SEC's favored equal-access theory on the one hand, and the courts' commitment to the fiduciary-cum-fraud model on the other) should be remedied by the adoption of a wrongful use theory of liability. The wrongful use model would limit the scope of insider trading liability to only that conduct that is economically harmful and morally wrong. Its scope of liability would be broader than the current regime's by capturing wrongful trading that does not involve the violation of fiduciary duties (for example, trading based on information acquired by outright theft), but it would be narrower than the current regime in that it would provide an express safe harbor for issuer-licensed insider trading (which, as the following chapters demonstrate, is not wrongful). The proposed reform would also improve clarity by offering statutory definitions of when information is "material" and "nonpublic," and a definition of when persons should be understood as trading "on the basis of" information. Trading in violation of a fiduciary duty of trust and confidence remains illegal under the proposed reform, but the duty of trust and confidence is expressly defined to improve ex ante certainty for traders. The proposed reform also expressly defines the requisite mental state for each element of insider trading liability. Finally, the proposed reform precludes derivative insider trading liability for controlling persons or employers who own the material nonpublic information that was traded upon, ensuring that innocent victims are never held liable for crimes perpetrated against them.

It is expected that the principal challenge to implementing the reforms outlined in Chapter 11 will be overcoming popular (and therefore political) resistance to liberalizing the regime to permit issuer-licensed insider trading. If the conclusions of the following chapters are credited, however, any such resistance is the product of a false consciousness that can be overcome by the open and honest discourse this book aims to spur.

PART I

Law

1

Early Development of Insider Trading Law in the United States

The origins of insider trading law in the United States are found in a series of nineteenth-century state court decisions. These cases were typically brought as private contract disputes over face-to-face stock transactions between senior corporate officers and outsiders, and the courts were not consistent in their approaches. By the time the modern federal statutory regime was adopted in the early 1930s, the state courts were split between two common law rules, neither one of which bears much resemblance to the current regime's approach.

1.1 THE NINETEENTH CENTURY AND THE MAJORITY RULE

Perhaps the earliest insider trading case came before the Alabama Supreme Court in 1836. In *Spence v. Whitaker*, William Whitaker, the treasurer and most active trustee of a joint-stock company, informed a shareholder, John Spence, that his recently acquired shares in the company were encumbered by a debt that would force their forfeiture if not paid immediately.[1] Spence asked whether dividends due on the shares would cover the debt and was informed by Whitaker that no dividends had been declared by the company.[2] Whitaker then volunteered a solution. He offered to buy six shares of Spence's stock at $92 a share to free up enough cash to cover the debt and remove the lien. Whitaker assured Spence that the offer reflected fair market value.[3] Spence had no independent means of verifying any of Whitaker's claims because Whitaker had not maintained the company's register of accounts as he was required to do by the firm's articles. Thus, believing he had no other choice, Spence agreed to proceed with the trade on Whitaker's terms. Spence later sought to

---

[1] Spence v. Whitaker, 3 Port. 297 (1836).
[2] Ibid. at 299.
[3] Ibid.

rescind the trade when he learned that there had never been a lien on his shares and his stock was in fact worth $415 a share at the time of the trade.[4]

The Alabama Supreme Court applied the elements of common law fraud to the facts of *Spence*. The general rule, persisting to this day, is that an agreement may be rescinded as fraudulent where it was intentionally induced by a statement the maker knew to be false, or where it was intentionally induced by active concealment of the truth.[5] Silence, or failure to disclose the truth, may also support an action for fraud where there is an independent duty to disclose some fact or facts.[6] The presence of a fiduciary or similar relation of trust and confidence between the parties is one consistently recognized basis for such a duty to disclose.[7] The court appeared to find evidence to support all three bases for fraud in *Spence*. Whitaker's false representations that Spence's shares were encumbered and that they had a book value of only $92 a share induced Spence to sell at one-quarter of their true value.[8] Moreover, Whitaker's failure to maintain the company's books was arguably an attempt at active concealment, preventing Spence and others from learning the truth.[9] More still, the court seemed to suggest that Whitaker's status as trustee, "in whom faith and confidence had been reposed, and whose agency imparted to him more intimate knowledge of the condition and value of the subjects of the trust, than the [beneficiary], or others, could possess," created a duty to disclose the truth about the encumbrance and value of the shares under these circumstances.[10] The court concluded that regardless of "whether the evidence of artifice, misrepresentation and fraudulent design" in this case would offer sufficient grounds to avoid the contract on their own, when considered together with the fact that Whitaker was trustee to Spence, these circumstances were "amply sufficient" to warrant rescission of the share sale as fraudulent.[11]

Though *Spence* clearly held that Whitaker had a duty to disclose the true value of the company shares to Spence prior to the sale, the court's reasoning left the precise nature and source of this duty ambiguous. Did the duty derive from Whitaker's insider position as treasurer and trustee alone, or did it stem from his insider status in combination with other factors such as his failure to maintain records and his misleading representations? Of course, a great deal turns on which rule a court follows. If a duty to disclose attaches by virtue of one's position as senior officeholder alone, then virtually every trade by senior management in possession of material nonpublic information would be fraudulent and therefore voidable.

---

[4] Ibid. at 324–25.
[5] See Restatement (Second) of Contracts at §§ 159–62 (1981).
[6] Ibid. at § 161. (Such silence is treated as "equivalent to an assertion that the fact does not exist.")
[7] Ibid. at § 161(d).
[8] See *Spence*, 3 Port. at 324–25.
[9] Ibid. at 325.
[10] Ibid. at 325–26.
[11] Ibid.

The New York courts took up the problem three decades later in *Carpenter v. Danforth*.[12] Francis Carpenter sold 136 shares of the National Bank Note Company to George Danforth, then a director of the company, for $60 a share ($10 more than par value). During negotiations, Danforth told Carpenter that he was prepared to offer more than any of the other officers would for the shares, and that he wanted the shares to increase his voting power at the upcoming shareholder meeting.[13] Within thirteen months of the sale, the company declared two dividends, one of 310 percent and one of 200 percent. Carpenter later sued to rescind the sale as fraudulent when he learned of these dividends.

Carpenter's principal argument was that Danforth's position as director placed him in a position of "trust and confidence" to all shareholders such that the stock sale must be declared void as fraudulent unless "Danforth paid a full and fair price for the stock" and also disclosed to Carpenter "every fact or circumstance known to him ... and not known to [Carpenter], material on the question of the value of the stock."[14] The court recognized this issue as being of "great" and, in this case, "controlling importance." It began with the observation that a corporation is not a living thing and can therefore only act by agents. A corporation's directors are the principal agents for managing the general affairs of that corporation, and such management will determine its profits. Since the value of the shareholder's stock is determined by the present value of its right to future dividends of profits, there is "a certain trust relation between shareholders and the directors of a corporation."[15] But, the court went on, "the trust put in the directors usually extends ... only to the management of the general affairs of the corporation, with a view to dividends of profits."[16] Directors "are not trustees for the sale of the stock of the corporation."[17] Consequently, the court held that the trust relation between Danforth as director and Carpenter as stockholder was real, but that it did not touch upon transactions in the stock itself "except so far as the good or bad management of the general affairs of a corporation by its directors, indirectly affects the value of the stock."[18] Thus, Danforth as director had no duty to Carpenter as shareholder to disclose any information advantage he may have had concerning the value of the corporation's shares prior to executing the sale. To rescind the sale for fraud, Carpenter would have to show that Danforth made some affirmative misrepresentation or that he took active measures to conceal the true state of the company's affairs from Carpenter. The court thus concluded that these facts could not support rescission for fraud.[19]

---

[12] Carpenter v. Danforth, 52 Barb. 581 (1868).
[13] Ibid. at 587.
[14] Ibid. at 583.
[15] Ibid. at 584.
[16] Ibid.
[17] Ibid.
[18] Ibid.
[19] Ibid. at 587–91.

After *Carpenter*, the trend continued in the direction of limiting the scope of the trust relationship between directors and shareholders to decisions pertaining to the management of the firm's business affairs, and not to transactions in the firm's shares. The Indiana Supreme Court took up the issue in *The Board of Commissioners of Tippecanoe County v. Reynolds*.[20] In this case, the president of the Indianapolis Railroad Company purchased (through an agent) 570 shares of the firm's stock from Tippecanoe County for $0.90 on the dollar of its face value. At the time of this purchase, the president was negotiating the sale of the company for more than ten times the price he paid the county. The county later claimed the sale was induced by fraud and sued the president for the difference between the price paid for the county's shares and the subsequent sale price. Despite the fact that the president had failed to declare dividends and had represented that the stock was not worth its face value, the court concluded there had been no affirmative misrepresentation or active concealment on the part of the president.[21] Consequently, the court held that the only live issue was whether the defendant, as president and director of the company, was "a trustee of the [county] as a stockholder, whereby it became his duty, as a purchaser of the stock, to pay a fair and adequate price for it ... and to disclose ... all the material facts within his knowledge, not known to the plaintiff, affecting the value of the stock."[22] Citing *Carpenter*, the court reasoned that the scope of directors' duties to shareholders is limited to the prudent management of the *company's* property. The stock held by the county was, however, its own property, over which neither the firm nor its officers had any "control, power, or dominion."[23] The court thus concluded it is "very clear" that "in the purchase of stock by a director from the holder, the relation of [trust] does not exist between them."[24] The decisions in *Carpenter* and *Tippecanoe County* were soon followed by decisions in a number of other jurisdictions,[25] and by the close of the nineteenth century the understanding that directors do not owe any special duties of trust and confidence to shareholders in connection with the purchase or sale of stock had become the majority rule.[26]

A few nineteenth-century courts did, however, recognize more expansive duties of trust and confidence for corporate officers. In *Fisher v. Budlong*,[27] for example, the shareholder of an insurance company sought advice from the firm's president as to the value of his shares. The president told the shareholder that the shares were worth

[20] The Bd. of Comm'rs of Tippecanoe Cnty. v. Reynolds, 44 Ind. 509 (1873).
[21] Ibid. at 512.
[22] Ibid. at 513.
[23] Ibid. at 515.
[24] Ibid. at 516.
[25] See, e.g., Deadrick v. Wilson, 67 Tenn. 108 (1874); Crowell v. Jackson, 23 A. 426 (N.J. 1891); Krumbhaar v. Griffiths, 25 A. 64 (Penn. 1892); Haarstick v. Fox, 33 P. 251 (Utah 1893).
[26] See, e.g., Paula J. Dalley, "From Horse Trading to Insider Trading: The Historical Antecedents of the Insider Trading Debate," *William and Mary Law Review* 39 (1998): 1299.
[27] Fisher v. Budlong, 10 R.I. 525 (1873).

significantly less than their par value and recommended that they be sold as soon as possible. The president then offered to find a buyer for the shares. A few days later, the president informed the shareholder that he had found a "good offer" at $2 less than par value. The shareholder agreed to sell, and the president demanded and was paid a commission for arranging the transaction. It later came to light that the president had purchased the shares for himself (through an intermediary) and that they were worth twice the price paid.[28] The Rhode Island Supreme Court recognized that a "vendor is not obliged to disclose all the circumstance within his knowledge which might affect the value of the thing sold."[29] Indeed, the court even affirmed that "a buyer should not be liable to a suit for deceit for misrepresenting a seller's chance of selling for a good price."[30] Nevertheless, the court held that any "peculiar relation implying confidence or leading to confidence" would "take the case out of the ordinary rule," and such a "peculiar relation" was present here.[31] According to the court, the "material point" in this case was the fact that the president "professed to be aiding the plaintiff in selling his stock, and getting a good price for it."[32] Indeed, proof that the president purported to act as agent on the seller's behalf was found in the fact that he demanded and received a commission for the sale. As a result, "the seller was led to repose a trust and confidence in the president".[33]

Had the court stopped there, it would be fair to say that *Fisher* was consistent with the majority rule because the "special relationship" between the president and shareholder seemed to turn on the president's position as agent for the sale of the shares rather than as officer of the firm. But the court went on to point out that, even apart from this agency relationship, the shareholder had a right to suppose that the defendant, as president of the corporation, knew the shareholder's situation and could be relied upon for his statements as to the value of the shares. Accordingly, the court noted that "although any single officer cannot perhaps be considered as standing in the relation of trustee to each stockholder," such a relationship is nevertheless "a reason for confidence, and more especially when this officer is the sole manager of the corporation, and the stockholder has a right to call on him for this very information."[34] But while *Fisher* suggested a more expansive scope for the relation of trust and confidence between corporate officers and shareholders, this rule was slow to gain adherents. Other nineteenth-century cases finding a special relationship between officers and shareholders that triggered a duty to disclose typically relied on some additional facts such as those found in *Spence*

---

[28] Ibid. at 526.
[29] Ibid. at 527.
[30] Ibid. at 528.
[31] Ibid.
[32] Ibid.
[33] Ibid. at 529.
[34] Ibid.

(e.g., evidence the insider was an agent for the transaction, misrepresentation, or concealment) beyond the officer's insider status.[35] But times were changing.

1.2 THE EARLY TWENTIETH CENTURY AND THE RISE OF THE MINORITY RULE: 1900 TO 1934

The close of the nineteenth century coincided with the rise of progressivism in American politics and realism in American jurisprudence. The pro-management, laissez-faire political attitudes so prevalent during the early years of the Industrial Revolution were challenged by a greater awareness of the associated problems of urbanization and income disparity. Unions were gaining power, and workers' rights began to take precedence over the ethic of economic expansion at any price. At the same time, the formalism of classical nineteenth-century contract law was being questioned by the new legal realism. Realists challenged the mechanical application of "outdated" legal principles such as caveat emptor as generating harsh results that favored the wealthy and powerful over the poor and oppressed. There was a strong push by legal scholars to measure historically received legal principles by the new social sciences, and to soften their application by appeal to considerations of fairness and social justice. Increased pressure was placed on the pro-management majority rule in insider trading cases as these progressive and realist ideas gained traction among politicians and judges in the early twentieth century.

In *Oliver v. Oliver*,[36] the president and director of Gate City Oil Company purchased 658 shares of the firm's stock at $110 a share from a shareholder without first disclosing that he had previously arranged for the profitable sale of one of the company's facilities, making the shares worth $185 a share. There was no evidence that the president had lied or actively taken measures to prevent the shareholder from learning of the shares' true worth. The facts did not therefore support rescission on grounds of fraudulent misrepresentation or active concealment. Rather, to avoid the sale, the shareholder was compelled to demonstrate that the president had an independent duty to disclose all facts material to the sale prior to entering into the agreement.

In taking up this issue, the Supreme Court of Georgia cautioned that courts "cannot put parties upon an equality which does not in fact exist. They cannot deprive one of the advantage which superior judgment, greater skill, or wider information may give."[37] For, quoting Chief Justice John Marshall's language in *Laidlaw v. Organ* (a case that is discussed in great detail in Chapter 6 of this book),[38]

---

[35] See, e.g., Mulvance v. O'Brien, 58 Kan. 463 (1897) (the president of a corporation had a duty to disclose where he acted as agent for the sale of the shareholders' stock and made various misrepresentations and engaged in active concealment in effecting the sale).

[36] Oliver v. Oliver, 118 Ga. 362 (1903).

[37] Ibid. at 233.

[38] Laidlaw v. Organ, 15 U.S. 178 (1817).

"it would be difficult to circumscribe the contrary doctrine within proper limits."[39] In short, "[c]ourts are created for the enforcement of civil contracts and are power- less to relieve against hard bargains, unless authorized so to do by some rule of civil law."[40] One such rule, however, is that a failure to disclose an information advan- tage may be fraudulent where the parties stand in a special relation of trust. The court then addressed the question of whether the relation that a director bears to an individual stockholder alone is enough to generate the duty to disclose. The court recognized the well-settled understanding that the director is trustee for the com- pany and therefore serves the interests of the "entire body of stockholders."[41] But it went further and observed that "the fact that he is trustee for all is not to be perverted into holding that he is under no obligation to each."[42]

Consistent with the legal realism of the day, the *Oliver* court refused to privilege legal form over substance. It concluded that the corporation is an artificial entity, and it is the individual shareholders who are the "real parties at interest." Conse- quently, no "process of reasoning and no amount of argument can destroy the fact that the director is, in a most important and legitimate sense, trustee for the stock- holder."[43] The director is not trustee in the strict sense of holding title to the shares or of being precluded from transacting with shareholders. Rather the director stands in the relation of "*quasi trustee* as to the shareholder's interest in the shares."[44] In reaching this conclusion, the court expressly refused to follow the majority rule's limitation of the scope of a director's duty of trust to the prudent management of the firm's actual property, which would exclude stock owned by shareholders. The court found that when a director purchases shares from a stockholder, "he is not buying paper, but in effect is buying an undivided and substantial interest in property which has been committed to the director's care, custody, and control."[45] The court therefore concluded that directors do indeed stand in the relation of fiduciary to individual shareholders and their shares. The court then held that the duties of a director as fiduciary of the shareholder's interests are as follows:

> Where the director obtains the information giving added value to the stock by virtue of his official position, he holds the information in trust for the benefit of those who placed him where this knowledge was obtained, in the well-founded expectation that the same should be used first for the company, and ultimately for those who were the real owners of the company. The director cannot deal on this information to the prejudice of the artificial being which is called the corporation, nor, on any

---

[39] *Oliver,* 118 Ga. at 233.
[40] Ibid.
[41] Ibid.
[42] Ibid.
[43] Ibid.
[44] Ibid. at 234.
[45] Ibid.

sound principle, can be permitted to act differently towards those who are not artificially but actually interested.[46]

In short, the *Oliver* court treated material nonpublic information concerning the value of the firm's shares as a firm asset held in trust first for the benefit of the firm and then secondarily (or by extension) for the benefit of the shareholders.[47] Hence, assuming such information can be disclosed without harm to the firm (the director's principal obligation as fiduciary), the court ruled the director's secondary quasi-fiduciary obligations to the shareholder create a duty to disclose prior to trading. If the information cannot be disclosed without harm to the firm, the director's status as fiduciary requires that he or she abstain from trading altogether. If, as in this case, the director trades without making the requisite disclosures to the shareholder, the sale must be set aside as fraudulent.[48]

While *Oliver* was the first case to recognize the director's relationship to individual shareholders in stock transactions as essentially fiduciary in nature, the Supreme Court of Kansas followed it just one year later in *Stewart v. Harris.*[49] In *Stewart*, the president of a bank availed himself of an information advantage to purchase twelve shares of the bank's stock from a shareholder for much less than their actual value. At trial, the jury was instructed that "the president or other managing officer of a corporation ... stands in the relation of a trustee to all the stockholders who are not themselves engaged in" its active management.[50] For a trustee, any purchase from a shareholder without "first having informed such stockholder of the true condition of the bank, and of the amount and value of its assets, is a fraud."[51] The jury found for the plaintiff, and the director appealed, complaining that these jury instructions were erroneous because they were inconsistent with majority rule. Quoting extensively from *Oliver* as a "well-considered case," the *Stewart* court adopted that court's reasoning and rule in affirming the trial court's instruction that a relation of trust exists between directors and ordinary shareholders, and that this relation gives rise to a duty to disclose or abstain from trading. In following *Oliver*, the court expressly rebuked the majority rule as articulated in *Tippecanoe County*[52] as leaving stockholders the "legitimate prey" of their corporation's directors. The *Stewart* court explained that it could not "give its approval to a course of dealing that will permit

---

[46] Ibid.

[47] Interestingly, the court's property rights–based rationale hints at conversion, in addition to breach of trust, as a possible ground for rescission when a director trades based on the firm's material nonpublic information.

[48] Ibid. at 234–35.

[49] Stewart v. Harris, 66 L.R.A. 261 (1904).

[50] Ibid. at 279.

[51] Ibid.

[52] The *Stewart* court recognizes *Tippecanoe County* as the "pioneer case to announce the doctrine" that directors sustain no trust relation to stockholders, despite the fact that *Carpenter* precedes it.

those occupying a trust relation to be unmindful of the trust, betray the confidence reposed, and profit by such betrayal."[53]

The *Oliver* and *Stewart* courts' contempt for the majority rule as antiquated and socially naïve reflected the legal realism that was making its way into the jurisprudential mainstream by this time. And though it remained the minority rule, the fiduciary model articulated by these courts continued to gain adherents in the early decades of the twentieth century.[54]

As the majority and minority rules vied for jurisdictions, the US Supreme Court addressed the question of insider trading for the first time in *Strong v. Repide*.[55] In *Strong* the Court reviewed the judgment of the Supreme Court of the Philippine Islands concerning the purchase of shares of the Philippine Sugar Estates Development Company by its president, director, and owner of three-quarters of the firm's shares. It appears the company's only assets were its real estate holdings in the Philippines, and that the political realities of the time were such that these holdings could not be developed and were worthless unless they could be sold to the government. The president, the government, and other interested parties had been engaged in prolonged negotiations that appeared to the general public to be going nowhere. In reality, the government had made a strong offer for the land and the president was holding out for a stronger offer. With the offer already on the table, the president engaged an intermediary to approach Erica and Richard Strong's agent (whose office was adjacent to the president's) and offer to purchase their 800 shares of the company at the current market price, which was much less than their value in light of the government's pending offer. At this time, the public perception remained that a deal was unlikely. The Strongs' agent agreed to sell their shares. The deal was announced two and a half months later, sending the share price up almost 1,000 percent. When the Strongs later learned that the president had been the true counterparty to their trade, they sought to rescind the sale as fraudulent.

Since the president made no affirmative misrepresentations to the Strongs' agent, the Court found the issue to be whether "it was the duty of the defendant, acting in good faith, to disclose to the agent of the [Strongs] the facts bearing upon or which might affect the value of the stock."[56] The Court was careful to weigh the precedent, citing the minority rule in *Oliver* and *Stewart*, as well as the majority rule in *Tippecanoe County*. The Court then proceeded to stake out a middle ground

---

[53] Ibid. at 281.
[54] For example, in Jacquith v. Mason, 99 Neb. 509, 514–16 (1916), the Supreme Court of Nebraska quoted extensively from *Oliver* and *Stewart* in finding the president and director of an insurance company owed a fiduciary duty to shareholders to disclose information of a pending tender offer before purchasing their shares well below the offer price.
[55] Strong v. Repide, 29 S. Ct. 521 (1909). Though the Court addressed the problem of trading based on information asymmetries in Laidlaw v. Organ, 15 U.S. 178 (1817), it did not take up the problem of true insider trading until this case.
[56] Ibid. at 430–31.

between the two approaches in what has come to be known as the "special facts" doctrine. According to the Court, even if it is conceded that the

> ordinary relations between directors and shareholders in a business corporation are not of such a fiduciary nature as to make it the duty of a director to disclose to a shareholder the general knowledge which he may possess regarding the value of the shares of the company, yet there are cases where, by reason of the special facts, such duty exists.[57]

The Court identified a number of special facts that, together, warranted taking this case out of the general rule. To begin, the defendant was not only president and director of the company, but he also owned three-quarters of the firm's shares, was administrator general of the company, and, by the other shareholders' acquiescence, was the chief negotiator with the government for the sale of the property. Moreover, this was not just the negotiation of a significant deal; it was for the sale of all of the company's assets, and he was the only person aware of the status of these negotiations. When combined, these facts placed the president more in the role of agent for the sale of the lands on behalf of the shareholders than as simply managing the assets of the company. Once the land was sold, there would be no assets left to manage. And, finally, concealing his identity when procuring the purchase of the stock by his agent indicated that he knew that making the offer himself would have put the Strongs on notice of a possible deal. He therefore took active measures to conceal this from them. As the Court put it, his "concealment of identity was not a mere inadvertent omission ... but was a studied and intentional omission, to be characterized as part of the deceitful machinations to obtain the purchase" at a reduced price.[58] The Court held that these special facts were enough to create a duty to disclose, even if the bare director-shareholder relationship would not generate such a duty on its own.

Though the special facts doctrine articulated in *Strong* is usually recognized as an alternative to the majority and minority rules, it is probably best thought of as offering an equitable exception to the majority rule. It takes care not to recognize a general fiduciary duty of directors to all shareholders as such. In this sense it is inconsistent with *Oliver*, *Stewart*, and other minority rule cases. Instead, like *Fisher* (and perhaps *Spence*) before it, it simply recognizes that sometimes, under the right circumstances, deceitful conduct on the part of a director may be so extreme that a duty to disclose arises where it would otherwise not exist. Again, this is entirely consistent with the majority rule. Regardless of whether it is thought of as a third

---

[57] Ibid. at 431. There is language in *Strong* suggesting that the Court read *Oliver* and *Stewart* as special facts cases (see, e.g., ibid.), but, as demonstrated previously, a close reading of those cases makes it clear that the courts were convinced that the "ordinary relations between directors and shareholders" was enough to create the fiduciary duty.

[58] Ibid. at 433.

rule, or as an equitable exception to the majority rule, the special facts doctrine was adopted by a number of jurisdictions in the early twentieth century.

The minority and majority rules reached their final pre-Securities Exchange Act expressions in the cases *Hotchkiss v. Fischer*[59] and *Goodwin v. Agassiz.*[60] In *Hotchkiss*, the Supreme Court of Kansas embraced perhaps the most extreme version of the minority rule. The widowed owner of 2,300 shares of the Elmhurst Investment Company was in need of cash and approached the president and director of the company to inquire as to the firm's financial fitness and the likelihood a dividend would be announced at the upcoming shareholders meeting. The director honestly stated that he could not be certain a dividend would be announced, but he supplied and explained all material facts regarding the financial condition of the company to the shareholder. He answered all of her questions truthfully, but he refused to respond to her inquiry as to the true "worth" of her shares. The director explained to her, "I have told you the conditions of the affairs of the company, and I will be glad to furnish you any further information," but as to the worth of the stock, that "is a matter you have to determine yourself."[61] The shareholder was concerned that, if no dividend was announced at the upcoming meeting, her shares would be worth less, so she decided to offer her shares for sale in advance. There was evidence that the market price for the shares at the time was between $1.00 and $1.15 a share. The director offered to buy her shares at $1.25 a share, and she accepted. The shares later proved to be worth three times this amount, and the shareholder sought to rescind the trade as induced by fraud.

The director's conduct appears to have been above reproach in many respects. He supplied all material information requested and explained it truthfully and accurately. He only refused to offer any prediction as to whether a dividend would be announced and his opinion as to the true value of the shares. The widow, by contrast, appeared to be fishing for material nonpublic information so as to determine whether she should sell her shares before or after the upcoming meeting, and at what price. Despite this, the court held that the director violated his fiduciary duty to the shareholder. It was not enough that the director provided the appropriate statements and explained them on their face because "[w]ithout being analyzed and interpreted, the statement[s] would contain little information respecting financial condition to a shareholder who did not acknowledge competency to interpret [them]."[62] The court went on, "[w]hen interpreted, the statement would reflect book value of shares. Book value might have little relation to market value, and might have still less relation to actual value."[63] The director's failure to engage his

---

[59] Hotchkiss v. Fischer, 136 Kan. 530 (1932).
[60] Goodwin v. Agassiz, 283 Mass. 358 (1933).
[61] *Hotchkiss*, 136 Kan. at 532.
[62] Ibid. at 534.
[63] Ibid.

institutional knowledge and expertise to interpret these facts *for* the shareholder prior to purchasing her shares violated the relation of "scrupulous trust and confidence" between director and shareholder.

Though the fiduciary model reflected in the minority rule was clearly gaining momentum in the first decades of the twentieth century, the majority of jurisdictions still rejected it. Moreover, looking ahead to Chapter 2 of this book, it would be a stretch to infer that even these early minority rule cases provided strong common law precedent for the expansive insider trading enforcement regime to come. Note some important asymmetries: first, the insiders in every one of these early cases held positions at the highest levels of corporate governance (presidents and directors); there is not the slightest hint that lower-level insiders would be recognized as standing in the relation of fiduciary to shareholders as they are today. Second, all of these early cases were brought as civil contract disputes, seeking nothing more than rescission of the trade or restitution of the benefits of the trade. None of these cases hint at the possibility of civil fines or criminal liability. Third, all of the early cases addressed thus far dealt with face-to-face transactions; none of them found a fiduciary duty for insiders to disclose material nonpublic information when trading over impersonal stock exchanges.

The problem of insider trading over impersonal exchanges was finally addressed just one year prior to the promulgation of the Securities Exchange Act of 1934 in *Goodwin*. Upon reading a newspaper article stating that the Cliff Mining Company had closed exploratory operations on a particular property, Goodwin sold 700 shares of the company's stock through brokers on the Boston Stock Exchange. It turns out that those 700 shares were purchased by two Cliff Mining Company directors who had been recently convinced by a geologist's theory that the property might be profitably mined after all. The geologist's new theory was not made public in order to allow for the purchase of mining rights on adjacent properties. The directors were not responsible for the newspaper article read by Goodwin, but he nevertheless sought to rescind the trade, claiming that he never would have sold his shares if he had known of the new theory and that the directors had a fiduciary duty to disclose their material nonpublic information prior to purchasing his shares.

The Supreme Judicial Court of Massachusetts forcefully rejected the claim that the directors stand in some fiduciary relation to shareholders when trading the company's shares. In doing so, the court reaffirmed prior Massachusetts precedent and noted that it was "supported by an imposing weight of authority in other jurisdictions."[64] The court recognized that a "rule holding that directors are trustees for individual stockholders with respect to their stock" exists, but "in comparatively few states."[65] Though the court embraced the rule that the director-shareholder

[64] *Goodwin*, 283 Mass. at 362.
[65] Ibid.

relationship alone creates no fiduciary duties in stock transactions, it followed *Strong* in appreciating that special facts or circumstances may nevertheless impose an equitable duty to disclose on the part of directors in face-to-face transactions. The court held that such special facts cannot, however, arise over impersonal exchanges. The court explained that

> [a]n honest director would be in a difficult situation if he could neither buy nor sell on the stock exchange shares of stock in his corporation without first seeking out the other actual ultimate party to the transaction and disclosing to him everything which a court or jury might later find that he then knew affecting the real or speculative value of such shares.[66]

The court pointed out that such a rule would be highly impractical, and that the "[f]iduciary obligations of directors ought not to be made so onerous that men of experience and ability will be deterred from accepting such office."[67] And, finally, echoing the still-lingering influence of legal formalism and the principle of caveat emptor, the *Goodwin* court emphasized that

> [l]aw in its sanctions is not coextensive with morality. It cannot undertake to put all parties to every contract on an equality as to knowledge, experience, skill and shrewdness. It cannot undertake to relieve against hard bargains made between competent parties without fraud.[68]

As one commentator later put it, the Supreme Judicial Court of Massachusetts seemed comfortable concluding that the directors had merely "exercised a perk of being an insider"[69] in buying Cliff Mining stock over the exchange.

*****

In sum, leading up to the promulgation of the Securities Exchange Act of 1934, which to this day provides the principal statutory support for the federal insider trading enforcement regime in the United States, the state common law of insider trading was split, with the majority of jurisdictions finding no fiduciary relation between senior management and individual shareholders in stock trading. Special facts might give rise to an equitable duty to disclose for senior management in face-to-face transactions, but not over anonymous exchanges. A minority of courts were prepared to recognize a fiduciary duty for senior management to disclose material nonpublic information to individual shareholders prior to any face-to-face transaction in the firm's shares, but it remained unclear whether even these jurisdictions

---

[66] Ibid.
[67] Ibid., 362–63.
[68] Ibid., 363.
[69] Rick Wartzman, "A 1920 Insider Trade Was Ruled by a Court to Be Merely a Perk," *Wall Street Journal* (July 3, 2002).

would extend this duty to trading over anonymous exchanges. No jurisdiction had recognized a duty to disclose for low-level insiders trading on the company's material nonpublic information. Finally, the early recorded cases addressed the problem of insider trading as a matter of contract law or restitution; no jurisdiction imposed civil fines or criminal liability for insider trading prior to the implementation of the federal statutory regime.

2

Federal Regulation and the Modern Era

The mechanization of agriculture in the decade following World War I increased productivity, but decreased the demand for labor in rural economies. This, combined with increasing expansion in the industrial sector, led Americans to migrate from rural communities to the cities in growing numbers. Urbanization generated new needs in construction, sanitation, household maintenance, and transportation. Answering these needs led to new technological advancements (e.g., automobiles and household appliances), the mass production of which in turn generated entirely new industries and job opportunities. This was the Roaring Twenties, a time of tremendous prosperity in the United States. The potential for economic expansion seemed limitless, and the spirit of optimism prevailed.

In the midst of this prosperity, more Americans found themselves with extra income and looked for investment opportunities. The stock market was rising, and stocks began to be seen as a smart and modern form of investment. Increasingly, however, stock buyers were investing less and speculating more. The term "investor" typically refers to those who purchase a stock after carefully considering its fundamentals and reaching the conviction that, based on these fundamentals, the company's shares will perform well over time. Investors buy to hold. The term "speculator," by contrast, typically refers to a trader who is less concerned with a stock's fundamentals than its potential for volatility in price – whether up or down. Speculators try to anticipate how others will react to price movements or events affecting a specific stock or the market in general, and then they "bet" accordingly. Despite the obvious risks associated with market speculation, Americans from all backgrounds began to speculate at an increasing rate, spurred by the fabulous profits being won by others around them. Those who did not have ready cash available borrowed money to buy stock. It became routine for brokers to lend small investors more than two-thirds of the price of the stock they were purchasing. This margin buying only increased speculation, and a market bubble of historic proportions began to form. That bubble burst in October 1929. Over a two-day period, the

Law

market lost 25 percent of its value, and it would plummet still further in the coming months.[1] The situation was aptly summarized by Albert Wiggin, then president of Chase National Bank:

> We are reaping the natural fruit of the orgy of speculation in which millions of people have indulged. It was inevitable, because of the tremendous increase in the number of stockholders in recent years, that the number of sellers would be greater than ever when the boom ended and selling took the place of buying.[2]

There was no single cause to the market collapse and the Great Depression that ensued, but the public demanded an explanation and response.

2.1 FEDERAL REGULATION OF THE MARKETS

In March 1932, the US Senate launched an investigation into the causes of the market crash. The investigation was eventually led by Ferdinand Pecora, an assistant district attorney for New York, and eventually became known as the Pecora Commission. Encouraged by the newly elected President Roosevelt, Pecora's hearings drew headlines by calling J. P. Morgan and other titans of American finance before the Senate to account for their roles in the events leading up to the crash. At the end of the day, conflicts of interest between the commercial and investment operations of banks, excessive speculation, and market manipulation through "stock pools" and by other means were identified by the commission as the principal market-based causes of the crash.[3]

Insider trading on material nonpublic information was condemned by the Pecora Commission Report as "evil" and "among the most vicious practices unearthed at the hearings."[4] Against this backdrop, one would expect one of the three major pieces of legislation promulgated in response to the hearings – the Banking Act of 1933, the Securities Act of 1933, and the Securities Exchange Act of 1934 – to address insider trading head on, but, with one very limited exception, they were entirely silent on the issue. Indeed, the legislative history for the Securities Exchange Act, which formed the Securities and Exchange Commission and provides the principal statutory support for the modern insider trading enforcement regime in

---

[1] The Dow Jones Industrial Average reached a height of 381.17 points on September 3, 1929. It dropped to 230.07 on October 29, 1929 (Black Tuesday). On July 8, 1932, the market reached its nadir at 41.22 points. The market would not return to its pre-crash high until November 23, 1954.

[2] See Frederick Kennard and Addison Hanne, *Boom & Bust: A Look at Economic Bubbles* (Morrisville, NC: Lulu.com, 2015): 46.

[3] Stock pools occur where groups of traders pool their resources to trade massive amounts of a single stock's shares to manipulate its price – either up or down.

[4] Henry G. Manne, *Insider Trading and the Stock Market* (New York: Free Press, 1966): 10 (quoting the transcript of the report).

the United States, suggested that regulating insider trading was just not one of its principal purposes.[5] Consistent with the focus of the Pecora hearings, the preamble to the Exchange Act repeatedly references market "manipulation" and "excessive speculation" as the problems that the act addresses, but there is no mention of insider trading.[6]

2.1.1 *Exchange Act Section 16 Restriction on Short-Swing Trading by Insiders*

Section 16(b) is the only provision of the Exchange Act that explicitly addresses insider trading. The statutory provision explains that its purpose is to prevent the "unfair use of information which may have been obtained by" an insider "by reason of his relationship to the issuer."[7] Through Section 16(b), Congress sought to "curb the evils of insider trading [by] . . . taking the profits out of a class of transactions in which the possibility of abuse was believed to be intolerably great."[8] Section 16(b) is, however, extremely limited in its scope.

To begin, its application is limited to "directors," "officers," and "principal stock-holders."[9] The act defines a director as "any director of a corporation or any person performing similar functions with respect to any organization, whether incorporated or unincorporated."[10] Although the definition of "officer" under Section 16 was the subject of some controversy in the decades following its adoption,[11] the SEC issued Rule 16a-1(f) in 1991 to bring some clarity. Under Rule 16a-1(f), an officer is

> an issuer's president, principal financial officer, principal accounting officer (or, if there is no such accounting officer, the controller), any vice president of the issuer in charge of a principal business unit, division or function (such as sales, administration

---

[5] See, e.g., Stephen Bainbridge, "Incorporating State Law Fiduciary Duties into the Federal Insider Trading Prohibition," *Washington and Lee Law Review* 52 (1995): 1189; Michael P. Dooley, "Enforcement of Insider Trading Restrictions," *Virginia Law Review* 66 (1980): 55–69.

[6] See 15 U.S.C. § 78(b).

[7] Ibid.

[8] Foremost-McKesson, Inc. v. Provident Sec. Co., 423 U.S. 232, 243 (1976).

[9] 15 U.S.C. § 78(p).

[10] 15 U.S.C. § 78c(7).

[11] The first definition of "officer" applied to Section 16 was that found in Exchange Act Rule 3b-2:

> The term "officer" means a president, vice president, secretary, treasurer or principal financial officer, comptroller or principal accounting officer, and any person routinely performing corresponding functions with respect to any organization whether incorporated or unincorporated.

17 C.F.R. § 240.3b-2. This definition, however, left it open whether one could be regarded as an officer based on one's title alone; it also left open the question of what "functions" might render one an "officer" for purposes of Section 16 even without a title. See, e.g., Stephen Bainbridge, *Insider Trading Law and Policy* (St. Paul, MN: Foundation Press, 2014): 220–23.

or finance), any other officer who performs a policy-making function, or any other person who performs similar policy-making functions for the issuer.[12]

A note to the rule also provides that anyone identified by an issuer as an "executive officer" in its SEC filings is presumed to be an "officer" for purposes of Section 16. Finally, the act defines a "principal stockholder" as one who is "directly or indirectly the beneficial owner of more than 10 percent of" that company's stock.[13]

In addition to applying to an extremely limited class of insiders, Section 16 as a whole imposes only very limited restrictions on their ability to trade. Section 16(a) requires that statutorily defined insiders report their holdings and transactions in a company's shares.[14] Section 16(b) then precludes statutory insiders from enjoying short-swing profits. It does this by providing that any profits an insider earns from a purchase and sale (or sale and purchase) of their firm's shares that occurs within a period of less than six months "shall inure to and be recoverable by the issuer," regardless of the insider's intentions when initially purchasing or selling the shares.[15] If the issuer does not bring a suit to recover profits resulting from such trading, the section grants to any security holder in the company a right of action on the issuer's behalf. Finally, Section 16(c) makes it unlawful for statutory insiders to sell their firm's equity securities short.[16]

In light of the repeated denunciations of insider trading in the legislative history and the Pecora hearings, Section 16 is truly remarkable for who and what it leaves out. For example, true insiders who have access to material nonpublic information but who do not fit the definition of director, officer, or principal shareholder are simply not covered. Section 16(b) liability for those who *are* covered is limited to disgorgement, and there is no provision for tipping liability. Moreover, covered insiders are not precluded from trading based on their firm's material nonpublic information outside the six-month window. For instance, Section 16(b) does not preclude an insider's sale of firm shares the day before an earnings miss is announced if that insider purchased all of her shares more than six months prior to the sale. More still, the SEC may not initiate civil charges for Section 16(b) insider trading, and such trading cannot form the basis of a criminal charge.[17] Given the anemic quality of the insider trading restrictions and enforcement provisions in

---

[12] 17 C.F.R. § 240.16a-1(f).

[13] 15 U.S.C. § 78p(a)(1).

[14] 15 U.S.C. § 78p(a).

[15] 15 U.S.C. § 78p(b).

[16] 15 U.S.C. § 78p(c). This section is sometimes referred to as the "anti-Wiggin provision." One of the most troubling revelations to come out of the Pecora hearings was the fact that Albert Wiggin, then president of Chase National Bank, profited by selling the company's common stock short while the firm's affiliates were making offsetting purchases totaling more than $800 million. Wiggin's aim was to drive down the stock price so he could repurchase it at a lower level. See Steve Thel, "The Original Conception of Section 10(b) of the Securities Exchange Act," *Stanford Law Review* 42 (1990): 385.

[17] See, e.g., Bainbridge, *Insider Trading Law and Policy*, 226.

Section 16(b), it is not surprising that the modern insider trading enforcement regime looks to another section of the act for its statutory support.[18]

2.1.2 *Section 10(b) and the Beginnings of Federal Insider Trading Enforcement*

The principal statutory foundation for the modern insider trading enforcement regime in the United States is Section 10(b) of the Exchange Act. This statute provides in relevant part:

> It shall be unlawful for any person, directly or indirectly, by the use of any means or instrumentality of interstate commerce or of the mails, or of any facility of any national securities exchange –
>
> . . .
>
> (b) To use or employ, in connection with the purchase or sale of any security registered on a national securities exchange or any security not so registered . . . any manipulative or deceptive device or contrivance in contravention of such rules and regulations as the commission may prescribe as necessary or appropriate in the public interest or for the protection of investors.[19]

Section 10(b) was designed as a general antifraud provision and was subsequently implemented as such by the SEC in Exchange Act Rule 10b-5, which provides:

> It shall be unlawful for any person, directly or indirectly, by the use of any means or instrumentality of interstate commerce, or of the mails or of any facility of any national securities exchange,
>
> (a) To employ any device, scheme, or artifice to defraud,
> (b) To make any untrue statement of a material fact or to omit to state a material fact necessary in order to make the statements made, in light of the circumstances under which they were made, not misleading, or
> (c) To engage in any act, practice, or course of business which operates or would operate as a fraud or deceit upon any person, in connection with the purchase or sale of any security.[20]

---

[18] Indeed, Section 16 may be better thought of as an anti–market manipulation provision than an insider trading law. Senior management knows that the markets will look to their trading behavior as reflecting their honest appraisal of the health of the firm. Prior to the market crash, insiders would sometimes play on these expectations, buying (or selling) shares for no other reason than to manipulate the share price. They would then sell (or buy) to take advantage of the artificial price movement. Section 16 is far more effective in protecting against such market manipulation than it is in preventing trading by insiders on material nonpublic information. I thank Professor George A. Mocsary for this point.

[19] 15 U.S.C. § 78(j).

[20] 17 C.F.R. § 240.10b-5.

Generally, criminal or civil liability under Section 10(b) or Rule 10b-5 is understood to require:

(1) Showing a material misrepresentation or omission or other deceptive or manipulative practice.
(2) Showing that such false or misleading statement was "material."
(3) Showing that the defendant acted with intent, to wit, "scienter."
(4) Showing that the defendant's deceptive conduct was "in connection with" the purchase or sale of the subject security.[21]

Though the modern insider trading enforcement regime draws its statutory and rule-based support from the general fraud provisions of Section 10(b) and Rule 10b-5, it took some time to develop. Indeed, it would be almost thirty years before the SEC would enlist its authority under Section 10(b) in an insider trading enforcement action. Why the delay?

First, as a matter of statutory interpretation, it is not surprising that the new SEC, federal prosecutors, and civil plaintiffs looked only to Section 16, and not to 10(b), as the act's only safeguard against insider trading. Thomas Corcoran, the Roosevelt administration's chief lobbyist in support of the act, testified, "Section 10(b) was intended as a catch-all to prohibit the creation of other devices not covered by more explicit sections of the Exchange Act."[22] Insider trading *was*, however, explicitly addressed in Section 16. Again, as noted previously, the preamble to Section 16(b) makes it clear that its purpose is to prevent the "unfair use of information which may have been obtained by" an insider "by reason of his relationship to the issuer." Congress then went on to define the scope and method of Section 16 insider trading enforcement with great precision. It is true that Section 16 is extremely narrow in its

---

[21] This summary of the general elements of Section 10(b) and Rule 10b-5 liability is quoted from William K. S. Wang and Marc I. Steinberg, *Insider Trading* (New York: Oxford University Press, 2010): 102. The US Supreme Court has also recognized an implied private right of action under Section 10(b). See, e.g., Herman & Maclean v. Huddleston, 459 U.S. 375, 380 (1983). In addition to meeting all four of the elements for civil or criminal liability outlined previously, a private civil plaintiff must also prove the following by a preponderance of the evidence:

    (1) Status as a purchaser or seller of a security.
    (2) Unless presumed, establishing reliance.
    (3) Possibly, demonstrating the (plaintiff's) exercise of requisite care.
    (4) Establishing loss causation (i.e., the requisite nexus between the defendant's violative conduct and such plaintiff's loss).
    (5) Showing damages and the monetary amount of such damages.

Wang and Steinberg, *Insider Trading*, 102–03.
[22] "The Securities Exchange Act of 1934 – Principles of Full Disclosure" (2002–2017). From the Securities and Exchange Commission Historical Society, *Fair to All People: The SEC and the Regulation of Insider Trading*, www.sechistorical.org/museum/galleries/it/fullDisclosure_a.php (accessed March 7, 2017) (paraphrasing Corcoran's testimony before the House of Representatives; Stock Exchange Regulation, House Hearing, Committee on Interstate and Foreign Commerce, 73rd Congress, 2nd Session (1934): 115).

reach and weak on enforcement, but, given Congress's extensive treatment of insider trading in the Pecora hearings and in the legislative history, this cannot be dismissed as an oversight. In sum, it would be odd for Congress to be aware of the problem of insider trading, expressly address it in one section of the act, but then leave the *real* restrictions and enforcement provisions pertaining to it to be teased out of some other section that does not reference insider trading at all.

Second, and perhaps more importantly, the common law of insider trading law at the time of the Exchange Act's adoption, as summarized in Chapter 1, still favored the majority rule with a special facts exception. The recognition of a fiduciary duty to disclose for insiders to all shareholders was still the minority view, and even those courts who avowed this minority rule had yet to impose it in transactions over anonymous exchanges, against low-level insiders, or as a matter of regulatory or criminal enforcement. At a minimum, had Congress intended to buck the common law and expand insider trading liability through Section 10(b), one would expect some express reference to this in the legislative history of that section, yet there is none.[23]

Third, it is important to appreciate that the motivating purpose of the act was to address and confront the causes of the market crash and to prevent further blows to an already debilitated economy. Recall that the consensus at the time was that excessive speculation and market manipulation through price rigging were the principal culprits of the market crash. Though insider trading was referenced in the Pecora hearings and legislative history as an evil, it was usually in connection with insiders trading to speculate and price-rig, not to take advantage of material nonpublic information.[24] This is perhaps why Section 16 focuses exclusively on short-swing trading and short sales – two notorious means of speculation and price rigging. As we shall see, true insider trading (trading based on material nonpublic information) could not be further from market manipulation or speculation. The insider who trades on material nonpublic information does not manipulate the market, but, if anything, forces the market price of a stock in the direction of its true value. Insider trading is also the opposite of speculation. Far from betting on how others will react to a sudden price change or market trend, the insider trader buys or sells from the standpoint of relative certainty – based on information reflecting the true state of the firm's current value.

Regardless of the reason, the SEC did not even attempt to enlist Section 10(b) and Rule 10b-5 to enforce an insider trading action (or even hint at the possibility of an action) until the 1960s. Prior to that time, the commission was content allowing insider trading to be enforced by private citizens through Section 16(b). Things

---

[23] See, e.g., Thel, "The Original Conception of Section 10(b) of the Securities Exchange Act."
[24] Indeed, even the notorious Albert Wiggin's short selling that inspired Section 16 of the Exchange Act was an example of speculation and stock price manipulation by an insider, not trading based on material nonpublic information.

changed, however, with the appointment of William Cary as chairman of the SEC by President John F. Kennedy in 1961. Cary, a Columbia law professor, immediately set overturning *Goodwin v. Agassiz* at the top of his agenda.[25] Cary was "convinced that states were not effective regulators of insider trading abuses in the national markets" and set to work to find ways to expand federal enforcement through the SEC.[26]

The SEC's first tack in expanding federal jurisdiction over insider trading was to broaden the scope of Section 16. In *Blau v. Lehman*,[27] a shareholder of Tide Water Associated Oil Company sought to recover short-swing profits from board member Joseph Thomas *and* from the brokerage firm Lehman Brothers, where the board member also happened to be a partner. The SEC advocated on behalf of the private litigant in favor of a broader interpretation of Section 16(b), whereby external partners of an insider as defined by Section 16 would be deemed an insider for purposes of liability under that section. The Supreme Court rejected this broader interpretation, holding that it was "Thomas, not Lehman Brothers as an entity, that was the director of Tide Water."[28] Justice Black's rejection of the commission's policy argument in support of the broader interpretation of Section 16 gives insight into the Court's understanding of insider trading vis-à-vis the Exchange Act at the time and is worth quoting at length:

> The argument of petitioner and the Commission seems to go so far as to suggest that § 16(b)'s forfeiture of profits should be extended to all persons realizing "short swing" profits who either act on the basis of "inside" information or have the possibility of "inside" information. One may agree that petitioner and the Commission present persuasive policy arguments that the Act should be broadened in this way to prevent "the unfair use of information" more effectively than can be accomplished by leaving the Act so as to require forfeiture of profits only by those specifically designated by Congress to suffer those losses. But this very broadening of the categories of person on whom these liabilities are imposed by the language of § 16(b) was considered and rejected by Congress when it passed the Act. Drafts of provisions that eventually became § 16(b) not only would have made it unlawful for any director, officer or 10% stockholder to disclose any confidential information regarding registered securities, but also would have made all profits received by anyone, "insider" or not, "to whom such unlawful disclosure" had been made

---

[25] Goodwin v. Agassiz, 283 Mass. 358 (1933). Recall from Chapter 1 that *Goodwin* offered the final expression of the "majority rule" of insider trading enforcement prior to the introduction of federal regulation. In *Goodwin*, the Massachusetts Supreme Court rejected the idea that corporate insiders owe a duty to disclose material nonpublic information to shareholders prior to trading over anonymous exchanges.

[26] "The SEC Takes Command – William Cary and the Special Study" (2002–2017). From the Securities and Exchange Commission Historical Society, *Fair to All People: The SEC and the Regulation of Insider Trading*, www.sechistorical.org/museum/galleries/it/takeCommand_a.php (accessed March 7, 2017).

[27] Blau v. Lehman, 368 U.S. 403 (1962).

[28] Ibid. at 410.

recoverable by the company. Not only did Congress refuse to give § 16(b) the content we are now urged to put into it by interpretation, but ... so far as the record shows this interpretation of § 16(b) was the view of the Commission until it intervened last year in this case.[29]

After *Blau*, the door to expanded insider trading enforcement through liberal interpretations of Section 16 seemed shut. Another tack was necessary. It was about this time that Cary and the SEC turned to another, more malleable provision of the Exchange Act to achieve their activist insider trading agenda – Section 10(b). Cary himself wrote the administrative opinion *In the Matter of Cady, Roberts & Company*,[30] which both rejected the majority state-law rule as articulated in *Goodwin* and reimagined Exchange Act Rule 10b-5 as providing a new federal basis for broad insider trading enforcement powers.

Cheever Cowdin was on the board of directors of Curtiss-Wright Corporation, but he was also a partner in the brokerage firm Cady, Roberts & Company. When Curtiss-Wright's board decided to reduce their dividends, Cowden immediately notified Robert Gintel, another partner at Cady, Roberts. The facts suggest that Cowden was under the false impression that this information had been made public when he shared it with Gintel.[31] Gintel, knowing that this information was both material and nonpublic, proceeded to sell shares of Curtiss-Wright for his managed accounts. The SEC then brought an enforcement action under Section 10(b) and Rule 10b-5.[32]

On their face, the facts did not support an obvious common law fraud claim. Certainly under *Goodwin* and the majority rule, the fact that Cowdin believed the information had already been made public when he disclosed it to Gintel, together with the fact that Gintel's subsequent trades were made over an anonymous exchange (and not face-to-face), was enough to avoid liability for fraud. Nevertheless, describing the case as one of first impression, Commissioner Cary proceeded to explain the commission's jurisdiction. To begin, Cary explained that Section 10(b) and Rule 10b-5 "are broad remedial provisions aimed at reaching misleading or deceptive activities, whether or not they are precisely and technically sufficient to sustain a common law action for fraud and deceit."[33] Instead, these provisions are intended to be interpreted expansively "to encompass the infinite variety of devices

---

[29] Ibid. at 411–13.

[30] In the Matter of Cady, Roberts & Co., 40 S.E.C. 907 (1961). It should be noted that *Cady, Roberts* was a settled case. As such, Cary's opinion was not subject to judicial review, nor was it subject to an adversarial testing of the facts and law. It is therefore more a speech than an adjudication. I thank Professor Andrew Vollmer for this point.

[31] Ibid. at 917 ("Cowdin probably assumed, without thinking about it, that the dividend action was already a matter of public information and ... he called registrant's office to find out the effect of the dividend news upon the market").

[32] The SEC also brought the action pursuant to Securities Act of 1933 Section 17(a), which shares almost identical terms with Section 10(b) of the Exchange Act. See 15 U.S.C. § 77q(a).

[33] *Cady, Roberts*, 40 S.E.C. at 910.

by which undue advantage may be taken of investors and others."[34] Having set the stage for a liberal interpretation of Section 10(b), Cary then went on to offer the SEC's first articulation of the Rule 10b-5 "disclose-or-abstain rule," whereby persons

> must disclose material facts which are known to them by virtue of their position but which are not known to persons with whom they deal and which, if known, would affect their investment judgment. Failure to make disclosure in these circumstances constitutes a violation of the anti-fraud provisions. If, on the other hand, disclosure prior to effecting a purchase or sale would be improper or unrealistic under the circumstances, we believe the alternative is to forego the transaction.[35]

Cary was careful to point out that, unlike the limited scope of Section 16(b), the restrictions imposed by Section 10(b) apply "to securities transactions by 'any person,'" not just traditional, high-level insiders.[36] Moreover, since it can be assumed material nonpublic information would affect a counterparty's investment judgment either way, it makes no difference for purposes of Section 10(b) liability that a purchase or sale was made over an anonymous exchange or face-to-face.[37] Cary explained that this broad duty to disclose or abstain is based on two elements:

> first, the existence of a relationship giving access, directly or indirectly, to information intended to be available only for a corporate purpose and not for the personal benefit of anyone, and second, the inherent unfairness involved where a party takes advantage of such information knowing it is unavailable to those with whom he is dealing.[38]

The reference to a "relationship giving access" in the first element seems to rely on the traditional state-law fiduciary model for the duty to disclose. This fiduciary justification is then supplemented by a property-based rationale, whereby the material nonpublic "information belong[s] to the corporation, and therefore any use of it by any individual for personal profit [falls] within the prohibitions of Rule 10b-5."[39] The second element seems to rest even more generally on the moral supposition that trading based on *any* material nonpublic information advantages is fundamentally unfair and that Section 10(b) and Rule 10b-5 therefore demand parity of information, or at least equal access, prior to trading. In any event, Cary pointed out that in considering these two elements, "we are not to be circumscribed by fine distinctions and rigid classifications."[40]

On so broad an interpretation, Cary had no trouble finding liability for Gintel, and derivatively for Cady, Roberts. Gintel received information about the reduced

---

[34] Ibid. at 911.
[35] Ibid.
[36] Ibid.
[37] Ibid.
[38] Ibid. at 912.
[39] "The SEC Takes Command – William Cary and the Special Study."
[40] *Cady, Roberts*, 40 S.E.C. at 912.

dividend directly from Cowden, a board member of the issuer. Gintel knew that this information was material and that it was nonpublic, even if Cowden himself did not know it was nonpublic when he shared it. Thus, even if Cowden's reasonable ignorance may have shielded him from liability for any breach of fiduciary duty, Gintel had no such excuse. His knowing and willing sale of the Curtiss-Wright shares constituted a misuse of the company's information to gain an unfair trading advantage over counterparties who had no similar access to this information, and it therefore violated Rule 10b-5.

Cary's opinion in *Cady, Roberts* was merely administrative and established no common law precedent, but its influence would soon reach the courts in *SEC v. Texas Gulf Sulphur Company*.[41] Texas Gulf Sulphur Company (TGS) began mineral exploration activities on the Canadian Shield in eastern Canada in 1957. In November 1963, the exploration group took a core sample that from visual inspection appeared to contain rich copper, zinc, and silver deposits. The president of TGS immediately instructed the exploration team to keep the results of the test drill confidential, to conceal the test hole, and to intentionally drill another barren hole in the same general vicinity of the strike. Under this cloak of secrecy, TGS promptly began acquiring the mineral rights to all the land adjacent to the strike from unwitting landowners. By March 1964, TGS had largely completed its land acquisitions around the test sight and resumed test drilling in the vicinity. A public announcement confirming that TGS had made a twenty-five million–ton ore strike was finally made on April 16, 1963. TGS shares closed at $17 on the day test drilling began at the strike site. The price had reached a price of $26 by the end of March when the land acquisition program was concluded. On the date the strike was announced, the price closed at $36 a share.

During the time between the November 1963 test drill and the April 1964 public announcement of the strike, several TGS officers, directors, and employees purchased TGS stock or calls, either personally or through agents, on the basis of confidential nonpublic information concerning the strike. Two TGS insiders selectively divulged information of the strike to others for use in purchasing TGS stock. The SEC brought an enforcement action against TGS and these traders.[42]

The Second Circuit opinion embraced Cary's interpretation of Rule 10b-5 from *Cady, Roberts* as demanding equal access to information as a matter of fundamental fairness. According to the court, Congress's purpose in Section 10(b) was to ensure that "all investors should have equal access to the rewards of participation in securities transactions," and be "subject to identical market risks."[43] Rule 10b-5 looks to achieve this goal by giving effect to the "justifiable expectation of the securities marketplace that all investors trading on impersonal exchanges have

---

[41] S.E.C. v. Texas Gulf Sulphur Co., 401 F.2d 833 (1968).
[42] See ibid. at 839–47.
[43] Ibid. at 851–52.

relatively equal access to material information."[44] Under the rule, anyone with access to "information intended to be available only for a corporate purpose and not for the personal benefit of anyone may not take advantage of such information knowing it is unavailable to those with whom he is dealing."[45] Such persons have a duty pursuant to Rule 10b-5 to either disclose such information or abstain from trading on it. The court made it very clear that this rule does not apply to insiders alone; indeed, it does not appear to require any special relationship to the source or the counterparty. According to the court, the "only regulatory objective [for Rule 10b-5] is that access to material information be enjoyed equally."[46] The duty to disclose or abstain from trading therefore applies to "anyone in possession of material inside information," regardless of insider status.[47] In this case, the TGS employees and their tippees "were not trading on an equal footing with the outside investors" and therefore violated their duty to disclose or abstain under Rule 10b-5. The court concluded that such "inequalities based upon unequal access to knowledge should not be shrugged off as inevitable in our way of life, or in view of the congressional concern in the area, remain uncorrected."[48]

With the Second Circuit's decision in *Texas Gulf Sulphur*, Cary's expansive interpretation of Section 10(b) and Rule 10b-5 finally enjoyed the courts' imprimatur. The SEC wasted no time in pressing this advantage and expanding its insider trading enforcement efforts over the next decade.[49] In *The Matters of Investors Management Co.*,[50] for example, the SEC seemed to continue to distance itself from the state common law fiduciary model for insider trading liability in favor of a strict equal-access model. In this case, investment advisors, mutual funds, and investment partnerships all received and traded on material nonpublic information they received from a broker-dealer who was underwriting the issuer's debentures. In finding the traders liable, the commission explained that

> one who obtains possession of material non-public corporate information, which he has reason to know emanates from a corporate source, and which by itself places him in a position superior to other investors, thereby acquires a relationship with respect to that information within the purview and restraints of the antifraud provisions.[51]

44 Ibid. at 848.
45 Ibid.
46 Ibid. at 849.
47 Ibid. at 848.
48 Ibid. at 851.
49 There were thirty-five reported insider trading actions brought by the SEC after *Texas Gulf Sulphur*. For an excellent summary of each of these cases, see the appendix to Michael P. Dooley, "Enforcement of Insider Trading Restrictions," *Virginia Law Review* 66 (1980): 1.
50 The Matters of Investors Management Co., 44 S.E.C. 633, WL 120502 (1971).
51 Ibid. at 644.

The departure from the fiduciary model appears complete in this articulation. There is no reference to any relationship of trust and confidence between the bearer of information and the corporate source, nor is there reference to the need of any such relationship to the counterparty. The "inherent unfairness" of trading based on such an information advantage seems enough to warrant Rule 10b-5 liability.[52]

The SEC had its way interpreting insider trading liability under Rule 10b-5 throughout the 1970s, without being checked by the courts. But this honeymoon period came to an abrupt end in 1980, when the Supreme Court looked at insider trading regulation pursuant to Section 10(b) for the first time in *Chiarella v. United States*.[53]

2.2 *CHIARELLA* TO *O'HAGAN*: THE SUPREME COURT WEIGHS IN

Though the SEC brought a number of civil insider trading enforcement actions in the decade following *Texas Gulf Sulphur*, the criminal enforcement of insider trading had yet to be addressed by the circuits. That changed when the Second Circuit recognized Section 10(b) insider trading as a criminal offense in *United States v. Chiarella*.[54] In his capacity as a "markup man" for a financial printer, Vincent Chiarella learned the identities of take-over targets in advance of the market. He then profited on this material nonpublic information by purchasing shares in the target companies in advance of the public announcements. Chiarella was not an insider at the firms whose stocks he traded, and his employer, having been engaged by the purchasing companies, also had no relationship to these take-over targets. Chiarella therefore had no fiduciary or fiduciary-like duties to the target firms or their shareholders. Under the equal-access model affirmed by the courts in *Texas Gulf Sulphur* and since developed by the SEC, however, such a special relationship was not deemed a crucial element of insider trading liability under Rule 10b-5. Chiarella was charged with and tried for insider trading. The district court allowed the jury to convict Chiarella on a finding that "he willfully failed to inform sellers of [the] target company securities that he knew of a forthcoming take-over bid that would make their shares more valuable."[55] In affirming the lower court, the Second Circuit offered its strongest approval to date of the SEC's favored parity-of-information or equal-access model for Rule 10b-5 insider trading liability: "[a]nyone – corporate insider or not – who regularly receives material nonpublic information may not use that information to trade in securities without incurring an

---

[52] Ibid. at 648.
[53] Chiarella v. United States, 445 U.S. 222 (1980).
[54] United States v. Chiarella, 588 F.2d 1359 (2d Cir. 1978), *rev'd* on other grounds, 445 U.S. 222 (1980). Section 10(b) is not a criminal statute, but Section 32(a) of the Exchange Act makes any willful violation of the act a crime. See 15 U.S.C. § 78ff(a).
[55] *Chiarella*, 445 U.S. at 224.

affirmative duty to disclose."[56] According to that court, Congress's intent behind the federal securities law was to create "a system providing equal access to information necessary for reasoned and intelligent investment decisions," and the use of material nonpublic information in trading undermines this goal by giving some traders an unfair advantage over their less informed counterparties.[57] Chiarella's conviction was appealed to the Supreme Court. The Supreme Court reversed, holding that while the trial court's jury instruction may have been consistent with the SEC's theory of insider trading liability, it was not consistent with Section 10(b) of the Exchange Act.

Writing for the Court, Justice Powell explained that though Section 10(b) is "aptly described as a catchall provision ... what it catches must be fraud."[58] Since the typical insider trading case involves a failure to disclose rather than an affirmative misrepresentation, the government must prove a duty to disclose to establish the fraud. Powell explained that the common law duty to disclose arises in such circumstances only when "one party has information 'that the other [party] is entitled to know because of a fiduciary or other similar relation of trust and confidence between them.'"[59] Powell noted that the idea that corporate insiders and stockholders share a relation of trust and confidence giving rise to such a duty to disclose "is not a novel twist of the law."[60] The SEC, of course, had recognized such a duty in *Cady, Roberts* and its progeny, and the federal courts recognized it in *Texas Gulf Sulphur* and other cases.[61] On the foundation of this precedent, the Court embraced what has come to be known as the "classical" theory of Section 10(b) insider trading liability: a corporate insider who seeks to benefit from material nonpublic information by trading in her own company's shares thereby violates a fiduciary or other similar relation of trust and confidence to the current or prospective shareholders of the company on the other side of the transaction and may incur Section 10(b) liability. Powell explained that recognizing such a "disclose-or-abstain" rule guarantees that those "who have an obligation to place the shareholder's welfare before their own, will not benefit personally [at the expense of those shareholders] through [the] use of material, nonpublic information."[62]

While avowing the classical theory of insider trading liability, the *Chiarella* Court expressly rejected the SEC and government's theory of Section 10(b) liability as enforcing "a system providing equal access to information necessary for reasoned and intelligent investment decisions," thereby ensuring certain buyers or sellers do

---

[56] *Chiarella*, 558 F.2d at 1365.

[57] Ibid. at 1362.

[58] *Chiarella*, 445 U.S. at 234–35.

[59] Ibid. at 228 (quoting Restatement (Second) of Torts § 551(2)(a) (1976)).

[60] Ibid. at 227. In reaching this conclusion, Powell relied on recent federal administrative decisions and case law, rather than the more than 100 years of state and federal jurisprudence summarized previously, to back this claim.

[61] Ibid. at 228.

[62] Ibid. at 230.

not enjoy an unfair advantage over less informed buyers and sellers.[63] According to the Court, the formulation of such a broad "parity-of-information" rule, which "departs radically from the established doctrine that duty arises from a specific relationship between two parties ... should not be undertaken absent some explicit evidence of congressional intent."[64] Neither the language of Section 10(b) nor its legislative history, however, offers evidence that Congress intended such a duty, or to impose a "parity-of-information" regime upon the securities markets.[65] An information advantage placing a trader on an unlevel playing field with her counterparties may be unfair, but not "every instance of financial unfairness constitutes fraudulent activity under §10(b)."[66]

There was therefore a twofold error in the lower courts' reasoning. First, by simply instructing the jury to "decide whether [Chiarella] used material nonpublic information at a time when he knew other people trading in the securities market did not have access to the same information," the trial court erroneously found Chiarella "owed a duty [of disclosure] to everyone; to all sellers, indeed, to the market as a whole."[67] Section 10(b) imposes a duty to disclose only where a relation of trust and confidence exists. Second, there were no grounds for Section 10(b) liability under the classical theory. Chiarella was not a corporate insider of the target companies and received no material nonpublic information from them. Thus, Chiarella violated no fiduciary or similar duty of trust and confidence by failing to disclose his material nonpublic information to the sellers on the other side of his transactions. In sum, the Court concluded that "the 1934 Act cannot be read more broadly than its language and the statutory scheme reasonably permit."[68] Section 10(b) is an antifraud provision, and, since Chiarella had no fiduciary relation with his counterparty, the government's theory of Section 10(b) fraud was misguided.

The government offered an alternative theory of Section 10(b) liability in its brief to the Court, arguing that Chiarella "breached a duty to the acquiring corporation when he acted upon information that he obtained by virtue of his position as an employee of a printer employed by the corporation."[69] The Court, however, refused to decide whether this alternative theory had merit because it was never presented to the jury in *Chiarella*.

Though *Chiarella* was a clear defeat for the government, there were some silver linings for the SEC. First and foremost, the Supreme Court placed its imprimatur on the classical theory of insider trading liability – both civil and criminal. This had not been a foregone conclusion, particularly given the weight of common law

---

[63] Ibid. at 232.
[64] Ibid. at 233.
[65] Ibid.
[66] Ibid. at 232.
[67] Ibid. at 231.
[68] Ibid. at 234.
[69] Ibid. at 235.

precedent reflected in *Goodwin* and the majority rule cases that preceded it. Second, though the Court refused to consider the government's proposed misappropriation theory of insider trading liability in *that case*, it did not reject that theory outright. Finally, the concurring and dissenting opinions of four of the nine justices in *Chiarella* suggested that they stood ready to recognize even broader theories of Section 10(b) insider trading liability. For example, Chief Justice Burger wrote in dissent that he "would read § 10(b) and Rule 10b-5 . . . to mean that a person who has misappropriated nonpublic information has an absolute duty to disclose that information or to refrain from trading."[70] Justice Blackmun, joined by Justice Marshall in dissent, would go even further. According to Blackmun, the majority's narrow focus on the need for a relation of trust and confidence before the duty to disclose arises favors form over substance and completely defeats Congress's intent behind Section 10(b) as "an intentionally elastic 'catchall' provision" to protect the "uninitiated investor."[71] Justice Blackmun would dispense with the need to establish a breach of trust – to either the source of the information or the counterparty – and would instead read the Section 10(b) duty to disclose as applying even more broadly to anyone who gains "access to confidential information that the honest investor no matter how diligently he tried, could not legally obtain."[72]

The SEC's reaction to the Supreme Court's decision in *Chiarella* was twofold. It began to develop a misappropriation theory through its enforcement actions in the hope of eventually receiving express approval from the courts. In addition, it looked beyond Section 10(b) for statutory authority to regulate insider trading. Just six months after the Supreme Court decision in *Chiarella* was handed down, the SEC adopted Exchange Act Rule 14e-3 to preclude all trading based on material nonpublic information in the limited context of tender offers.[73]

By the early 1980s, the era of the corporate take-over was underway and, once financed by Michael Milken's junk bond empire, would eventually reach a fevered pitch. A whole new breed of insider traders, the likes of Ivan Boesky and Dennis Levine, thrived in the volatility created by these take-overs. Since most of these traders would receive their material nonpublic information from sources other than the take-over target, *Chiarella* dealt a crippling blow to the SEC's enforcement powers in this area. Rule 14e-3 gave them the weapon they needed by imposing a broad disclose-or-abstain rule upon anyone possessing "material information that relates to a tender offer by another person which information he knows or has reason to know is nonpublic and was acquired, directly or indirectly, from that person or the issuer of the securities" being targeted by the offer.[74] Note that though the scope

---

[70] Ibid. at 240.

[71] Ibid. at 246.

[72] Ibid. at 247.

[73] 17 C.F.R. § 240.14e-3. Rule 14e-3 was adopted pursuant to the SEC's authority under Sections 14(e) and 23(a) of the Exchange Act. 15 U.S.C. §§ 78n(e) and 78w(a) respectively.

[74] Tender Offers, Exchange Act Release No. 17,120, 20 SEC Docket 1350 (Sept. 4, 1980).

of the rule is limited to tender offers,[75] it requires no fiduciary or similar relation of trust between the trader and the source of the information as a basis for the duty to disclose or abstain. It is therefore, at least in this respect, broader in scope than the classical theory articulated by the majority in *Chiarella*, and even broader than the misappropriation theory advocated by Chief Justice Burger in his *Chiarella* dissent. It is beyond dispute that the facts of *Chiarella* would have given rise to Rule 14e-3 liability.

As the SEC scrambled to fill gaps in its enforcement authority in the wake of *Chiarella*, it was dealt yet another stinging setback by the Supreme Court in *Dirks v. S.E.C.*[76] This case addressed the problem of tippee liability under the classical theory. Raymond Dirks was a securities analyst specializing in the insurance sector. He received a tip from a former officer of Equity Funding of America, Ronald Secrist, that the company's assets were vastly overstated as a result of corporate fraud. Secrist "urged Dirks to verify the fraud and disclose it publicly."[77] Dirks investigated the claim and confirmed its truth.[78] Though Dirks did not trade in Equity Funding himself, he told a number of his clients of what he had learned; they sold out of their positions, and word spread. The stock's price dropped from $26 a share to $15 a share during Dirks's two-week investigation. Also during this time, Dirks encouraged the *Wall Street Journal* to write an article about the fraud, but, fearing a libel suit, it declined to do so. The fraud was confirmed soon thereafter, and the firm entered into receivership. Rather than applaud Dirks's efforts to uncover this fraud, however, the SEC brought an enforcement action against him for encouraging his clients to trade based on the tip he received from Secrist.

The SEC had advanced the following theory of tippee liability for Section 10(b) insider trading: "Where tippees – regardless of their motivation or occupation – come into possession of material information that they know is confidential and know or should know came from a corporate insider, they must either publicly

---

[75] The rule itself does not define "tender offer," but the Southern District of New York provided a multifactored standard that has been adopted by a number of jurisdictions:

> (1) active and widespread solicitation of public shareholders for the shares of an issuer; (2) solicitation made for a substantial percentage of the issuer's stock; (3) offer to purchase made at a premium over the prevailing market price; (4) terms of the offer are firm rather than negotiable; (5) offer contingent on the tender offer of a fixed number of shares, often subject to a fixed maximum number to be purchased; (6) offer open only a limited period of time; (7) offeree subjected to pressure to sell his stock.

Wellman v. Dickenson, 475 F. Supp. 783, 823–24 (S.D.N.Y. 1979).

[76] Dirks v. S.E.C., 463 U.S. 646 (1983).

[77] Ibid. at 649.

[78] Indeed, the fraud was startling in its scope and magnitude. Employees at the company reportedly held "forgery parties," where they passed around phony insurance contracts and signed them. See George A. Mocsary, "Statistically Significant Deaths: Disclosing Drug Harms to Investors (and Patients) under SEC Rule 10b-5," *George Washington Law Review* 82 (2013): 170.

disclose that information or refrain from trading."[79] Justice Powell, writing once again for the Court, rejected this theory as rooted in the false premise "that the antifraud provisions [of Section 10(b)] require equal information among all traders."[80] As the Court "emphasized in *Chiarella*, mere possession of nonpublic information does not give rise to a duty to disclose or abstain; only a specific [fiduciary-like] relationship does that."[81] The SEC sought to distinguish this case from *Chiarella*, however, because "Dirks' receipt of inside information from Secrist, an insider, carried Secrist's [fiduciary] duties [to disclose or abstain] with it, while Chiarella received the information without the direct involvement of an insider and thus inherited no duty to disclose or abstain."[82] Powell noted, however, that the SEC could not explain "why the [mere] receipt of nonpublic information from an insider automatically carries with it the fiduciary duty of the insider" without running afoul of *Chiarella's* holding.[83] Moreover, as a matter of public policy, Powell suggested that imposing so broad a disclose-or-abstain rule on all tippees would inhibit market analysts in fulfilling their valuable role in preserving a healthy market. For "[i]t is commonplace for analysts to ferret out and analyze information, and this often is done by meeting with and questioning corporate officers and others who are insiders."[84] Nevertheless, just because persons who receive material nonpublic information from insiders do not *always* acquire a duty to disclose or abstain does not mean they *never* do. Powell therefore laid down the test for tipper-tippee insider trading liability.

The *Dirks* Court held that any disclose-or-abstain duties that a tippee may incur will be crucially derivative; meaning they can only arise from her "role as a participant after the fact in the insider's breach of a fiduciary duty."[85] Thus,

> a tippee assumes a fiduciary duty to the shareholders of a corporation not to trade on material nonpublic information only when the insider has breached his fiduciary duty to the shareholders by disclosing the information to the tippee and the tippee knows or should know that there has been a breach.

The first step in determining Rule 10b-5 tippee liability is therefore to determine whether the tip itself constituted a breach of fiduciary duty. Powell explained that all "disclosures of confidential corporate information are not inconsistent with the duty insiders owe to shareholders." For example, insiders may sometimes disclose information they do not perceive to be material or nonpublic to analysts with the company's best interests in mind. To constitute a breach of fiduciary duty to the

---

79 *Dirks*, ibid. at 651. Note that this is essentially the same broad disclose-or-abstain obligation imposed by the SEC's freshly minted Rule 14e-3 in the context of tender offers.

80 Ibid. at 657.

81 Ibid at 656, n.15.

82 Ibid.

83 Ibid.

84 Ibid. at 658.

85 Ibid. at 659.

shareholders, the insider must seek to personally benefit (directly or indirectly) from the disclosure of the firm's information. The Court therefore held that "[a]bsent some personal gain, there has been no breach of duty to stockholders. And absent a breach by the insider, there is no derivative breach" by the tippee.[86]

The SEC argued that this rule would effectively destroy Section 10(b) enforcement of insider tippee trading because "it would be a rare situation when parties could not fabricate some ostensibly legitimate business justification for transmitting the information."[87] Powell explained, however, that proving the insider's purpose would not require reading his mind – there are a number of objective facts and circumstances that can support the inference of a personal benefit. In addition to evidence of actual pecuniary gain or reputational benefits on the part of the insider, there may be

> a relationship between the insider and the recipient that suggests a *quid pro quo* from the latter, or an intention to benefit the particular recipient. The elements of fiduciary duty and exploitation of nonpublic information also exist when an insider makes a gift of confidential information to a trading relative or friend. The tip and trade resemble trading by the insider himself followed by a gift of the profits to the recipient.[88]

Powell explained that while such proof may sometimes be difficult for the government to provide, and such determinations may be difficult for the courts to make, it is nevertheless crucial that some guidance be offered for those market players whose "daily activities must be limited and instructed by the SEC's inside-trading rules," and "the rule adopted by the SEC in this case would have no limiting principle."[89]

With this test in place, the Court had little difficulty finding that Dirks acquired no Section 10(b) duty to disclose or abstain from trading Equity Funding shares as a result of Secrist's tip. Secrist was motivated by nothing more than the desire to expose the ongoing fraud at the company. He neither expected nor received any personal benefit in exchange for the tip. He therefore violated no fiduciary duty to the Equity Funding shareholders by disclosing to Dirks information pertaining to the fraud. Absent a breach by Secrist, there could be no derivative breach by Dirks.

In just a three-year span, the Supreme Court had dealt two devastating blows to the SEC's once burgeoning insider trading enforcement regime. The SEC turned to Congress to stem the tide. Upon the SEC's urging, Congress passed, and President Reagan signed into law, the Insider Trading Sanctions Act of 1984 (ITSA).[90] The act significantly strengthened the SEC's enforcement power by permitting it to

---

[86] Ibid. at 662.
[87] Ibid. at 663.
[88] Ibid. at 664.
[89] Ibid.
[90] Insider Trading Sanctions Act of 1984, Pub. L. No. 98–376, 98 Stat, 1264 (codified as amended in scattered sections of 15 U.S.C.).

seek treble damages (or three times actual insider trading profits or losses avoided) in its civil actions. One would expect the SEC to have also fought for a statutory definition of insider trading that would legislatively overturn the Supreme Court's decisions in *Chiarella* and *Dirks*, but no definition of insider trading was included in the act. Broader definitions were proposed by some in Congress, but, remarkably, SEC Chairman John Shad cautioned against a statutory definition.[91] The concern was that any express definition would undermine the SEC's flexibility in enforcement. As Professor Stephen Bainbridge put it, there was a fear "that any definition would have to be either so broad as to be unworkable or so narrow as to reduce the SEC's and the courts' flexibility to address new forms of trading."[92]

Emboldened by the passage of ITSA, and confronted with a leveraged buyout frenzy that had reached a fevered pitch, the SEC pressed on with bigger and more sensational insider trading enforcement actions in the mid-1980s. This was the era of the Predators Ball and the "decade of greed." Hollywood had indicted the culture of insider trading in the hit movie *Wall Street*, and the SEC and DOJ were getting big headlines by bringing down the likes of Ivan Boesky on insider trading charges. Throughout this period, and despite its uncertain legal status, the SEC and DOJ continued to rely upon the misappropriation theory of Section 10(b) insider trading liability in civil and criminal enforcement actions. In 1987, the misappropriation theory went before the Supreme Court again in *Carpenter v. United States*.[93]

R. Foster Winans, a *Wall Street Journal* reporter, was prosecuted for trading in advance of the publication of his daily column, which offered buy or sell recommendations on selected stocks. The column was widely read and typically had an impact on the price of the stocks mentioned in it. The *Journal's* official policy was that, prior to publication, the content of the column was the *Journal's* confidential information.[94] In violation of this confidentiality requirement, the reporter entered into an arrangement with brokers whereby he would give them advance notice of the column's recommendations in exchange for a share of their trading profits. Over a four-month period, the scheme netted the participants trading profits of $690,000. Winans and other participants in the scheme were convicted under the federal mail and wire fraud statutes, as well as under the misappropriation theory of Section 10(b) insider trading liability. The district court accepted the government's misappropriation theory of insider trading liability, holding that Winans's breach of confidentiality and concealment of the scheme constituted a fraud on the *Journal*. The court held that the fraud was "in connection with" the purchase or

[91] "Raising the Stakes – Corporate Take-Overs and Insider Trading Scandals in the 1980s" (2002–2017). From the Security and Exchange Commission Historical Society, *Fair to All People: The SEC and the Regulation of Insider Trading*, www.sechistorical.org/museum/galler ies/it/raisingStakes_a.php (accessed March 7, 2017).

[92] Bainbridge, *Insider Trading Law and Policy*, 143 n. 30.

[93] Carpenter v. United States, 484 U.S. 19 (1987).

[94] Ibid. at 23.

sale of securities, despite the fact that the *Journal* (the only victim of the fraud) was not a counterparty to any of Winans's transactions, because "the scheme's sole purpose was to buy and sell securities at a profit based on advance information of the column's contents."[95] The Second Circuit affirmed, and the convictions were appealed to the Supreme Court.

Justice Powell vigorously lobbied the other justices to grant certiorari "in order to reject the misappropriation theory once and for all."[96] Powell was convinced that, pursuant to *Chiarella*, "liability for failure to disclose material information about a transaction under Rule 10b-5 arose only if premised on a relationship of trust and confidence between parties to that transaction."[97] He managed to convince Chief Justice Renquist and Justice O'Connor of this argument and certiorari was granted. After all of these efforts, however, Justice Powell retired from the Court and was not replaced before *Carpenter* was argued. Had Powell remained on the bench, the misappropriation theory would have likely been dead. Without him, however, the Court split, four-to-four, on the validity of the government's misappropriation theory of Section 10(b) insider trading liability, leaving the conviction to stand.[98]

Though *Carpenter* was not itself a defeat for the SEC's misappropriation theory, it signaled that one may be imminent. Harvey Pitt, who would later become chairman of the SEC, warned that the *Carpenter* decision left "the Commission's own enforcement tools in a state of limbo," and Professor James Cox testified before Congress that the decision cast "a menacing shadow on the continued effective enforcement of insider trading rules."[99] With things thus left in the air, the commission returned to Congress for help, this time with a proposed statutory definition of insider trading based on the misappropriation theory it defended in *Carpenter*. The result of these efforts was the Insider Trading and Securities Fraud Enforcement Act of 1988 (ITSFEA).[100] In addition to increasing criminal fines and prison sentences for insider trading, ISTFEA enacted Section 20A of the Exchange Act, which grants a private right of action for those who trade contemporaneously with insider traders.[101] The act also included a "bounty provision," permitting the SEC to offer

---

[95] Ibid. at 24.

[96] "Counterattack from the Supreme Court – Carpenter v. United States" (2002–2017). From the Securities and Exchange Commission Historical Society, *Fair to All People: The SEC and the Regulation of Insider Trading*, www.sechistorical.org/museum/galleries/it/counterAttack_d.php#ftn43 (accessed March 7, 2017).

[97] Ibid.

[98] *Carpenter*, 484 U.S. at 24.

[99] Both of these quotes are drawn from SEC Commissioner Joseph Grundfest's speech before the Federal Bar Association on January 26, 1988. Joseph Grundfest, Commissioner, Securities and Exchange Commission, Address at the Federal Bar Association, "Is the Sky Really Falling? The State of Insider Trading Law after the Winin's Decision" (January 26, 1988) (transcript available from the SEC).

[100] Insider Trading and Securities Enforcement Act of 1988, Pub. L. No. 100–704, 102 Stat. 4677 (codified as amended in scattered sections of 15 U.S.C.).

[101] 15 U.S.C. § 78t-1.

those who inform against insider traders a bounty of up to 10 percent of any civil penalties that are recovered.[102] Perhaps most significantly, ITSFEA extended the civil penalty of treble damages to all "controlling persons"[103] who "knew or recklessly disregarded the fact that [a] controlled person was likely to engage in the act or acts constituting the violation and failed to take appropriate steps to prevent such act or acts before they occurred."[104] The legislative history suggests that one of the principal purposes behind the act was to "increase the economic incentives" for controlling persons to "supervise vigorously their employees."[105] Indeed, the failure to adopt and implement effective insider trading compliance programs and procedures can sometimes stand as evidence of "reckless disregard" under this provision.[106] Noticeably absent from the act, however, was any statutory definition of insider trading. It seems that, as with ITSA, by the time ITSFEA had been hammered out, members of the commission and of Congress had reached the conclusion that any express definition of insider trading would ultimately "narrow [rather than enhance] the SEC's ability to bring enforcement actions."[107] For this reason, despite the recent setbacks before the Supreme Court, then Commissioner Joseph Grundfest and others were convinced that it was best to put proposed legislation that would define insider trading on the "back burner" and instead continue to allow the law of insider trading "to evolve on a case-by-case basis in the courts."[108]

The legal validity of the SEC's misappropriation theory therefore remained in limbo for almost two decades until the Supreme Court finally embraced it in *United*

---

[102] Exchange Act Section 21A(e); 15 U.S.C. § 78u-1(e).

[103] Although ITSFEA does not expressly define "controlling person," the legislative history makes clear that its meaning is adopted from Section 20(a) of the Exchange Act. The Committee Report summarized its meaning as follows:

> "Controlling person" may include not only employers, but any person with power to influence or control the direction or the management, policies, or activities of another person. "Control" is inferred from possession of such power, whether or not it is exercised. The Committee expects the Commission and courts to continue to interpret the term "controlling person" on a case-by-case basis according to the factual circumstances.

H.R. Rep. No. 100–910, at 17 (1988), as reprinted in 1988 U.S.C.C.A.N. 6043, 6054 (citations omitted). See generally Howard M. Friedman, "The Insider Trading and Securities Fraud Enforcement Act of 1988," *North Carolina Law Review* 68 (1990): 465 (discussing the history and implications of ITSFEA).

[104] Exchange Act Section 21A(b)(1)(A); 15 U.S.C. § 78 u-1(b)(1)(A). Issuers were subject to derivative liability for their employees' insider trading violations under Section 20(a) of the Exchange Act, but they were not subject to treble damages.

[105] Wang and Steinberg, *Insider Trading*, 814–15 (quoting H.R. Rep. No. 100–910, at 17).

[106] See ibid. at 884–85; Robert A. Prentice, "The Future of Corporate Disclosure: The Internet, Securities Fraud, and Rule 10b-5," *Emory Law Journal* 47 (1998): 83; Alan M. Weinberger, "Preventing Insider Trading Violations: A Survey of Corporate Compliance Programs," *Securities Regulation Law Journal* 18 (1990): 184–85.

[107] See Jonathan R. Macey, *Insider Trading: Economics, Politics, and Policy* (Washington, DC: The AEI Press, 1991): 64 (quoting Congressman John Dingell).

[108] Grundfest, "Is the Sky Really Falling?"

States v. O'Hagan.[109] James O'Hagan was a partner at a law firm that represented Grand Metropolitan PLC in a potential tender offer for Pillsbury Company. O'Hagan did not actually work on the take-over himself, but learned of it from others in his firm. Based on this nonpublic information, O'Hagan acquired positions in Pillsbury and profited by more than $4.3 million when the take-over was finally announced. Since O'Hagan was neither an actual nor a constructive insider at Pillsbury, he was criminally charged under the SEC's misappropriation theory of Rule 10b-5 insider trading liability, as well as for trading on material nonpublic information pertaining to a tender offer in violation of Rule 14e-3. O'Hagan appealed his convictions, challenging both the legality of the misappropriation theory of Rule 10b-5 insider trading and the SEC's authority in adopting Rule 14e-3. The Eighth Circuit reversed the convictions, holding that the misappropriation theory of insider trading liability was inconsistent with Section 10(b) and that the SEC had exceeded its Section 14(e) rulemaking authority in adopting Rule 14e-3 because it imposes criminal liability without a breach of fiduciary duty. The Supreme Court reversed and reinstated the convictions.

Justice Ginsburg's majority opinion began by distinguishing the misappropriation theory of Section 10(b) liability in question from the "traditional" or "classical" theory.[110] Under the classical theory, liability is incurred when actual corporate insiders ("officers, directors, and other permanent insiders of a corporation, but also … attorneys, accountants, consultants, and others who temporarily become fiduciaries of a corporation") trade on the basis of the company's material nonpublic information. Such trading "qualifies as a 'deceptive device' under § 10(b) … because 'a relationship of trust and confidence [exists] between the shareholders of the corporation and those insiders who have obtained confidential information by reason of their position with that corporation.'"[111] The misappropriation theory, by contrast, holds that liability is incurred where anyone (insider or not) "misappropriates confidential information for securities trading purposes, in breach of a duty owed to the source of the information."[112] Here, "[i]n lieu of premising liability on a fiduciary relationship between company insider and purchaser or seller of the company's stock, the misappropriation theory premises liability on a fiduciary-turned-trader's deception of those who entrusted him with access to confidential information."[113]

Though, as an outsider, O'Hagan could not be found liable for Section 10(b) insider trading under the classical theory, Justice Ginsburg explained that he *was* liable under the misappropriation theory. O'Hagan satisfied the "deceptive device or contrivance" element of Section 10(b) because he pretended loyalty as a fiduciary of

---

[109] United States v. O'Hagan, 521 U.S. 642 (1997).
[110] Ibid. at 651.
[111] Ibid. at 651–52.
[112] Ibid. at 652.
[113] Ibid.

Grand Metropolitan in order to gain its confidential information pertaining to the tender offer.[114] The "in connection with the purchase or sale of any security" element of Section 10(b) was met when O'Hagan acquired a position in the target company based on this information. It did not matter that the deception was committed against the source while the harm was imposed upon the market; Ginsburg pointed out that "a fraud or deceit can be practiced on one person, with resultant harm to another person or group of persons."[115] It also did not matter that the misappropriated information could possibly have been used for some purpose other than securities trading; that the information was "of a sort that misappropriators ordinarily capitalize upon to gain no-risk profits through the purchase or sale of securities" was enough to satisfy the "in connection with" requirement.[116]

In embracing the misappropriation theory, Ginsburg reasoned that, insofar as the impact on the parties and the market is the same in both cases, it makes no sense to hold a lawyer like O'Hagan liable under Section 10(b) if he works for a law firm representing the target of a take-over (as required under the classical theory) but not if he works for a law firm representing the bidder (which would be the result if the misappropriation theory of Section 10(b) liability were to be rejected). The Court found that the language of Section 10(b) does not require this odd result. In fact, Ginsburg pointed out that these two theories of Section 10(b) liability are complementary:

> The classical theory targets a corporate insider's breach of duty to shareholders with whom the insider transacts; the misappropriation theory outlaws trading on the basis of nonpublic information by a corporate "outsider" in breach of a duty owed not to a trading party, but to the source of the information.[117]

The Court also recognized Exchange Act Rule 14e-3 for the first time, though with qualifications. Section 14(e) authorizes the SEC to "define, and prescribe means reasonably designed to prevent, such acts and practices as are fraudulent, deceptive, or manipulative."[118] The Eighth Circuit had held that the SEC exceeded its rulemaking authority in adopting Rule 14e-3(a) because the rule permits liability for fraud regardless of whether a trader's nondisclosure violated some fiduciary duty. In reaching this conclusion, the Eighth Circuit held that the term "fraud" must mean the same in Sections 14(e) and 10(b). In reversing the Eighth Circuit, the Supreme Court focused on the prophylactic nature of Section 14(e)'s mandate. Ginsburg explained that a "prophylactic measure, because its mission is to prevent, typically encompasses more than the core activity prohibited," in this case,

---

[114] Ibid. at 653–54.
[115] Ibid. at 656 (quoting Barbara Bader Aldave, "Misappropriation: A General Theory of Liability for Trading on Nonpublic Information," *Hofstra Law Review* 13 (1984): 120.
[116] Ibid. at 656.
[117] Ibid. at 652–53.
[118] 15 U.S.C. § 78n(e).

fraudulent activity.[119] Consequently, "under § 14(e), the Commission may prohibit acts not themselves fraudulent under the common law or § 10(b), if the prohibition is 'reasonably designed to prevent . . . acts and practices [that] are fraudulent.'"[120] At least on the facts of *O'Hagan* and "other cases of this genre," the Court held that the rule's application was reasonably designed to prevent fraud and did not therefore exceed the SEC's congressional mandate. The Court did, however, leave the door open to revisiting the question under different facts.

The Supreme Court did not address the issue of insider trading again until two decades later in the tipper-tippee case *Salman v. United States*.[121] This case is treated in Chapter 3. At this point it is sufficient to note that the *Salman* Court did little more than reaffirm its prior holdings in *Chiarella*, *Dirks*, and *O'Hagan*.

2.3 SEC RULEMAKING AND OTHER TWENTY-FIRST-CENTURY DEVELOPMENTS

With its decision in *O'Hagan*, the Supreme Court at long last gave its imprimatur both to the misappropriation theory of Section 10(b) insider trading liability and, albeit qualifiedly, to Rule 14e-3. The SEC did not have the parity-of-information or equal-access regime it aspired to, but it had shored up two powerful theories of Section 10(b) liability to address both insider (the classical theory) and outsider (the misappropriation theory) trading. Nevertheless, the Supreme Court's continued insistence on the fiduciary-cum-fraud model still left nagging gaps in coverage, some of which had been filled by Rule 14e-3, but, in 2000, the SEC attempted to fill others with the adoption of new rules.

2.3.1 *Use versus Possession and the Adoption of Rule 10b5–1*

In addition to establishing the duty to disclose, common law fraud requires a finding of scienter (the mental state of intent to deceive or manipulate). Accordingly, the Supreme Court has consistently insisted that liability under Section 10(b) and Rule 10b-5 requires a finding of this mental state. For example, in *Ernst & Ernst v. Hochfelder*,[122] the Supreme Court looked to the language and legislative history of Section 10(b) in reaching the conclusion that mere negligence could not support liability under Rule 10b-5. The Court explained that the "words 'manipulative or deceptive' used in conjunction with 'device or contrivance' strongly suggest that § 10(b) was intended to proscribe knowing or intentional misconduct,"[123] and

---

[119] *O'Hagan*, 521 U.S. at 672–73.
[120] Ibid. at 673.
[121] Salman v. United States, 137 S.Ct. 420 (2016).
[122] Ernst & Ernst v. Hochfelder, 425 U.S. 185 (1976).
[123] Ibid. at 197.

"[t]here is no indication ... that § 10(b) was intended to proscribe conduct not involving scienter."[124] The element of scienter can, however, complicate the already difficult task of insider trading enforcement.

As we have seen, Section 10(b) prohibits insiders from trading in their own company's shares only if they do so based on material nonpublic information. But there are any number of alternative, innocent explanations an insider might offer for the sale of shares: diversifying her portfolio, paying for a child's upcoming wedding or college tuition, building a new house, buying a boat, etc. Such alternative motives are easy to manufacture and difficult to disprove.

Historically, the SEC sought to overcome this challenge by taking the position that the element of scienter in Rule 10b-5 could be satisfied by the insider's knowing possession of material nonpublic information, regardless of whether it is proved the information actually caused the relevant transaction. This strategy met with mixed results in the courts. In *United States v. Teicher*,[125] an attorney fed material non-public information about his firm's corporate client's merger and acquisition plans to others who then traded on that information. The tippee traders were convicted of insider trading pursuant to Section 10(b) and Rule 10b-5. These traders appealed their convictions by challenging, inter alia, the jury instruction that embraced the SEC's possession standard. In dicta, the Second Circuit endorsed the SEC's posses-sion standard, noting that (1) the "in connection with" language of both Section 10 (b) and Rule 10b-5 is to be interpreted flexibly; (2) the mere possession standard comports with the "disclose-or-abstain" maxim that is so often quoted in insider trading jurisprudence; and (3) the "knowing possession" standard has the practical benefit of simplifying the task of enforcement.[126]

In *SEC v. Adler*,[127] however, the Eleventh Circuit rejected the SEC's knowing possession standard. *Adler* involved a corporate director's sale of shares in his own firm's stock while in knowing possession of material nonpublic information. The director offered the defense that the sale in question was part of a trading plan that predated his acquisition of the material nonpublic information in question. The court began its analysis by noting that while Section 10(b) and Rule 10b5-1 do not expressly address the question of whether an insider's mere possession of material nonpublic information at the time of the trading is enough to establish liability, their language "suggests a focus on fraud, deception, and manipulation."[128] Next the court recognized that the Supreme Court has repeatedly indicated, if only in dicta, that the element of scienter for insider trading under Section 10(b) and Rule 10b5–1 requires proof the insider or misappropriators "use[d]," "[took] advantage of," or

---

[124] Ibid. at 202.
[125] United States v. Teicher, 987 F.2d 112 (2d Cir. 1993).
[126] Ibid. at 120.
[127] S.E.C. v. Adler, 137 F.3d 1325 (11th Cir. 1998).
[128] Ibid. at 1333.

traded "on the basis of" material nonpublic information.[129] In addition, the court pointed out that even the SEC has been inconsistent on the issue of "use versus possession."[130] Ultimately, the *Adler* court concluded the "use test" is the most appropriate because it "best comports with the language of § 10(b) and Rule 10b-5, and with the Supreme Court precedent."[131]

Nevertheless, in a nod to the difficulty the SEC faces in proving use in this context, where "the motivations for the trader's decision to trade are difficult to prove and peculiarly within the trader's knowledge," the court held that "when an insider trades while in possession of material nonpublic information, a strong inference [of use] arises."[132] The insider can, however, "rebut the inference by adducing evidence that there was no causal connection between the information and the trade."[133] Later that same year, the Ninth Circuit joined the Eleventh Circuit in expressly rejecting the SEC's possession test in *United States v. Smith*,[134] this time in the context of a criminal insider trading case. The *Smith* court relied heavily on the reasoning of *Adler*.

With two circuits rejecting the SEC's knowing possession test in the same year, the trend in the courts appeared to be in favor of requiring a causal connection between the possession of material nonpublic information and trading to establish liability under Section 10(b) and Rule 10b-5.[135] Rather than risk further erosion of its enforcement power by the courts, the SEC proposed Rule 10b5–1 a year later, in December 1999,[136] and it was adopted in October 2000.[137]

The preliminary note to Rule 10b5–1 explains that the rule "defines when a purchase or sale constitutes trading 'on the basis of' material nonpublic information in insider trading cases brought" under Section 10(b) and Rule 10b-5.[138] The note adds that the law of insider trading is "otherwise defined by judicial opinions construing Rule 10b-5, and Rule 10b5–1 does not modify the scope of insider trading law in any other respect."[139]

---

[129] Ibid. at 1333–34

[130] Ibid. at 1335 n. 26.

[131] Ibid. at 1337–38.

[132] Ibid. at 1337.

[133] Ibid.

[134] United States v. Smith, 155 F.3d 1051, 1070 (9th Cir. 1998).

[135] Much of the following summary first appeared in John P. Anderson, "Anticipating a Sea Change for Insider Trading Law: From Trading Plan Crisis to Rational Reform," *Utah Law Review* 2015 (2015): 349–50.

[136] See Selective Disclosure and Insider Trading, Exchange Act Release No. 33–7787, Fed. Sec. L. Rep. (CCH) ¶ 82,846 (Dec. 20, 1999).

[137] See Selective Disclosure and Insider Trading: Final Rule, 65 Fed Reg. 51,716 (Aug. 24, 2000) (to be codified at 17 C.F.R. pts. 240, 243, 249).

[138] Trading "on the Basis of" Material Nonpublic Information in Insider Trading Cases, 17 C.F.R. § 240.10b5–1 (2014).

[139] Ibid.

Section (a) of Rule 10b5–1 incorporates both the classical and misappropriation theories of insider trading by expressly providing that among the "manipulative and deceptive devices" prohibited by Section 10(b) and Rule 10b-5 is included the purchase or sale of a security "on the basis of" material nonpublic information "in breach of a duty of trust or confidence that is owed directly, indirectly, or derivatively, to the issuer of that security," its shareholders, "or to any other person who is the source of the material nonpublic information."[140] The "use versus possession" issue is then addressed in Section (b) by defining "on the basis of" for purposes of the rule as nothing more than being "aware" of material nonpublic information at the time of the trade. In defining "on the basis of" in terms of "awareness," one commentator noted "the SEC may have indulged in some linguistic legerdemain ... arguably transforming a phrase that connotes a deliberate act ... into something less."[141]

Though the SEC chose the term "aware" rather than "possess," it appears to be a distinction without much of a difference. The final release announcing the rule's adoption explains that "the goals of insider trading prohibitions ... are best accomplished by a standard closer to the 'knowing possession' standard," but, nevertheless, the SEC recognizes that "an absolute standard based on knowing possession, or awareness, could be overbroad in some respects."[142] The release explains that the "new rule attempts to balance these considerations by means of a general rule based on 'awareness' of the material nonpublic information, with several carefully enumerated affirmative defenses."[143] The sole perceivable distinction between knowing possession and the awareness standard adopted appears to be the availability of affirmative defenses in 10b5–1(c) of the rule, which we return to in Chapter 4.

2.3.2 *The Duty of Trust and Confidence and the Adoption of Rule 10b5–2*

One of the principal complications to insider trading enforcement under the classical theory after *Dirks* was establishing the relevant breach of fiduciary duty in tipper-tippee cases. A clear implication of *Dirks* was that an insider's disclosure of material nonpublic information to, for example, seek advice from a trusted family member or friend (who then violates this trust by trading on the information) would not result in insider trading liability under the classical theory for either the insider

---

[140] Ibid. § 240.10b5–1(a); see also Carol B. Swanson, "Insider Trading Madness: Rule 10b5–1 and the Death of Scienter," *University of Kansas Law Review* 52 (2003): 191.

[141] Allan Horwich, "The Origin, Application, Validity, and Potential Misuse of Rule 10b5–1," *Business Lawyer* 62 (2007): 921–22.

[142] Selective Disclosure and Insider Trading: Final Rule, 65 Fed Reg. 51,727 (Aug. 24, 2000) (to be codified at 17 C.F.R. pts. 240, 243, 249).

[143] Ibid.

or the tippee because the disclosure was not motivated by self-dealing. Such disclosures are, however, as one might expect, quite common.

After *O'Hagan*, the SEC could, with new confidence, avail itself of the misappropriation theory to fill enforcement gaps under the classical theory. It was no longer necessary to find a breach of fiduciary or other duty on the part of an insider to form the basis of Section 10(b) insider trading liability. Outsiders and confidants of even well-meaning insiders could now be liable for their trading on material nonpublic information, so long as such trading violated a relation of trust and confidence to the *source* of the information. *O'Hagan*, *Carpenter*, and other cases had established that certain business relationships (such as attorney-client and employer-employee) were themselves enough to establish the requisite relation of trust and confidence. The case law remained unclear, however, as to what types of contractual, family, or other "non-business relationships" might give rise to such a duty. Just as in the "use versus possession" context, the SEC had suffered a recent setback to its preferred interpretation. In *United States v. Chestman*,[144] the Second Circuit held that the marriage relationship alone does not create a relationship of trust and confidence sufficient to generate a duty to disclose under the misappropriation theory. The court held that absent an "express agreement of confidentiality," or a "pre-existing fiduciary-like relationship" between family members, there would not be sufficient basis for Section 10(b) misappropriation trading liability.[145] With *O'Hagan* decided, however, the SEC was emboldened to exercise its rulemaking authority to settle the debate with the adoption of Rule 10b5–2 in 2000.

Rule 10b5–2 provides a "non-exclusive definition of circumstances in which a person has a duty of trust or confidence for purposes of the 'misappropriation' theory of insider trading" under Section 10(b) and Rule 10b-5.[146] By defining the relevant duty as one of "trust *or* confidence" as opposed to "trust *and* confidence" as the Supreme Court articulated it in *Chiarella*, *Dirks*, and *O'Hagan*, the SEC from the outset attempted to expand the scope of 10b-5 insider trading liability to potentially encompass trading on information that is shared in confidence but outside a fiduciary or fiduciary-like relationship of trust.[147] This expanded scope is reflected in the three duty-creating circumstances defined by the rule, none of which appear to require anything more than an expectation of mere confidentiality:

(1) Whenever a person agrees to maintain information in confidence;
(2) Whenever a person communicating the material nonpublic information and the person to whom it is communicated have a history, pattern, or practice of sharing confidences, such that the recipient of the

---

[144] United States v. Chestman, 947 F.2d 551 (2d Cir. 1991), cert. denied, 503 U.S. 1004 (1992).
[145] Ibid. at 571.
[146] 17 C.F.R. § 240.10b5–2.
[147] See, e.g., Donna Nagy, "Insider Trading and the Gradual Demise of Fiduciary Principles," *Iowa Law Review* 94 (2009): 1369.

information knows or reasonably should know that the person communicating the material nonpublic information expects that the recipient
will maintain its confidentiality; or

(3) Whenever a person receives or obtains material nonpublic information
from his or her spouse, parent, child, or sibling; provided, however, that
the person receiving or obtaining the information may demonstrate that
no duty of trust or confidence existed with respect to the information,
by establishing that he or she neither knew nor reasonably should have
known that the person who was the source of the information expected
that the person would keep the information confidential.[148]

The first of these circumstances offers the most obvious deviation from the fiduciary-
cum-fraud framework established by the Supreme Court by requiring nothing
more than an agreement of confidentiality to create the requisite duty. In *SEC v.
Cuban*,[149] for example, the SEC relied on a purported agreement to keep information of a company's upcoming private investment in public equity (PIPE)
offering confidential to support its charge that Mark Cuban's subsequent sale of
shares in that company constituted insider trading under the misappropriation
theory. The district court rejected the SEC's argument, holding that Section 10(b)
insider trading liability requires "more than an express or implied promise merely to
keep information confidential. It must also impose on the party who receives the
information the legal duty to refrain from trading on or otherwise using the information for personal gain."[150] The court emphasized that "nondisclosure and nonuse
are logically distinct," and misappropriation insider trading liability based on a
contractual relationship must be founded on an express or implied agreement to
both.[151] But even if the *Cuban* district court's restriction on Rule 10b5–2 were
ultimately upheld, as Professor Bainbridge pointed out, the simple fact that it
permits the requisite duty to be founded on a mere contractual relationship (as
opposed to a richer fiduciary-like relation) may have already stretched the model
articulated in *Chiarella* and *Dirks* "to its breaking point."[152]

2.3.3 *Equal Access and Adoption of Regulation Fair Disclosure*

However much the SEC may have stretched the Supreme Court's fiduciary-cum-
fraud model to fill enforcement gaps through its adoption of Rules 10b5–1 and
10b5–2, the Court's repeated insistence that Section 10(b) only regulates fraud has

---

[148] 17 C.F.R. § 240.10b5–2(b)(1)-(3).
[149] S.E.C. v. Cuban, 634 F.Supp.2d 713 (2009), vacated and remanded, 620 F.3d 551 (5th
Cir. 2010).
[150] Ibid. at 725.
[151] Ibid.
[152] Bainbridge, *Insider Trading Law and Policy*, 170.

presented an insurmountable obstacle to the commission's use of that statute to implement the parity-of-information or equal-access regime it has sought since *Cady, Roberts*. For example, after *Dirks*, it became quite clear that no interpretation of Section 10(b) would prevent well-meaning insiders from disclosing material nonpublic information to analysts or others (who might then choose to trade on it), so long as the disclosure looks to advance the firm's interests. The SEC would therefore have to look to some statutory authority other than Section 10(b) to preclude such disclosures, and this is precisely what it did with the adoption of Regulation FD (Fair Disclosure).[153]

Regulation FD requires that when issuers or persons acting on their behalf disclose "material nonpublic information to certain enumerated persons (in general, securities market professionals and holders of the issuer's securities who may well trade on the basis of the information), [they] must make public disclosure of that information."[154] If the selective disclosure is intentional, the rule requires that the information be "simultaneously" disclosed to the general public; if it is unintentional, then it must be disclosed "promptly."[155] The SEC claimed that Regulation FD is motivated by the same policy interests and concerns that drive the regulation of insider trading pursuant to Rule 10b-5 – ensuring a "level playing field" for investors, bolstering "confidence in the fairness of the markets," and preventing the exploitation of "unerodable informational advantages."[156] Nevertheless, the commission is equally clear that Regulation FD "is not an antifraud rule," but rather an "issuer disclosure rule" adopted pursuant to the SEC's authority under Sections 13(a) and 15(d) of the Exchange Act, and Section 30 of the Investment Company Act of 1940.[157] As such, Regulation FD does not create new duties under Section 10(b) or any of the other "antifraud provisions of the federal securities laws or in private rights of action."[158] Consequently, it is unclear how, if at all, the adoption of Regulation FD affects the law of insider trading. The potential consequences of Regulation FD for the law of insider trading are addressed further in Chapter 3.

2.3.4 *Stop Trading on Congressional Knowledge Act of 2012*

In 2011, Peter Schweizer published his book *Throw Them All Out*, in which he exposed some of the dubious means by which politicians manage to increase their personal wealth 50 percent faster than the average American. Among the most

---

[153] 17 C.F.R. § 243.100–103.
[154] Selective Disclosure and Insider Trading: Final Rule, 2000 WL 1200556 (Aug. 24, 2000).
[155] 17 C.F.R. § 243.100(a)(1)-(2).
[156] Selective Disclosure and Insider Trading: Final Rule, 2000 WL 1200556 (Aug. 24, 2000).
[157] Ibid.
[158] Ibid.

common congressional investment tools highlighted by Schweizer's study was, not surprisingly, trading on material nonpublic information.[159] Schweizer cited a study finding that:

- The average American investor underperforms the market.
- The average corporate insider, trading his own company's stock, beats the market by 7 percent a year.
- The average hedge fund beats the market by 7 percent and 8 percent a year.
- The average senator beats the market by 12 percent a year.[160]

The release of Schweizer's book was soon followed by a scathing expose on the CBS TV news magazine *60 Minutes*, highlighting many of the congressional trades chronicled in the book. The resulting public outcry spurred Congress to action, and the Stop Trading on Congressional Knowledge (STOCK) Act was signed into law just a few months later, on April 4, 2012.

There was never any question that members and employees of Congress are subject to the same Section 10(b) insider trading restrictions as everyone else. There was, however, a concern that the law had not recognized a fiduciary duty for congressional insiders to refrain from personally benefiting from the confidential information they might acquire by virtue of their position within the government. Without a clear fiduciary duty to the source (in this case, the government or the public), there could be no insider trading liability pursuant to the misappropriation theory.[161] The STOCK Act closed this perceived loophole by amending Section 21A of the Exchange Act to expressly provide that "each Member of Congress or employee of Congress owes a duty arising from a relationship of trust and confidence" to Congress, the government, and the public "with respect to material, nonpublic information derived from such person's position ... or gained from the performance of such person's official responsibilities."[162]

The STOCK Act's ultimate effectiveness in changing the stock-trading habits of members of Congress and their employees remains to be seen, but the initial signs are not encouraging. It took three years for the SEC to initiate its first investigation under the act. Brian Sutter, then a staffer for the House Ways and Means Committee, was alleged to have tipped a lobbyist about an upcoming Medicare decision, who then immediately passed the tip along to hedge funds that traded on it. Almost immediately after the SEC began investigating Sutter, lawyers for the House of

---

[159] Peter Schweizer, *Throw Them All Out* (New York: Houghton Mifflin Harcourt, 2011).

[160] Ibid. at xvi.

[161] See Jeanne Schreoder, "Taking Stock: Insider and Outsider Trading by Congress," *William and Mary Business Law Review* 5 (2014): 165 (STOCK Act was motivated by the lack of clarity in applying the misappropriation theory of insider trading in the governmental context).

[162] 15 U.S.C. § 78u-1(g).

Representatives moved to block it, claiming that it violated the separation of powers and was therefore unconstitutional.[163] Regardless of the validity of the constitutional challenge, with Congress controlling the SEC's budget and responsible for confirming its commissioners, it is highly unlikely that the STOCK Act will be enforced aggressively.

****

These first two chapters have offered an overview of the historical development of insider trading law in the United States. To take stock: from the beginning, state courts addressed insider trading within the context of common law fraud. The majority rule was that insiders could avail themselves of material nonpublic information when trading in their own companies' shares so long as they did not make any affirmative misrepresentations or actively conceal material nonpublic information. Importantly, however, the majority of the early state courts did not recognize any fiduciary or other duty on the part of insiders to disclose material nonpublic information to shareholders prior to trading absent special circumstances. By the late nineteenth century, however, a growing number (though still a minority) of courts began to recognize a fiduciary-like relationship between senior management and shareholders that gives rise to a duty to disclose material nonpublic information to shareholders prior to trading at arm's length. Nevertheless, at the time of the adoption of the Securities Exchange Act of 1934, no court had recognized a fiduciary duty to disclose for insiders who were not members of senior management, nor for any insider trading over an anonymous exchange. Moreover, all of these early state-law cases were essentially contract disputes, with the plaintiff seeking rescission and restitution. No civil fines or criminal liability was imposed.

Even after the promulgation of the Exchange Act and the advent of federal regulation of the securities markets, there was no attempt by the SEC or prosecutors to regulate insider trading for almost thirty years, other than under the limited provisions of Section 16. When the SEC did begin to regulate insider trading pursuant to Section 10(b) of the Exchange Act in the early 1960s, it did not justify it on the fiduciary-cum-fraud basis articulated in the early state court cases, but rather in terms of fairness (ensuring equal access to market information – or perhaps even parity of information) and promoting market confidence. The Supreme Court ultimately rejected the SEC's favored equal-access regime, holding that whatever Section 10(b) regulates, it must be some form of fraud. Since that time, the SEC has been forced to live within this fiduciary-cum-fraud framework, though it has fought to expand it to better approximate the equal-access framework by pushing creative

---

[163] See Lee Fang, "Congress Tells Court that Congress Can't Be Investigated for Insider Trading," Theintercept.com (May 7, 2015), https://theintercept.com/2015/05/07/congress-argues-cant-investigated-insider-trading/.

theories of liability (such as the misappropriation theory) and by exercising its rulemaking authority (such as with the adoption of Rules 14e-3, 10b5–1, 10b5–2, and Regulation FD).

The narrative that emerges is nothing like a linear progression toward a coherent theory of insider trading liability – it is quite the opposite. The modern insider trading regime exploded on the scene in the early 1960s in a new form barely contemplated by prior state court decisions – the equal-access theory. This theory was vehemently rejected by the Supreme Court as contrary to law in the early 1980s, and since that time the law's evolution has resembled something like a tug of war between regulators and the courts. As the next chapter demonstrates, this tension between regulators and the courts has resulted in a great deal of legal uncertainty.

3

The Problem of Vagueness in the Law

Though the SEC and courts have offered inconsistent accounts of the underlying principles and overarching goals informing the insider trading regime in the United States, it is nevertheless tempting to conclude that after *United States v. O'Hagan* a relatively clear and consistent test for liability has emerged. It looks something like this: absent an affirmative misrepresentation, Section 10(b) insider trading liability can arise only from fraudulent deception through the breach of a duty to disclose. The duty to disclose can be breached in two circumstances. First, under the classical theory, the duty is breached where an insider trades (or tips) on the basis of material nonpublic information in violation of a relation of trust and confidence to the firm's shareholders. Second, under the misappropriation theory, the duty is breached where *anyone* trades (or tips) based on material nonpublic information in violation of a relation of trust and confidence to the source of the information (whomever that may be). Tippee liability is derivative upon an original tipper's breach under either of the preceding theories.

On closer inspection, however, the façade of clarity and consistency crumbles. The goal of this chapter is to expose the weak underbelly of insider trading jurisprudence in the United States. Absent any significant guidance by statute or rule, insider trading's common law development has brought little if any clarity to the key elements of the crime. For example, few scholars, regulators, or courts can agree on what information qualifies as "material" or "nonpublic," or even on what it means to trade "on the basis of" information. Still more concerning, the SEC and the courts are even at odds concerning what counts as a "relation of trust and confidence," the very foundation for the duty to disclose. These problems of vagueness in the law are then amplified further in the context of derivative tipper and tippee liability. In short, this chapter shall expose each of the elements of Section 10(b) insider trading liability developed in Chapter 2 as exceedingly vague, and sometimes incoherent. Chapter 4 will show that this ambiguity and incoherence in the law has left market participants unable to plan their trading to avoid liability without taking sides in a number of ongoing scholarly debates, splits among circuits, and conflicting direction from the SEC and the courts. The result is an inefficient, unfair, and irrational insider trading enforcement regime that is in need of reform.

3.1 WHEN IS INFORMATION MATERIAL?

In *Basic Inc. v. Levinson*,[1] the Supreme Court held that information is material for purposes of Section 10(b) liability if "there is a substantial likelihood that a reasonable shareholder would consider it important" in making a trading decision.[2] In addition, "there must be a substantial likelihood that the disclosure of the omitted fact would have been viewed by the reasonable investor as having significantly altered the 'total mix' of information made available."[3] But, as Professor Joan MacLeod Heminway explained, "[t]he facial simplicity" of this definition "masks the complexities encountered by transaction planners" and others in applying it.[4]

The qualitative materiality standard articulated in *Basic* is subject to multiple interpretations.[5] For example, who is the "reasonable shareholder" or "reasonable investor"?[6] Is she small or institutional, a short-term speculator or long-term investor?[7] What constitutes the "total mix" of information?[8] And, under any reading, the *Basic* standard demands a fact-intensive analysis that will expose even the most thoughtful and diligent advance planning to second guessing by regulators and the courts ex post.[9] For example, information concerning a potential problem or opportunity for an issuer may be judged so speculative at the time of a proposed trade that advance disclosure would be misleading to the public.[10] But if the trade is executed without disclosure, and the problem or opportunity later comes to pass, it will often appear material in retrospect.[11] This example illustrates the problem raised by the awareness of contingent or "soft" information in advance of a trade.

---

[1] Basic Inc. v. Levinson, 485 U.S. 224 (1988).

[2] Ibid. at 231–32 (quoting TSC Indus., Inc. v. Northway, Inc., 426 U.S. 438, 449 (1976) (articulating this definition of materiality in the context of proxy solicitations)).

[3] Ibid. at 231–32 (quoting *TSC Indus.*, 426 U.S. at 449).

[4] Joan MacLeod Heminway, "Materiality Guidance in the Context of Insider Trading: A Call for Action," *American University Law Review* 52 (2003): 1138–39.

[5] Much of the following discussion of vagueness in the law of insider trading first appeared in John P. Anderson, "Solving the Paradox of Insider Trading Compliance," *Temple Law Review* 88 (2016): 273–311.

[6] Heminway, "Materiality Guidance in the Context of Insider Trading," 1152.

[7] See, e.g., Donald C. Langevoort, "Commentary: Stakeholder Values, Disclosure, and Materiality," *Catholic University Law Review* 48 (1998): 98 ("[I]nvestors are not homogeneous.").

[8] Heminway, "Materiality Guidance in the Context of Insider Trading," 1152–53.

[9] See ibid. at 1140 ("[T]his failure of [regulatory] guidance may ... lead to allegations that there has been a failure of adequate disclosure, even with thoughtful advance planning.").

[10] See A. C. Prichard, "Markets as Monitors: A Proposal to Replace Class Actions with Exchanges as Securities Fraud Enforcers," *Virginia Law Review* 85 (1999): 936–37.

[11] See ibid.

Soft information is information that "inherently involves some subjective analysis or extrapolation, such as projections, estimates, opinions, motives, or intentions."[12] As Professors William Wang and Marc Steinberg explained, such information "does not necessarily relate to expectations regarding the future, but may include any statement that cannot be factually supported, whether due to a lack of substantiating data or because the information consists primarily of subjective evaluations or opinions."[13] In *Basic*, the Supreme Court addressed the problem of soft information by suggesting that its materiality should be determined "upon a balancing of both the indicated probability that the event will occur and the anticipated magnitude of the event in light of the totality of the company activity."[14] But, rather than improve clarity, the *Basic* probability-magnitude test has itself been criticized as vague and unhelpful.

The *Basic* probability-magnitude test appears at first blush to be modeled after the famous Learned Hand formula from tort law.[15] Under that formula, liability is determined by weighing the product of the probability of injury and its "gravity" against the "burden of adequate precautions."[16] If the former is greater than the latter, then liability is imposed for failure to take adequate precautions.[17] But the *Basic* test adopts only half of the equation. It offers nothing corresponding to the "burden of adequate precautions" value in the Hand formula.[18] In other words, the *Basic* formula offers no objective threshold for materiality. As Professor Stephen Bainbridge put it, the Court "never tells us how high a probability or how large a magnitude is necessary for information to be deemed material."[19] Consequently, insiders who trade based on speculative information must do so "knowing that a jury, acting with the benefit of hindsight, may reach a different conclusion about how probability and magnitude should be balanced" than they do at the time of the trade.[20]

---

[12] William K. S. Wang and Marc I. Steinberg, *Insider Trading* (New York: Oxford University Press, 2010) (quoting Bruce A. Hiler, "The SEC and the Courts' Approach to Disclosure of Earnings Projections, Asset Appraisals, and Other Soft Information: Old Problems, Changing Views," *Maryland Law Review* 46 (1987): 1116).

[13] Ibid.

[14] *Basic*, 485 U.S. at 238 (quoting S.E.C. v. Texas Gulf Sulphur Co., 401 F.2d 833, 849 (2d Cir. 1968)); see also United States v. Smith, 155 F.3d 1051, 1065–6 (9th Cir. 1998) (concluding that the soft information at issue was material).

[15] See Stephen M. Bainbridge, *Insider Trading Law and Policy* (St. Paul, MN: Foundation Press, 2014): 67.

[16] United States v. Carroll Towing Co., 159 F.2d 169, 173 (2d Cir. 1947).

[17] Ibid. ("[I]f the probability be called P; the injury, L; and the burden, B; liability depends upon whether B is less than L multiplied by P: i.e., whether B [is] less than PL.").

[18] See Bainbridge, *Insider Trading Law and Policy*, 67.

[19] Ibid.

[20] Ibid.

Finally, there is the disturbing problem of "bootstrapping" by courts when making materiality determinations.[21] In *SEC v. Texas Gulf Sulphur Co.*, the Second Circuit explained that "a major factor in determining whether" information is material "is the importance attached to the [information] by those who knew about it."[22] And, according to the court, an insider's choice to trade can by itself serve as an indication of such importance.[23] In *Basic*, the Supreme Court confirmed that "trading (and profit making) by insiders can serve as an indication of materiality."[24] But if trading alone can indicate materiality, then, as Professor Bainbridge has argued, "the materiality requirement becomes meaningless because all information in the defendant's possession when he or she traded would be material."[25]

In sum, the lack of a clear and objective standard permits almost any information to be deemed material for purposes of insider trading liability, at least with the benefit of hindsight. Such flexibility can be quite useful to the SEC and prosecutors. Consequently, it should come as no surprise that the SEC has openly resisted efforts to bring greater clarity to the definition of materiality.[26] But even if a trader who is charged with insider trading stands little chance of mounting a defense based on the immateriality of the information he possessed, one might think it possible to defend on the claim that it was public at the time of trading. It turns out, however, that the test for whether information is public is no clearer than that for materiality.

3.2 WHEN IS INFORMATION NONPUBLIC?

In his dissenting opinion in *Dirks*, Justice Harry Blackmun expressed frustration that

[t]he SEC seemingly has been less than helpful in its view of the nature of disclosure necessary to satisfy the disclose-or-refrain duty. The [SEC] tells persons

---

[21] Ibid. at 68.

[22] *Texas Gulf Sulphur*, 401 F.2d at 851.

[23] Ibid. ("[T]he timing by those who knew of it of their stock purchases and their purchases of short-term calls – purchases in some cases by individuals who had never before purchased called or even TGS stock – virtually compels the inference that the [information was material].").

[24] *Basic*, 485 U.S. at 140 n. 18.

[25] Bainbridge, *Insider Trading Law and Policy*, 68.

[26] See Heminway, "Materiality Guidance in the Context of Insider Trading," 1140 (noting that the SEC "purposefully has left ambiguous the effect of applying the existing materiality standard to any specific factual situation"); see also Selective Disclosure and Insider Trading, Exchange Act Release No. 43,154, 65 Fed. Reg. 51,716, 51,721 (Aug. 24, 2000) (acknowledging that "materiality judgments can be difficult," but that the SEC does not "believe an appropriate answer to this difficulty is to set forth a bright-line test"); John M. Fedders, "Qualitative Materiality: The Birth, Struggles, and Demise of an Unworkable Standard," *Catholic University Law Review* 48 (1998): 42 (pointing out that the SEC has "stubbornly refused to promulgate rules designed to fill in the details of a broadly stated qualitative standard or materiality").

with inside information that they cannot trade on that information unless they disclose; it refuses, however, to tell them how to disclose.[27]

Blackmun added, "This seems to be a less than sensible policy, which it is incumbent on the [SEC] to correct."[28] Despite this admonition, the SEC has yet to issue a rule on proper disclosure – on when information will be deemed public for purposes of insider trading liability.[29] This poses a problem because, as two commentators put it, "[w]hile on its face the concept might seem simplistic, the dividing line between public and nonpublic information is porous."[30]

In the absence of a statute or rule defining when information becomes public, the SEC and the courts have applied two tests: the "dissemination and absorption" test and the "efficient market" test.[31]

Under the dissemination and absorption test, to become public, information must first be "disseminated in a manner calculated to reach the securities marketplace in general through recognized channels of distribution."[32] Courts have understood the requirement that the disclosure be "general" to mean that it must not favor "any special person or group."[33] So, for example, courts have found appearances on the Dow Jones broad tape[34] or on the Reuters Financial Report wire service[35] to be sufficient dissemination, but dissemination over less recognized wire systems (e.g., AutEx) has been found insufficient because it reached only a limited number of subscribers.[36] Dissemination is, however, only half the test. The information must also be "*absorbed* by the investing public," and absorption is not necessarily simultaneous with dissemination.[37] As the court explained in *Texas Gulf Sulphur*, "[w]here the news is of a sort which is not readily translatable into investment action, insiders may not take advantage of their advance opportunity to evaluate

---

[27] Dirks v. S.E.C., 463 U.S. 646, 678 (1983) (Blackmun, J. dissenting).

[28] Ibid.

[29] See Wang and Steinberg, *Insider Trading*, 145 (noting that the SEC has not issued a rule on proper disclosure and has preferred to adopt a case-by-case, fact-based approach). Even Regulation Fair Disclosure (Regulation FD) (adopted in 2000) does not define "nonpublic." 17 C.F.R. §§ 243.100–243.103 (2016).

[30] Bradley J. Bondi and Steven D. Lofchie, "The Law of Insider Trading: Legal Theories, Common Defenses, and Best Practices for Ensuring Compliance," *New York University Journal of Law and Business* 8 (2011): 170.

[31] See Wang and Steinberg, *Insider Trading*, 143.

[32] In the Matter of Certain Trading in the Common Stock of Faberge, Inc., 1973 WL 149283 (May 25, 1973).

[33] *Dirks*, 463 U.S. at 653 n. 12 (quoting *Faberge, Inc.*, 1973 WL 149283, at *6).

[34] See *Texas Gulf Sulphur Co.*, 401 F.2d at 854 (noting that information remains nonpublic "until [it] could reasonably have been expected to appear over the media of widest circulation, the Dow Jones broad tape").

[35] See, e.g., DuPont Glore Forgan, Inc. v. Arnold Bernhard & Co., 73 Civ. 3071, 1978 WL 1062, at *7 (S.D.N.Y. Feb. 27, 1978).

[36] See, e.g., *Faberge, Inc.*, 1973 WL 149283, at *6.

[37] Wang and Steinberg, *Insider Trading*, 145.

the information by acting immediately upon dissemination."[38] It is, however, unclear just when information becomes translatable into investment action, and opinions vary dramatically.[39] Some courts have suggested that absorption occurs as little as fifteen minutes after information hits the wire.[40] In *SEC v. Ingoldsby*,[41] however, the court held that information of a change in leadership remained nonpublic nine days after a press release and eight days after it was highlighted in a *Wall Street Journal* article because the issuer was small and the information had not been fully digested by the relevant investing public.[42]

The omnipresence of the Internet has made the question of dissemination and absorption of information still more unpredictable and inscrutable.[43] Companies can now "functionally" disseminate information without filing it with the SEC or releasing it to a public news source (e.g., by posting it on Twitter, Facebook, a LISTSERV, the company website, etc.).[44] But there is no guarantee that such functional dissemination will be recognized as legally sufficient by the SEC.[45] At the end of the day, market participants are simply left guessing as they navigate these "murky waters."[46]

Though the SEC has pushed the dissemination and absorption method as its preferred test for whether information is nonpublic for the purpose of Section 10(b) insider trading liability,[47] its vagueness has led some courts to adopt an alternative

---

[38] *Texas Gulf Sulphur*, 401 F.2d at 854 n. 18.

[39] See, e.g., Robert A. Prentice, "The Internet and Its Challenges for the Future of Insider Trading Regulation," *Harvard Journal of Law and Technology* 12 (1999) (noting that "there is no clear rule regarding what period of time constitutes a reasonable period for absorption . . . [and] [r]esults . . . have varied widely" based on the issuer and the nature and complexity of the information).

[40] See Billard v. Rockwell Int'l Corp., 526 F. Supp. 218, 220 (S.D.N.Y. 1981) (quoting 2 Alan R. Bromberg & Lewis D. Lowenfels, *Securities Fraud & Commodities Fraud* § 7.4(7)(B) (1967)).

[41] S.E.C. v. Ingoldsby, Civ. A. No. 88–1001-MA, 1990 WL 120731 (D. Mass. May 15, 1990).

[42] Ibid. at *5.

[43] Bondi and Lofchie, "The Law of Insider Trading," 170 ("Due to the prevalence of online message boards, social networking, and blogs, information and rumors about companies can spread quickly to millions of interconnected investors. In some cases those rumors are leaked by company insiders. The growth of so-called watchdog groups, such as Wikileaks, have generated a new level of uncertainty as to what information is considered 'nonpublic.'").

[44] See, e.g., Prentice, "The Internet and Its Challenges for the Future of Insider Trading Regulation," 279.

[45] See Selective Disclosure and Insider Trading: Final Rule, 2000 WL 1201556, at 16 (Aug. 24, 2000) (noting that posting on a corporate website is not sufficient for "public disclosure" under Regulation FD); Wang and Steinberg, *Insider Trading*, 146–47 (suggesting that certain methods of disseminating information on the Internet may not satisfy the dissemination and absorption approach); Prentice, "The Internet and Its Challenges for the Future of Insider Trading Regulation," 279–93 (discussing available technology for the release of information that the SEC has not yet provided guidance on).

[46] Prentice, "The Internet and Its Challenges for the Future of Insider Trading Regulation," 279.

[47] Bondi and Lofchie, "The Law of Insider Trading," 171–72 (the SEC has "clung" to the dissemination and absorption theory).

method based on the "efficient capital market hypothesis" (ECMH).[48] The ECMH comes in "weak," "semi-strong," and "strong formulations."[49] The weak formulation holds that stock prices are entirely random – not affected by past events – and are therefore impossible to predict with any certainty. The strong formulation reaches the same conclusion (that stock prices cannot be predicted) by a different route. It holds that *all* current information (both public and private) is immediately impounded in the price of stocks; trying to "beat" the market with superior information is therefore an exercise in futility. The semi-strong formulation of the ECMH is the most widely accepted; it "posits that at any given time, share prices in an efficient market will incorporate all publicly available information relating to publicly traded companies (in addition to general information about the economy as a whole)."[50] It is the latter, semi-strong version of the ECMH that has informed some courts in determining whether information is public for purposes of insider trading liability. Under this efficient market approach, information is considered public when it is impounded in the price of the stock by traders in the active investment community, regardless of whether the issuer has disclosed the information by public announcement or SEC filing. In *United States v. Libera*, a trader was charged under the misappropriation theory for purchasing prerelease copies of a stock-picking column in *Business Week* magazine from employees of the magazine's printer and then trading on them.[51] Part of Libera's defense was that the information was already public because trading records showed that stocks highlighted in the article regularly increased in trading volume and price a full day before the magazine hit the stands. The Second Circuit agreed that

> information may be considered public for Section 10(b) purposes even though there has been no public announcement and only a small number of people know it. The issue is not the number of people who possess it but whether their trading has caused the information to be fully impounded in the price of the stock.[52]

After all, information can hardly be misused for trading profits after it is fully reflected in the price of the stock. Even while accepting the ECMH model, however, the Second Circuit rejected Libera's argument because, in his case, the stocks typically continued to increase in volume and price even after the magazine's release to the general public, and this was evidence that the information had been only partially impounded at the time of his trading. Nevertheless, *Libera* confirms that, under the ECMH approach, information may be regarded by the courts as

---

[48] See Ronald J. Gilson and Reinier H. Kraakman, "The Mechanisms of Market Efficiency," *Virginia Law Review* 70 (1984): 555–65 (providing an excellent summary of the ECMH).

[49] See generally Eugene F. Fama, "Efficient Capital Markets: A Review of Theory and Empirical Work," *Journal of Finance* 25 (1970): 383 (providing the first modern articulation of the efficient capital market hypothesis and its division into weak, semi-strong, and strong forms).

[50] Prentice, "The Internet and Its Challenges for the Future of Insider Trading Regulation," 277.

[51] United States v. Libera, 989 F.2d 596 (2d Cir. 1993).

[52] Ibid. at 601.

"public" for purposes of insider trading liability without a prior announcement, and even though the broad investing public has no direct access to it.[53]

The ECMH approach, however, generates problems of its own. It may be possible for an expert witness and jury to look at a stock's price charts months or years later and determine whether information was impounded, but it is far more difficult for traders to make this determination at the moment of trading. After all, how can one know in advance of one's trade whether a sufficient number of traders in the active investment community are aware of the relevant information? One cannot simply monitor price movement. No movement in stock price could reflect prior impoundment, a lack of dissemination, or the introduction of offsetting collateral information. Some price movement may reflect only partial impoundment, as in *Libera*, or it may reflect the impact of other, entirely collateral, information. There is simply no way to be certain ex ante.

In sum, the SEC and the courts have set a demanding threshold for publicity (dissemination and absorption, or impoundment). Absent explicit conditions of satisfaction it is often impossible for traders to know whether the threshold has been crossed at the time of trading. But, at the end of the day, just how worrisome should ambiguity in the elements of materiality and publicity be, given that Section 10(b) insider trading liability is a form of common law fraud requiring scienter? Should not an insider (or anyone else) at least be able to trade with confidence so long as she is not trading firm shares strategically on the basis of material nonpublic information, but rather to diversify or to gain access to cash? The SEC and the courts frequently give different answers to this question.

3.3 TRADING "ON THE BASIS OF" INFORMATION AND THE DEMANDS OF SCIENTER

Recall from Chapter 2 that in Rule 10b5–1(b) the SEC defines trading "on the basis of" inside information as trading while "aware" of material nonpublic information.[54] Though the SEC did not expressly define the scienter element of 10b-5 liability in terms of "knowing possession," the release suggested that awareness means the same thing, explaining that "the goals of insider trading prohibitions ... are best accomplished by a standard closer to the 'knowing possession' standard."[55] The SEC claimed its adoption of 10b5–1(b) did not diminish the element of scienter required for insider trading liability under Section 10(b) and Rule 10b-5.[56] However, a number of commentators have suggested that the rule change draws insider trading

---

[53] Ibid.
[54] 17 C.F.R. § 240.10b5–1(b) (2016).
[55] Selective Disclosure and Insider Trading: Final Rule, 2000 WL 1197687 (Aug. 24, 2000).
[56] Selective Disclosure and Insider Trading, 2000 WL 1201556, at 22 (Aug. 15, 2000) ("Scienter remains a necessary element for liability under Section 10(b) of the Exchange Act and Rule 10b-5 thereunder, and Rule 10b5–1 does not change this.").

closer to being a strict liability offense and have questioned the SEC's authority for the change.[57] This move away from the element of scienter is particularly controversial in light of the Supreme Court's clear statement in *Hochfelder* that Section 10 (b) "was intended to proscribe knowing or intentional conduct."[58] Thus, with the experts, the SEC, and the federal courts potentially at odds over the proper definition of "on the basis of" as it relates to the mental element of insider trading liability, traders are forced to take sides. And when the mere awareness test under Rule 10b5–1(b) is combined with vagueness in the definitions of materiality and publicity, a conservative insider may decline to trade altogether. For, as demonstrated previously, corporate insiders will almost never enjoy complete confidence that they are not "aware" of *some* information that could be deemed material and nonpublic in hindsight. Though the federal courts may be ready to vindicate an insider who did not use inside information *strategically* (indeed some courts have simply "ignored the adoption of Rule 10b5–1"[59]), few individuals are ready to trade and then litigate the statutory authority for 10b5–1(b) to test the theory.

3.3.1 *Trading Plans Bring Little Certainty and Create New Problems*

The SEC was aware of the chilling effect the new "awareness" test might have on insiders who wish to trade their firm's shares for legitimate reasons, and adopted Rule 10b5–1(c) in an attempt to address it.[60] Rule 10b5–1(c) provides, inter alia, that an affirmative defense to insider trading is available to those who trade company shares through a qualified trading plan ("Trading Plan" or "Plan").[61] To qualify, a Plan must be written and specify the amount, price, and date of the securities to be purchased or sold, or it must include "a written formula or algorithm" that determines the Plan transactions.[62] A qualifying Plan must have been entered into while the insider was unaware of material nonpublic information, and the insider is not permitted to have any subsequent influence "over how, when, or whether to effect

---

[57] See, e.g., Allan Horwich, "The Origin, Application, Validity, and Potential Misuse of Rule 10b5–1," *Business Lawyer* 62 (2007): 921–22; Carol B. Swanson, "Insider Trading Madness: Rule 10b5–1 and the Death of Scienter," *University of Kansas Law Review* 52 (2003): 196–99; Kevin E. Warner, "Rethinking Trades 'on the Basis of' Inside Information: Some Interpretations of SEC Rule 10b5–1," *Boston University Law Review* 83 (2003): 306.

[58] Ernst & Ernst v. Hochfelder, 425 U.S. 185, 197 (1976).

[59] Donald C. Langevoort, "'Fine Distinctions' in the Contemporary Law of Insider Trading," *Columbia Business Law Review* 2013 (2013): 439.

[60] Much of the following analysis of Rule 10b5–1(c) Trading Plans first appeared in John P. Anderson, "Anticipating a Sea Change for Insider Trading Law: From Trading Plan Crisis to Rational Reform," *Utah Law Review* 2015 (2015): 339–89.

[61] 17 C.F.R. § 240.10b5–1(C)(1)(i)(A)(3) (2016). The rule also recognizes affirmative defenses for trades pursuant to a binding contract under 10b5–1(C)(i)(A)(1) or instruction under 10b5–1(C)(i)(A)(2).

[62] 17 C.F.R. § 240.10b5–1(C)(1)(i)(B)(2).

[Plan] purchases or sales."[63] Finally, a Trading Plan provides an affirmative defense to insider trading liability only when it was "entered into in good faith."[64]

According to Linda Chatman Thomsen, former director of the SEC Division of Enforcement, part of the rationale for adopting 10b5–1(c) Trading Plans was "to give executives opportunities to diversify or become more liquid through the use of plans with prearranged trades without facing the prospect of an insider trading investigation."[65] In other words, the SEC implicitly admitted that its preferred "knowing possession" test (now reflected in the strict "awareness" test under 10b5–1(b)) made it very difficult for insiders to trade without the risk of liability outside of these Plans. As one commentator put it, "if executives [did] not have access to the 10b5–1 plans, they [would] never be able to sell their stock."[66] Once Trading Plans became available, firms immediately began availing themselves of them. Indeed, since the adoption of Rule 10b5–1(c) in 2000, the use of Trading Plans by corporate insiders has become pervasive, accounting for billions of dollars of trading each year. Yet, despite the SEC's intentions, the affirmative defenses under Rule 10b5–1(c) have left too many problems unresolved, and created some new ones.

To begin, 10b5–1(c)'s requirement that Trading Plans be entered into at a time when insiders are not aware of material nonpublic information leaves traders in much the same position they would be in without the rule. They still must determine whether some future jury might deem them aware of material nonpublic information at the time the Plan is adopted. Absent clear statutory or regulatory guidance, however, this determination can be exceedingly difficult to make, if not impossible. In other words, the affirmative defenses under Rule 10b5–1(c) simply push the predicament of legal and factual uncertainty back to the date of a Trading Plan's adoption, rather than the date of the trade. To make matters worse, the regulatory scrutiny of this decision has increased exponentially in light of recent studies reflecting that insiders are using Trading Plans to beat the market.

In August 2005, the *Wall Street Journal* reported initial results of a study by Professor Alan Jagolinzer reflecting that insiders using Trading Plans were beating the market on average by 5.6 percentage points.[67] Professor Jagolinzer's subsequently published article explained that Trading Plan participants' stock sales "tend

---

[63] Ibid.

[64] 17 C.F.R. § 240.10b5–1(C)(1)(ii).

[65] Linda Chatman Thomsen, Director of Division of Enforcement, US Securities and Exchange Commission, Opening Remarks before the 15th Annual NASPP Conference (Oct. 10, 2007).

[66] Sougata Mukherjee, "The Dangerous Game Corporate Executives Are Playing," *Triangle Business Journal* (last modified Dec. 11, 2012), www.bizjournals.com/triangle/blog/2012/12/the-dangerous-game-corporate.html.

[67] Tony Cooke and Serena Ng, "Moving the Market – Tracking the Numbers/Street Sleuth: Insiders Prosper Despite SEC Rule; Even with Planned Trades, Executives Still Can Beat Overall Market Performance," *Wall Street Journal*, sec. C3 (Aug. 5, 2005).

to follow price increases and precede price declines."[68] Moreover, the study showed that Trading Plan initiations (which usually include sell orders) "are associated with subsequent adverse news disclosures and that early [Trading Plan] termination is associated with positive firm performance."[69] From these results, Professor Jagolinzer concluded that insiders are using Trading Plans to trade "strategically."[70] In November 2012, the *Wall Street Journal* followed up with its own study suggesting the strategic use of Trading Plans by insiders.[71] It found that while 1,418 of the executives who traded in their own company's shares during the period of the study recorded average gains (or avoided average losses) of 10 percent, only half that number recorded losses of 10 percent or more.

These studies led to increased media scrutiny of Trading Plans and calls for the SEC to address the issue. It is likely the SEC will respond to this pressure with a rule change imposing greater restrictions on Plan use. Indeed, the *Wall Street Journal* quoted a fund manager as stating that he would be "shocked" if the SEC does not reform 10b5–1 to prevent the strategic use of Trading Plans by insiders.[72] And as market participants wait for the SEC's next move to address this controversy over Trading Plans, SEC staff comments and guidance on the issue have only clouded Trading Plan use in increased uncertainty.

For example, the chief counsel of the SEC's Division of Corporate Finance stated that he would "love to catch" an insider abusing Trading Plans "and use him as an example."[73] He added that the SEC is "looking for [a] big [Trading Plan] case to send a message."[74] But while the SEC has made it clear that it is after insiders who are using Trading Plans "for cover" while they trade on material nonpublic information, as Professor Allan Horwich noted, the SEC has not explained "how such conduct violate[s] the law or under what circumstances an affirmative defense under Rule 10b5–1 would not be available."[75]

There is evidence that one of the principal means of manipulating Trading Plans to beat the market is selective termination.[76] The SEC has affirmed that, all things

---

[68] See Alan D. Jagolinzer, "SEC Rule 10b5–1 and Insiders' Strategic Trade," *Management Science* 55 (2009): 224.

[69] Ibid.

[70] Ibid. at 225–26.

[71] Susan Pulliam and Rob Barry, "Executives' Good Luck in Trading Own Stock," *Wall Street Journal* (Nov. 27, 2012), www.wsj.com/articles/SB10000872396390444100404577641463717344178.

[72] Jean Eaglesham and Rob Barry, "Trading Plans Under Fire: Despite 2007 Warning, Experts Say Loopholes Remain for Corporate Insiders," *Wall Street Journal* (Dec. 13, 2012), www.wsj.com/articles/SB10001424127887324296604578177734024394950.

[73] Yin Wilczek, "No Conclusion on 10b5–1 Plans, but SEC Monitoring Situation, Official Says," *Securities Law Daily* (BNA) (Apr. 18, 2013).

[74] Ibid.

[75] Horwich, "The Origin, Application, Validity, and Potential Misuse of Rule 10b5–1," 951, n. 181.

[76] See, e.g., Cooke and Ng, "Moving the Market" ("I just think [selective termination is] such a major loophole in terms of that particular rule. . . . [It allows insiders to] get rid of the bad trades

being equal, the act of terminating an existing Trading Plan while aware of material nonpublic information does not violate securities laws because it does not involve the sale or purchase of a security.[77] The power to terminate a Plan based on material nonpublic information, however, effectively permits insiders to create a cost-free option to buy or sell a company's shares. And studies indicate that insiders are using early Plan terminations in precisely this way. For example, Jagolinzer's study reflects that 46 percent of sampled Plan terminations preceded positive news events for the company, while only 11 percent preceded negative news events.[78] Technically, strategic early Plan terminations exploit a loophole in Rule 10b5–1(c) and therefore remain within the letter of the law. Nevertheless, the SEC has issued vague threats and ambiguous guidance insisting its enforcement arm can reach this conduct. For example, the SEC qualified its approval of early Plan terminations by warning that (1) such terminations may deprive an insider of the affirmative defense for prior transactions under the Plan, and (2) frequent early terminations may raise concerns over whether an insider established a new Plan in good faith.[79] This guidance is subject to multiple interpretations, but the gist seems to be that if an insider engages in frequent or otherwise suspicious Plan terminations, the SEC may conclude either that the Plan was never qualified because the insider had material nonpublic information at adoption, or that the insider was using early Plan termination "as part of a plan or scheme" to evade the *spirit* (if not the letter) of 10b-5.[80]

As we have seen, however, the problem is that the SEC and the courts often have very different ideas of what the *spirit* of Section 10(b) and Rule 10b-5 is. With the SEC and the courts often far apart concerning the purpose and scope of Section 10 (b) insider trading liability, it is no help to suggest that compliance officers approve only those Trading Plans that are consistent with the spirit of the law. Instead, conscientious traders are forced to be exceedingly conservative in their use of Trading Plans. But compelling such conservatism undermines the usefulness of

---

and keep what look like the good trades." (quoting then Associate Professor Constance Bagley, Harvard Business School)); Horwich, "The Origin, Application, Validity, and Potential Misuse of Rule 10b5–1," 951 ("It is not a violation of Rule 10b-5 for someone who has established a Plan to terminate the Plan to abort a sale that would have taken place pursuant to the Plan at a disadvantageous price, when the person who created the Plan has come to know that there are undisclosed material positive developments at the company that would likely cause the price of the stock to increase after the Plan sale."); Jagolinzer, "SEC Rule 10b5–1 and Insiders' Strategic Trade," 224 ("Finally, the SEC allows participants to terminate plans before events or changes in firm performance that might negatively affect their trade returns."); Stanley Veliotis, "Rule 10b5–1 Trading Plans and Insiders' Incentive to Misrepresent," *Business Law Journal* 47 (2010): 329–30 (asserting that there is a loophole by which an individual may terminate the plan at any time).

[77] See US Securities and Exchange Commission, Compliance and Disclosure Interpretations: Exchange Act Rules, Question 120.27 (Feb. 13, 2012).

[78] Jagolinzer, "SEC Rule 10b5–1 and Insiders' Strategic Trade," 235.

[79] See US Securities and Exchange Commission, Compliance and Disclosure Interpretations: Exchange Act Rules, Questions 120.18 and 120.19 (Feb. 13, 2012).

[80] 17 C.F.R. § 240.10b5–1 (c)(1)(ii) (2016).

the 10b5–1(c) affirmative defenses for their intended purpose – to permit insiders to diversify their portfolios without the threat of insider trading liability under the strict "awareness" regime imposed by Rule 10b5–1(b). In other words, by cracking down on the strategic use of Trading Plans, the SEC further weakens its claim that scienter remains alive and well after the adoption of 10b5–1(b), and leaves insiders with little legal certainty when trading their own companies' shares.

Finally, the SEC rejected comments suggesting that the 10b5–1(c) affirmative defenses should be understood as part of a nonexclusive safe harbor. The SEC explained that "adding a catch-all defense or redesignating the affirmative defenses as non-exclusive safe harbors would effectively negate the clarity and certainty that the rule attempts to provide."[81] The result is that an insider who trades while aware of material nonpublic information but who presents incontrovertible evidence that that information was not a cause of the trading will nevertheless be liable under the Rule 10b5–1 test for insider trading if the proof does not fit squarely within the rule's enumerated affirmative defenses. In other words, it appears the rule leaves the door open for one to be found liable for insider trading without intent to deceive. Such a result seems to fly in the face of the courts' interpretation of Section 10(b) as requiring proof of scienter.

3.3.2 *Scienter and Tipper-Tippee Liability*

Still more ambiguity and confusion surround the element of scienter in the context of tipper-tippee insider trading liability. Again, the Supreme Court has held that Section 10(b) liability, as a form of fraud, requires "intentional misconduct."[82] In *Dirks*, however, the Supreme Court used the following language to define a tippee's derivative insider trading liability:

> A tippee assumes a fiduciary duty to the shareholders of a corporation not to trade on material nonpublic information only when the insider has breached his fiduciary duty to the shareholders by disclosing the information to the tippee and the tippee knows or *should know* that there has been a breach.[83]

The "should know" language gives the impression that the objective reasonable person standard for mere negligence is sufficient to establish the requisite mens rea for tippee liability. How does one reconcile the seemingly objective test articulated in *Dirks* with the subjective test of intentionality required by *Hochfelder*? As Professor J. Kelly Strader has explained, given "the common understanding of securities fraud as an intentional crime, the only rational explanation of the [*Dirks*] Court's

---

[81] Selective Disclosure and Insider Trading: Final Rule, 2000 WL 1197687 (Aug. 24, 2000).
[82] See *Hochfelder*, 425 U.S. at 197.
[83] *Dirks*, 463 U.S. at 660 (emphasis added).

of the language ["should know" is] that it was being sloppy."[84] Whatever the explanation, this lack of consistency and precision by the Supreme Court has left the lower courts in complete disarray concerning the appropriate mens rea for tipper-tippee insider trading liability. This uncertainty has in turn opened the door to what Professor Donald Langevoort refers to as the "most jarring recent development" in the law of insider trading, "the emergence of recklessness" as a basis for tipper-tippee liability.[85]

Before focusing on the specific problem of mens rea in the context of tipper-tippee insider trading liability, it is helpful to survey some generally accepted categories. Model Penal Code (MPC) Section 2.02 recognizes four types of culpability, ranked from most to least culpable: purpose, knowledge, recklessness, and negligence.[86] One acts purposefully with respect to the element of a crime when it is one's "conscious object to engage in conduct of that nature or to cause that result." One acts knowingly when one is "aware" of the relevant "nature" or "attendant circumstances" or "practically certain" result of one's conduct. One acts recklessly when one "consciously disregards a substantial and unjustifiable risk that the material element [of a crime] exists or will result" from one's conduct. One acts negligently when one "should be aware of a substantial and unjustifiable risk that the material element [of a crime] exists or will result" from one's conduct.

In the context of insider trading, it is important to place two further culpability terms on the spectrum outlined previously: "willfulness" and "willful blindness." While Section 10(b) is not a criminal statute, Section 32(a) of the Exchange Act provides that anyone who "willfully violates" the act is criminally liable.[87] The act does not, however, define the term "willful." Webster's Dictionary defines the term as "done deliberately" or "intentional,"[88] and the MPC defines the term as equivalent to knowing conduct.[89] Some courts and commentators have suggested that it requires "a conscious awareness that one is acting wrongfully."[90] Thus, at a minimum, it seems that "willfulness" requires intentional (i.e., purposeful or knowing) conduct, but it may also require a consciousness that one's conduct is wrongful or morally culpable.[91]

---

[84] J. Kelly Strader, "(Re)Conceptualizing Insider Trading: United States v. Newman and the Intent to Defraud," *Brooklyn Law Review* 80 (2015): 1473.

[85] Langevoort, "'Fine Distinctions' in the Contemporary Law of Insider Trading," 435.

[86] Model Penal Code § 2.02(2)(a)-(d).

[87] 15 U.S.C. 78ff(a).

[88] *Webster's Third New International Dictionary* 2617 (1986).

[89] See Model Penal Code § 2.02(8) ("A requirement that an offense be committed willfully is satisfied if a person acts knowingly with respect to the material elements of the offense, unless a purpose to impose further requirements appears.").

[90] See Strader, "(Re)Conceptualizing Insider Trading," 1445 (citing Samuel W. Buell, "Novel Criminal Fraud," *New York Law Review* 81 (2006): 1985).

[91] See Samuel W. Buell and Lisa Kern Griffin, "On the Mental State of Consciousness of Wrongdoing," *Law and Contemporary Problems* 75 (2012): 145 ("To act with consciousness of

"Willful blindness" (sometimes referred to as "conscious avoidance") is a level of mens rea recognized by the MPC and the common law as satisfying the requirement of knowledge.[92] The Supreme Court has defined "willful blindness" as follows: "(1) the defendant must subjectively believe that there is a high probability that a fact exists and (2) the defendant must take deliberate actions to avoid learning of that fact."[93] Thus, on the MPC spectrum, the Supreme Court recognizes willful blindness as roughly equivalent to knowledge – holding that a "court can properly find willful blindness only where it can almost be said that the defendant actually knew." Without question, the Court sees willful blindness as a more demanding test than recklessness (where one "merely knows of a substantial and unjustified risk of . . . wrongdoing") and negligence (where one "should have known of a similar risk but, in fact, did not").[94]

At common law, the general rule is that crimes are "intentional" only when done purposefully or knowingly (to include willful or with willful blindness), while crimes done recklessly or negligently are "unintentional."[95] Those who would strictly adhere to the Supreme Court's requirement in *Hochfelder* of intentional conduct for Section 10(b) liability follow Professor Strader in concluding that the Court's "should know" language in *Dirks* may be written off as "sloppy" and read the law as requiring, at a minimum, the showing of willful blindness for tippee liability. Those convinced that the objective language in *Dirks* should be given meaningful effect will push for the recognition of unintentional mental states of recklessness or perhaps even negligence as sufficient for all, or at least some, of the elements of tippee liability. Neither scholars nor the courts have reached anything close to a consensus on the issue. Indeed, a brief survey of recent cases within the Second Circuit (which includes Manhattan and is therefore the most important jurisdiction for insider trading jurisprudence) reflects a startling lack of consistency and clarity on the issue.

In *SEC v. Obus*, for example, the Second Circuit held that "tippee liability can be established if a tippee knew *or had reason to know* that confidential information was initially obtained and transmitted improperly (and thus through deception), and if

---

wrongdoing would simply be to act knowing that one is engaged in any sort of moral transgression").

[92] Though the MPC does not specifically reference "willful blindness," scholars have recognized § 2.02(7), "Requirement of Knowledge Satsified by Knowledge of High Probability," as a willful blindness provision. See Strader, "(Re)Conceptualizing Insider Trading," 1447.

[93] Global-Tech Appliances, Inc. v. S.E.C. S.A., 563 U.S. 754, 769 (2011).

[94] Ibid. at 770.

[95] See Strader, "(Re)Conceptualizing Insider Trading," 1444. See also United States v. U.S. Gypsum Co., 483 U.S. 422, 445 (1978) ("[I]t is now generally accepted that a person who acts (or omits to act) intends a result of his act (or omission) under two quite different circumstances: (1) when he consciously desires that result, whatever the likelihood of that result happening from his conduct; and (2) when he knows that the result is practically certain to follow from his conduct, whatever his desire may be as to that result.").

the tippee intentionally or *recklessly*" traded on that information.[96] In the same year, after referring to the circuit court's decision in *Obus* as "Delphic," the Southern District of New York held in *United States v. Whitman* that derivative insider trading liability may be incurred if a tippee "had a *general understanding* that the insider [tipper] was improperly disclosing inside information for personal benefit,"[97] suggesting that consciousness of the mere risk of tipping for personal benefit (very close to the definition of recklessness) is sufficient.[98] Just one year later, however, in *United States v. Goffer*, the Second Circuit held that tippee liability requires a showing that the tippee "knew or consciously avoided knowing that" the tip "was based on nonpublic information illegally disclosed in breach of a fiduciary duty,"[99] suggesting that only intentional (as opposed to reckless or negligent) conduct is sufficient for tippee liability. The *Goffer* court did not cite to the mens rea standard it had set just one year before in *Obus*, nor did it suggest that it was deviating from that standard in *Goffer*. Most recently, in *United States v. Newman*, the Second Circuit stated that tippee liability requires proof that the tippee "knew, or deliberately avoided knowing, that the information originated with insiders," but then two sentences later used the familiar *Dirks* "knew, or should have known" language to make the same point without explanation.[100] It might be argued that the dissonance between, for example, *Obus* and *Goffer* can be explained by the fact that *Obus* is a civil enforcement case and *Goffer* is criminal. But this fails to explain the "general understanding" test in *Whitman*, and it also fails to explain the Second Circuit's repeated reliance on *Dirks* (also a civil case) in articulating the mens rea for criminal cases such as *Newman*. Moreover, even if limited to the civil setting, the unintentional mens rea of recklessness would still be inconsistent with the Second Circuit's express recognition of scienter as an element of both civil and criminal Section 10(b) insider trading violations. For, as explained previously, scienter requires intentional conduct.[101]

To complicate matters further, courts sometimes strive to reconcile *Hochfelder* and *Dirks* by splitting the baby and applying different mens rea to different elements of insider trading liability. For example, in *Obus*, the Second Circuit explained that the *Dirks* "knows or should know" standard goes to "the tippee's knowledge that the tipper breached a duty" (implying that negligence may be enough for this element), but then applied "*Hochfelder's* requirement of intentional ... [or] reckless ...

---

[96] S.E.C. v. Obus, 693 F.3d 276, 288 (2012) (emphasis added). *Obus* also contemplates that even reckless tipping may incur insider trading liability. Ibid. at 287 (explaining that recklessly discussing material nonpublic information over the phone when a close friend is within earshot may be enough to incur tipper liability).

[97] United States v. Whitman, 904 F. Supp. 2d 363, 371 (S.D.N.Y. 2012).

[98] See Strader, "(Re)Conceptualizing Insider Trading," 1474–75.

[99] United States v. Goffer, 721 F.3d 113, 125 (2d Cir. 2013).

[100] United States v. Newman, 773 F.3d 438, 455 (2d Cir. 2014).

[101] See, e.g., Joan MacLeod Heminway, "Willful Blindness, Plausible Deniability and Tippee Liability: SAC, Steven Cohen, and the Court's Opinion in *Dirks*," *Transactions* 15 (2013): 55.

conduct . . . to the tippee's eventual use of the tip."[102] Moreover, courts often use familiar mens rea terms "like recklessness" or "should know" while giving them a novel meaning in the context of tippee liability.[103] Still more confusingly, some courts have invented new mens rea terms altogether. As noted previously, it is unclear whether the *Obus* court intended its "had reason to know" language to be meaningfully different from the objective "should know" of *Dirks*. And one is left entirely guessing when it comes to determining what the *Whitman* court intended by its "general understanding" requirement. All this has led to a great deal of head scratching. As Professor Strader put it, the resulting "imprecision is enough to give a law professor a headache, much like reading a bad exam answer."[104]

These ambiguities in the mens rea requirements for insider trading are not just matters of academic hairsplitting. As Professor Langevoort explained, "there can be significant differences in coverage depending on which articulation" of the mens rea requirement is relied upon.[105] Indeed, it is easy to see how the level of mens rea required can make all the difference in the world to market analysts, who regularly receive market information that is several levels removed from its original source. For example, the type or specificity of information alone may be enough to put one on objective or subjective notice of the significant *risk* that the original source of the information is an insider. While mere awareness of this risk (without more) would not be enough to satisfy the intentional mens rea requirements of knowledge or willful blindness, it may be enough to satisfy the test of recklessness. Absent clear direction from the SEC or the courts, the prudent analyst would not therefore pass along or trade upon information reflecting even the remotest risk of insider entanglement.[106] The result is that ambiguity in this area of insider trading law has almost certainly had a significant chilling effect on the flow and use of market information among analysts and other market players. These and other inefficiencies resulting from ambiguity in the law are addressed in Chapter 4.

3.4 WHEN DOES A "RELATION OF TRUST AND CONFIDENCE" ARISE? AND WHEN IS IT BREACHED?

Though controversial as an inference from the state common law that preceded the Exchange Act (see Chapter 1), it has been well-established since *Chiarella* that all

---

[102] *Obus*, 693 F.3d at 288.

[103] See, e.g., Langevoort, "'Fine Distinctions' in the Contemporary Law of Insider Trading," 436–37 (explaining that courts "diverge quite noticeably when it comes to explaining precisely what recklessness is," ranging from "negligence plus" to requiring an "extra element of subjective awareness").

[104] Strader, "(Re)Conceptualizing Insider Trading," 1478.

[105] Langevoort, "'Fine Distinctions' in the Contemporary Law of Insider Trading," 437.

[106] See, e.g., ibid. at 456 ("the message here is that recipients of valuable information should assume that it is tainted, and not trade unless they are fairly sure it is legitimately theirs to take advantage of").

insiders – meaning all corporate employees – stand in a fiduciary relation of trust and confidence to shareholders for purposes of insider trading liability. The courts are also fairly clear and consistent on when a technical outsider might be treated as a temporary insider: anyone who receives a firm's material nonpublic information by virtue of being engaged by that firm (e.g., as an underwriter, accountant, attorney, consultant, etc.) is deemed a temporary insider of that firm and thereby acquires the insider's fiduciary duties to its shareholders. As Justice Powell explained in *Dirks*, the basis for recognizing temporary insider status for these technical outsiders is "that they have entered into a special confidential relationship in the conduct of the business of the enterprise and are given access to information solely for corporate purposes."[107] This logic is sound. Anyone hired to do work for a firm – and given access to material nonpublic information in the performance of those duties – will stand in precisely the same functional relation to that firm's shareholders as would an actual employee of the firm, at least when it comes to trading on that firm's material nonpublic information. The boundaries and notice of temporary insider status are clear as well. It is hard to imagine a situation in which an outsider might be engaged by a firm without knowing it. The existence of the requisite fiduciary relation between insider and shareholder (and who will count as an insider) therefore stands as one of the few settled and salient points of American insider trading law.

The courts and SEC have not, however, been so clear and consistent in identifying who assumes a fiduciary or similar relation of trust and confidence under the misappropriation theory. Even before the Supreme Court embraced the misappropriation theory in *O'Hagan*, the Second Circuit noted in *United States v. Chestman* that a "broad expansion of 10b-5 liability" results from extending its focus beyond the "fiduciary/shareholder" relation to "fiduciary breaches of any sort," particularly if "the add-on, a 'similar relationship of trust and confidence,' is construed liberally."[108] In *Chestman*, Kieth Loeb was informed by his wife (who was the niece of the company's president) that Walbaum, Inc. was the subject of a pending tender offer. Loeb's wife cautioned him not to share the information with anyone because disclosure "could possibly ruin the sale."[109] Despite this warning, Loeb shared the information with his stockbroker, Robert Chestman, who then proceeded to purchase shares in the company for himself and his clients. Chestman was convicted of insider trading under the misappropriation theory.[110] He appealed this conviction on the theory that there was no fiduciary or similar relation of trust and confidence between Loeb and his wife.

---

[107] *Dirks*, 463 U.S. at 655.
[108] United States v. Chestman, 947 F.2d 551, 567 (2d Cir. 1991).
[109] Ibid. at 555.
[110] Chestman was also convicted for violations of Rule 14e-3(a) and for wire fraud. While his wire fraud and 10b-5 convictions were overturned by the Second Circuit, the Rule 14e-3(a) convictions were upheld.

The Second Circuit had yet to find the fiduciary-like relationship necessary for misappropriation liability outside the employer-employee context. In taking up the question presented in *Chestman*, the court noted that it would "tread cautiously in extending the misappropriation theory to new relationships, lest our efforts to construe Rule 10b-5 lose method and predictability, taking over 'the whole corporate universe.'"[111] In an effort to restrain liberal construction, the court noted that the term "similar" in "fiduciary or *similar* relation of trust and confidence" must be given meaningful effect.[112] To qualify, the relationship must be the "functional equivalent" of a common law fiduciary relationship.[113] This means that it "cannot be imposed unilaterally" by simply sharing a confidence with someone.[114] It also requires some manner of "discretionary authority and dependency" such that "[o]ne person depends on another – the fiduciary – to serve his interests."[115] The beneficiary must entrust the fiduciary with property (in this case, information) for the sole purpose that the property will be used for the beneficiary's advantage. "Because the fiduciary obtains access to this property to serve the ends of the fiduciary relationship, he becomes duty-bound not to appropriate the property for his own use."[116] Though some spouses or other family members may stand in such a relationship, the Second Circuit held that Loeb did not. His wife entrusted the confidential information to him, but not with any reasonable expectation that he would use it for her or the company's benefit. Loeb was not an employee of Walbaum, and there was no evidence that Loeb had been brought into the family's "inner circle," where the company's management was discussed on a regular basis. Moreover, there was no indication that the Loebs' marital relationship was "characterized by influence or reliance of any sort," or that the disclosure served the interests of Loeb's family in any way. Since there was no fiduciary or similar relation between Loeb and his wife, his disclosure to Chestman did not constitute a breach of duty and the latter's Rule 10b5–1 conviction was therefore reversed.

3.4.1 Trust "and"/"or" Confidence

As noted in Chapter 2, the SEC responded to the Second Circuit's *Chestman* decision by adopting Rule 10b5-2, which provides a "non-exclusive definition of circumstances in which a person has a duty of trust or confidence for purposes of the 'misappropriation' theory of insider trading" under Rule 10b-5.[117] The details

---

[111] *Chestman*, 947 F.2d at 567 (quoting United States v. Chiarella, 588 F.2d 1358, 1377 (2d Cir. 1978)).

[112] Ibid. at 568.

[113] Ibid.

[114] Ibid. at 567.

[115] Ibid. at 568.

[116] Ibid. at 569.

[117] 17 C.F.R. § 240.10b5–2.

of the rule are laid out in Chapter 2; it is revisited here to draw attention to the uncertainty it has generated. To begin, by redefining the relevant relationship as simply one of "trust or confidence," the SEC departs radically from precedent. This articulation eliminates the "fiduciary or similar" language that the Second Circuit identified in *Chestman* as so vitally important to keeping the relation from losing "method and predictability." The *Chestman* court made a point of emphasizing that without "the adjective 'similar,' interpretation of a 'relationship of trust and confidence' becomes an exercise in question begging." For, "when one en*trusts* a secret (read *confidence*) to another, there then exists a relationship of trust and confidence."[118] As evidence that the SEC intended to achieve just such a question-begging result, Rule 10b5–2 also substituted the disjunctive "trust *or* confidence" for the Supreme Court's conjunctive "trust *and* confidence," thus opening the door that the Second Circuit feared in *Chestman* would subsume "the whole corporate universe" under the rule. As noted in Chapter 2, the three duty-creating circumstances defined by the rule serve to illustrate just how far the SEC deviates from the courts in interpreting the requisite relationship by focusing exclusively on the expectation of confidentiality (whether express or inferred by prior dealings or by familial relationship). The fiduciary-like elements found to be so crucial by the Supreme Court in *Chiarella*, *Dirks*, and *O'Hagan* (and by the Second Circuit in *Chestman*) are entirely absent. Moreover, there is the concern that, if the relationship is limited to maintaining confidence alone, how does trading (which is done over anonymous exchanges) result in a breach of confidence? Trading is not itself a disclosure. Unsurprisingly, the courts have pushed back against the SEC's exercise of rulemaking discretion in Rule 10b5–2,[119] in some cases questioning the validity of the rule altogether.[120] The result is yet another crucial element of insider trading liability with respect to which regulators and the courts are far apart – leaving market participants guessing as to what trading is permissible versus criminal.

3.4.2 Personal Benefit Test

A related controversy between regulators and the courts concerns the circumstances under which the fiduciary-like duty to shareholders or the source of the information is breached. As noted in Chapter 2, the *Dirks* Court made it clear that, to trigger insider trading liability, the insider or misappropriator's trading or tipping must be

---

[118] *Chestman*, 947 F.2d at 568.
[119] See, e.g., S.E.C. v. Cuban, 634 F.Supp.2d 713 (N.D. Tex. 2009), vacated and remanded, 620 F.3d 551 (5th Cir. 2010). See discussion of this case in Chapter 2.
[120] Langevoort, "'Fine Distinctions' in the Contemporary Law of Insider Trading," 445 (some courts have questioned the validity of Rule 10b5–2(a) on the ground that trading does not constitute a breach of confidentiality and, moreover, a promise of confidentiality is not necessarily fiduciary).

motivated by some direct or indirect personal benefit.[121] This element is always satisfied when the insider or misappropriator actually trades on the material non-public information, but the requirement of a personal benefit can be more difficult to establish in tipper-tippee cases. This was the missing element in *Dirks*. Recall that in that case a company insider disclosed material nonpublic information to Dirks in order to expose a fraud within the company – not to benefit personally. As a result, there was no breach of fiduciary duty by the insider in making the disclosure, and therefore no derivative liability for Dirks when he traded on the information. Sensitive to the SEC's concern that this personal benefit test will make tipper-tippee liability difficult to prove because "it would be a rare situation when the parties could not fabricate some ostensibly legitimate business justification for transmitting the information," the Court offered examples of objective facts that regulators could look to in identifying the existence of a personal benefit:

> there may be a relationship between the insider and the recipient that suggests a quid pro quo from the latter, or an intention to benefit the particular recipient. The elements of fiduciary duty and exploitation of nonpublic information also exist when an insider makes a gift of confidential information to a trading relative or friend. The tip and trade resemble trading by the insider himself followed by a gift of the profits to the recipient.[122]

Though the SEC and prosecutors have never challenged the validity of the personal benefit requirement set forth in *Dirks*, the Second Circuit recently accused the government of "selectively parsing" the courts' admittedly "Delphic" dicta concerning the personal benefit test to render the requirement meaningless.[123] In *United States v. Newman*, two remote tippees were charged with derivative liability for purported fiduciary breaches by two tippers from whom they were many levels removed. No evidence was offered that either of the original insider tippers had received any monetary or other direct compensation for their tips. In one case, the insider tipper disclosed material nonpublic information concerning Dell Com-puter's earnings to an acquaintance from business school who had offered him some career advice. In the other case, an insider at NVIDIA passed along material nonpublic information concerning that company's earnings to a casual acquaint-ance at church. The Second Circuit concluded that if these facts were sufficient to establish a personal benefit on the part of the insider tippers then "practically anything would," and "the personal benefit requirement would be a nullity."[124] If the personal benefit requirement is to have any meaning at all, then an indirect

---

[121] *Dirks*, 463 U.S. at 662 ("Thus, the test is whether the insider personally will benefit, directly or indirectly, from his disclosure. Absent some personal gain, there has been no breach of duty to stockholders.").

[122] Ibid. at 664.

[123] *Newman*, 773 F.3d at 447.

[124] Ibid. at 452.

benefit based on a gift of information to a trading relative or friend requires at least "a meaningfully close personal relationship that generates an exchange that is object- ive, consequential, and represents at least a potential gain of a pecuniary or similarly valuable nature."[125]

Unsurprisingly, the Second Circuit's decision in *Newman* called a number of past and pending insider trading civil and criminal enforcement cases into question.[126] *United States v. Salman* was another remote tippee case in which the original tipper, Maher Kara, shared material nonpublic information he acquired through his position at Citigroup with his brother, Michael Kara. Michael then shared the information with Salman, his brother-in-law. Absent evidence that Maher received any monetary compensation from his brother in exchange for the information, the government relied on the fact of their familial relationship as itself sufficient evidence of a soft benefit under *Dirks*. Salman argued that the brothers' often contentious relationship was not sufficiently close to license the inference that the gift of information from Maher to Michael was motivated by a "potential gain of a pecuniary or similarly valuable nature" under *Newman*. The Ninth Circuit declined to follow *Newman* to the extent that it could be read to support Salman's argument. For, according to the Ninth Circuit, to do so would require it "to depart from the clear holding of *Dirks* that the element of breach of fiduciary duty is met where an 'insider makes a gift of confidential information to a trading relative or friend.'"[127]

The tension between the Ninth and Second Circuits, and the Second Circuit and the SEC, on this crucial issue cast a vast swath of trading under a cloud of uncertainty. Is trading such as that conducted by Newman and Salman perfectly legal, or is it criminal behavior for which they were deserving of many years in prison? The Supreme Court granted certiorari in *Salman v. United States* to settle the question.[128] The Court had not addressed the issue of insider trading in twenty years, and there was a great deal of speculation among scholars and regulators as to whether, in addition to settling the personal benefit question, the Court might also take this opportunity to resolve some of the other ambiguities in the law outlined previously. When the opinion came out in the winter of 2016, however, most were surprised that the Court had waited so long to say so little.

---

[125] Ibid.

[126] See, e.g., Matthew Goldstein and Ben Protess, "U.S. Attorney Preet Bharara Challenges Insider Trading Ruling," *The New York Times* (Jan. 23, 2015) (noting that the *Newman* decision had already spurred a number of persons recently convicted of insider trading to request rehearings and causing Bharara to complain that the decision would "limit the ability to prosecute people who trade on leaked information"). See also Richard Hill, "SEC Still Bringing Insider Trading Cases Despite *Newman* Loss," *Securities Law Reporter* 47 (Dec. 21, 2015): 2397 (noting that the SEC is having to "work harder to establish a relationship that helps satisfy the court's personal benefit standard" after *Newman*).

[127] United States v. Salman, 792 F.3d 1087, 1094 (9th Cir. 2015).

[128] Salman v. United States, 137 S.Ct. 420 (2016).

The Supreme Court unanimously upheld Salman's conviction. Justice Samuel Alito's opinion is remarkable for its brevity (comprising only eight pages and two footnotes), and it is perhaps best summarized by the following line: "We adhere to *Dirks*, which easily resolves the narrow issue presented here."[129] Quoting extensively from *Dirks*, the Court affirmed that "a tippee's liability for trading on inside information hinges on whether the tipper breached a fiduciary duty by disclosing the information."[130] A tipper breaches such a fiduciary duty only when disclosing "the inside information for a personal benefit."[131] This personal benefit must be proven by "objective criteria," such as evidence of a "pecuniary gain or reputational benefit that will translate into future earnings."[132] But the benefit need not be concrete or something of a "pecuniary or similarly valuable nature." As the Court held in *Dirks*, it may also be inferred from evidence that an insider made "a gift of confidential information to a trading relative or friend." In such gift-giving cases, the "tip and trade resemble trading by the insider followed by a gift of the profits to the recipient."[133] The Court concluded that "Salman's conduct is in the heartland of *Dirks's* rule concerning gifts."[134] The tipper provided the inside information to a "close relative" – his older brother, who was the best man at his wedding, with whom he had a "very close relationship," and whom he "lov[ed] ... very much."[135] Indeed, the record indicated that at one point the tipper offered his brother money, but his brother "asked for the information instead."[136] In sum, the Court held that the case involved "precisely the 'gift of confidential information to a trading relative' that *Dirks* envisioned."[137]

In carefully limiting its decision to the facts of that case, the *Salman* Court left the most important open questions concerning the personal benefit test unanswered. By noting that *Salman* involved precisely the type of gift to a trading relative or friend that *Dirks* envisioned, the Court implied there are some gifts to relatives and friends not envisioned by that test. For example, would the Court have reached the same result in a case where a gratuitous tip was made to a more remote relative, or to a mere acquaintance – as was the case in *Newman*? The *Salman* Court admitted that its decision did nothing to change the fact that "determining whether an insider personally benefits from a particular disclosure ... will not always be easy for courts,"

---

[129] Ibid. at 427.
[130] Ibid. at 423.
[131] Ibid.; see also ibid. at 427 ("the disclosure of confidential information without personal benefit is not enough").
[132] Ibid. at 427.
[133] Ibid.
[134] Ibid. at 429.
[135] Ibid. at 424.
[136] Ibid.
[137] Ibid.

but then concluded that "there is no need for us to address those difficult cases today."[138] In short, while *Salman* could not have been clearer in stating that the *Newman* "tangible benefit" test is not a necessary condition for tipper-tippee liability in *all* cases, it left the door open for courts to conclude that it is necessary in *some* (and perhaps even *most*) cases.[139]

Another ambiguity concerning the personal benefit requirement in the tipper-tippee context centers on what Professor Franklin A. Gevurtz has termed the "daisy-chain" problem.[140] It is clear from *Dirks* (and now *Salman*) that derivative tippee liability requires that the original tipper personally benefit from the initial tip, but the law is unclear as to whether the original tipper must also benefit from every subsequent tip in the daisy chain to maintain derivative liability for the remote tippees. For example, under the facts of *Salman*, though the original tipper Maher's familial relationship with the initial tippee Michael was sufficiently close for Maher's gift of information to constitute a personal benefit, must Maher also have benefited from Michael's subsequent tipping of Salman for the latter to incur derivative Section 10(b) liability? Or is it enough that Maher benefited from the gift to Michael and Michael benefited from the gift to Salman, even if Maher did not benefit (directly or indirectly) from the gift to Salman? Or is any benefit by Michael (or any subsequent tipper) irrelevant to derivative liability so long as Maher benefited from the gift to Michael?[141]

If the rule is that all remote tipper-tippee liability presupposes a benefit that is ultimately enjoyed by the original tipper, then a further complication arises when one asks whether that benefit must have been subjectively contemplated by the original tipper, or whether an objective benefit is sufficient. Consider a scenario in

---

[138] Ibid. at 429.
[139] Indeed, uncertainty surrounding the rigor of the "personal benefit" test for tipper-tippee liability after *Salman* increased still further as this book went to press. On August 23, 2017, a split panel of the Second Circuit decided United States v. Martoma, 2017 WL 3611518. In it, the majority held that the Supreme Court's decision in *Salman* not only overruled *Newman's* tangible benefit test, but also abrogated its holding that gifts of material nonpublic information will result in a personal benefit to the tipper only where there is a "meaningfully close personal relationship" between the tipper and tippee. Judge Rosemary Pooler filed a strongly worded dissenting opinion in *Martoma*, complaining that:

> In holding that someone who gives a gift *always* receives a personal benefit from doing so, the majority strips the long-standing personal benefit rule of its limiting power. What counts as a "gift" is vague and subjective. Juries, and more dangerously, prosecutors, can now seize on this vagueness and subjectivity. The result will be liability in many cases where it could not previously lie.

2017 WL 3611518, p. 11. It is rare for a panel to overturn Second Circuit precedent, so it is almost certain that Martoma will seek en banc review by the entire Second Circuit. Barring success before the entire Second Circuit, Martoma will likely petition the Supreme Court.
[140] See Franklin A. Gevurtz, "The Overlooked Daisy Chain Problem in Salman," *Boston College Law Review Electronic Supplement* 58 (2016): 18.
[141] See ibid. at 19.

which Maher gives material nonpublic information to his brother Michael on the express condition that he trade on the information, but not tip others. In this case it might be said that Michael's subsequent tip to Salman objectively benefits Maher (if only because it benefits his brother), but such benefit was not subjectively contemplated by Maher. There has been remarkably little treatment of this issue by scholars or the courts,[142] perhaps because prosecution of remote tippers and tippees is only a very recent phenomenon. For example, in *Newman*, the Second Circuit noted that "the Government has not cited, nor have we found, a single case in which tippees as remote as Newman ... have been held criminally liable for insider trading."[143] Nevertheless, as *Newman* and *Salman* demonstrate, the issue is real but unresolved. The daisy-chain problem therefore offers yet another example of how the line between legal and criminal trading is blurred by ambiguity in the law.

3.5 CREATIVE EXPANSIONS OF LIABILITY

Many scholars joined the SEC and prosecutors in expressing concern that the Second Circuit's decision in *Newman* opened "a disturbing loophole" for insider trading resulting from gratuitous tipping,[144] at least some of which (as explained previously) seems to have been left intact by the Supreme Court's decision in *Salman*.[145] Some of these scholars scrambled to identify novel theories of liability from within the existing regulatory framework to capture such conduct.[146]

For example, Professors Michael Guttentag and Donna Nagy have each argued to the conclusion that the entire *Dirks* framework has been rendered functionally obsolete by subsequent common law and regulatory developments, including (1) the Supreme Court's endorsement of the misappropriation theory in *O'Hagan*, (2) recent state court decisions offering more expansive accounts of what conduct constitutes a breach of fiduciary duty in the corporate context, and (3) the SEC's adoption of Regulation FD.[147]

First, Guttentag pointed out that when the Supreme Court endorsed the misappropriation theory in *O'Hagan*, it expanded the set of persons whose deception could trigger insider trading liability from including just counterparties to also

---

[142] See ibid. at 22.

[143] *Newman*, 773 F.3d at 448.

[144] Donna M. Nagy, "Beyond Dirks: Gratuitous Tipping and Insider Trading," *Journal of Corporation Law* 42 (2016): 22.

[145] But see *Martoma*, 2017 WL 3611518 (2d Cir. 2017) (the August 23, 2017 Second Circuit panel decision overruling the "meaningfully close personal relationship" test for when a tipper receives a personal benefit in a gift-giving context). This decision was pending en banc and perhaps Supreme Court review at the time this book went to press.

[146] Many of the following points were first made in John P. Anderson, "Poetic Expansions of Insider Trading Liability," *Journal of Corporation Law* 43 (2018): 367.

[147] See Nagy, "Beyond Dirks"; Michael D. Guttentag, "Selective Disclosure and Insider Trading," *Florida Law Review* 69 (2017).

including sources of material nonpublic information. In so ruling, the Court also opened the door to new types of deception capable of triggering Section 10(b) insider trading liability. According to Guttentag, the "types of deceptive conduct that a misappropriator might engage in when taking information from the source are far more numerous than the silence that constitutes the only type of deception that can take place on an impersonal securities market."[148] For example, a misappropriator may gain access to material nonpublic information by affirmative conduct. If the fraud is affirmative, there is no need to prove fraud by silence, and therefore no need to show the breach of a fiduciary relation of trust and confidence (and therefore no need to prove a personal benefit).[149]

Second, even if courts continue to insist that the breach of a fiduciary-like duty is required for insider trading liability under the misappropriation theory, one's fiduciary duties to the source of material nonpublic information (e.g., to one's employer) are different from one's duties as an insider to shareholders. Consequently, while the duty to refrain from self-dealing may be the only relevant fiduciary duty under the classical theory (where the beneficiary is a current or prospective shareholder), there is no reason to think it is the only relevant fiduciary duty under the misappropriation theory (where the beneficiary is the source of the information). Nagy has pointed out that some recent Delaware cases have broken down traditional common law limits on fiduciary duties as they pertain to corporate officers and employees, expanding them beyond the classical understanding of a duty of loyalty (involving self-dealing) to the more general duty of good faith.[150] This fiduciary duty of good faith demands more than refraining from self-dealing. It requires that fiduciaries always act in the "best interest of the corporation."[151] Consequently, "where the fiduciary acts with the intent to violate applicable positive law, or where the fiduciary intentionally fails to act in the face of a known duty to act," she breaches her fiduciary duty to the firm.[152] If courts and regulators were to adopt this expanded understanding of fiduciary duty in applying the misappropriation theory, any tipping of material nonpublic information that violates a firm's internal policies or external laws (regardless of personal benefit) would be sufficient to establish a fiduciary breach and therefore to predicate insider trading liability.

Third, the promulgation of Regulation FD in 2000 introduced another significant change to the post-*Dirks* legal landscape. As explained in Chapter 2, Regulation FD requires that whenever an issuer (or certain defined persons acting on its behalf)

---

[148] Guttentag, "Selective Disclosure and Insider Trading," 545.

[149] Guttentag cited S.E.C. v. Dorozhko, 574 F. 3d 42 (2d Cir. 2009), as an example of a case in the court that recognized insider trading could be incurred by deception without a breach of fiduciary duty.

[150] See Stone v. Ritter, 911 A.2d 362 (Del. 2006); The Walt Disney Company Derivative Litigation, 906 A.2d 27 (Del. 2006); see also Nagy, "Beyond Dirks," 42–45.

[151] *Disney*, 906 A.2d at 67.

[152] Ibid.

discloses material nonpublic information concerning the issuer or its shares to market professionals or those who are likely to trade the firm's shares, they must simultaneously disclose that information to the general investing public. Both Guttentag and Nagy have suggested that the adoption of Regulation FD significantly changed the moral and legal tableau from what it was seventeen years before when *Dirks* was decided.[153] One of the principal justifications advanced by Justice Powell in defense of the personal benefit test in *Dirks* was that it would protect space for legitimate selective disclosures to further the issuer's interests and speed information to the market. Guttentag and Nagy have both argued that this space for selective disclosure once preserved by *Dirks* was closed by Regulation FD. Many of these disclosures are now illegal. Moreover, since the adoption of Regulation FD, most firms have adopted internal rules that selective disclosures of material nonpublic information would violate. Consequently, any such selective disclosure would deceive the source of the information (the firm) by feigning fidelity while violating its disclosure rules, and by violating the law.

In sum, considering the expanded reach of *O'Hagan* alongside new common law articulations of fiduciary duty and Regulation FD, Guttentag and Nagy both argue that regulators can sidestep the personal benefit test altogether when applying the misappropriation theory. Moreover, since most scholars agree that any insider trading cases brought under the classical theory could also be brought under the misappropriation theory,[154] the result is that the *Dirks* personal benefit test is rendered functionally obsolete.

The arguments offered by Guttentag and Nagy are as controversial as they are creative. First, in recognizing the fraud-on-the-source theory in *O'Hagan*, the Supreme Court certainly could have recognized any form of deceptive conduct toward the source as a form of affirmative misrepresentation – thereby dispensing with the need to establish a fiduciary duty to disclose or abstain as an element of fraudulent insider trading – but it did not do so. Instead, Justice Ginsburg's opinion explained that "[d]eception through nondisclosure is central to liability under the misappropriation theory."[155] And the Court explicitly cabined the type of deceptive nondisclosure that triggers such liability as the "breach of a fiduciary duty owed to the source of the information."[156] In doing so, the Court clearly intended to establish symmetry between the classical and misappropriation theories. It would therefore be a stretch to suggest that it nevertheless contemplated that the personal benefit test would apply under the former but not the latter. In support of this reading, courts

[153] See Nagy, "Beyond Dirks," 36–41; Guttentag, "Selective Disclosure and Insider Trading," 540–44.
[154] See, e.g., Donald C. Langevoort, *Insider Trading Regulation, Enforcement & Prevention*, Vol. 18, § 6–1 (New York: Thomson Reuters, 2015).
[155] *O'Hagan*, 521 U.S. at 643.
[156] Ibid. at 654.

have consistently held that the basic elements of tipper-tippee liability are the same under the classical and misappropriation theories.[157]

Second, while it is true that Delaware has expanded its understanding of fiduciary disloyalty to include any conduct reflecting bad faith, the relevance of this state common law development to Section 10(b) insider trading liability is dubious. For instance, Nagy cited no Delaware precedent suggesting that violating a fiduciary duty of good faith without self-dealing would suffice as proof of criminal fraud in that state. The relevant Delaware cases recognize a spectrum of corporate culpability in the context of shareholder derivative suits, ranging from mere negligence (least culpable), to bad faith that does not involve self-dealing (more culpable), to bad faith involving self-dealing (most culpable).[158] Absent some precedent to the contrary, it should be assumed that Delaware still requires bad faith at the highest culpability level (involving self-dealing) as a predicate for criminal fraud. But even if the Delaware law has changed in this important respect, it is a stretch to suggest that this somehow overturns more than three decades of federal precedent interpreting Section 10(b) insider trading liability as requiring self-dealing.

Finally, there is express language in Regulation FD that precludes its violations from predicating Section 10(b) insider trading liability. Rule 101(c) of Regulation FD excludes tipping "in breach of a duty of trust or confidence to the issuer" from the regulation's coverage.[159] Since both *O'Hagan* and SEC Rule 10b5-2 require the violation of some duty of trust and confidence as an element of misappropriation liability, Section 101(c) makes it logically impossible for a violation of Regulation FD to provide the basis of insider trading liability under the misappropriation theory: if an insider's tipping violates a duty of trust and confidence to the issuer, then by definition it cannot violate Regulation FD. If tipping does not violate a duty of trust and confidence, it may violate Regulation FD, but by definition it cannot support misappropriation liability. Section 102 of Regulation FD confirms that the SEC intended this logical separation, providing that no "failure to make a public disclosure required solely by [Regulation FD] shall be deemed to be a violation of

---

[157] See, e.g., *Newman*, 773 F.3d at 446 ("The elements of tipping liability are the same, regardless of whether the tipper's duty arises under the 'classical' or the 'misappropriation' theory."). Since neither party in *Salman* disputed the application of the *Dirks* personal benefit test to misappropriation cases, the Supreme Court noted that it "need not resolve the question" and proceeded on the "assumption" that the test applies in both contexts. *Salman*, 137 S. Ct. at note 2. The Court may therefore revisit the issue should theories such as those presented by Nagy and Guttentag gain traction among prosecutors and the lower courts.

[158] See Nagy, "Beyond Dirks," 43–44.

[159] 17 C.F.R. § 243.101(c). Guttentag and Nagy both noted Rule 101(c)'s exclusion, but suggested that it was included only to ensure that issuers do not incur Regulation FD liability for the actions of rogue employees. See Guttentag, "Selective Disclosure and Insider Trading," 542; Nagy, "Beyond Dirks," 38. This explanation ignores, however, that the express language of Rule 101(c) functions to preclude Regulation FD liability for the insider employee who acts "in breach of a duty of trust or confidence to the issuer" as well.

Rule 10b–5."[160] This clear statement that Regulation FD does not affect Section 10 (b) insider trading liability seems designed to foreclose precisely the end run around *Dirks* that Guttentag and Nagy would like to make.

Nevertheless, to say that Guttentag's and Nagy's arguments are controversial and require some creative interpretive leaps is not to say that the SEC or prosecutors would not resort to them – or that some courts would not eventually follow them. Recall that the misappropriation theory was itself a creative response to a setback before the Supreme Court in *Chiarella*. The very fact that these novel theories of liability are being pondered and espoused by respected legal scholars – and just waiting to be tested by regulators and enterprising prosecutors – offers yet another example of just how ambiguous, volatile, and uncertain the scope of insider trading liability is in the United States today.

*****

This chapter has identified some of the ways in which the current insider trading regime in the United States is plagued by vagueness and ambiguity. This state of affairs must not be permitted to persist. For, as Chapter 4 will demonstrate, vagueness and ambiguity in the current regime have real moral and economic consequences for individuals and the markets.

---

[160] 17 C.F.R. § 243.102. Guttentag argued that Rule 102 was not intended to shield individuals from insider trading liability pursuant to Rule 10b-5, only to protect issuers from private rights of action pursuant to Rule 10b-5 for violations of Regulation FD. Guttentag, "Selective Disclosure and Insider Trading," 542. The problem with this argument is that Rule 102 is not limited by its language to private rights of action. It is a blanket exclusion.

4

Injustice, Incoherence, and Irrationality

Time for Regime Change

As Chapters 1 and 2 demonstrated, insider trading law in the United States has not developed in a linear fashion. Prior to the adoption of the Securities Exchange Act of 1934, there was no sense that insider trading over anonymous exchanges could incur civil, much less criminal, liability. And, with the limited exception of Section 16, there is no indication that Congress intended to change this with the promulgation of the Exchange Act and the subsequent creation of the Securities and Exchange Commission. It was not until the 1960s that the SEC decided Section 10(b) of the Exchange Act proscribed insider trading, and by that time the SEC was convinced that this meant pretty much any trading based on material nonpublic information. The SEC read Section 10(b) as guaranteeing a level playing field for investors, which for it meant that all market participants should share equal access to material information. About two decades later, the Supreme Court rejected the SEC's theory of insider trading liability, holding that, whatever Section 10(b) proscribes, it must involve fraudulent deception, and the classical and misappropriation theories of insider trading liability emerged. Despite the Supreme Court's admonishments, the SEC continued to bring cases consistent with its preferred equal-access theory and then adopt rules (sometimes with dubious statutory support) to circumvent any judicial setbacks. For example, the SEC adopted Rule 14e-3 to help negate the impact of *Chiarella*, Regulation FD, and Rule 10b5–2 in reaction to *Dirks*, and Rule 10b5–1 when the federal courts failed to side with it in the use-versus-possession debate. In short, the SEC has regulated as if we function under an equal-access (and sometimes even parity-of-information) regime, despite the fact that the governing statute and the courts have made it clear that we do not. The SEC apparently prefers to ask forgiveness rather than permission.

Of course, if it is an equal-access or parity-of-information regime that the SEC wants, it could have it at any time by simply asking Congress. Congress has demonstrated time and again that it is ready to support the SEC's campaign against insider trading with increased penalties. The SEC has, however, passed on opportunities to define the law of insider trading, preferring flexibility of enforcement over certainty in authority. As Chapter 3 explained, one consequence of this decision has been significant vagueness and ambiguity surrounding the elements and reach of insider trading liability in the United States. The aim of this chapter is to argue that the SEC's apparent preference for ambiguity over certainty has led to an insider trading regime that is unjust, incoherent, and irrational. The current regime is therefore in serious need of reform.[1]

4.1 THE CURRENT REGIME IS UNJUST

Regardless of what one thinks of the moral permissibility of insider trading in general, the current insider trading enforcement regime in the United States is unjust. The vagueness and ambiguity of its elements offer insufficient notice of criminal wrongdoing and invite abuse of regulatory and prosecutorial discretion.

4.1.1 *Insufficient Notice of Crime*

The fact that insider trading has never been defined by statute leaves us with the "jurisprudential scandal that [it] is largely a federal common law offense."[2] The Western liberal jurisprudential tradition is suspicious of common law crimes like insider trading because they often violate the principle of legality, which is sometimes expressed in the Latin phrase *nullum crimen sine lege*.[3] The principle of legality holds that "there must be no crime or punishment except in accordance with fixed, reasonably specific, and fairly ascertainable preestablished law."[4] This principle gives expression to our shared intuition that justice requires that persons be given reasonable notice of when criminal sanctions will be imposed. Otherwise persons would be left helpless in planning their lives to avoid such sanctions. The same moral intuition informs our repugnance toward ex post facto laws.[5]

The history of insider trading enforcement in the United States offers a sad illustration of the perniciousness of common law crimes. For example, federal regulators imposed sanctions on individuals pursuant to the "equal-access" model of insider trading liability for more than two decades before this model was rejected by the Supreme Court as inconsistent with its ultimate statutory authority in

---

[1] Much of the following analysis concerning the injustice, incoherence, and irrationality of the current insider trading enforcement regime in the United States first appeared in John P. Anderson, "The Final Step to Insider Trading Reform: Answering the 'It's Just Not Right!' Objection," *Journal of Law, Economics & Policy* 12 (2016): 279–302.

[2] Jeanne Schroeder, "Taking Stock: Insider and Outsider Trading by Congress," *William and Mary Business Law Review* 5 (2014): 163.

[3] See, e.g., David A. J. Richards, *The Moral Criticism of Law* (Belmont, CA: Wadsworth Publishing Co., 1977): 195.

[4] Ibid.

[5] Ex post facto laws are, of course, unconstitutional pursuant to US Const. art. I §§ 9, 10.

Section 10(b).[6] Moreovoer, despite the fact that the Supreme Court's decision in *Chiarella* left the legal status of the misappropriation theory of insider trading liability uncertain, regulators continued to enforce it for the next seventeen years before it finally received the Court's imprimatur in *O'Hagan*.[7] The SEC and prosecutors continue to press for broader insider trading enforcement authority, and, again, they would rather ask forgiveness than permission from the courts. Without a statutory definition, market participants are just left guessing as to whether that expanded authority will be recognized by some judge. Most would rather settle than take the risk. This is precisely the injustice the principle of legality looks to avoid.

It is worth noting that simply codifying the current working definition of insider trading would not solve the problem. Injustice due to inadequate notice would persist because, as demonstrated in Chapter 3, the current definition's terms are themselves hopelessly vague. Both the classical and misappropriation theories impose liability on those who seek to "benefit" from trading "on the basis of" "material" "nonpublic" information in violation of a "fiduciary or other similar relation of trust and confidence," but few agree on the definition of any one of these terms. In *Connally v. General Construction Company*, the Supreme Court held that a law violates due process when a person of "common intelligence must necessarily guess at its meaning."[8] Some scholars have suggested that the law against insider trading is unconstitutionally vague.[9] Indeed it is hard to disagree with Steven Cohen, founder of S.A.C. Capital Advisors, LP, and the target of multiple insider trading investigations, when he said, "It's my belief that the rule [against insider trading] is vague, and therefore . . . as a lawyer, you can interpret it in lots of different ways."[10] As Professor Homer Kripke put it more generally, "fraud" in Rule 10b-5 has "come to mean anything that the SEC dislikes because by picking cases in which it can dramatically describe the facts, the SEC hopes that the facts will carry the law."[11] The concern that regulators may exploit vagueness in the law to pursue their own institutional or even personal agendas was shared by Justice O'Connor in *Kolender v. Lawson*:[12]

---

[6] The *Chiarella* Court explained that the SEC's formulation of such a broad "parity-of-information rule," which "departs radically from the established doctrine that duty arises from a specific relationship between parties . . . should not be undertaken absent some explicit evidence of congressional intent." Chiarella v. United States, 445 U.S. 222, 233 (1980).

[7] United States v. O'Hagan, 521 U.S. 642, 652–53 (1997).

[8] Connally v. Gen. Constr. Co., 269 U.S. 385, 391 (1926).

[9] See, e.g., Homer Kripke, "Manne's Insider Trading Thesis and Other Failures of Conservative Economics," *Cato Journal* 4 (1985): 949.

[10] Greg Ferrell, "SAC's Cohen May Face SEC Suit as Deposition Hurts Case," *Bloomberg* (Feb. 19, 2013), www.bloomberg.com/news/articles/2013-02-19/sac-s-cohen-may-face-sec-suit-as-deposition-hurts-case.

[11] Kripke, "Manne's Insider Trading Thesis and Other Failures of Conservative Economics," 949.

[12] Kolender v. Lawson, 461 U.S. 352 (1983).

the more important aspect of vagueness doctrine "is not actual notice, but ... the requirement that a legislature establish minimal guidelines to govern law enforcement." Where the legislature fails to provide such minimal guidelines, a criminal statute may permit "a standardless sweep [that] allows policemen, prosecutors, and juries to pursue their personal predilections."[13]

US Circuit Court Judge Barrington Parker expressed this concern during oral argument in *United States v. Newman*[14] when he challenged the government's "amorphous theory" of insider trading liability as leaving "all these institutions at the mercy of the government."[15] And there is evidence suggesting that abuse of discretion has occurred in the context of insider trading enforcement.

4.1.2 *Abuse of Discretion*

Some have noted that enforcement officials and prosecutors are wont to "exploit the hostile reaction [insider trading] provokes among the general public" to "generate positive publicity" for themselves (or to deflect criticism) in the wake of market downturns.[16] For instance, in the wake of the subprime mortgage meltdown of 2008, the government needed "a white collar scandal that it could tout as having successfully prosecuted to satisfy the public's demand for Wall Street scalps."[17] Insider trading prosecutions offered the anodyne for wounded political reputations: "insider trading was viewed as the easiest way to restore the [SEC's] reputation following the Madoff catastrophe and the image hit taken in the aftermath of the financial crisis."[18] The government's "amorphous theories" of insider trading liability permitted it to rack up scores of white collar scalps at a near perfect conviction rate. And these efforts put the United States Attorney for the Southern District of New York, Preet Bharara, on the cover of *Time* magazine with the headline "This Man Is Busting Wall St."[19] The fact that insider trading had nothing to do with the financial collapse seemed unimportant. Decades before, some alleged that then United States Attorney Rudolph Giuliani sensationalized his insider trading cases in the 1980s to build support for his imminent bid for public office.[20]

---

[13] Ibid. at 358 (quoting Smith v. Goguen, 415 U.S. 566, 574–75 (1974)).
[14] United States v. Newman, 773 F.3d 438 (2d Cir. 2014).
[15] See Nate Raymond, "U.S. Prosecutor Grilled over Insider Trading Definition in Key Appeal," *Reuters* (April 22, 2014), www.reuters.com/article/insidertrading-appeal-idUSL2N0NE0 OR20140422 (quoting US Circuit Judge Barrington Parker).
[16] Peter Henning, "What's So Bad about Insider Trading Law," *The Business Lawye* (2015): 762.
[17] Charles Gasparino, *Circle of Friends* (New York: Harper Collins, 2013): 155.
[18] Ibid. at 201.
[19] "This Man Is Busting Wall St.: Prosecutor Preet Bharara Collars the Masters of the M(*Time* (Feb. 13, 2012), http://content.time.com/time/covers/0,16641,20120213,00.html.
[20] James B. Stewart, *Den of Thieves* (New York: Simon & Schuster Paperbacks, 1991

It has also been suggested that insider trading enforcement has been exploited by the SEC in its turf wars with other agencies over money, jurisdiction, and prestige. Professor Stephen Bainbridge explained that, according "to one widely accepted theory of bureaucratic behavior, administrators can maximize their salaries, power, and reputation by maximizing the size of their agency's budget."[21] And Professor Jonathan Macey has claimed that the SEC's "politicization of the insider trading issue" enabled it to "double its budget by arguing that more resources were necessary to combat [what it had convinced the public was a] dire national emergency."[22]

It is clear that money matters to prosecutors and the SEC every bit as much as it does to the insider traders they prosecute. For instance, in the 1980s, the SEC reached a $100 million settlement with Ivan Boesky, but they needed him to sell his portfolio to get it. The SEC worried that news of Boesky's arrest would send the market into a tailspin (including those stocks in Boesky's portfolio), so it "directed Boesky to begin liquidating some of his holdings during the two weeks preceding the announcement."[23] In other words, the SEC directed Boesky to trade on the material nonpublic information of his own charges and settlement arguably to protect its $100 million fine. The other arbitrageurs (and regular traders) betting alongside Boesky were livid when news of the SEC's complicity hit. The irony was not lost on the press either. The *Washington Post* ran a front-page story titled "Wall Street Lambastes SEC Action: Agency Reportedly Let Boesky Sell Off Stocks in Advance."[24] One trader, David Nolan, noted that "[t]he SEC has unwittingly aided one of the largest insider trading scams in history." Not long after providing this quote to the *Washington Post*, Mr. Nolan himself was investigated for insider trading, which raises another concern.[25]

As one journalist put it, the "government, being the government, can always find something to charge you with, and they will do so if you rub their noses in it."[26] Vague and amorphous prohibitions like those geared toward insider trading are ready weapons for government agencies to retaliate against political enemies or to bully those who refuse to do their bidding. In 2014, Nelson Obus, whose hedge fund was the target of an insider trading enforcement action, authored a *Wall Street Journal* commentary entitled "Refusing to Buckle to SEC Intimidation."[27] In this article, Obus painted the picture of a twelve-year SEC enforcement process that was short on substance and long on political motives. Vagueness in the law and virtually

---

[21] Stephen Bainbridge, "Incorporating State Law Fiduciary Duties into the Federal Insider Trading Prohibition," *Washington and Lee Law Review* 52 (1995): 1246.

[22] Jonathan R. Macey, *Insider Trading: Economics, Politics, and Policy* (Washington, DC: The AEI Press, 1991): 4.

[23] Stewart, *Den of Thieves*, 337.

[24] *Washington Post* (Nov. 21, 1987): A1.

[25] Stewart, *Den of Thieves*, 345.

[26] Gasparino, *Circle of Friends*, 230.

[27] Nelson Obus, "Refusing to Buckle to SEC Intimidation," *Wall Street Journal* (June 24, 2014), www.wsj.com/articles/nelson-obus-refusing-to-buckle-to-sec-intimidation-1403651178.

unlimited resources permitted the SEC to press even a weak case for more than a decade at a cost of $12 million in legal fees. According to Obus, the SEC attempted to "bully" him into a settlement, but he refused to admit guilt when he had done nothing wrong. Obus expressed concern that "not many small firms could be expected to weather such a storm from a system that provides regulators with every incentive to overreach without repercussions," and he worried that most targets would be forced to "settle or falsely admit wrongdoing."[28]

4.2 THE CURRENT REGIME IS INCOHERENT

The current insider trading enforcement regime in the United States is also incoherent. This incoherence is due to the fact that it is driven by two competing and irreconcilable rationales. As explained in Chapters 2 and 3, the SEC and federal prosecutors continue to press for an equal-access regime through their rulemaking authority and enforcement discretion. The judiciary, on the other hand, remains committed to the fiduciary-cum-fraud-based model reflected in the language of Section 10(b). Since these theories of liability reach different traders and trading, the result is a schizophrenic enforcement regime. With the house so divided against itself, the unsurprising result is that neither model is effectively implemented.

4.2.1 *Current Regime Is Under-Inclusive per Equal-Access Model*

To begin, if the current regime is judged by the SEC's own stated goal of achieving a "level playing field" by guaranteeing that all market participants have equal access to information, then it is woefully under-inclusive in its reach.[29] There are a number of forms of knowing securities trading based on material nonpublic information that are not proscribed under the fiduciary-based enforcement regime, some of which have already been identified in Chapters 2 and 3.

4.2.1.1 Eavesdropping or Luck

Both the classical and misappropriation theories require the existence of a fiduciary or similar duty of trust and confidence. The classical theory requires that the party trading on material nonpublic information have a fiduciary-like relationship with the counterparty to the transaction, and the misappropriation theory requires that she have such a relationship to the source of the information. Consequently, courts

---

[28] Ibid.

[29] See, e.g., Marc I. Steinberg, "Insider Trading Regulation – A Comparative Analysis," *International Law* 37 (2003): 158 ("The goal that ordinary investors play on a level playing field with market professionals, having equal access to material nonpublic information, no longer survives under Section 10(b) insider trading jurisprudence.").

have found no Section 10(b) liability where an outsider acquires material nonpublic information by sheer luck or by eavesdropping on the conversation of insiders.

For example, Barry Switzer, the successful college and NFL football coach, overheard an insider privately discussing material nonpublic information concerning a publicly traded company while Switzer was sunbathing on the bleachers at his son's track meet.[30] Switzer immediately acquired positions in the company and encouraged his friends to do the same. When the information was finally announced, Switzer and his friends profited from a 16.5-point jump in the stock's price.

Recall that, under *Dirks*, tippee liability is derivative upon the insider's (or misappropriator's) breach of duty in providing the tip. Because the insider in this case had no idea Switzer was eavesdropping on his private conversation, he did not breach a fiduciary duty to his stockholders, and therefore the court found no liability for the insider or Switzer. Section 10(b) simply "does not bar trading on the basis of information inadvertently revealed by an insider."[31] Switzer and his friends were allowed to keep and enjoy their profits from trading on this information advantage over the market.

4.2.1.2 Tipper Fails to Benefit

As explained in Chapters 2 and 3, tippee liability under Section 10(b) arises only where the insider (or misappropriator) somehow benefits by the disclosure. Absent some personal gain, there has been no breach of duty to the stockholders or the source. The personal benefit requirement precluded liability in *Dirks*, and its absence can result in perfectly legal trading based on material nonpublic information in a multitude of contexts.

Consider the facts of *SEC v. Maxwell*,[32] in which the SEC brought an enforcement action against David Maxwell and his barber of fifteen years, Elton Jehn. Jehn knew Maxwell worked for a publicly traded company and repeatedly asked him for inside information. One day Maxwell came in for a haircut and told Jehn there was a "rumor" some buyers were "interested" in his company. Maxwell was in charge of his company's due diligence efforts in advance of a merger. He had been specifically instructed to keep information of the upcoming merger confidential and not to use the information for personal benefit. Jehn proceeded to leverage everything he had to purchase positions in the company's stock. When the merger was announced, Jehn sold his position at a profit of $191,954.57.

The court ruled there could be no Section 10(b) liability for either Maxwell or Jehn because there was no evidence Maxwell benefited from the disclosure directly

---

[30] See S.E.C. v. Switzer, 590 F. Supp. 756, 761–63 (W.D. Okla. 1984).
[31] Ibid. at 766.
[32] S.E.C. v. Maxwell, 341 F. Supp. 2d 941 (S.D. Ohio 2004).

or indirectly. The court found that, given "the parties' relative stations in life, any reputational benefit to . . . Maxwell in the eyes of his barber is extremely unlikely to have translated into any meaningful future advantage."[33] The relationship between the two was "no more than the relationship between a barber and his client."[34] Thus, as in *Switzer*, Jehn used material nonpublic information to gain an advantage over the market and was allowed to enjoy his near $200,000 in profits free of civil or criminal liability.

4.2.1.3 Announcing Intent to Trade

The Supreme Court explained in *O'Hagan* that full disclosure of intent to trade forecloses Section 10(b) liability under the misappropriation theory:

> Because the deception essential to the misappropriation theory involves feigning fidelity to the source of information, if the fiduciary discloses to the source that he plans to trade on the nonpublic information, there is no "deceptive device" and thus no § 10(b) violation – although the fiduciary-turned-trader may remain liable under state law for breach of a duty of loyalty.[35]

In fact, as Justice Thomas pointed out in his *O'Hagan* dissent, "were the source expressly to authorize its agents to trade on the confidential information – as a perk or bonus perhaps – there would likewise be no § 10(b) violation."[36]

As explained in Chapter 2, in *Carpenter v. United States*,[37] a *Wall Street Journal* reporter was prosecuted for trading in advance of the publication of his daily column offering recommendations with respect to selected stocks, in violation of a confidentiality agreement with the *Journal*. Although the reporter deceived his employer, at oral argument in *O'Hagan*, the government explained that if he "had gone to the *Wall Street Journal* and said, look, you know, you're not paying me very much. I'd like to make a little bit more money by buying stock, the stocks that are going to appear in my . . . column . . . [then] there would have been no deception of the

---

[33] Ibid. at 948.
[34] Ibid. at 947. As explained in Chapter 3, after United States v. Newman, 773 F.3d 438, 452 (2d Cir. 2014), which held that the tipper must have a "meaningfully close personal relationship" with a tippee in order for a gift of material nonpublic information to qualify as personally benefiting the tipper, one would have expected the same result in the Second Circuit. On August 23, 2017, however, a split Second Circuit panel reversed *Newman* on this point in United States v. Martoma, 2017 WL 3611518 (2d Cir. 2017). That decision was pending en banc review before the Second Circuit, and potentially Supreme Court review, at the time this book went to press. If the *Martoma* decision is upheld, query whether the facts of *Maxwell* now support a conviction for insider trading in the Second Circuit.
[35] United States v. O'Hagan, 521 U.S. 642, 655 (1997).
[36] Ibid. at 689 (Thomas, J., concurring in the judgment in part and dissenting in part).
[37] Carpenter v. United States, 484 U.S. 19 (1987).

Wall Street Journal," and therefore no Section 10(b) liability.[38] The government's point was not that the *Journal's* prohibition of such trading alone grounded the liability in *Carpenter*. In fact, the *Carpenter* Court explicitly rejected the argument that the reporter's "conduct in revealing prepublication information was no more than a violation of workplace rules."[39] The government in *O'Hagan* was emphasizing the fact that the key to the reporter's criminal liability in *Carpenter* was his sham promise not to reveal the *Journal's* confidential information to support his scheme to share profits from trading on that information prior to publication. Without this element of deception, there would be no Section 10(b) liability.

4.2.1.4 Not Selling/Not Buying

Another circumstance in which one appears to be able to gain an advantage over the market by making investment decisions based on material nonpublic information without incurring Section 10(b) liability occurs when insiders or misappropriators refrain from buying or selling securities that they otherwise would have bought or sold. In such circumstances, there can be no Section 10(b) liability because there has been no securities transaction – only an omission. Nevertheless, such decisions based on material nonpublic information have the same market effect. As Professor Henry Manne put it, "[r]efraining from selling stock that would otherwise have been sold has exactly the same economic effect on market price as a decision to buy the same number of shares."[40] Manne went on:

> The upshot of all this is that people can make abnormal profits in the stock market simply by knowing when *not* to buy and when *not* to sell. They will not make as much perhaps as if they could trade on the information more efficiently, but nonetheless they will still make supra-competitive returns.[41]

As noted in Chapter 3, the SEC only enhanced insiders' ability to profit from such strategic abstention by recognizing Rule 10b5–1(c) trading plans in 2000. The selective termination of Rule 10b5–1 trading plans effectively grants insiders a cost-free option to buy or sell based on material nonpublic information.

---

[38] *O'Hagan*, 521 U.S. at 689 n.5. It remains an open question, however, whether this safe harbor in *O'Hagan* should be read to extend to the brazen misappropriator who discloses her intent to trade to the source and then trades over the source's vigorous objection. A straightforward reading of *O'Hagan* leaves one with the impression that the Court intended to leave such cases to be addressed by state law, not Section 10(b). See ibid. at 655. But some courts have read the *O'Hagan* safe harbor to exclude the brazen misappropriator. See, e.g., S.E.C. v. Rocklage, 470 F.3d 1 (1st Cir. 2006); see also Stephen Bainbridge, *Securities Law: Insider Trading*, 2d ed. (New York: Foundation Press, 2007): 118–20.

[39] *Carpenter*, 484 U.S. at 27.

[40] Henry G. Manne, "Insider Trading and Property Rights in New Information," *Cato Journal* 4 (1985): 938.

[41] Ibid.

4.2.2 *Current Regime Is Over-Inclusive from Standpoint of Fraud-Based Rationale*

If, however, the current enforcement regime is instead judged by the fiduciary-cum-fraud standard articulated by the courts, it is over-inclusive in at least two crucially important respects.

4.2.2.1 Absence of Scienter

First, common law fraud requires some knowing deception or "scienter." Accordingly, the Supreme Court has consistently held that Section 10(b) fraud requires some "knowing or intentional misconduct." However, as explained in Chapter 3, in promulgating Rule 10b5–1(b) in 2000, the SEC seems to have effectively dropped the requirement of scienter for insider trading liability. Again, the prelude to Rule 10b5–1 explains that the rule "defines when a purchase or sale constitutes trading 'on the basis of' material nonpublic information in insider trading cases brought" under Section 10(b) and SEC Rule 10b-5. Rule 10b5–1(b) then goes on to define the mental state requirement that trading be "on the basis of" material nonpublic information as demanding nothing more than "awareness" (or mere possession) of material nonpublic information while trading. The result is that an insider who sells shares for no other reason than to pay for her husband's emergency heart transplant is nevertheless liable for insider trading if she happened to be in possession of material nonpublic information at the time of the trade. As Professor Allan Horwich put it, "the SEC may have indulged in some linguistic legerdemain, arguably transforming a phrase that connotes a deliberate act … into something less."[42] Indeed, another commentator went so far as to suggest that Rule 10b5–1 converted insider trading into a strict liability offense,[43] which is clearly inconsistent with the Supreme Court's announcement that though Section 10(b) was designed as a catchall, "what it catches must be fraud."[44]

4.2.2.2 Absence of Deception

A second important way in which the current enforcement regime is over-inclusive under the fraud-based model is its proscription of issuer-licensed insider trading. "Issuer-licensed" insider trading is defined in Chapter 9, and the explanation for why its proscription is inconsistent with a fraud-based theory of insider trading is deferred to that chapter as well. For now, the promissory note is offered for the

---

[42] Allan Horwich, "The Origin, Application, Validity, and Potential Misuse of Rule 10b5–1," *Business Lawyer* 62 (2007): 921.

[43] Carol B. Swanson, "Insider Trading Madness: Rule 10b5–1 and the Death of Scienter," *University of Kansas Law Review* 52 (2003): 155.

[44] *Chiarella*, 445 U.S. at 234–35.

conclusion that such trading is not deceptive and cannot therefore be coherently articulated as a form of Section 10(b) fraud.

In sum, the current insider trading enforcement regime in the United States comprises two incompatible theories of liability that have so far resisted synthesis: the equal-access theory promoted and enforced by regulators, and the fraud-cum-fiduciary theory that continues to be upheld by the courts. The result is an incoherent and sometimes schizophrenic regime that, as a whole, makes little sense under either theory.

4.3 THE CURRENT REGIME IS IRRATIONAL

In addition to being unjust and theoretically incoherent, the current insider trading enforcement regime is also irrational because it tends to undermine many of the concrete values (e.g., shareholder value, market liquidity, and cost of capital) it purports to promote. Moreover, in the context of corporate criminal liability, the current insider trading enforcement regime is objectively irrational in that it punishes victims for the crime.

4.3.1 *The Paradox of Insider Trading Compliance*

Regulators demand the impossible when they require issuers to design and implement effective insider trading compliance programs because, as demonstrated in Chapter 3, neither the SEC nor Congress has defined this crime with any specificity. This problem of uncertainty is then compounded by the threat of heavy civil and criminal sanctions for violations.[45] Placed between this rock and hard place, issuers tend to adopt overbroad insider trading compliance programs, which comes at a heavy price in terms of corporate culture, cost of compensation, share liquidity, and cost of capital. The irony is that, since all of these costs are passed along to the shareholders, insider trading enforcement under the current regime has precisely the opposite of its intended effect.[46]

4.3.1.1 Strong Compliance or Else!

Firms with weak compliance programs stand to incur derivative civil and criminal liability for the insider trading of their employees, and the penalties (both reputational and monetary) are stiff. To begin, the Insider Trading and Securities

---

[45] See, e.g., Stephen Bainbridge, "Incorporating State Law Fiduciary Duties into the Federal Insider Trading Prohibition," 1189 (noting that insider trading "carries penalties that can only be described as draconian").

[46] Much of the following analysis first appeared in John P. Anderson, "Solving the Paradox of Insider Trading Compliance," *Temple Law Review* 88 (2016): 273.

Fraud Enforcement Act of 1988 (ITSFEA)[47] extended the civil penalty of treble damages[48] – once limited to actual traders under the Insider Trading Sanctions Act of 1984 (ITSA)[49] – to all "controlling persons."[50] Under ITSFEA, issuers may incur derivative liability if they "knew or recklessly disregarded the fact [a] controlled person was likely to engage in the act or acts constituting the violation and failed to take appropriate steps to prevent such act or acts before they occurred."[51] The failure to adopt and implement effective insider trading compliance programs and procedures can sometimes stand as evidence of "reckless disregard" under Section 21A(b)(1)(A).[52] The legislative history reflects that the intent behind ITSFEA was to "increase the economic incentives" for controlling persons to "supervise vigorously their employees."[53] Measured by this goal, ITSFEA appears to have had its desired effect. Most issuers have adopted strict insider trading compliance policies and procedures despite the fact that they are not expressly required to do so under ITSFEA.[54] As one sample insider trading compliance policy explains: "[o]nerous penalties may be assessed against the Company for the insider trading violations of its employees. Accordingly, if the Company does not take active steps to adopt preventive policies

---

[47] See Insider Trading and Securities Fraud Enforcement Act of 1988, Pub. L. No. 100–704, 102 Stat. 4677 (codified in scattered sections of 15 U.S.C. § 78 (2012)).

[48] Firms are subject to penalties not exceeding "the greater of [$1,525,000], or three times the amount of the profit gained or loss avoided as a result of such controlled person's violation." 15 U.S.C. § 78u-1(a)(3). The penalty was last adjusted for inflation in 2013. Adjustments to Civil Monetary Penalty Amounts, 2013 WL 1154360 (Feb. 27, 2013).

[49] Insider Trading Sanctions Act of 1984, Pub. L. No. 98–376, 98 Stat. 1264 (codified in scattered sections of 15 U.S.C. § 78 (2012)). Congress "[d]id not extend the treble penalties of ITSA to controlling persons or to employers under principles of respondeat superior." William K. S. Wang and Marc I. Steinberg, *Insider Trading* (New York: Oxford University Press, 2010): 812.

[50] Although ITSFEA does not expressly define "controlling person," the legislative history makes clear that its meaning is adopted from Section 20(a) of the Exchange Act. The Committee Report summarized its meaning as follows:

> "Controlling person" may include not only employers, but any person with power to influence or control the direction or the management, policies, or activities of another person. "Control" is inferred from possession of such power, whether or not it is exercised. The Committee expects the Commission and courts to continue to interpret the term "controlling person" on a case-by-case basis according to the factual circumstances.

H.R. Rep. No. 100–910, at 17 (1988), as reprinted in 1988 U.S.C.C.A.N. 6043, 6054 (citations omitted). See generally Howard M. Friedman, "The Insider Trading and Securities Fraud Enforcement Act of 1988," *North Carolina Law Review* 68 (1990): 465 (discussing the history and implications of ITSFEA).

[51] 15 U.S.C. § 78u-1(b)(1)(A). Issuers were subject to derivative liability for their employees' insider trading violations under Section 20(a) of the Exchange Act, but they were not subject to treble damages.

[52] See Wang and Steinberg, *Insider Trading*, 884–85.

[53] See ibid. at 814–15.

[54] A 1996 survey found that more than 92% of sample firms had adopted a written policy regulating insider trading. Ibid. at 807 n. 3 (citing J. C. Bettis, J. L. Coles, and M. L. Lemmon, "Corporate Policies Restricting Trading by Insiders," *The Journal of Financial Economics* 57 (2000): 192.

and procedures covering securities transactions by Company personnel, the consequences could be severe."[55]

In addition to the risk of stiff civil penalties under ITSFEA, the Federal Sentencing Guidelines offer issuers an added incentive to adopt insider trading compliance policies and procedures.[56] Under the Sentencing Guidelines, an issuer can significantly reduce its "culpability score" for insider trading and other offenses by having an effective compliance and ethics program in place.[57] Moreover, the Justice Department has made it clear that the adoption and implementation of effective compliance programs will impact the decision to prosecute firms for the actions of their employees.[58]

4.3.1.2 Challenges and Costs of Compliance

Thus, to avoid treble damages under ITSFEA and criminal liability under Section 10(b), firms must implement strong compliance policies designed to prevent insider trading. But ambiguity in the law leaves issuers with no clear sense of what conduct is actually proscribed by law. This places issuers in an awkward position. If they do not implement effective compliance programs, they risk serious civil and criminal

---

[55] Steven Chasin, "Insider v. Issuer: Resolving and Preventing Insider Trading Compliance Policy Disputes," *UCLA Law Review* 50 (2003): 862 n. 9 (quoting Dale E. Short and Yvonne E. Chester, "Form: Sample Insider Trading Policy," from Joseph F. Troy and William D. Gould (eds.), *Advising and Defending Corporate Directors and Officers* (San Francisco, CA, California Continuing Legal Education of the Bar, 1998): 437).

[56] See US Sentencing Guidelines Manual, § 8B2.1 (providing standards for organizational compliance programs).

[57] See US Sentencing Guidelines Manual, § 8C2.5(f); see also Ellen S. Podgor, "Educating Compliance," *American Criminal Law Review* 46 (2009): 1528 n. 37 ("Companies can reduce their culpability score by three points when they have in place an effective compliance and ethics program."). Note, however, that a 2004 amendment to the Federal Sentencing Guidelines created a

> [r]ebuttable presumption, for purposes of subsection (f)(1), that the organization did not have an effective compliance and ethics program if an individual – (i) within high-level personnel of a small organization; or (ii) within substantial authority personnel, but not within high-level personnel, of any organization, participated in, condoned, or was willfully ignorant of, the offense.

US Sentencing Guidelines Manual, § 8C2.5(f)(3)(B)(i)-(ii).

[58] See Memorandum from Larry D. Thompson, Deputy Att'y Gen., US Dep't of Justice, to Heads of Dep't Components, US Att'ys 8 (Jan. 20, 2003) ("Compliance programs are established by corporate management to prevent and to detect misconduct and to ensure that corporate activities are conducted in accordance with all applicable criminal and civil laws, regulations, and rules. The Department encourages such corporate self-policing, including voluntary disclosures to the government of any problems that a corporation discovers on its own."). The 2006 memorandum from Deputy Attorney General Paul McNulty replaced the Thompson Memorandum, but it preserved the policy toward compliance programs. See Press Release, US Dep't of Justice, US Deputy Attorney General Paul J McNulty Revises Charging Guidelines for Prosecuting Corporate Fraud (Dec. 12, 2006).

sanctions, as well as reputational damage, should one or more of their employees be found guilty of insider trading. But how can issuers implement policies to reliably prevent conduct that is not defined with any specificity?

There are a number of insider trading control mechanisms employed by issuers, including (1) a published ban on any trading in an issuer's shares based on material nonpublic information (i.e., self-policing), (2) requiring preclearance for trading, and (3) the imposition of "blackout periods." Predictably, ambiguities in the law of insider trading create significant challenges to designing and implementing each of these control mechanisms, and answering these challenges translates directly into significant costs to firms.

4.3.1.2.1 CANNOT RELY ON SELF-POLICING Ambiguity in the law of insider trading presents serious challenges for issuers in articulating and implementing effective self-policing plans. At a minimum, self-policing requires educating employees by offering an everyday language definition of the proscribed conduct. Once employees are educated, the policy must then set out the nature of the controls that will be in place to identify noncompliance and incentivize compliance. The obstacles to designing and implementing such a policy for insider trading should by now be obvious.

Again, it is generally understood that issuers' employees violate the law against insider trading when they seek to benefit by trading (or tipping) on the basis of material nonpublic information in violation of some fiduciary or other similar relation of trust and confidence. But simply parroting these words in a written compliance policy is unhelpful without also offering definitions of its key elements. As explained in Chapter 3, however, crucial elements of this definition (e.g., materiality, publicity, the relevant mental state, and the nature of the relation of trust and confidence) remain uncertain. Thus, giving expression to these terms with sufficient specificity to guide conduct pursuant to a written self-policing policy requires that issuers first take sides in ongoing scholarly debates, splits among circuits, and conflicting direction from the SEC and the courts. In doing so, issuers are forced to guess, and risk guessing incorrectly.

Consequently, issuers who rely exclusively on self-policing policies have three options, none of which are good. First, an issuer can adopt a written policy that bans employees from trading in its shares based on material nonpublic information without defining the key terms. But this defeats the goals of effective compliance (i.e., preventing violations while insulating the firm from liability when violations occur) by leaving employees without a clear sense of what conduct is proscribed. Second, an issuer can adopt a written ban on insider trading that actually defines key terms such as "material," "nonpublic," and "based on" in everyday language that can educate and guide the conduct of its employees. But this strategy risks contradiction by the ex post interpretations of regulators or the courts. Third, an issuer can adopt a "play-it-safe" approach by banning all (or nearly all) trading in firm shares by employees. But this tactic is highly inefficient – precluding vast numbers of perfectly legal trades – and would virtually eliminate equity as a form of employee compensation.[59] Thus, an insider trading compliance policy that relies exclusively on self-policing would be vague and therefore unhelpful, well-defined and therefore risky, or blanket and therefore highly inefficient. The result is that, in practice, issuers tend to adopt written policies that proscribe insider trading without defining it with specificity,[60] but they then supplement this written ban with other control mechanisms, such as preclearance for trading and blackout periods. Supplementing self-policing with these control mechanisms does not, however, resolve the problem of insider trading compliance in the face of legal ambiguity.

4.3.1.2.2 AMBIGUITY AND PROBLEMS FOR PRECLEARANCE Given the uncertainties and risks associated with reliance on self-policing, many commentators recommend that issuers adopt preclearance procedures for employee trades, but preclearance is not without its own challenges. The same ambiguities in the law that preclude effective self-policing will hinder compliance officers in making appropriate preclearance decisions. The problem of ambiguity in the law is then compounded by compliance officers' limited access to facts regarding employees' knowledge and motives for trading. Compliance officers are therefore required to exercise a great deal of discretion in preclearing insider trades and, given the incentives, this often leads to inefficient results. Consider the following scenario.

Imagine the chief financial officer (CFO) of ABC Corp. requests preclearance for the sale of 10,000 shares of ABC stock pursuant to the company's compliance plan.[61] The CFO explains that he wants to sell because he needs cash to cover the down payment and closing costs for the purchase of a new home. Six months prior, ABC Corp. publicly announced that its president would be retiring and that a successor would be named soon. Two days prior to the CFO's preclearance request, ABC Corp. posted a press release on its website announcing that ABC's senior vice president of marketing would be the new president. The news was picked up and noted by the *Wall Street Journal* that same day. For years, it had been assumed by analysts that this senior vice president would be the president's successor. Indeed, a

---

[59] Firms that adopt such play-it-safe insider trading compliance policies could still use stock and stock options as a form of compensation, but the value of the compensation would be diminished significantly by the fact that employees could not liquidate their shares or exercise their options until after leaving the firm. This would also create a perverse incentive for employees to leave the firm to diversify their portfolio – or to leave whenever the stock is performing well.

[60] See, e.g., Alan J. Berkeley, "Form of Summary Memorandum and Sample Corporate Policy on Insider Trading," *ABA Business Law Course Material Journals* 29 (2005): 58–60 (offering a general definition of insider trading along with the suggestion that, when in doubt about whether information is "material" or "nonpublic," employees should "assume that the information is").

[61] This hypothetical first appeared in Anderson, "Solving the Paradox of Insider Trading Compliance," 288–93.

number of analysts had already issued reports operating under the assumption that this senior vice president would get the nod. These analyst reports agreed that, given the senior vice president's similar background and management style, the change would not affect ABC's operations. The stock price has remained steady since the press release was posted.

Before clearing the CFO's trade, the compliance officer must determine whether it is based on material nonpublic information. Is news of the new president's identity "public"? As explained in Chapter 3, the compliance officer gets little to no help from the statutes and rules in answering this question. Applying the dissemination and absorption test, the compliance officer must consider whether news of the leadership change has been disseminated through recognized sources in a manner calculated to reach the general market. Indications from the SEC suggest that ABC posting the release on the company's website alone would not be sufficient. Still, publication in the *Wall Street Journal* is likely to be regarded as a recognized source of distribution with general reach. But dissemination is only half the test; the compliance officer must also determine whether the information has been absorbed (i.e., whether it is "readily translatable into investment action") by the investing public. The answer is not obvious here. As noted in Chapter 3, the *Ingoldsby* court held that information concerning a change in leadership had not been sufficiently absorbed a full nine days after it was highlighted in the *Wall Street Journal* because it had not been fully digested by the relevant investing public.[62] Applying the efficient market approach (i.e., trying to determine whether the information has been impounded in the price of the stock) will not help the compliance officer here either. In this case it is impossible for the compliance officer to know ex ante whether the information has reached a sufficient number of traders in the active investment community for ABC shares. It is no help for the compliance officer to look to the share price to determine whether the information has been impounded because it has remained static. This could reflect (1) the information has reached the active investment community and was not deemed material (as prior analyst reports would suggest), (2) it has not yet reached the active investment community (as in *Ingoldsby*), or (3) its effect has been offset by other information. In the midst of such uncertainty, and in light of the significant risks of guessing incorrectly, a prudent compliance officer would likely act under the assumption that the information is nonpublic. But there remains the question of materiality.

Is news of the new president's identity material? On the one hand, in light of the surrounding circumstances and related analyst buzz, the compliance officer might conclude that the new president's identity would not be considered important by the reasonable investor, or as altering the "total mix" of information available, because the market had long assumed this was ABC's succession plan. On the other hand, the compliance officer might worry that any change in leadership is per se important

[62] S.E.C. v. Ingoldsby, CIV. A. No. 88–1001-MA, 1990 WL 120731, at 5 (D. Mass. May 15, 1990).

to investors. Indeed, Regulation FD explicitly identifies "changes in control or in management" as information that may be material.[63] In making the materiality determination, courts will sometimes look to the market's reaction upon disclosure.[64] Here the compliance officer might look at the static price and conclude that information regarding the change in leadership is not material. But while price movement is a factor, courts have held it is not dispositive, and, as noted previously, here there may be the concern that two days has not provided enough time for the market to absorb the information.[65]

Moreover, the preclearance decision cannot focus exclusively on facts of which the compliance officer is aware. Given the CFO's position, he may know of future earnings or other financial information not available to the compliance officer but that may nevertheless be material. The compliance officer will ask the CFO if he is aware of any such information, but he can never be certain that the CFO has provided an honest answer.

To complicate matters further, the CFO may not know whether he is aware of material nonpublic information. He is no doubt privy to a great deal of soft information about which he has formed opinions concerning the future performance of the company, but he may not know whether such information is sufficiently crystallized or important to count as material. As explained in Chapter 3, even if the CFO is completely forthright with the compliance officer by sharing all of the soft information that he possesses, the *Basic* probability-magnitude test will likely be useless to the compliance officer in making a decision ex ante. For example, the CFO may have learned that there is a 5 percent chance that one of ABC's leading products may have to be recalled. The magnitude is great, but the probability is low. The *Basic* test provides no threshold for determining when the product of probability and magnitude equals materiality, so the compliance officer must guess. In guessing, the compliance officer recognizes that, should the recall actually occur, a future jury will judge his decision in hindsight. Even more concerning, the compliance officer must consider the fact that, under *Texas Gulf Sulphur* and *Basic*, jurors may take the mere fact that the CFO traded while in possession of this soft information as itself "an indication of materiality."[66]

Thus, as one commentator put it, given the subtlety of the question, and the limited information available, "it may be almost impossible for [a compliance] officer to make [a materiality] determination empirically."[67] When in

---

[63] Selective Disclosure and Insider Trading: Final Rule, 65 Fed Reg. 51,727 (Aug. 24, 2000).

[64] See, e.g., S.E.C. v. Tome, 638 F. Supp. 596, 623 (S.D.N.Y. 1986) (finding that a jump in price from thirty dollars per share to forty-five dollars per share immediately upon public announcement of a tender offer was an indication of materiality).

[65] See, e.g., United States v. Bilzerian, 926 F.2d 1285, 1298 (2d Cir. 1991) (stating that a price change – or lack thereof – is not dispositive of materiality).

[66] Basic, Inc. v. Levinson, 485 U.S. 224, 240 n.18 (1988) (citing S.E.C. v. Texas Gulf Sulphur Co., 401 F.2d 833, 851 (1968)).

[67] Chasin, "Insider v. Issuer," 868.

doubt, a prudent compliance officer will therefore err on the side of finding the information material.

But trading by an insider is illegal only if it is done "on the basis of" material nonpublic information, and our CFO has represented that he is trading only because he needs cash to close on his new house. If our compliance officer applies Rule 10b5–1(b), however, she must ignore the CFO's stated purpose for the sale of the ABC shares and focus strictly on the question of whether he is currently "aware" of any material nonpublic information. Again, this places the compliance officer in a difficult position. As noted previously, it will be very difficult for the compliance officer to determine whether the CFO is "aware" of any material nonpublic information – either because the CFO may be untruthful or because, without clear regulatory guidance, neither he nor the compliance officer may be able to answer this question with any certainty. Thus, the prudent default is to assume awareness of material nonpublic information and deny clearance for the trade. As noted in Chapter 3, there are good reasons for concluding that the SEC exceeded its authority in adopting the mere awareness standard under Rule 10b5–1, but, of course, the compliance officer is not expected to put the firm or her employment at risk to challenge the rule.

Thus, with potential firm liability and the compliance officer's own employment on the line, she will have every incentive to play it safe and refuse preclearance for trades in the face of such uncertainty. This conservative approach leads, however, to a number of adverse consequences for the firm and its shareholders.

First, the CFO may bear ill will toward the compliance officer. Since the CFO told the compliance officer that he is not aware of any material nonpublic information and wishes to trade only to close on his house, then, when the trade is not approved, the CFO may assume the compliance officer determined that he was untruthful. Such ill will can undermine the spirit of cooperation and mutual respect that is vitally important to a strong compliance culture and a strong firm. To avoid this potential for in-house conflict, the firm may choose to shift preclearance decisions to outside counsel, but this comes at a significant cost to the firm and therefore the shareholders.[68] At a minimum, such difficult compliance decisions are likely to be a distraction for management, which also affects share value.[69]

Second, corporate insiders typically receive a large portion of their compensation in firm shares.[70] Equity compensation holds value for insiders only if it can be

---

[68] Joan MacLeod Heminway, "Materiality Guidance in the Context of Insider Trading: A Call for Action," *American University Law Review* 52 (2003): 1180–82 (noting that the costs to a firm and its shareholders in turning to outside counsel to make compliance decisions are increased by ambiguity in the law).

[69] Ibid. at 1177–80 (noting that vagueness in insider trading law distracts management from focusing on business and operations, which negatively impacts stockholder value).

[70] M. Todd Henderson, "Insider Trading and CEO Pay," *Vanderbilt Law Review* 64 (2011): 508 (reporting that between 1999 and 2008, "the average public company executive earned more than half her total pay in the form of stock options or restricted stock").

liquidated without much difficulty. Thus, any restrictions the company places on its employees' ability to monetize firm shares will devalue them as compensation, requiring the company to offer more shares to achieve the same remunerative effect in the future.[71] In the previous example, the compliance officer's denial of preclearance devalued ABC shares to the CFO. This costs ABC (and therefore its shareholders) because the CFO is now more likely to demand a comparative increase in ABC shares (or cash) in his next negotiation of compensation.[72]

Third, in part because equity has become a leading component of corporate compensation packages, insider ownership typically accounts for a large proportion of a given issuer's outstanding shares. As Professor Jesse Fried pointed out, "Although U.S. firms are commonly thought to have relatively diffuse ownership, average insider ownership in publicly-traded firms is . . . surprisingly high."[73] Professor Fried cites one study suggesting that directors and officers own an average of 24 to 32 percent of a given firm's equity. This figure excludes insiders' stock options, "which would further increase their effective equity ownership."[74] With so many shares in the hands of insiders, it stands to reason that significant restrictions on their trading will decrease liquidity. This, in turn, will increase firms' cost of capital.[75]

Of course, a compliance officer could avoid these costs by adopting a liberal approach to preclearance, but, in light of the ambiguities in the law, she would thereby risk exposing the company to civil and criminal insider trading liability. There appear to be no good options for an effective preclearance strategy under the current insider trading regime.

4.3.1.2.3 AMBIGUITY AND PROBLEMS FOR BLACKOUT PERIODS Another insider trading compliance strategy for issuers is the implementation of "blackout periods" in lieu of (or in addition to) a preclearance program. A blackout period is a date range within which issuers preclude their officers and directors from trading in a corporation's shares. A "trading window" is a period during which relevant employees are permitted to trade – the flip side of the coin to a blackout period.[76] The

---

[71] Ibid. at 509–10 (noting that when the insiders cannot trade without restrictions, the value of the shares is reduced, which causes an "increase [in] the amount of shares necessary to achieve the same incentive effects").

[72] Heminway, "Materiality Guidance in the Context of Insider Trading," 1174–77 (contending that vagueness in the law leads to delayed or foregone transactions).

[73] Jesse M. Fried, "Insider Trading via the Corporation," *Pennsylvania Law Review* 162 (2014): 804.

[74] Ibid. at 804 n. 11.

[75] See Yakov Amihud and Haim Mendelson, "Asset Pricing and the Bid-Ask Spread," *The Journal of Financial Economics* 17 (1986): 249 (explaining that the greater the liquidity of a security, the lower the expected return required by investors, which decreases the firm's cost of capital).

[76] Robert A. Barron, "Some Comments on the Pre-Clearance Procedure," *Securities Regulation Law Journal* 37 (2009): 387–88 (using coin analogy).

duration of blackout periods will vary from issuer to issuer, and they are not always fixed. For example, many issuers impose regular blackout periods around the quarterly disclosure process – typically beginning three or four weeks prior to scheduled disclosure and ending forty-eight hours after filing. It is assumed that such blackout periods will cover the time period during which officers and directors are most likely to have access to material nonpublic information. As one commentator suggested, "[B]ecause of the substantial and wide-ranging disclosures required in these [quarterly filings] . . . there is a relatively low probability that an insider who trades during the time immediately following their dissemination will be deemed to have traded on material nonpublic information."[77] Firms do not, however, always limit blackout periods to disclosure seasons; they will often close an otherwise open trading window if new material information arises that is not yet ripe for disclosure.[78]

The SEC has not prescribed set blackout periods or trading windows, so they are typically set by issuers on the advice of counsel or at the discretion of compliance officers.[79] In the midst of the legal ambiguity in the law of insider trading, however, the exercise of discretion in setting trading windows and blackout periods creates many of the same problems and runs many of the same risks as preclearance.

Again, in addition to regular blackout periods around quarterly filings, compliance officers will close otherwise open trading windows when employees become aware of material nonpublic information concerning a company. But, as Professor Stephen Bainbridge has noted, "[a]n issuer always has undisclosed information about numerous different aspects of its business," and "[b]y the time all of that information has been disseminated publicly . . . new undisclosed information doubtless will have been developed."[80] So, just as with the preclearance decision, there will rarely be a point in time when compliance officers can set trading windows with confidence – particularly given the reality that their ex ante materiality and publicity determinations will be judged by regulators, prosecutors, and jurors ex post with the benefit of hindsight.

This leaves compliance officers or corporate counsel making blackout period decisions with the same bad choices they face in the preclearance programs. They can adopt a conservative strategy and extend blackout periods to all but a few small trading windows immediately following quarterly filings. Such restrictive blackout policies will, however, decrease the value of shares issued by firms as compensation to employees by limiting their liquidity. Again, this means firms will have to issue more shares to achieve the same remunerative and incentive effect, at great cost

[77] Ibid. at 383.
[78] See, e.g., Stephen Bainbridge, *Insider Trading Law and Policy* (St. Paul, MN: Foundation Press, 2014): 155.
[79] Barron, "Some Comments on the Pre-Clearance Procedure," 387.
[80] Bainbridge, *Insider Trading Law and Policy*, 154.

to their existing shareholders. In addition, as with preclearance, implementing so conservative a policy might affect a firm's cost of capital (by decreasing liquidity). Finally, implementing extended blackout periods will force insiders to make large trades in short, periodic spurts, which will likely have an unnatural impact on the price and trading volume of the firm's shares during trading windows.[81] Such concentrated trading may attract unwarranted (and therefore misleading) market attention.

The alternative for firms, however, is no better. By adopting a more liberal approach and limiting the imposition of blackout periods to only rare circumstances in which there is widespread knowledge within the firm of market-moving, material nonpublic information (say, in the midst of merger or tender offer negotiations), a compliance officer risks exposing a company to significant civil or criminal liability.

Ultimately, as with self-policing and preclearance, ambiguity in the law of insider trading leaves a conscientious compliance officer with few good options in designing and implementing an effective trading window policy.

4.3.1.3 The Paradox of Compliance for Issuers

To take stock, vagueness in the law translates into uncertainty for issuers in the design and implementation of their insider trading compliance programs. This uncertainty, when combined with the threat of significant reputational and economic sanctions for "ineffective" compliance programs, typically leads firms to adopt a "play-it-safe" approach. Issuers design and implement compliance regimes that are marked by highly restrictive preclearance decision-making and extended blackout periods.

Stingy preclearance and lengthy blackout periods, however, come at a heavy price to firms in terms of corporate culture, cost of compensation, share liquidity, and cost of capital. If the issuer is rational, then the magnitude of such inefficiencies will be a direct function of the ambiguity in the law (which is great) and the severity of the sanctions for violation (which are stiff). This is the paradox of insider trading compliance for issuers: ambiguity in the law combined with the threat of stiff reputational damage and legal sanctions creates a perverse incentive to adopt compliance programs that are highly inefficient and ultimately costly to shareholders. Thus, ironically, the very insider trading regulations that were implemented to increase value for shareholders may be having the opposite effect.

---

[81] See Peter J. Romero and Alan L. Dye, "Insider Trading under Rules 10b5–1 and 10b5–2," in *Postgraduate Course in Federal Securities Law*, SHO13 A.L.I-A.B.A. 893, 901 (2002) ("Open market sales by [insiders] ... often attract unwanted attention, due to the perception of many investors that such sales may reflect a lack of confidence in the company.").

4.3.2 *Victim Punished for the Crime – Corporate Criminal Liability*

The current insider trading regime is irrational and absurdly overbroad in that it threatens corporate victims of insider trading with criminal liability for the very crimes that were perpetrated against them.[82]

4.3.2.1 Corporate Criminal Liability Generally

The United States Supreme Court first recognized corporate criminal liability in *New York Central & H.R.R. Co. v. United States*. A railroad company and its assistant traffic managers were convicted for the payment of illegal rebates on the shipment of sugar. Despite the objection that imposing criminal liability on a corporation "is in reality to punish the innocent stockholders," the Court applied the civil doctrine of respondeat superior to uphold the railroad's conviction.[83] The Court explained that, "in the interest of public policy," it is necessary to extend the civil doctrine of vicarious liability to the criminal context in those circumstances where law could not otherwise be "effectually enforced."[84] Without corporate criminal liability, circumstances might arise where firms would be free to set up and profit from morally hazardous incentive structures that entice their employees to break the law. In such circumstances, the employees might end up in jail, but the firm and its shareholders would be permitted to just replace those employees in the same structure and persist in profiting risk free from illegal conduct. The Court concluded that it simply could not "shut its eyes to the fact that the great majority of business transactions in modern times are conducted through [corporations]."[85] To give corporations "immunity from all punishment because of the old and exploded doctrine that a corporation cannot commit a crime would virtually take away the only means of effectually controlling the subject-matter and correcting the abuses aimed at."[86]

The *New York Central* Court laid out a basic two-part test for when corporations may be held criminally liable for the acts of their employees: (1) the employee must perform the criminal act within the scope of their employment, and (2) the corporation must be an intended beneficiary of the act.[87] Subsequent courts have, however, interpreted these elements quite expansively – arguably beyond the scope intended by the *New York Central* Court. For example, in *United States v. Hilton Hotels Corp.*, the Ninth Circuit held that the employee's authority need only be

---

[82] Much of the following analysis first appeared in John P. Anderson, "When Does Corporate Criminal Liability for Insider Trading Make Sense?," *Stetson Law Review* 46 (2016): 147.
[83] New York Central & H.R.R. Co. v. United States, 212 U.S. 481, 492 (1909).
[84] Ibid. at 494–95.
[85] Ibid. at 495.
[86] Ibid. at 495–96.
[87] New York Central & H.R.R. Co. v. United States, 212 U.S. 481, 494–95 (1909).

apparent, and it may be found even where the employee acts contrary to express company policy or instructions.[88] Some courts have gone so far as to find that even criminal actions beyond the scope of an employee's real or apparent authority might be attributed to the corporation if management or the board does not take active measures to stop it.[89]

The test for whether an employee's criminal act was "with the intent to benefit the corporation" has also been interpreted quite liberally.[90] The employee's action need not actually benefit the corporation to satisfy the test[91]; in fact it can prove detrimental to the corporation.[92] Indeed, it need not even be the case that the employee's primary intent was to benefit the firm[93]; acts motivated principally by self-interest may be imputed to the corporation where a jury might find that at least part of the employee's motivation – "however befuddled" – was to benefit the corporation.[94] Indeed, Professor John Hasnas has suggested that corporate liability may be found where, absent any clear intent to benefit the firm, employees could have reasonably *believed* the firm would benefit.[95]

Ultimately, the two-part *New York Central* test for corporate criminal liability has been interpreted so liberally by the courts that it has, as one commentator put it, been rendered "almost meaningless."[96] The practical reality is that whether a

---

[88] United States v. Hilton Hotels Corp., 467 F.2d 1000, 1004 (9th Cir. 1973); see also United States v. Basic Contr. Co., 711 F. 2d 570, 573 (4th Cir. 1985) (holding that the lower court properly instructed the jury that corporate intent can be shown by the actions or statements of those who "have *apparent* authority to make policy for the corporation" and recognizing that a corporation can be held criminally responsible even when an employee's acts "were against corporate policy or express instruction.") (emphasis added).

[89] See, e.g., Cont'l Baking Co. v. United States, 281 F.2d 137, 149 (6th Cir. 1960).

[90] See, e.g., Pamela H. Bucy, "Corporate Ethos: A Standard for Imposing Corporate Criminal Liability," *Minnesota Law Review* 75 (1991): 1102–03 (discussing the requirement that a criminal act be committed with the intent to benefit the corporation and how an act can satisfy that requirement when the corporation received no benefit from the offense and those within the corporation were unaware of the conduct when it occurred).

[91] See, e.g., Standard Oil Co. of Tex. v. United States, 307 F.2d 120, 128 (5th Cir. 1962) (stating that an actual benefit to the corporation is not necessary to create liability).

[92] See, e.g., United States v. Automated Med. Lab., Inc., 770 F.2d 399, 406–07 (4th Cir. 1985).

[93] See, e.g., ibid. (stating that liability can exist when an agent acts for both his or her own benefit and for the corporation's benefit); United States v. Gold, 743 F.2d 800, 823 (11th Cir. 1984) (finding that an employee must intend to benefit the corporation only "in part").

[94] United States v. Sun-Diamond Growers of Cal., 138 F.3d 961, 970 (D.C. Cir. 1998). See also Local 1814, Int'l Longshoremen's Ass'n, AFL-CIO v. NRLB, 735 F.2d 1384, 1395 (D.C. Cir. 1984) ("[T]he acts of an agent motivated partly by self-interest – even where self-interest is the predominant motive – lie within the scope of employment so long as the agent is actuated by the principal's business purposes 'to any appreciable extent.'").

[95] John Hasnas, "The Centenary of a Mistake: One Hundred Years of Corporate Criminal Libaility," *American Criminal Law Review* 46 (2009): 1333 (citing Steere Tank Lines v. United States, 330 F.2d 719, 722–4 (5th Cir. 1964), as holding that "a corporation could be liable for the illegal actions of truck drivers who reasonably could believe the corporation benefited from and demanded such actions.").

[96] Bucy, "Corporate Ethos," 1102.

corporation is or is not charged for the crimes of its employees is less a function of the two-part *New York Central* test than it is a matter of prosecutorial whim.[97] This breadth in prosecutorial discretion leaves corporations extremely vulnerable and "invites abuse."[98]

In January 2003, then Deputy Attorney General Larry D. Thompson issued a memorandum offering guidelines for prosecutors in the exercise of their discretion to charge a corporation with a criminal offense. The Thompson Memorandum encouraged prosecutors to consider factors such as the "nature and seriousness of the offense," the "pervasiveness of wrongdoing within the corporation," the "adequacy of the corporation's compliance program," and the corporation's "voluntary disclosure of wrongdoing and its willingness to cooperate."[99] Most controversially, in determining whether a corporation was willing to "cooperate," the Thompson Memorandum permitted prosecutors to consider (1) whether a firm was willing to waive its "attorney-client and work product protection" and (2) whether it has declined to pay attorneys' fees for implicated employees.[100] These latter factors demonstrate just how far the Department of Justice managed to leverage its virtually limitless discretion to prosecute corporations to force firms to effectively "[sign] on as deputy prosecutorial agents" against themselves and their own employees.[101] The government may, however, have been a bit too aggressive in pressing its advantage. Backlash from business groups, civil liberties organizations, and judges ultimately forced the Department of Justice to soften its stance somewhat.[102] In December 2006, then Deputy Attorney General Paul McNulty issued new guidelines that, while retaining most of the same language from the Thompson Memorandum, now requires that prosecutors seek approval from the deputy attorney general before requesting that firms waive privilege and allows consideration of advancing attorneys' fees for employees only under extraordinary circumstances.[103] Nevertheless, a recent memorandum issued by then deputy attorney general Sally Quillian Yates looked to recover some of this lost ground and functionally revive the privilege waiver demand by requiring that entities turn over "all relevant facts" in order to

---

[97] *Sun-Diamond Growers*, 138 F.3d at 970 (providing "the only thing that keeps deceived corporations from being indicted for the acts of their employee-deceivers is not some fixed rule of law or logic but simply the sound exercise of prosecutorial discretion").

[98] Hasnas, "The Centenary of a Mistake," 1354.

[99] Memorandum from Larry D. Thompson, Deputy Attorney General, US Department of Justice, to Heads of Department Components and All US Attorneys (Jan. 20, 2003).

[100] Ibid.

[101] Hasnas, "The Centenary of a Mistake," 1354.

[102] See, e.g., Ashby Jones, "Thompson Memo Out, McNulty Memo In," *Wall Street Journal* (Dec. 12, 2006).

[103] Memorandum from Paul J. McNulty, Deputy Attorney General, US Department of Justice, to Heads of Department Components and All US Attorneys (Dec. 12, 2006).

receive "any" cooperation credit.[104] In sum, vast prosecutorial discretion continues to leave the government holding all the cards. As former US Attorney Preet Bharara once put it, "the corporation is particularly ill-equipped to defend itself . . . against the power of prosecutors to prove *virtually any corporate entity guilty upon showing criminal conduct on the part of at least one employee.*"[105] In other words, corporations have no choice but to "cooperate," and prosecutors are free to decide what that means.[106]

Even before the Thompson, McNulty, and Yates Memoranda, the Federal Sentencing Guidelines, promulgated in 1991, imposed essentially the same incentive structure on corporations to self-police and "cooperate" with the government. Under the Sentencing Guidelines, a corporation reduces its culpability score by maintaining "effective compliance and ethics programs," and by "self-reporting, cooperation, or acceptance of responsibility."[107] Though these credits under the Sentencing Guidelines are offered in the form of post-conviction carrots, they end up functioning as hefty pre-indictment sticks when coupled with limitless prosecutorial discretion under the courts' liberal interpretations of *New York Central*. These Sentencing Guidelines, like the previously described DOJ memoranda, effectively deputize corporations against their employees and themselves.[108]

But recall that the guiding policy behind *New York Central's* recognition of corporate criminal liability was to fill an enforcement gap – to create otherwise absent incentives for firms to police the conduct of their own employees. In other words, effectively deputizing firms to perform a law enforcement function was precisely the Supreme Court's objective. Presumably the idea was that the clear benefits of increased enforcement would outweigh the inevitable harm of punishing innocent shareholders. Even keeping this broad policy justification in mind, however, corporate criminal liability in the context of insider trading is often irrational. For, it turns out that in three of the four circumstances under which a corporation is subjected to criminal liability for the insider trading of its employees, it (or its shareholders) is by theory of law also the principal victim of that same trading. This leads to the absurd result that the victim is liable for the crime.

---

[104] Memorandum from Sally Quillian Yates, Deputy Attorney General, US Department of Justice, to Heads of Department Components and All US Attorneys (Sept. 9, 2015).

[105] Preet Bharara, "Corporations Cry Uncle and Their Employees Cry Foul: Rethinking Prosecutorial Pressure on Corporate Defendants," *American Criminal Law Review* 44 (2007): 70–71 (emphasis added).

[106] See generally Lisa Kern Griffin, "Compelled Cooperation and the New Corporate Criminal Procedure," *New York University Law Review* 82 (2017): 311 (examining the constitutional implications of the corporate cooperation doctrine).

[107] US Sentencing Guidelines Manual, § 8A1.1 at 499, § 8B2.1 at 509 (2015).

[108] Hasnas, "The Centenary of a Mistake," 1354 ("[T]he New York Central standard brings almost irresistible pressure on corporations to do whatever they can to avoid indictment, which means signing on as deputy prosecutorial agents") (footnote omitted).

4.3.2.2 Absurdity of Corporate Criminal Liability for True Insider Trading under the Classical Theory

As explained in Chapter 2, under the classical theory, when a true insider (whether the issuer itself, a board member, senior management, or a low-level employee) profits by trading in the firm's shares based on material nonpublic information, the fraud is said to be perpetrated on the counterparty. In such cases, the counterparty will always be a current or prospective shareholder who, as such, is owed a fiduciary or similar duty of trust and confidence that warrants disclosure prior to trading. The insider profits by deception, and the current or prospective shareholder with whom she trades is identified as the victim of this deception.

Corporate criminal liability for insider trading exposes firms to significant monetary fines.[109] Moreover, history suggests that the uncertainty accompanying a criminal indictment alone can cause a corporation's sources of capital to evaporate, ultimately resulting in the firm's collapse.[110] Who suffers these consequences? As Professor Hasnas explained, "[t]o the extent that such a loss cannot be passed along to consumers, it is the owners of the corporation, the shareholders, who incur the penalty."[111] But, while almost all corporate criminal liability forces innocent shareholders to bear the punishment, the case of insider trading is unique in that, as explained previously, the theory of criminal liability itself also identifies these same shareholders as the victims. Consequently, shareholders are forced to suffer the crime and the punishment!

Recall that in *New York Central*, the Court weighed the concern that imposing corporate criminal liability might sometimes force innocent shareholders to pay a price for the corporation's crimes. With this concern in mind, the Court nevertheless held that corporate criminal liability may still be warranted in those cases where no other effective means of protecting the public are available. The Court presumably reasoned that in such cases, the wrong of penalizing innocent shareholders was outweighed by the wrong of leaving innocent victims unprotected or by the wrong of undermining the policy advanced by the relevant statute. But this rationale cannot justify corporate criminal liability for the true insider trading of an employee under the classical theory. Imposing harsh penalties on the innocent shareholders whom the theory of liability also identifies as the victims of the crime is just plain absurd, and does not jibe with the Court's reasoning in *New York Central*.

---

[109] Exchange Act Section 32(a) provides that an insider trading violation by a person "other than a natural person" is subject to a fine of up to $25,000,000.

[110] The collapse of Drexel Burnham Lambert in the 1980s is instructive. See, e.g., Stewart, *Den of Thieves* (chronicling the demise of Drexel).

[111] Hasnas, "The Centenary of a Mistake," 1339.

Law

4.3.2.3 Absurdity of Corporate Criminal Liability for True Insider Trading under the Misappropriation Theory

As a number of scholars have pointed out, there is no reason that true insiders cannot also incur Section 10(b) liability for insider trading based on the misappropriation theory.[112] When a true insider incurs Section 10(b) liability under the misappropriation theory, the fraud is actually perpetrated on the issuer. The *O'Hagan* Court explained that "[a] company's confidential information ... qualifies as property to which the company has a right of exclusive use. The undisclosed misappropriation of such information, in violation of a fiduciary duty ... constitutes fraud akin to embezzlement."[113]

The irrationality of derivative corporate criminal liability for the true insider trading of a firm's employees under the misappropriation theory is even more blatant than under the classical theory. The absurdity of holding a firm criminally liable for its employees' embezzlement is palpable, but this is precisely what corporate criminal liability for true insider trading amounts to under the misappropriation theory. Certainly the policy rationale behind *New York Central* cannot support corporate criminal liability under such circumstances.

4.3.2.4 Absurdity of Corporate Criminal Liability for Source-Employee Outsider Trading

The Supreme Court first recognized the misappropriation theory to fill a gap in the classical theory's coverage – namely that it failed to capture outsiders who look to profit by trading on material nonpublic information in breach of a fiduciary or similar duty of trust and confidence. The *O'Hagan* Court held that since the impact on the parties and the market is the same in both cases, it makes little sense to hold a lawyer like O'Hagan liable under Section 10(b) if he works for a law firm representing the target of a take-over (as he would be under the classical theory), but not if he works for the bidder.

This section focuses on "source-employee" outsider trading under the misappropriation theory. Here the outsider misappropriation trading is done by an employee of the information's source. Such insider trading is perpetrated by an employee against his employer. Take, for example, the case of *Carpenter v. United States*.[114] In that case, a *Wall Street Journal* reporter was prosecuted for trading in advance of

---

[112] See, e.g., Donald C. Langevoort, *Insider Trading: Regulation, Enforcement & Prevention*, Vol. 18, § 6–1 (New York: Thomson Reuters, 2015) ("Virtually all cases that could be brought [under the classical theory] can also be styled as misappropriation cases"); Wang and Steinberg, *Insider Trading*, 492 ("In most instances, both the Commission and private plaintiffs could recast a classical special relationship case as involving 'misappropriation'").

[113] *O'Hagan*, 521 U.S. at 654.

[114] *Carpenter*, 484 U.S. at 19.

the publication of his daily stock-picking column. The column was popular and usually had an impact on stock prices. The *Journal's* policy was that, prior to publication, the content of the column was the *Journal's* confidential information. In violation of this policy, the reporter R. Foster Winans entered into an arrangement whereby he and others would profit by trading on this information in advance of publication. Under liberal interpretations of the *New York Central* test, however, there was nothing other than the exercise of prosecutorial discretion that prevented the *Journal* from being indicted for Winan's trading. This, as Professor Jonathan Macey pointed out, is "ironic in light of the fact that the Supreme Court 'went to great lengths to indicate that the [*Journal*] had been victimized by Winans and his cohorts.'"[115]

4.3.2.5 When Corporate Criminal Liability for Insider Trading Does Make Sense

There is one form of derivative corporate criminal liability for insider trading that makes sense – "third-party" insider/outsider trading. Third-party insider/outsider trading occurs where the violation of fiduciary or similar duty of trust and confidence that makes the trading fraudulent is committed against someone other than the trader's employer or shareholders. Third-party traders are typically tippees, who may be held derivatively liable under either the classical or misappropriation theories of liability. But they might also be held directly liable under the misappropriation theory where they trade in violation of a fiduciary or similar duty of trust and confidence to someone other than their employer. Of course, only third-party traders whose trading might somehow be interpreted as within the scope of their employment under *New York Central* are relevant here.[116] Third-party traders fitting this description are typically employed within the financial industry.

Imagine that Timmy, a trader for the hedge fund ABC Capital, pays an insider at Big Strike Mining Corporation for material nonpublic information concerning the company's recent discovery of a major gold deposit in North Dakota. Timmy purchases all of the Big Strike Mining shares he can get his hands on for ABC Capital. ABC makes millions after the announcement, and Timmy receives a generous bonus. Who are the victims of Timmy's insider trading? As explained previously, under the classical theory, the counterparties to the trading are the victims, and under the misappropriation theory, Big Strike is the victim. ABC Capital is not a victim under either theory. Moreover, Timmy's trades benefited

---

[115] Macy, *Insider Trading: Economics, Politics, and Policy* (Washington, DC: The AEI Press, 1991): 66 (quoting Harvey L. Pitt and Karen L. Shapiro, "Securities Regulation by Enforcement: A Look Ahead at the Next Decade," *Yale Journal on Regulation* 7 (1990): 240–41.

[116] For example, even under the most liberal interpretation, the *New York Central* test would not license derivative corporate liability for Dunkin' Donuts when one of its cashiers trades in Apple shares based on an illegal tip from an insider at Apple.

ABC and were squarely within his scope of employment under *New York Central*. Consequently, by contrast to the three other types of derivative corporate insider trading already analyzed, holding ABC Capital derivatively liable under Section 10(b) for Timmy's insider trading does not suffer from the irrationality of holding the victim liable for the crime.

Moreover, consider the ABC Capital example in light of the policy considerations informing *New York Central*. Despite the risk that corporate criminal liability will often punish innocent shareholders for the crimes of the firm's employees, the Court held that such liability was warranted where, absent the incentives for self-regulation imposed by the threat of corporate criminal liability, there would be no other effective means of protecting the public from morally hazardous incentives set by the corporation. This is precisely the situation presented by third-party trading through hedge funds like ABC Capital and other financial service firms. Nevertheless, the fact that one of the four forms of derivative corporate liability for insider trading is not manifestly absurd is hardly encouraging. Reform is clearly needed.

The objection is anticipated that this is all much ado about nothing in that corporations are rarely indicted for insider trading, and, when they are, it is precisely the firms that deserve it – namely those whose employees are engaging in third-party insider trading.[117] But this tells only half of the story. Prosecutors are mindful of the often disastrous, and therefore politically harmful, collateral consequences of a corporate indictment. Experience has taught them that the mere threat of an indictment gives them all the power they need to force a change in a firm's compliance practices, force a corporation to cooperate in the government's investigation of the firm or its employees, or force a corporation to otherwise cooperate with the government's political goals. The recent increase in Deferred Prosecution Agreements and the recent Yates Memorandum are clear reflections of this strategy. As Professor Hasnas put it,

> It has become apparent that the purpose of corporate criminal liability is not to punish corporations, but to force them to cooperate in the prosecution of their employees. This is evidenced by the constantly increasing number of federal criminal investigations of business organizations that end in Deferred Prosecution Agreement coupled with a constantly decreasing number which end with corporate indictments and convictions. It is anachronistic to think of the purpose of corporate prosecution as the imposition of punishment upon conviction. Today, it is corporate indictment that is the punishment and lack of cooperation that is the offence.[118]

---

[117] Prior to the 1988 indictment of Drexel Burnham Lambert, only individuals had been indicted for insider trading. See Harry First, *Business Crime* (Westbury, NY: The Foundation Press, 1990): 159. This indictment, and the events surrounding it, ultimately led to the firm's collapse in 1990. For a brilliant account of this, see James B. Stewart's *Den of Thieves*. Since the collapse of Drexel Burnham, very few firms have been indicted for insider trading, and most of those that have were held derivatively liable for third-party insider trading.

[118] Hasnas, "The Centenary of a Mistake: One Hundred Years of Corporate Criminal Liability," 1354.

As explained in the previous section, the mere threat of corporate criminal indictment for the insider trading of a corporation's employees has forced issuers to adopt overbroad insider trading compliance programs that come at a heavy price in terms of corporate culture, cost of compensation, share liquidity, and cost of capital. Moreover, recent criminal investigations of employee use of Exchange Act Rule 10b5–1(c) trading plans have also put issuers on the defensive concerning the possible insider trading of their employees. The concern raised in this section is that *any* leverage derived by prosecutors from (1) the threat of indicting issuers for the insider trading of their employees under either the classical or misappropriation theories, or from (2) the threat of indicting source companies for the insider trading of their employees under the misappropriation theory, is irrational and illegitimate.

*****

This chapter has made the argument that, regardless of what one thinks of the propriety of the practice of insider trading, the current enforcement regime in the United States is manifestly unjust, incoherent, and irrational. It is unjust because it gives insufficient notice of criminal liability and invites abuse of prosecutorial discretion due to its lack of statutory guidance and its exceedingly vague common law elements. It is incoherent because it is guided by two competing and mutually exclusive paradigms, the SEC's favored equal-access model versus the courts' insistence that Section 10(b) is exclusively an antifraud provision. It is irrational because, due to the paradox of compliance for issuers and the fact that derivative corporate liability holds the victims liable for the crime of insider trading, the current regime actually undermines most of the values it purports to advance. For these reasons alone, the current enforcement regime is in clear need of reform.

Once it is decided that reform is needed, the next question is what form it should take. This book takes it for granted that the normative task of legal reform is to make a society's positive laws reflect its shared critical conceptions of the good, the right, and the efficient. The ideal insider trading reform will therefore reflect a proper balance of each of these core values. To this end, Part II of this book engages in this normative task by identifying and weighing the principal ethical and economic implications of insider trading. But before concluding Part I's summary of the current state of the law and its problems, it would be prudent to consider the experiences of other nations in regulating insider trading and determine what if any lessons might be learned. Chapter 5 will therefore offer a brief survey of insider trading regulation outside the United States.

5

The Global Experience

Current and historical insider trading enforcement regimes around the world may be roughly grouped along the following spectrum: (1) laissez-faire or caveat emptor regimes, which permit all trading on material nonpublic information, so long as there is no affirmative fraud (actual misrepresentations or concealment); (2) fiduciary-cum-fraud regimes, which recognize a duty to disclose or abstain from trading, but only for those who share a recognized duty of trust and confidence (with either the counterparty to the trade or the source of the information, or both); (3) equal-access regimes, which preclude trading by those who have acquired information advantages from sources that are closed to other market participants (regardless of whether such trading violates a duty of trust and confidence); and (4) parity-of-information regimes, which strive to prohibit all trading on information asymmetries (regardless of the source).

Outside of the United States, most countries adopted the laissez-faire approach to insider trading regulation until the 1980s. As explained in Chapter 2, it was around this time that the SEC was struggling for expanded powers and resources to combat insider trading in the United States. The SEC was pushing for an equal-access (or perhaps even parity-of-information) regime, but the Supreme Court pushed back, insisting that the statutory authority extended only to a fiduciary-cum-fraud regime.[1] In addition to pressing for expanded insider trading regulation in the United States (or perhaps as a coordinated aspect of these efforts), around this time the SEC also began using its considerable international clout to "prod" foreign governments to adopt regulations as part of a "global crusade against insider trading."[2] This crusade

---

[1] See Chiarella v. United States, 445 U.S. 222 (1980), and Dirks v. S.E.C., 463 U.S. 646 (1983).
[2] See Amir Licht, "The Mother of All Path Dependencies: Toward a Cross-Cultural Theory of Corporate Governance Systems," *Delaware Journal of Corporate Law* 26 (2001): 195 (adoption of insider trading laws in the European Union largely a product of US "prodding"); Joan MacLeod Heminway, "Disparate Notions of Fairness: Comparative Insider Trading Regulation in an Evolving Global Landscape," in Sanford R. Silverburg (ed.), *International Law:*

bore much fruit, reflected in the recent implementation of a myriad of insider trading enforcement regimes around the world.

5.1 THE RECENT RISE OF INSIDER TRADING REGULATION ON THE WORLD SCENE

The European markets crashed alongside the US markets in 1929, but no European countries thought to respond with insider trading regulation. It simply was not on their radar. It was not until 1980 that, due in part to pressure from the United States, the United Kingdom promulgated the Companies Act, which, for the first time, included a specific (though limited) criminal offense for insider trading.[3] Few countries on the European continent followed the United Kingdom's lead. As of 1986, only three of the European Community members regulated insider trading.[4] Things began to change, however, in 1989 when, also due in part to US prompting, the European Council passed the Directive Coordinating Regulations of Insider Dealing mandating that member states regulate insider trading.[5] At the time this directive was adopted, twelve of the European Community's members had no insider trading regulations whatsoever.[6] Since the 1989 directive's adoption, however, all twelve of these countries have complied with the mandate to implement insider trading regulations.

The story is similar elsewhere around the world. In the East, Japan responded to US pressure by adopting an insider trading law in 1988.[7] Hong Kong made insider

Contemporary Issues and Future Developments (Boulder, CO: Westview Press, 2011): 111, 119 ("the SEC has executed [a] global crusade against insider trading").

[3] See Companies Act 1980, §§ 68–73. Up to 1980, the UK common law refused to recognize that company directors and other executives owed fiduciary duties to shareholder counterparties when trading in company shares. See, e.g., Percival v. Wright (1902), 2 Ch. 421. This is probably still true as a matter of civil law in the United Kingdom. See Kern Alexander, "UK Insider Dealing and Market Abuse Law: Strengthening Regulatory Law to Combat Market Misconduct," in Stephen Bainbridge (ed.), *Research Handbook on Insider Trading* (Northampton, MA: Edward Elgar Publishing, Inc., 2013): 407, 410.

[4] Viveca Hostetter, "Turning Insider Trading Inside Out in the European Union," *California Wester International Law Journal* 30 (1999): 186 (noting that as of 1986, only the United Kingdom, Denmark, and France regulated insider trading).

[5] See Council Directive 89/592/EEC of November 13, 1989 coordinating regulations on insider dealing, 1989 O.J. (L 334) 30. See also Katja Langenbucher, "Insider Trading in European Law," in Bainbridge, *Research Handbook on Insider Trading*, 429; Heminway, "Disparate Notions of Fairness," 119 ("The United States, acting through the SEC, was an impetus behind ... the EC Directive.").

[6] See Thomas C. Newkirk and Melissa A. Robertson, "Insider Trading – A U.S. Perspective" (speech, Cambridge, England, Sept. 19, 1998), US Securities and Exchange Commission, www.sec.gov/news/speech/speecharchive/1998/spch221.htm.

[7] See FTPA, §§ 166, 167; SEA §§ 190–92, 190–93; see also J. Mark Ramseyer, "Insider Trading Regulation in Japan," in Bainbridge, *Research Handbook on Insider Trading*, 347; Heminway, "Disparate Notions of Fairness," 118 (Japanese "insider trading regulation was implemented in 1988 in response to pressure from the United States and other developed states").

trading illegal in 1991.[8] India created its Securities and Exchange Board to regulate insider trading in 1992. China had no regulations pertaining to insider trading until 1993, and its complete enforcement regime was not in place until 1998.[9] And Russia enacted its first insider trading law in 2010.[10] In the global South, South Africa adopted insider trading regulations in 1989. Colombia and Costa Rica made insider trading illegal in 1990.[11] And Argentina, Chile, and Peru adopted insider trading regulations in 1991.[12] All told, 77 of the 87 countries that had insider trading laws on the books by the year 2000 adopted them after 1980.[13] The average year of adoption for developed countries was 1990, and the average year of adoption for undeveloped countries was 1991.[14] In fact, of the 103 countries that had established stock exchanges as of a 2000 study, only 16 had yet to adopt insider trading regulations.[15]

No one approach has been taken. In what follows, some representative insider trading enforcement regimes from around the globe are summarized.

5.1.1 *Japan*

As an occupying power, the United States essentially imposed the Japanese Securities and Exchange Act on the country in 1948 (1948 Act). The 1948 Act combined provisions from the US Securities Act of 1933 and the Securities Exchange Act of 1934.[16] Similar to its US counterparts, the only provision of the 1948 Act that expressly addressed insider trading was Section 189, its equivalent to Section 16 of the US Exchange Act. The most important aspect of this provision (its reporting requirement) was, however, repealed by the Japanese Diet in 1953, and Section 189 has been all but abandoned since.[17] The 1948 Act also included a Section 10(b) equivalent, but Japan never used this provision to address insider trading. As Professor J. Mark Ramseyer put it, "Japanese prosecutors and judges stayed with the

---

[8] See James H. Thompson, "A Global Comparison of Insider Trading Regulations," *International Journal of Accounting and Financial Reporting* (2013): 3.

[9] See ibid. See also Hui Huang, "The Regulation of Insider Trading in China: Law and Enforcement," in Bainbridge, *Research Handbook on Insider Trading*, 304.

[10] See The Federal Law No. 224-FZ dated 27 July 2010 "On Prevention of Illegitimate Use of Inside Information and Market Manipulation and on Amendments to Certain Laws of the Russian Federation."

[11] See Laura Nyantung Beny, "The Political Economy of Insider Trading Laws and Enforcement: Law vs. Politics? International Evidence," in Bainbridge, *Research Handbook on Insider Trading*, 266, 287. Beny's data is drawn from an empirical study by Utpal Bhattacharya and Hazem Daouk, "The World Price of Insider Trading," *The Journal of Finance* 57 (2002): 75.

[12] Beny, "The Political Economy of Insider Trading Laws and Enforcement," 287–88.

[13] Ibid. at 287–89.

[14] Ibid.

[15] Ibid. This number of countries failing to regulate insider trading has since grown smaller, though no comprehensive study provides an updated number.

[16] See Ramseyer, "Insider Trading Regulation in Japan," 352.

[17] See ibid.

American SEC's original plan for the rule."[18] Insider trading was therefore left virtually unregulated until 1988, when the Japanese Diet passed extensive amendments to its existing securities laws (1988 Amendments).[19] In addition to reintroducing its Section 16 analogue, Japan's 1988 Amendments introduced a limited equal-access insider trading enforcement regime.[20]

The 1988 Amendments lay out the Japanese insider trading enforcement regime with admirable specificity. The statute prohibits covered persons from trading in a firm's shares while in possession of material nonpublic information acquired by virtue of their relationship to that firm. The persons covered by the prohibition are defined by an exhaustive list. The list includes the issuer's employees, major shareholders, outside counsel, persons in contractual privity with the issuer, and former insiders.[21] The 1988 Amendments also prohibit trading in a target by any "person who acquires information from his affiliation (whether by employment, stock holdings, legal authority, or contractual ties) to the acquirer in a tender offer."[22] Finally, the Japanese regime prohibits trading by any tippee who received material nonpublic information directly and intentionally from an insider. Interestingly, however, remote tippees are typically free to trade under the Japanese regime,[23] and tippers were not subject to insider trading liability in Japan until a recent 2013 statutory amendment imposed such liability.[24]

The 1988 Amendments define material information as any information "that an investor would consider important in deciding whether to buy or sell."[25] They then

---

[18] See ibid. at 354.

[19] Law No. 75 of 1988.

[20] See Ramseyer, "Insider Trading Regulation in Japan," 352. This provision, which is now codified as §§ 163 and 164 of the Financial Instruments and Exchange Act (FIEA), has a reporting requirement under § 163, and § 164 then provides:

> For the purpose of preventing the unfair use of secrets obtained by an officer or principal shareholder of a listed company by reason of his office or status, any profit realized by him from any purchase of a specified security of the listed company and sale within a period of six months, or from any sale of a specified security and purchase within a period of six months, shall be recoverable by the listed company.

[21] See FIEA § 166(a).

[22] Ramseyer, "Insider Trading Regulation in Japan," 356 (paraphrasing FIEA § 167).

[23] See ibid. ("Because the ban covers only those who hear from a defined insider, secondary and tertiary tippees may freely trade."). But note that courts have interpreted the statute to impose liability on remote tippees when an insider tipper intends to convey material nonpublic information to a third party through an intermediary or agent. See, e.g., Hiroko Tabuchi, "Japanese Insider Trading Case Ensnares U.S. Firm," *The New York Times* (June 8, 2012) (describing a Japanese insider trading prosecution of a trader who "had learned of [an offering] through a securities consultancy, whose source was an employee at the offering's lead underwriter"). I thank Masa Yamamoto for bringing this exception to the general rule that remote tippees are not liable under Japanese law to my attention.

[24] See FIEA §167–2, Paragraphs 1 and 2.

[25] Ramseyer, "Insider Trading Regulation in Japan," 356.

offer a nonexclusive list of types of information that are material. The statute authorized the Japanese Financial Services Agency (FSA) to issue a rule on when information is "public." The FSA did so, providing that information is public twelve hours after its disclosure to at least two media outlets.[26]

The Japanese model is not fraud-based, and therefore requires no breach of fiduciary duty or scienter as elements of the crime. In this sense, it has broader reach than the US model.[27] But it is narrower than the US regime in insofar as it does not generally impose remote tippee or misappropriation liability.[28] The Japanese model also differs from the US regime by defining both who counts as an "insider" and what information counts as "material" and "nonpublic" by statute or rule, allowing it to avoid at least some of the pitfalls of legal ambiguity (detailed in Chapter 4) that have plagued the common law development of these elements under US law.[29]

5.1.2 Western Europe

The first coordinated European attempt to regulate insider trading came in 1989 with the adoption of the Market Abuse Directive (MAD). MAD defined inside information as

> [i]nformation of a precise nature which has not been made public, relating, directly or indirectly, to one or more issuers of financial instruments or to one or more financial instruments and which, if it were made public, would be likely to have a

---

[26] See ibid. at 357.

[27] See Heminway, "Disparate Notions of Fairness," 121–29.

[28] Ibid. at 118. FIEA § 167 does restrict outsider trading by affiliates of tender offerors (similar to Rule 14e-3's restriction), but the law imposes no broad misappropriation liability. See Ramseyer, "Insider Trading Regulation in Japan," 356.

[29] Ibid. at 124–28. The Japanese law defines insiders to include "corporate officers, employees, agents and shareholders having access to corporate records; those with statutory authority over the corporation; and those who come to know material facts in contracting with the corporation (and the officers, employees, and agents of contracting parties that are entities)." Ibid. at 124. Concerning materiality,

> [t]he Japanese insider trading statute contains a laundry list of important facts that can trigger the insider trading prohibition. These include: management decisions about issuing securities, reductions in capital, stock splits, alterations in dividends, mergers, purchases or sales in whole or in part of a business, dissolution and marketing a new product; disasters or damages to the corporation; changes in principal shareholders; events causing delisting of a security; differences between actual and forecasted sales and profits; any other events listed by Cabinet Ordinance; and, finally, other important facts involving management, business or assets of the corporation which would material affect investment decisions.

> Franklin A. Gevurtz, "The Globalization of Insider Trading Prohibitions," *The Transactional Lawyer* 15 (2002): 73–74. Though the Japanese statute's laundry list certainly offers greater certainty than the US standard, its final "catchall" provision still leaves it open to charges of ambiguity.

significant effect on the prices of those financial instruments or on the price of related derivative financial instruments.[30]

This definition was recently recodified in the Commission's Market Abuse Regulation (MAR), which, as of July 2016, unified Europe's insider trading law under a single code.[31] Under this definition, whether information would have a "significant effect" depends on whether "a reasonable investor would be likely to use [it] as part of the basis of his investment decisions."[32] The European definition appears similar to the materiality standard embraced by courts in the United States, though some suggest European courts have interpreted it even more broadly.[33] Aside from the obvious concern that too broad a definition of inside information might have a chilling effect on information gathering by market professionals, European disclosure requirements generate another risk: Europe, unlike the United States, links issuer disclosure requirements to MAR's definition of inside information, requiring disclosure of all information meeting that definition, irrespective of trading or selective disclosure by insiders. This has led some scholars to express the concern that too broad an interpretation of "inside information" by regulators and the courts risks increasing volatility by "flooding the markets with irrelevant information."[34]

Under MAR, insider trading liability arises "any time a person possesses inside information and uses that information" to trade or tip.[35] The regulation makes it clear that the prohibition applies not only to classic and constructive insiders, but to any person "who possesses inside information ... where that person knows or ought to know that it is inside information."[36] Though the regulation requires that one both "possess" and "use" inside information to incur liability, the European Court of Justice has recognized a rebuttable presumption of use from possession.[37]

MAR's application to any person who possesses inside information renders it more expansive than the fraud-based US model (which requires a breach of fiduciary or similar duty of trust and confidence) and more expansive than the Japanese model (which does not generally impose remote tippee liability or misappropriator

---

[30] MAD Art. 1 para. 1 sub-para. 1. See Langenbucher, "Insider Trading in European Law," 432.
[31] See MAR, Art. 7 para. 1(a). MAR went live on July 3, 2016. See "New EU rules to fight insider dealing and market manipulation in Europe's financial markets take effect" (July 1, 2016), http://europa.eu/rapid/press-release_IP-16-2352_en.htm.
[32] MAR, Art. 7 para. 4, available at http://eur-lex.europa.eu/legal-content/EN/TXT/?uri=CELEX:32014R0596.
[33] See Langenbucher, "Insider Trading in European Law," 442.
[34] Ibid. at 445–47; but see George A. Mocsary, "Statistically Insignificant Deaths: Disclosing Drug Harms to Investors (and Patients) under SEC Rule 10b–5," *George Washington Law Review* 82 (2013): 162 (questioning the idea that too much information can be a problem for markets). MAR Art. 17 requires that an "issuer shall inform the public as soon as possible of inside information which directly concerns that issuer."
[35] MAR Art. 8 para. 1; Art. 10 para 1.
[36] MAR Art. 8 para. 4.
[37] See Langenbucher, "Insider Trading in European Law," 435–36.

liability). When coupled with its broad definition of inside information and its presumption of use from possession, the European model offers something very close to a parity-of-information regime.[38] In sum, the European model offers a streamlined approach to insider trading enforcement that enjoys the advantage of relative clarity and simplicity, though perhaps at the price of overbreadth.

5.1.3 *Australia*

Australia's insider trading enforcement regime has been described as "the most expansive in the world."[39] Under Australia's Corporations Act of 2001, "information" is defined broadly to include even "matters of supposition and other matters that are insufficiently definite to warrant being made known to the public; and matters relating to the intentions or likely intentions of a person."[40] The Australian courts have confirmed that this language is to be given the expansive interpretation that its everyday sense suggests.[41] "Inside information" is then defined simply as any information that is "not generally available," and if it were generally available, "a reasonable person would expect it to have a material effect on the price or value" of a security.[42] Information is deemed "generally available" if it is "readily observable."[43] With inside information so defined, the act imposes insider trading liability upon *any* person who knowingly "possesses inside information" and trades in the relevant security or tips another who is likely to trade.[44]

The Australian model is clearly more expansive than the US regime by failing to require the breach of a fiduciary or similar duty of trust or confidence. Anyone who possesses inside information is deemed an insider under the Corporations Act. By imposing liability on misappropriators and remote tippees, the Australian law is also more expansive than the Japanese model. It is arguably also even more expansive than the already broad European model, due to its liberal definition of "inside information" (lacking any requirement that the information be "precise" or specific) and because it makes no reference to "use" of the inside information as an element

---

[38] Only Australia's regime (discussed later), which restricts trading by any "person" who "possesses inside information," surpasses the European model for expansiveness in coverage.

[39] See Gordon Walker and Andrew F. Simpson, "Insider Trading Law in New Zealand," in Bainbridge, *Research Handbook on Insider Trading*, 386, 396 (the "Australian regime is the most expansive in the world").

[40] Corporations Act 2001 § 1042A.

[41] See Keith Kendall and Gordon Walker, "Insider Trading in Australia," in Bainbridge, *Research Handbook on Insider Trading*, 365, 371 (citing the New South Wales Court for the holding that "information may be imprecise" and the Federal Court for the proposition that information includes a "person's internal thought processes").

[42] Corporations Act 2001 § 1042A.

[43] Corporations Act 1042C(1)(a).

[44] Corporations Act 2001 §§ 1043A(1)-(2). It should be noted that this broad definition is subject to a number of express exceptions and defenses detailed under the act. See Kendall and Walker, "Insider Trading in Australia," 380–82.

of liability; the use-versus-possession debate is therefore settled by statute. In sum, it is as close to a true parity-of-information regime as can be found on the world scene. And the Australian model has had some geographic influence: though New Zealand initially modeled its regime directly upon the US fiduciary model, it has since followed Australia in adopting the same parity-of-information approach.[45]

5.1.4 *Canada*

Perhaps the most unusual characteristic of the Canadian insider trading enforcement regime is that it lacks a national securities regulator.[46] As was the case in the United States prior to the adoption of the Securities Act of 1933 and the Exchange Act of 1934, Canadian securities laws are adopted and enforced at the provincial level. The most important province for purposes of insider trading regulation is Ontario, home of the Toronto Stock Exchange.[47]

Ontario's insider trading law is set forth in its Securities Act of 1990, which provides in relevant part that "no person or company in a special relationship with an issuer shall purchase or sell securities of the issuer with the knowledge of a material fact or material change with respect to the issuer that has not been generally disclosed."[48] The statute also prohibits disclosing material undisclosed information unless the disclosure is "in the necessary course of business."[49] The Ontario regime limits trading and tipping by those in a "special relationship" with the issuer, but it is not a fraud-based regime. Unlike the US regime, it does not impose insider trading liability on anyone who breaches a fiduciary or similar duty of trust and confidence by trading on material nonpublic information. This leaves open the possibility that misappropriators who would be held liable under US law may not be liable for the same trades in Ontario if they do not stand in the statutorily defined relationship to the issuer.[50] Despite this difference, the Ontario statute's definition of those in a "special relationship with an issuer" is sufficiently broad to cover most persons who would be liable under both the classical and misappropriation theories in the United

---

[45] See Walker and Simpson, "Insider Trading Law in New Zealand," 388.

[46] See Laura Nyantung Beny and Anita Anand, "Private Regulation of Insider Trading in the Shadow of Lax Public Enforcement: Evidence from Canadian Firms," *Harvard Business Law Review* 3 (2013): 224.

[47] See ibid. at 224. Most other Canadian provinces model their securities laws on the Ontario regime.

[48] Securities Act, R.S.O. 1990, §76(1).

[49] Securities Act, R.S.O. 1990, §76(2).

[50] The recent enforcement actions against Canadian investment banker Richard Moore reflect this difference. He was held liable by US regulators under the misappropriation theory, but was not found liable for insider trading by Canadian regulators. See Barbara Schecter, "How the SEC and the OSC differ in their approaches to trading offenses," *Financial Post* (April 22, 2013), http://business.financialpost.com/legal-post/how-the-sec-and-the-osc-differ-in-their-approaches-to-trading-offences.

States, including tippees.[51] Moreover, since the Canadian model does not require showing the breach of a fiduciary or similar duty of trust and confidence, it is conceivable that it might cover some trading and tipping that would not be covered by the US regime. Finally, the Ontario model is distinguished from its US counterpart by permitting short-swing profits by corporate insiders, so long as the trading does not otherwise violate the law. In other words, there is no counterpart to the US Exchange Act's Section 16(b), and firms that are listed on both Canadian and US exchanges are exempt from Section 16(b) in the United States.[52]

5.1.5 *Russia*

The Russian Federation did not recognize "inside information" or "insider trading" as legal concepts until July 2010, when it enacted its Law on Counteracting the Illegitimate Use of Insider Information and Market Manipulation and on the Amendment of Certain Legislative Acts of the Russian Federation (the Law).[53] Though the Russian Law was enacted in 2010, its provisions pertaining to criminal liability did not go into effect until July 30, 2013. Since that time, the Russian Federation has issued notice of only two insider trading investigations and no convictions.[54] Absent significant enforcement action and precedent, interpretation of the new Law must involve some speculation. Nevertheless, there are a number of provisions worthy of note.

To begin, the Law appears to offer a significant departure from other jurisdictions in its definition of "inside information." It defines inside information as "any precise and specific non-public information the disclosure of which may significantly affect the price of a particular financial instrument, foreign currency and/or commodity," *and* that is included in an exhaustive list of types of inside information published by

---

[51] For example, the Ontario statute defines "person or company that is in a special relationship with an issuer" to include any person who is employed by or affiliated with the issuer, any person or company that is considering or evaluating whether to make a take-over bid on the issuer, any person or company considering or evaluating whether to become party to a reorganization or merger with the issuer, any person or company engaging in any business activity with the issuer, and any person or company that "learns of a material fact or material change with respect to the issuer from any other person or company described in this subsection, including a person or company described in this clause, and knows or ought to reasonably have known that the other person or company is a person or company in such a relationship." Securities Act, R.S.O., 1990, §76(5).

[52] See 17 C.F.R. § 240.16b (2011); see also Beny and Anand, "Private Regulation of Insider Trading in the Shadow of Lax Public Enforcement," 226.

[53] Federal Law No. 224-FZ. Prior to the adoption of the Law, the Federal Law on the Securities Market No. 39-FZ, which was enacted in April 1996, proscribed only trading on nonpublic "official information" (*sluzhebnaya informatsia*).

[54] See Market Misconduct: Detected Cases of Market Manipulation and Illegal Use of Insider Information, http://www.cbr.ru/eng/finmarket/inside_detect/.

certain public authorities and issuers themselves.[55] Defining inside information by reference to an exhaustive statutorily imposed list provided by regulators and also by issuers is uncommon among insider trading regimes.[56] Depending on how this provision is implemented by regulators and issuers, it may provide greater certainty for market participants than regimes operating under nothing more than a vague standard for materiality.

The Russian Law's restrictions on trading appear to be quite broad, prohibiting all trading or tipping while in possession of inside information, regardless of insider status. In this respect, the Russian model appears to tend toward the parity-of-information regimes in Europe and Australia. It rejects the American fiduciary model and extends its reach beyond that of the Japanese regulation by imposing liability on misappropriators and remote tippees. Similar to the Japanese model, however, the Law offers an exhaustive list of those who count as "insiders."[57] The Russian Law also requires that legal entities maintain a list of all of their statutory insiders, and must notify everyone of their inclusion on the list. Similar to the case in Europe, the Law generally requires the public disclosure of inside information by issuers and certain other market participants.[58] Though presumably one does not need to be a statutorily defined insider to possess inside information and therefore have a duty not to trade, another unique characteristic of the Russian Law is that its statutorily defined insiders share the *additional* duty to report all of their transactions to the relevant issuer.[59] Finally, all legal entities with respect to which inside information exists are required to develop and implement insider trading monitoring and compliance programs.[60]

5.1.6 *China*

The China Securities Regulatory Commission (CSRC) oversees the world's second largest securities market. China began implementing its insider trading enforcement regime on a piecemeal basis in the early 1990s, but the key provisions of the current regime were laid out in the Securities Law of the People's Republic of China (Securities Law), which was promulgated in 1998.

---

[55] Federal Law No. 224-FZ, Article 2(1). See Larisa Afanasyeva and Philipp Windemuth, "Russia's New Law on Insider Trading and Market Manipulation," *Orrick*, www.orrick.com/Insights/2011/03/Russias-New-Law-on-Insider-Trading-and-Market-Manipulation (quoted text from this translation).

[56] For example, though the Japanese law defines materiality by statute, the list it provides of the types of information generally regarded to be material is not exhaustive. See, e.g., Ramseyer, "Insider Trading Regulation in Japan," 356.

[57] Federal Law No. 224-FZ, Article 4.

[58] Federal Law No. 224-FZ, Article 8.

[59] Federal Law No. 224-FZ, Article 10.

[60] Federal Law No. 224-FZ, Article 11.

Article 75 of the Securities Law defines inside information broadly as "information that concerns the business or finance of a company or may have a major effect on the market price of the securities thereof and hasn't been publicized in securities trading."[61] The article then provides a list of the types of information that will satisfy this definition, including any "major event,"[62] plan to distribute dividends,[63] change in equity structure,[64] acts by senior management exposing the company to liability,[65] or plans to be acquired.[66] Though most commentators interpret the list to be exhaustive (similar to the Russian model), it concludes with a "catchall" category, "[a]ny other important information that has been recognized by the securities regulatory authority under the State Council as having a marked effect on the trading prices of securities," which provides regulators with great flexibility to add categories as needed.[67]

Article 73 restricts the use of inside information. At first blush, it seems to embrace a broad equal-access model, providing that any "insider who has access to any insider information of securities trading or who has unlawfully obtained any insider information is prohibited from taking advantage of the insider information ... to engage in any securities trading."[68] However, Article 74 goes on to offer an exclusive list of who counts as an "insider who has access to insider information" so as to narrow the scope of liability mostly to those who would be recognized as having a fiduciary duty to shareholders under the classical theory in the United States.[69] Tippers, tippees, and those who would qualify as misappropriators under US law are

---

[61] Securities Law, Art. 75 (quoted language from translation provided by Chinese Ministry of Commerce, China.Org.Cn, available at www.china.org.cn/english/government/207337 .htm).

[62] Securities Law, Art. 75(1). What constitutes a major event is defined by Article 62 of the Securities Law.

[63] Securities Law, Art. 75(2).

[64] Securities Law, Art. 75(3).

[65] Securities Law, Art. 75(6).

[66] Securities Law, Art. 75(7).

[67] Securities Law, Art. 75(8) (quoted language from translation provided by Chinese Ministry of Commerce, China.Org.Cn, available at www.china.org.cn/english/government/207337 .htm); for example, though a nonpublic earnings forecast is not expressly included in the Article 75 list, the CSRC has held that it is included in the Article 75(8) catchall category. See Huang, "The Regulation of Insider Trading in China," 308.

[68] Securities Law, Art. 73 (quoted language from translation provided by Chinese Ministry of Commerce, China.Org.Cn, available at www.china.org.cn/english/government/207337 .htm).

[69] See Securities Law, Art. 74 (1)-(7). The scope of the Article 74 definition of "insider" extends beyond those covered by the classical theory in the United States by also including the "functionary of the securities regulatory body, and other personnel who administer the issuance and transaction of securities pursuant to their statutory functions and duties." Art. 74 (5). Article 74 also includes a "catchall" provision that grants general authority to regulators under the State Council to prescribe other categories. Art. 74 (7). The CSRC has, however, yet to issue guidance in the interpretation of this latter provision. See Huang, "The Regulation of Insider Trading in China," 308.

conspicuously absent from the Article 74 list of "insiders." This gap is, however, filled by Article 76, which provides that

> [a]ny insider who has access to insider information or has unlawfully obtained any insider information on securities trading may not purchase or sell the securities of the relevant company ... or advise any other person to purchase or sell such securities.[70]

By precluding insiders with access to inside information from advising others to purchase shares in the relevant security, Article 76 clearly imposes liability on tippers. The status of tippees and misappropriators remained ambiguous, however, until the Supreme People's Court and the Supreme People's Procuratorate issued guidance in 2012 explaining when information is "unlawfully obtained."[71] As Professor Hui Huang summarized the Judicial Interpretation, information is "unlawfully obtained" under Article 76 if it is obtained:

> (1) through such means as theft, cheating, tapping, spying, extraction, bribery and private trading; (2) from the close relatives of primary insiders, or people with other types of close relationships with primary insiders; (3) from people who have contact with primary insiders during the sensitive period of the inside information.[72]

These three categories appear broad enough to cover those who would be counted as tippees and misappropriators under the US model, but they also seem to go further by including thieves, "extractors," and those who obtain the information from primary insiders, presumably for any reason at all. There is no indication that a breach of fiduciary or similar duty of trust and confidence is requisite for insider trading liability under the statute.

Some scholars have suggested that the Securities Law reflects an attempt to "transplant" the US classical and misappropriation theories of liability to China by simply listing the categories of persons and conduct held liable under the US model.[73] But without embracing the common law fiduciary model that underpins the US regime, China is left with statutory definitions and principles that do not obviously cohere. Article 73 suggests a broad equal-access regime, but Article 74's definitions of who counts as an "insider" indicates a far more limited scope, along the lines of the American classical theory. Article 76 then seems to find insider trading liability beyond even the American misappropriation theory, again making it look more like an equal-access regime. At the end of the day, one is left with

---

[70] Securities Law, Art. 76 (quoted language from translation provided by Chinese Ministry of Commerce, China.Org.Cn, available at www.china.org.cn/english/government/207337 .htm).

[71] Judicial Interpretation on Several Issues Concerning the Application of Insider Trading Law in Criminal Cases (promulgated on March 29, 2012, effective from June 1, 2012). See Huang, "The Regulation of Insider Trading in China," 305.

[72] Ibid. at 309.

[73] See ibid. at 303.

the impression that China attempted to borrow aspects of the fiduciary and equal-access models found elsewhere around the world on an ad hoc basis, without giving much thought to whether or how they might cohere.[74] As with Russia, however, the true scope of China's nascent insider trading regime will be revealed only through enforcement actions brought by its regulators and interpreted by its tribunals, and there have been relatively few of these actions to date.

5.1.7 *India*

India implemented a statutory overhaul of its insider trading regulations in January 2015 (2015 Regulation), which makes it the newest insider trading regime among large market economies. India passed its first insider trading enforcement laws in 1992, but they suffered from numerous ambiguities and were almost never enforced.[75] In 2013, the Securities and Exchange Board of India (SEBI) appointed a committee to propose reforms. The 2015 reforms were based on the committee's 2015 report. The new regime defines the elements of insider trading liability with greater specificity than the old regulatory model, but it also broadens its scope.

Like so many other regimes around the world, India rejected the US fiduciary model in favor of a broad equal-access regime, and the 2015 Regulation made its scope still broader. Under the 2015 Regulation, insiders are prohibited from trading "in securities that are listed or proposed to be listed on a stock exchange when in possession of unpublished price sensitive information."[76] In predicating liability on mere possession of inside information, the 2015 Regulation represents a significant departure from the former regime, which required proof of actual use. Moreover, the 2015 Regulation defines "insider" broadly as "any person who is: (i) a connected person; or (ii) in possession of or having access to unpublished price sensitive information."[77] The regulation then defines "unpublished price sensitive

---

[74] See ibid. at 316 ("China's insider trading law appears to have transplanted both the equality of access theory and the fiduciary-duty-based theories consisting of the classical theory and the misappropriation theory").

[75] Indian authorities did bring one high-profile case against Hindu Lever and some of its employees for trading on inside information concerning a pending merger of Brooke Bond. The appellate authority did not, however, uphold the charges, finding that the information was publicly available at the time of the trades. See Umakanth Varottil, "The Long and Short of Insider Trading Regulation in India," *NSE Center for Excellence in Corporate Governance* (April 2016), www1.nseindia.com/research/content/res_QB13.pdf.

[76] 2015 Regulation, Chapter II, 4(1), www.sebi.gov.in/cms/sebi_data/attachdocs/14213195 19608.pdf.

[77] Ibid. at Chapter I, 2(1)(g). "Connected Person" is also defined generally as

> [a]ny person who is or has during the six months prior to the concerned act been associated with the company, directly or indirectly, in any capacity including by reason of frequent communication with its officers or by being in any contractual, fiduciary or employment relationship or by being a director, officer or an employee of the company or holds any position including a professional or business relationship between himself and the company

information" as "any information, relating to a company or its securities, directly or indirectly, that is not generally available which upon becoming generally available, is likely to materially affect the price of the securities."[78] Recognizing that, with the net of insider trading liability cast so broadly, Indian corporate insiders who are compensated in firm shares may never be able to liquidate them for innocent purposes (e.g., for portfolio diversification) without incurring liability, the 2015 Regulation offers a number of affirmative defenses. For example, insiders are permitted to trade pursuant to trading plans.[79] These trading plans are similar to those authorized under SEC Rule 10b5–1(c), but have some unique characteristics. For example, the trading plans must be approved by a firm's compliance officer. The first trade under the plan cannot take place until six months after its creation, and no trades under the plan may take place in the twenty days preceding the due date for the firm's financial filings, or within two days after they are filed. The trading plans are "irrevocable," thus precluding the possibility of strategic termination so prevalent in the United States (see Chapter 4). Perhaps most significantly, compliance officers are required to publish the trading plan with stock exchanges upon the plan's approval.[80]

Finally, the 2015 Regulation imposes a broad restriction on the "communication or procurement" of unpublished price sensitive information "except where such communication is in furtherance of legitimate purposes, performance of duties or discharge of legal obligations."[81] Absent a clear definition of what constitutes a "legitimate purpose," some have expressed concern that these limitations are "too restrictive, leading to a virtual freeze in communication."[82]

Like so many other newly minted insider trading enforcement regimes around the world, only time will tell how and to what extent India's will be implemented. Nevertheless, under any interpretation, the new insider trading enforcement regime in India offers improved clarity over its predecessor, and broadens its scope of liability.

whether temporary or permanent, that allows such person, directly or indirectly, access to unpublished price sensitive information or is reasonable expected to allow such access.

Ibid. at Chapter II, 2 (1)(d)(i). The regulation then goes on to offer a nonexclusive list of persons who qualify as connected persons.

[78] Ibid. at Chapter I, 2 (1)(n). This definition then goes on to offer a nonexclusive list of information that will typically qualify: "(i) financial results; (ii) dividends; (iii) change in capital structure; (iv) mergers, de-mergers, acquisitions, delistings, disposals and expansion of business and such other transactions; (v) changes in key managerial personnel; and (vi) material events in accordance with the listing agreement." Ibid.

[79] Ibid. at Chapter II, 5.

[80] Ibid.

[81] Ibid. at Chapter II, 3(1).

[82] Jayashree P. Upadhyay, "Insider Trading: New Rules Confound India, Inc.," *Business Standard* (Dec. 20, 2015), www.business-standard.com/article/opinion/insider-trading-new-rules-confound-india-inc-115122000686_1.html.

5.2 TREND TOWARD UNIVERSALITY

Though approaches may differ, there is no denying that there has been a significant global trend toward insider trading regulation in the last three decades. To gain some sense of the vector of this trend, consider a 2002 study by Professors Uptal Bhattacharya and Hazem Daouk. That study showed that during the first third of the twentieth century, there were no laws regulating insider trading. In the second third of the century, only the United States regulated it. By the close of the century, however, every developed country and four-fifths of emerging market countries had insider trading laws on the books.[83] It is tempting to draw some strong conclusions from this remarkable trend:

(1) Near-universal adoption of insider trading prohibitions reflects a global cultural recognition that insider trading is wrong, inefficient, and otherwise undermines healthy markets.

(2) Though the United States was for many years the only country regulating insider trading, the recent trend toward near-universal regulation has proven its importance and validity.

(3) Near-universal adoption of insider trading regulations proves that insider trading proscriptions are enforced the world over and – based on (2) – this is a sign of progress.

Indeed, many within the SEC have hastened to draw just these conclusions. As Thomas C. Newkirk, then associate director, Division of Enforcement, stated:

> [T]he European Economic Community has formally recognized the importance of insider trading prohibitions by passing a directive requiring its members to adopt insider trading legislation. The preamble to the directive stresses the economic importance of a healthy securities market, recognizes that maintaining healthy markets requires investor confidence and acknowledges that investor confidence depends on the "assurance afforded to investors that they are placed on an equal footing and that they will be protected against the improper use of inside information." These precepts echo around the world as reports of increased insider trading regulation and enforcement efforts are daily news.[84]

Far from indicating a rapid cultural convergence, however, the very need for the European directive (and now regulation) suggests that, as indicated previously, many European countries were unwilling to adopt insider trading regulations absent compulsion, and that many countries who have adopted them do not enforce them.[85] This raises the concern that the recent international trend toward insider trading regulation does not reflect an emerging consensus regarding the evils of

---

[83] Bhattacharya and Daouk, "The World Price of Insider Trading," 89–90.
[84] Newkirk and Robertson, "Insider Trading – A U.S. Perspective."
[85] See Beny, "The Political Economy of Insider Trading Laws and Enforcement," 266.

insider trading, but instead reflects the phenomenon of regulatory ritualism. Recent examples of ritualism in the context of international human rights are instructive and warrant caution against drawing hasty conclusions from perceived universality.

5.3 PROBLEM OF REGULATORY RITUALISM: THE EXAMPLE OF HUMAN RIGHTS

To a great extent, the modern international human rights regime was set forth in a series of post–World War II treaty documents.[86] These documents largely reflect the rights agenda of the wealthy Western liberal democracies that guided their drafting and that incentivized their adoption by poorer, non-Western states. Despite its relatively provincial beginnings, on its face the modern human rights system has been a dramatic success, achieving almost universal acceptance in the international community. For instance, the International Covenant on Civil and Political Rights (ICCPR) has 169 state members and the International Covenant on Economic, Social, and Cultural Rights (ICESCR) has 164 state members.[87] Such broad acceptance is particularly remarkable given that both of these covenants require member states to incorporate the treaties' numerous guarantees (e.g., protections against arbitrary arrest or detention, prohibition of torture, right to habeas corpus, fair trial rights, freedom of movement, freedom of expression, freedom of the press, freedom of religion, right to vote, racial and gender equality under the law, right to health care, right to education, etc.) into their municipal law. As with the example of insider trading, it is tempting to draw some conclusions from this apparent international convergence:

(1) The near-universal adoption of these human rights instruments reflects a dramatic trend toward universal cultural and political embrace of the values reflected in these instruments.

(2) Though the modern human rights regime was born of once controversial Western liberal cultural values, the recent trend toward near-universal acceptance confirms the validity of these values.

(3) The near-universal adoption of these treaties proves that these rights are in fact being protected within the member states and – based on (2) – this is a sign of progress.

---

[86] The principal treaty documents are the United Nations Charter (UNC) (1945), the Universal Declaration of Human Rights (UNDHR) (1948), the International Covenant of Civil and Political Rights (ICCPR) (1976), and the International Covenant of Economic, Social, and Cultural Rights (ICSECR) (1976). Together these instruments are typically referred to as the International Bill of Rights. All except the UNDHR are legally binding treaties. The UNDHR is merely hortatory in nature.

[87] Data provided by the United Nations Human Rights Office of the High Commissioner of Human Rights, available at http://indicators.ohchr.org/.

Although it is tempting to draw these conclusions, it would be hasty.

In his seminal book *Social Theory and Social Structure*, Professor Robert Merton identified five modes of adaptation to normative orders imposed upon individuals or cultures from the outside: conformity, innovation, ritualism, retreatism, and rebellion.[88] Ritualism "occurs when there is no acceptance of particular normative goals, but great deference is paid to the formal institutions that support them. It can be defined as 'acceptance of institutionalized means for securing regulatory goals while losing all focus on achieving the goals or outcomes themselves.'"[89]

Professor Hilary Charlesworth has developed this concept of ritualism in her international human rights scholarship. Human rights ritualism is understood "as a way of embracing the language of human rights precisely to deflect real human rights scrutiny and to avoid accountability for human rights abuses."[90] Countries that adapt to the contemporary international human rights regime ritualistically "accept human rights treaty commitments to earn international approval, but they resist the changes that the treaty obligations require."[91] Far from atypical, Charlesworth has shown that "rights ritualism is a more common response than an outright rejection of human rights standards and institutions."[92] By simply going through the motions of outwardly ratifying international treaties, but taking no steps to implement and/or enforce their provisions, countries have found that they can enjoy all of the carrots associated with membership in the international human rights community while avoiding all the sticks reserved for outsiders.[93] The human rights regime is complicit in this charade because the perceived universality that ritualism provides lends authority to the regime.

---

[88] Robert Merton, *Social Theory and Social Structure* (New York: Free Press, 1968).

[89] Hilary Charlesworth, "Swimming to Cambodia: Justice and Ritual in Human Rights after Conflict," *Australian Year Book of International Law* 29 (2010): 12 (quoting John Braithwaite, Valerie Braithwaite, and Toni Makkai, *Regulating Aged Care: Ritualism and the New Pyramid* (Northampton, MA: Edward Elgar Publishing, Inc., 2007).

[90] Charlesworth, "Swimming to Cambodia," 12.

[91] Ibid. at 13.

[92] Ibid. at 12.

[93] Charlesworth offered the Cambodian experience as just one example. The UN-brokered 1991 Paris Peace Agreement (winning a cease-fire between Cambodia and Vietnam) made a brokered peace contingent on Cambodia's willingness to guarantee its citizens all the rights and freedoms embodied in the UDHR and the human rights covenants. Cambodia then ratified both the ICCPR and ICESCR (as well as the Convention against Torture and the Convention on the Rights of the Child) in 1992. Since that time, "there has been a great deal of human rights talk in Cambodia but very little actual progress on the protection of human rights." Ibid. at 9. And this strategy of human rights ritualism "seems to have been successful for Cambodia in flying under the radar of international scrutiny." Ibid. at 13–14. There is a rich literature identifying examples of human rights ritualism elsewhere. See, e.g., Melanie O'Brien, "Ritualism and the Erosion of Human Rights," *New Mandala* (Feb. 29, 2016), www.newmandala.org/ritualism-and-the-erosion-of-human-rights/; Hilary Charlesworth and Emma Larking (eds.), *Human Rights and the Universal Periodic Review: Rituals and Ritualism* (Cambridge: Cambridge University Press, 2014).

Appreciating the fact of pervasive human rights ritualism forces us to question the aforementioned conclusions (1) through (3). In other words, given the prevalence of ritualism, near-universal ratification of the International Bill of Rights tells us almost nothing about: (1) the universal cultural and political embrace of the core values reflected in those instruments; (2) the validity of those values; and (3) whether the associated rights are actually being protected in member states, or even whether they *should* be protected.

Historical similarities suggest that the recent trend toward near-universal regulation of insider trading on the global stage may also be explained by the phenomenon of ritualism. Consider the example of Germany, Europe's largest economy. As one commentator stated, for "a long time, Germany represented a capital marketplace which refused to take regulation of insider trading seriously."[94] Non-binding insider trading guidelines were adopted in Germany in 1970, but "they were only a voluntary code of behavior to which one had to subject oneself to expressly."[95] Germany grudgingly acquiesced to regulating insider trading after the 1989 Directive was adopted because it had no choice – and because it recognized that, without the regulations, "it would lose its reputation as a developed market."[96] Even still, Germany delayed adoption of insider trading regulations for another five years (until 1994), two years after the Directive's 1992 deadline.[97]

Outside of Europe, other international bodies began associating carrots and sticks with the adoption of insider trading regulations. For example, in 1998, the International Organization of Securities Commissions (IOSCO) included an insider trading regulation among its "Objectives of Securities Regulation."[98] Not only are 85 percent of the world's markets members of IOSCO, but the World Bank and International Monetary Fund use IOSCO's objectives to review the "financial health" of countries. Moreover, the United States's considerable influence on international market policies cannot be underestimated. As previously noted, Europe's as well as Japan's adoption of insider trading regulations was all but forced on them "as part of an international effort to encourage insider trading regulation consistent with the predominant U.S. model."[99] Consequently, as one commentator

---

[94] Jeorg Hartman, "Insider Trading: An Economic and Legal Problem: How Would O'Hagan Come Out under the New German Securities Trading Act," *Gonzaga Journal of International Law* 1 (1997–1998): 2.

[95] Ibid.

[96] Ibid.

[97] Heminway, "Disparate Notions of Fairness," 119.

[98] Objectives and Principles of Securities Regulation, OICU-IOSCO, www.iosco.org/library/pubdocs/pdf/IOSCOPD154.pdf.

[99] Heminway, "Disparate Notions of Fairness," 115, 118.

explained, the "convergence of laws [pertaining to insider trading] can be attributed to convergence of cultural attitudes only marginally. For the most part, competitive pressures, primarily from the U.S. [and international bodies under American influence], [are] playing a major role as well."[100]

Further proof of an absence of cultural consensus concerning the regulation of insider trading is found in evidence of enforcement – or lack thereof. As Professor Laura Nyantung Beny has pointed out, "enforcement, rather than enactment" is the best measure of a country's commitment to regulations "because it requires an expenditure of scarce resources" and "demonstrates political and legal will to give the insider trading prohibition teeth."[101] It is true that recent decades have witnessed an explosion of insider trading regulations finding their way to the statute books, but, as in the context of human rights, this does not mean they are being enforced.

For example, even the United Kingdom, which was out in front of Europe in adopting insider trading regulation, lags far behind the United States in enforcement and has earned a reputation as a "light touch jurisdiction."[102] Predictably, German adoption was followed by weak enforcement, and many European countries (e.g., Austria, Ireland, and Luxembourg) had not enforced their laws at all as of the latest comprehensive worldwide data collection.[103] Moreover, Austria, Bulgaria, Slovakia, the Czech Republic, Estonia, Finland, and Slovenia did not impose criminal sanctions for insider trading and market manipulation until the European Commission forced the issue by adopting the Directive on Criminal Sanctions for Market Abuse (CSMAD), requiring that "Member States ... ensure that the criminal offences of insider dealing and market manipulation are subject to criminal sanctions."[104] There would be no need for this directive if some European countries were not resisting criminal liability for insider trading. Other developed economies such as Japan, Canada, Russia, China, Hong Kong, and New Zealand have also been

---

[100] Licht, "The Mother of All Path Dependencies," 195.

[101] Beny, "The Political Economy of Insider Trading Laws and Enforcement," 280.

[102] See Thompson, "A Global Comparison of Insider Trading Regulations," 6; Alexander, "UK Insider Dealing and Market Abuse Law," 407.

[103] Beny, "The Political Economy of Insider Trading Laws and Enforcement," 287.

[104] See "EU calls for criminal penalties for insider trading," *EU Business* (Oct. 17, 2011), www.eubusiness.com/news-eu/finance-economy.cxy. See also Commission Proposal for a Directive of the European Parliament and of the Council on criminal sanctions for insider dealing and market manipulation, recital (15), COM (2011) 654 final (Oct. 20, 2011); "European Commission seeks criminal sanctions for insider dealing and market manipulation to improve deterrence and market integrity," *European Commission Press Release*, http://europa.eu/rapid/press-release_IP-11–1218_en.htm. CSMAD went into effect on July 3, 2016. See "New framework on Market Abuse published in the Official Journal," *European Commission Press Release*, http://europa.eu/rapid/midday-express-12–06–2014.htm?locale=en.

historically weak with respect to insider trading enforcement.[105] And what little enforcement there is in these countries is often attributable to outside (usually US) political influence.[106]

The tale of enforcement is still bleaker for emerging market countries. Of the sixty-seven emerging market countries that had enacted insider trading regulations as of 2000, a whopping forty-seven had yet to bring a single enforcement action by 2000.[107] Oman adopted insider trading regulations in 1988, but failed to bring its first enforcement action until 1999.[108] Another remarkable illustration of regulatory ritualism in this context is provided by India. As noted previously, India adopted insider trading regulations in 1992; however, it took its regulators "17 years to realize the term 'insider trading' did not literally mean insider within the company."[109] Even after this "humbling" realization, a 2011 review found that India had yet to win a single insider trading conviction.[110]

These facts suggest that the recent global trend toward the adoption of insider trading laws may be explained by regulatory ritualism. And, just as in the context of human rights, evidence of ritualism should force us to pause before drawing hasty conclusions from the near-universal regulation of insider trading. Specifically, given the prevalence of ritualism, the near-universal adoption of insider trading laws alone tells us very little about the universal cultural and political embrace of the policy rationales that purportedly inform their insider trading regulations, nor does pervasive regulation support the validity of those rationales. Indeed, the evidence suggests that the majority of states that have adopted insider trading regulations do not enforce them with any vigor (if at all). In fact, as is often the case in the human rights context, the lack of enforcement suggests that many countries may have adopted insider trading laws precisely to deflect international scrutiny of their markets.

---

[105] See, e.g., Beny and Anand, "Private Regulation of Insider Trading in the Shadow of Lax Public Enforcement," 229 ("Because of lax public enforcement and the rarity of private enforcement, insider trading has been viewed as being relatively prevalent in Canada."); Beny, "The Political Economy of Insider Trading Laws and Enforcement," 287 (noting that, as of 2000, neither China nor New Zealand had enforced their insider trading laws even once); Thompson, "A Global Comparison of Insider Trading Regulations," 7–15 (noting minimal enforcement in Hong Kong and minimal fines for insider trading in Japan); Walker and Simpson, "Insider Trading Law in New Zealand," 402–04 (pointing out that, as of 2013, there had been no high-profile insider trading enforcement actions in New Zealand).

[106] Heminway, "Disparate Notions of Fairness," 118 (noting that increased enforcement in Japan was "a response to pressure from the United States").

[107] Beny, "The Political Economy of Insider Trading Laws and Enforcement," 287–89.

[108] Ibid. at 288.

[109] Thompson, "A Global Comparison of Insider Trading Regulations," 8.

[110] Ibid.

5.4 LESSONS FROM THE INTERNATIONAL EXPERIENCE

What lessons are learned from the international experience of insider trading regulation? To begin, the comparative analysis in this chapter suggests that there is no single way to organize an insider trading regime. Europe and Australia offer examples of broad parity-of-information regimes. Japan, Canada, Russia, and India embody variations of the equal-access model. And countries that do not (or did not) regulate insider trading at all offer current and historical examples of laissez-faire regimes. It is instructive that markets have functioned under all of these models with varying degrees of success. Moreover, the international experiences vary in other ways. Canada offers a working model of insider trading regulation that is left to provincial governments. All of the regimes summarized in this chapter are statute-based, in contrast to the common law development in the United States. Many of these statutes define elements of insider trading liability with great specificity, and some (for example, in Russia) permit issuers to aid in these definitions. All of these lessons and examples will prove useful in the following chapters (and particularly in Chapter 11), as the focus turns from the description of what the law of insider trading *is* in the United States and around the world, to the normative enterprise of determining what it *ought* to be.

The international lesson of regulatory ritualism should also be borne in mind as focus turns to the debate over the ethics of insider trading and to proposed reforms for the US regime. For example, one who advocates liberalization of the current enforcement regime (less enforcement) may rejoice in the fact that evidence of ritualism removes a number of arrows from the quiver of those who defend broad and vigorous insider trading regulation. First, the problem of ritualism significantly weakens claims of regulatory inevitability and global consensus that are often enlisted against liberalization. Second, far from proving the argument for insider trading regulation, the reality that most of the developed and technologically advanced markets in the world have insider trading laws on the books but choose not to enforce them argues strongly against many of the traditional policy justifications for insider trading regulation. Third, the evidence of insider trading ritualism also suggests that even the appearance of global consensus (based on the number of insider trading laws on the books) is quite flimsy. To the extent that these laws were adopted as a result of external pressure from the United States or other international bodies (and not from a genuine cultural embrace of the rules or the rationales behind them), they will remain on the books only so long as those incentives remain unchanged. Just as recent shifts in global political and economic power from West to East and North to South have tested the viability of the Western corpus of human rights that are embraced only ritualistically, those same shifts may also test the continued recognition of insider trading regulation as an international norm for markets.

For those who are convinced that a broad and vigorous insider trading enforcement regime is necessary in the United States and elsewhere around the world, the evidence of insider trading ritualism should be interpreted as a call to action. If most American market participants, regulators, legislators, politicians, and judges are truly convinced that markets cannot be fair, efficient, or inspire confidence unless insider trading is regulated, then they will need to do a better job of convincing other cultures of this. US incentives and influence may have been enough to get these laws on the books in other countries, but, as Professor Marc Steinberg noted, the likelihood that "'admired' executives may be faced with criminal prosecution in a culture that has declined to embrace the evils of such 'gentlemen' offenses" is low.[111] To overcome the problem of insider trading ritualism in resisting cultures, it will be necessary to switch from incentives to persuasion as the preferred method of influence. Economic arguments should be demonstrated rather than assumed. Some excellent empirical work to this end has begun,[112] but much more is needed.[113] And the equally important ethical justifications should be made explicit by appeal to paradigms and tropes familiar to the target culture. Such "enlightenment missions" should strive to appeal directly (and in a culturally sensitive manner) to the constituencies within that country who are directly affected by insider trading abuses: "corporate insiders, bankers, brokers, judges, legislators, and the investing public."[114]

*****

[111] Marc I. Steinberg, "Insider Trading Regulation – A Comparative Analysis," *International Law* 37 (2003): 169–70.

[112] See, e.g., Bhattacharya and Daouk, "The World Price of Insider Trading" (empirical study finding that the cost of equity in a country does not change after the introduction of insider trading laws, but decreases significantly after the first prosecutions); Laura Nyantung Beny, "Insider Trading Laws and Stock Markets around the World: An Empirical Contribution to the Theoretical Law and Economics Argument," *Journal of Corporation Law* 32 (2007): 237 (finding that "more stringent insider trading laws are generally associated with more dispersed equity ownership, greater stock price accuracy and greater stock market liquidity"); Beny, "The Political Economy of Insider Trading Laws and Enforcement," 266 (finding that a country's political system – not its legal or financial system – best explains its proclivity to regulate insider trading); Beny and Anita, "Private Regulation of Insider Trading in the Shadow of Lax Public Enforcement," 215 (finding that Canadian firms tend to be "super-compliant" with insider trading laws despite lax enforcement, suggesting that such enforcement enhances corporate performance).

[113] Beny's 2007 study identified some challenges to empirical research in the field of insider trading, noting that "the sample of available countries is quite small and there may be differences among them in data reliability." Beny, "Insider Trading Laws and Stock Markets around the World," 281. Beny also recognized that the problem of ritualism must be accounted for in empirical studies, noting that it is "possible that some countries enacted insider trading laws merely in response to external pressure, resulting in rote transplantation of foreign insider trading laws unrelated to such countries' financial, legal, and institutional characteristics." Ibid. Moreover, empirical studies suggesting that the adoption and enforcement of insider trading laws correlate to increased volume and liquidity must confront the significant counterexample of Japan. As Ramseyer noted, within two years of the Diet declaring insider trading criminal in 1988, "the volume of shares traded plummeted, and the market capitalization of Japanese firms disappeared. Two decades later, the market has yet to recover." Ramseyer, "Insider Trading Regulation in Japan," 347.

[114] Steinberg, "Insider Trading Regulation – A Comparative Analysis," 171.

Even (or especially) as exporters of the norms of insider trading regulation, our insider trading enforcement regime in the United States would benefit a great deal from a more frank discourse concerning the economic and ethical implications of insider trading regulation within our own culture. And, faced with symptoms of insider trading ritualism elsewhere around the world, meaningful insider trading enforcement outside the United States may not even get off the ground without such discourse. Just such a serious and in-depth analysis of the economic, ethical, and cultural implications of insider trading is the subject of Part II of this book. It would be irresponsible and unproductive to propose reforms to our insider trading regime without first identifying and weighing these normative stakes.

Ethics

6

From Cicero to *Laidlaw*

Two Thousand Years of Debate over the Propriety of Information Asymmetries

The problem of when, if ever, persons should be permitted to profit from information asymmetries in the purchase or sale of something is, of course, not limited to insider trading; it has divided jurists and philosophers for thousands of years. It therefore pays to preface an ethical and economic analysis of the specific problem of insider trading with a general survey of the history of ideas pertaining to the broader problem of information asymmetries in exchanges.

6.1 CICERO AND THE STOICS

Imagine you are a hardworking and entrepreneurial grain merchant in first-century BCE Alexandria. You learn that shortages have driven grain prices sky-high on the distant Greek island of Rhodes. Wasting no time, you set your employees to work at filling the hold of your ship with grain and otherwise preparing for the dangerous journey across the Mediterranean Sea. News travels quickly, and a number of other Alexandrian merchants also start rushing to get their grain to Rhodes. Your diligence pays off, however, and you are the first to arrive at the island. The buyers are lined up at the docks in a mood of excitement and celebration. As you hoped, the market price is ten times what you could fetch in Alexandria. But, of course, this price is based on the buyers' assumption that the current state of scarcity will persist. You, however, know something the buyers do not. You know that hundreds of other ships laden with grain are just days, if not hours, behind you. Should you disclose this material information to the islanders and take a lesser price for your grain, or should you take advantage of the islanders' mistaken assumption that their scarcity will persist?

The preceding scenario is based on one Marcus Tullius Cicero presented in *De Officiis* ("On Duties"). Cicero authored this treatise in 44 BCE, in his final days,[1]

---

[1] At Mark Antony's bidding, Cicero was branded an enemy of the state soon after Julius Caesar's death. After months on the run, Cicero was finally tracked down and executed by a centurion on December 7, 43 BCE.

and he styled it in the form of a letter offering guidance to his son on how to live a good and virtuous life. The grain merchant's dilemma was introduced to address the question of whether there can ever be a conflict between expedience and morality. Cicero was a jurist and philosopher of the Stoic school, and he noted that two of the most "profound" Stoic thinkers were divided over whether the grain merchant should disclose to the buyers.

Antipater of Tarsus embraced a parity-of-information approach, arguing that the grain dealer should disclose "all the facts" to ensure the buyer is not "uninformed of any detail that the seller knows."[2] After all, the buyer is your fellow man and "it is your duty to consider the interests of your fellow-men" as your own, and "to serve society."[3] For Antipater, the grain merchant's decision was made simple by the recognition that his interests should be "the interest of the community."[4]

Diogenes of Babylon, Antipater's mentor and predecessor as head of the Stoic school, held a different view. For Diogenes, the grain seller had every right to try to get the highest price the market would bear for his grain, so long as he did not make any express misrepresentation or take affirmative steps to conceal the truth. On this approach, resembling the modern rule of caveat emptor, the seller could say, "I have imported my stock … I have offered it for sale; I sell at a price no higher than my competitors – perhaps even lower, when the market is overstocked. Who is wronged?"[5] Moreover, Diogenes was convinced that Antipater's parity-of-information model reduced to absurdity: for if the moral demand that we consider the interests of others requires that we level all advantages that are acquired without wrong, then "we should not sell anything at all, but freely give everything away" until all inequalities are eliminated.[6]

On the one hand, as Diogenes suggested, Antipater's advice comes off as utopian and perhaps even misguided. Is it realistic to expect that in all matters we are to regard others' interests as equal to or superior to our own? For example, common sense dictates that we sometimes favor our own family over the interests of others. And we take for granted that we are at least occasionally permitted to go to a movie or treat ourselves to a scoop of ice cream despite the fact that inequalities might be mitigated by spending that money on vaccinations or food for the less fortunate. There is always something more we can do to improve the conditions of others; but we may strip life of all its joy by strictly demanding these sacrifices of ourselves. Moreover, many economists would argue that organizing a society around such egalitarian principles may make everyone worse off. A society benefits from its

[2]   Walter Miller (trans.), *Cicero, De Officiis* (Cambridge, MA: Harvard University Press, 1913): 321.
[3]   Ibid.
[4]   Ibid.
[5]   Ibid.
[6]   Ibid. at 23.

citizens' hard work and intelligence, and allowing persons to profit from information and other advantages is sometimes an effective means of incentivizing their exercise.

On the other hand, even absent express misrepresentation or concealment, wouldn't there be something hard-hearted and perhaps even vicious in taking advantage of the islanders' desperate situation to earn fabulous margins they would never agree to with complete information? In other words, there does seem to be something base and shameful in the failure to disclose, and Diogenes' laissez-faire ethic fails to account for this.

Having introduced the problem, Cicero shared his own judgment. He concluded that the grain seller should disclose the market information to the islanders prior to the sale, but his reasoning was opaque. Cicero began by pointing out that "merely holding one's peace about a thing *does not* constitute concealment."[7] In making this point, Cicero seemed to anticipate the modern common law rule that concealment (if it is to be regarded as the legal equivalent of a misrepresentation) requires some affirmative *action* calculated to prevent one's counterparty from learning a fact.[8] But Cicero then muddied the waters somewhat when he went on to insist that the grain seller would nevertheless be guilty of concealment by failing to disclose news of the arriving grain to the islanders "when it is in their interest to know it."[9] This latter claim can be reconciled with the preceding statement that silence alone does not constitute concealment only by concluding that Cicero used the term "conceal-ment" broadly to cover *any* violation of a duty to disclose. But what triggered the grain seller's duty to disclose in the hypothetical?

Cicero appears to have concluded that such a duty arises any time one's counter-party to a transaction might benefit from disclosure. In other words, he implicitly adopted Antipater's parity-of-information principle. Cicero offered no argument in support of this conclusion, just an appeal to common sense: "[W]ho fails to discern" that, in keeping his peace, the grain seller would be "shifty, sly, artful, shrewd, underhand, cunning, [and] one grown old in fraud and subtlety?"[10] This appeal will be unsatisfying to anyone who, like Diogenes, fails to share Cicero's ethical intuition favoring information egalitarianism.

6.2 THE SCHOLASTICS

Early Christian theologians tended to side with Cicero and Antipater on the problem of information asymmetries in exchanges, but did so by appeal to Biblical

---

[7] Ibid. at 325–27.
[8] The Restatement (Second) of Contracts provides that concealment must be some "*[a]ction* intended or known to be likely to prevent another from learning a fact." § 160 (1981). According to the Restatement, when such action occurs, it will be regarded as "equivalent to an assertion that the fact does not exist." Ibid.
[9] Miller, *Cicero, De Officiis*, 327.
[10] Ibid. at 327.

premises and upon pain of sin. For these Scholastic jurists, the Golden Rule – that "whatever you wish that others would do to you, do also to them" – settles the question.[11] Since "no man wishes to buy a thing for more than it's worth," no man should ever "sell a thing to another man for more than it's worth."[12] By the same token, a seller should reveal any information asymmetry they themselves would want revealed if they were the counterparty. To fail to disclose under such circumstances is to sin, and any contract founded in sin cannot be recognized by the law.[13]

St. Thomas Aquinas did not go so far as Cicero and other theologians in demanding that a party level *all* apparent information asymmetries a counterparty would want revealed when negotiating a purchase or sale. For Aquinas, "a man need not always give another the help or counsel which would be for his advantage in any way."[14] If, however, an information asymmetry relates to a defect in the subject matter of an exchange that would force a loss on the ignorant counterparty (i.e., rendering it worth less than the agreed-upon price), then justice demands disclosure. For Aquinas, the legal constructs of buying and selling are "established for the common advantage of both parties."[15] Whatever "is established for the common advantage, should not be more of a burden to one party than to another."[16] Consequently, "to sell a thing for more than it's worth, or to buy it for less than it's worth, is in itself unjust and unlawful."[17] So, for example, Aquinas concluded that if the subject matter of an exchange is defective, the defect is hidden and not reflected in the price, and the seller knows of the defect without disclosing it, "the sale will be illicit and fraudulent, and the seller will be bound to compensation for the loss incurred."[18]

But how should Aquinas's rule be applied to the problem of Cicero's grain merchant? Aquinas's demand for disclosure focused on "defects" not reflected in the contract price. The grain in Cicero's example was not, however, defective. Perhaps the answer is found in Aquinas's more general principle that "to sell a thing for more than it's worth, or to buy it for less than it's worth, is in itself unjust and unlawful.". There is, however, a problem. Aquinas seemed to assume that the

---

[11] Book of Matthew, Ch. 7:12.
[12] St. Thomas Aquinas, *Summa Theologica*, Vol. III, Part II, Second Section, Q. 77, Art. 1 (Fathers of the English Dominican Province, trans.) (Charleston, SC: BiblioBazaar, 2007). Aquinas did not offer his own view here; he simply stated one commonly held view. See also Wim Decock, *Theologians and Contract Law* (Leiden: Martinus Nijhoff Publishers, 2013) (the idea that contracting parties might "try to outwit each other was seen in radical opposition to the Golden Rule (*lex naturalis*) that you do not do to others what you would not have done to you").
[13] See generally Decock, *Theologians and Contract Law*, 507–604 (summarizing the Scholastic notion of "commutive justice" and fairness in exchanges).
[14] Aquinas, *Summa Theologica*, Vol. III, Part II, Second Section, Q. 77, Art. 1.
[15] Ibid.
[16] Ibid.
[17] Ibid.
[18] Ibid. at Q. 77, Art. 3.

"worth" of that which serves as the subject matter of an exchange can be determined objectively at the moment of contracting. Worth is, however, always relative. If worth is determined by market value, then which is the relevant market, and at what time? In Cicero's example, should the worth of the grain be determined by the market price in Alexandria upon the merchant's departure? Should it be determined by the market price in Rhodes upon his arrival? Or should it be determined by the seller's estimate of the market price in Rhodes after subsequent shipments arrive? Nothing in Aquinas's articulation of the rule prevents one from saying with Diogenes that the seller would force no loss upon the purchaser if he sold the grain at the market price in Rhodes upon his arrival, and consequently that the failure to disclose would be neither fraudulent nor illicit. Aquinas's notion of "objective value" has only become more problematic as the centuries have passed and markets have grown more dynamic and complex.[19]

6.3 CHIEF JUSTICE JOHN MARSHALL AND *LAIDLAW V. ORGAN*

Almost two thousand years after Cicero posed his hypothetical, Chief Justice John Marshall confronted very similar facts in *Laidlaw v. Organ*.[20] On December 24, 1814, British and American officers signed the Treaty of Ghent to end the War of 1812. But in those days it often took a month or more for news to reach America from Europe. In the meantime, hostilities continued. In January 1815, General Andrew Jackson led US forces to a decisive victory over the British in the Battle of New Orleans. Even after this defeat, a British fleet continued to impose a blockade on the Port of New Orleans. The blockade had a crippling effect on exports like

---

[19] As Professor Morton Horowitz explained, the development of extensive markets by the early nineteenth century

> contributed to a substantial erosion of belief in theories of objective value and just price. Markets for future delivery of goods were difficult to explain within a theory of exchange based on giving and receiving equivalents in value. Futures contracts for fungible commodities could only be understood in terms of a fluctuating conception of expected value radically different from the static notion that lay behind contracts for specific goods; a regime of markets and speculation was simply incompatible with a social imposed standard of value. The rise of a modern law of contract, then, was an objective value which lay at the foundation of the eighteenth century's equitable idea of contract.

Morton Horowitz, *The Transformation of American Law 1780–1860* (Cambridge MA: Harvard University Press, 1977), 180–81.

[20] Laidlaw v. Organ, 15 U.S. 178 (1817). *Laidlaw* is sometimes referred to as the earliest recorded case of insider trading, despite the fact that it does not involve the purchase or sale of securities. Others suggest that the earliest recorded example of insider trading in modern history occurred in 1815 when Nathan Mayer Rothschild raced across the English Channel to buy government bonds at the Exchange before news of Wellington's victory at Waterloo was announced. See, e.g., Bernhard Bergmans, *Insider Information and Securities Trading: A Legal and Economic Analysis of the Foundations of Liability in the USA and the European Community* (Boston, MA: Graham & Trotman, 1991): 3. Even if this story is not apocryphal (as some allege it to be), the events of *Laidlaw* still predate it by a few months.

tobacco, which was selling well below its pre-blockade price. By February 18, news of the treaty and the end of the war finally reached the British ships blockading the city. That evening, three men, Messrs. Livingston, White, and Shepherd, visited the British fleet and brought news that the blockade was lifted back into the city. It was agreed that a public announcement would be made at 8 AM the following morning.[21]

The reported facts are vague, but it appears Mr. Shepherd shared this (still nonpublic) news with his brother. Shepherd's brother then conveyed the information to his business partner, Hector M. Organ, in the early morning hours of February 19. Later that morning, "soon after sunrise," Organ called upon an agent for the commodity traders Peter Laidlaw & Co. and offered to purchase 111 hogsheads of tobacco for $7,544.[22] The trader may have been taken aback by Organ's rush to conclude the contract so early on a Sunday morning because he reportedly asked "if there was any news which was calculated to enhance the price or value of the article about to be purchased."[23] Organ apparently made no reply.[24] The parties then entered into the contract. As expected, the market price for tobacco soared 30 to 50 percent hours later when news of the treaty hit the streets of New Orleans.[25] Laidlaw subsequently claimed fraud and refused to deliver the tobacco. Organ sued for breach of contract. The trial court issued a directed verdict on behalf of Organ, and Laidlaw appealed the decision to the US Supreme Court.

In making its case, Laidlaw asked the Court to adopt the civil law rule that "[s]upression of material circumstances within the knowledge of the vendee, and not accessible to the vendor, is equivalent to fraud, and vitiates the contract."[26] In support, Laidlaw relied on the French natural law jurist Robert Joseph Pothier as persuasive authority. Pothier, like the Enlightenment jurists Hugo Grotius and Samuel von Pufendorf before him, offered secular justifications for the Scholastic principles of strict equality in contracting.[27] Pothier recognized the distinction

---

[21] *Laidlaw*, 15 U.S. at 182–83.

[22] A hogshead is a wooden barrel containing about 1,000 pounds of tobacco. The reported facts suggest that Organ had already begun negotiations with Laidlaw for the tobacco on the evening of February 18, before he learned that the blockade was to be lifted. See ibid. at 183. This helps explain how he managed to conclude a deal prior to 8 AM the following morning.

[23] Ibid. at 183.

[24] Ibid. at 189.

[25] Ibid. at 183.

[26] Ibid. at 184–85.

[27] See Decock, *Theologians and Contract Law*, 598–601. Decock explained the influence of the Scholastics' conception of strict equality on the theories of exchange espoused by Grotius, Pufendorf, and Pothier. For example, Decock pointed out that, like the Scholastics, Grotius demanded not only "equality between what is given and exchanged in a contract ... but also equality of information before the parties enter into the contract ... and equality of voluntary consent." Ibid at 600–01.

between "the forum of conscience and the forum of law," and that they are not coextensive.[28] But he argued that there is a necessary convergence between the two when giving effect to the demands of good faith in commercial transactions.[29] For Pothier, *good faith* in the sale of goods "not only forbids the assertion of falsehood, but also all reservation concerning that which the person with whom we contract has an interest in knowing, touching the thing which is the object of the contract."[30]

Pothier's parity-of-information principle was similar to Cicero's (indeed, he references Cicero's example of the grain merchant in its exposition), but he offered a more complete justification. Pothier began with the claim that good faith in contracting requires that the parties strive for equality in bargaining and the underlying exchange. Echoing Aquinas, Pothier held that failing to disclose information that is material to one's counterparty is "fatal to this equality" because "the moment that one acquires a knowledge of this object superior to the other, he has an advantage over the other in contracting."[31] Moreover, equity "requires that what the one party gives should be the equivalent of what he receives, and that neither party should wish to profit at the expense of the other."[32] If one party takes advantage of an information asymmetry to buy a good for less than it is worth, then she cannot in good faith regard the exchange as equitable. And this is true whether the information relates to an "intrinsic vice of the thing" or to indirect market conditions bearing on its value.[33] Pothier went even further than Aquinas and suggested that the failure to disclose material information may show bad faith even where the contract is entered into on fair terms. For, even when the terms are equitable, withholding material information undermines the counterparty's autonomy and freedom of choice. The counterparty should be left "perfectly at liberty" to contract or not contract "even for a fair price, if that price does not suit" her.[34] It is therefore "unjust to lay a snare for this liberty" by failing to disclose information material to the counterparty's decision.[35]

Applying Pothier's principle, Laidlaw argued that Organ's failure to disclose his knowledge of the Treaty of Ghent deprived the trading house of an informed choice and forced it to negotiate its contract on unequal footing. Laidlaw had no access to information concerning the treaty, which was "monopolized by the messengers from the British fleet."[36] Indeed, news of peace was particularly unexpected given that the smoke had hardly settled from the Battle of New Orleans just a few weeks before. The deception was then exasperated when Organ remained silent in

---

[28] *Laidlaw*, 15 U.S. at 185.
[29] Ibid.
[30] Ibid. at n. c (quoting Pothier, *De Vente*, Article I § 233).
[31] Ibid.
[32] Ibid. (quoting Pothier, *De Vente*, Article III § 241).
[33] Ibid. (quoting Pothier, *De Vente*, Article I § 236).
[34] Ibid. (quoting Pothier, *De Vente*, Article I § 237).
[35] Ibid.
[36] Ibid. at 194.

response to Laidlaw's inquiry as to whether there was any news that would enhance the price of the tobacco. According to Laidlaw, "[t]his reserve, when such question was asked, was equivalent to a false answer, and as much calculated to deceive as the communication of the most fabulous intelligence."[37] For these reasons, Laidlaw concluded that Organ violated his good faith duty to share his material nonpublic information of the treaty, and the contract should therefore be set aside for fraudulent nondisclosure.

According to Organ, the only issue for the Court to decide was "whether the sale was invalid because the vendee did not communicate information, which he received precisely as the vendor *might* have got it had he been equally diligent or equally fortunate."[38] Organ's reply made three points in support of enforcing the contract.

First, even if there had been a duty to disclose news of the treaty, Laidlaw waived this right when its agent failed to demand that Organ respond to his inquiry concerning any news affecting the market for tobacco. This waiver argument strove to turn one of the trading house's strongest facts against it.

Second, even assuming arguendo that Organ's conduct was shameful or otherwise worthy of contempt, this alone did not give rise to a legally enforceable right. Grounds for contempt are not grounds for rescission, and Laidlaw admitted as much by recognizing the distinction between the "forum of conscience" and the "forum of law." Indeed, Organ argued that the facts of this case demonstrated the need for this distinction. For "[i]t is a romantic equality that is contended for on the other side. Parties never can be precisely equal in knowledge, either of facts or of the inferences from such facts, and both must concur in order to satisfy the rule contended for."[39] Organ concluded that so expansive a standard of good faith in contracting would be unreasonable and impracticable, and it has ever been recognized in the common law jurisdictions of England and the United States. If good faith in contracting demanded so much of parties, then certainly the "maxim of caveat emptor could never have crept into the law."[40]

Third, absent a duty to disclose, fraud requires some overt deception by words or conduct. In this case, however, there was "no circumvention or maneuver practiced by the vendee, unless rising earlier in the morning, and obtaining by superior diligence and alertness that intelligence by which the price of commodities was regulated, be such."[41] In sum, Organ seemed to suggest that while Laidlaw's pious talk of complete information equality might be appropriate for Sunday school

[37] Ibid. at 189–90.
[38] Ibid. at 193.
[39] Ibid. at 193–94.
[40] Ibid. at 193.
[41] Ibid.

classes, the common law should continue to recognize that such a standard would be impracticable and unreasonable in the rough-and-tumble world of modern commerce.

Chief Justice Marshall's opinion for the Court was so brief it can be quoted here in its entirety:

> The question in this case is, whether the intelligence of extrinsic circumstances, which might influence the price of the commodity, and which was exclusively within the knowledge of the vendee, ought to have been communicated by him to the vendor? The court is of opinion that he was not bound to communicate it. It would be difficult to circumscribe the contrary doctrine within proper limits, where the means of intelligence are equally accessible to both parties. But at the same time, each party must take care not to say or do any thing tending to impose upon the other. The court thinks that the absolute instruction of the judge was erroneous, and that the question, whether any imposition was practiced by the vendee upon the vendor ought to have been submitted to the jury. For these reasons the judgment must be reversed, and the cause remanded to the district court of Louisiana, with directions to award a *venire facias de novo*.[42]

Marshall's opinion made it clear that overt deception (by words or conduct) *does* give rise to a duty to disclose, and the case was remanded because the trial court erred in taking this issue away from the jury. The case did not, however, become canonical for this holding; rather, it continues to be cited to this day for Marshall's dictum that there is, all things being equal, no duty to disclose an information advantage in a bargaining transaction.[43] But Marshall's judgment that disclosure was not required on these facts was just as unsatisfying as Cicero's judgment two thousand years prior that it was. The only indication of the Court's basis for refusing to recognize a duty to disclose information of these "extrinsic circumstances" is found in Marshall's commonsense claim that it "would be difficult to circumscribe the contrary doctrine within proper limits, where the means of intelligence are equally accessible to both parties." Jurists and scholars continue to debate the meaning, limits, and wisdom of these words.

That Marshall appeared to limit the scope of the rule to information asymmetries concerning "extrinsic circumstances" suggests one rationale. Courts in the early nineteenth century used to draw an equitable distinction between disclosure duties pertaining to intrinsic information (concerning the "nature, character, condition, title, safety, use, or enjoyment, &c., of the subject matter of the contract, such as natural or artificial defects") and extrinsic information (concerning circumstances "accidentally connected" with the contract, but which "may enhance or diminish its value or price ... such, as facts respecting peace or war, rise or fall of markets,

---

[42] Ibid. at 194. An order of venire facias de novo is a writ for summoning a new jury to try the facts.
[43] See, e.g., Joseph M. Perillo, *Calamari and Perillo on Contracts*, 6th ed. (St. Paul, MN: Thomson Reuters, 2009): § 9.20 at 302.

character of the neighborhood ... or the like circumstances").[44] While information concerning hidden intrinsic defects may be accessible to the seller, they are not always accessible to the buyer. Extrinsic defects, by contrast, are equally accessible to both. This distinction suggests an equitable basis for the rule in considerations of justice and fairness. On this reading, the Court would have required disclosure if, say, the roles had been reversed and the seller had failed to disclose a hidden defect in the tobacco itself (e.g., hidden mold) because it would have been unfair to place the risk of this defect on a buyer who had no means of discovering it. Since the information asymmetry in *Laidlaw* pertained to an extrinsic circumstance, fairness did not require disclosure because that information was equally accessible to both parties.[45] Marshall's statement that disclosure is not required "where the means of intelligence are equally accessible to both parties" supports this reading. Though the distinction between extrinsic and intrinsic facts has fallen from use, the modern distinction between hidden defects (which must sometimes be disclosed) and obvious defects (which usually need not be disclosed) is often justified by appeal to this same principle of equal access.[46]

But reading *Laidlaw* as decided on the equitable principle of fairness through equal access is problematic on the facts. Recall that Organ's partner's brother was the source of Organ's information asymmetry. Laidlaw not only failed to have equal access to this information at the time of contracting, but it seems clear the trading house had no access to this information at all. Consequently, if *Laidlaw* is a case where the source of the information asymmetry was "equally accessible" to both parties, it is hard to imagine any situation where information would *not* be equally accessible. It is therefore doubtful that Marshall intended either the extrinsic-intrinsic distinction or the principle of equal access to offer a meaningful constraint on the rule of the case. Indeed, the facts of the case suggest that Marshall was endorsing a clean break from the egalitarian principles of Roman civil law in favor of a harsh rule of caveat emptor, reflecting the laissez-faire attitudes gaining momentum in early nineteenth-century America.[47] Modern scholars continue to debate the doctrine of caveat emptor on grounds of ethics as well as efficiency.

---

[44] See Joseph Story, *Commentaries on Equity Jurisprudence as Administered in England and America* (Boston, MA: Charles C. Little & James Brown Publishers: 1836): § 207–10. Indeed, Story cites to *Laidlaw* in drawing the distinction. See § 207 n. 1.

[45] See Kim Lane Scheppele, "'It's Just Not Right': The Ethics of Insider Trading," *Law and Contemporary Problems* 56 (1993): 132.

[46] Ibid. at 133.

[47] See, e.g., Paula J. Dalley, "From Horse Trading to Insider Trading: The Historical Antecedents of the Insider Trading Debate," *William & Mary Law Review* 39 (1998): 1319 (noting that *Laidlaw* is the most frequently cited pronouncement of caveat emptor); see also M. H. Hoeflick, "Laidlaw v. Organ, Gulian Verplanck, and the Shaping of Early Nineteenth Century Contract Law: A Tale of a Case and a Commentary," *University of Illinois Law Review* 1991 (1991): 57 (*Laidlaw* established a "more pragmatist and harsher American contracts rule").

6.4 REACTION TO *LAIDLAW* AND THE MODERN
SCHOLARLY DEBATE

The nineteenth-century American jurist Gulian Verplanck authored a book challenging Marshall's decision in *Laidlaw* just a few years after it was handed down.[48] Verplanck cynically pointed out that the common law notion of caveat emptor tells the seller, "Be honest, if you choose to be so." To the buyer it says, "Be vigilant – consider yourself as surrounded by thieves and sharpers – trust no man – look upon every one who buys or sells as a rogue."[49] For Verplanck, however correct Marshall's decision may seem based on the "necessities of trade," those who "form their moral judgments from their unstudied impressions of right and wrong, will find it somewhat revolting to their notions of sound morality."[50] For this reason, Verplanck was convinced that the "odious maxim of *Caveat Emptor* with all its trains of absurdities and contradictions, should be for ever expelled from our courts."[51] Verplanck did not, however, go so far as to adopt the parity-of-information standard espoused by Cicero and Pothier, and reflected in the civil law tradition at the time. To the extent that this demand for parity of information would deprive merchants of information advantages earned by honest labor, skill, and acumen, Verplanck was convinced such a rule would push "notions of morality to an unreasonable extent" and therefore defeat its own object. Its remedy falls "as short of the true rule of justice, as its theory goes beyond it."[52]

For Verplanck, commonsense morality does not require that we act as saints would when conducting business, but neither does it leave every person to fend for herself in a Hobbesian state of nature. Verplanck pointed out that everyone buying and selling tobacco in New Orleans at the time understood and shared in their current price calculations that the English blockade was the principal cause for the depressed tobacco prices. Some tobacco traders used their research, acumen, and hunches to bet that tobacco prices would soon rise and won; others bet in the other direction and lost. Such speculation based on asymmetric opinion and inference is expected and even necessary in a healthy commodities market, and common sense does not demand that these traders share their disparate information and reasoning with one another. The moral status of a trader changes, however, when she obtains certain knowledge that a material fact presupposed by the current market price is false. This is because a basic assumption of her counterparty is that no such knowledge exists. If the counterparty were aware that such knowledge existed, he would not enter into an agreement until it had been fully investigated.

---

[48] Gulian C. Verplanck, *An Essay on the Doctrine of Contracts* (1825, reprinted Clark, NJ: The Lawbook Exchange Ltd., 2006).

[49] Ibid. at 215.

[50] Ibid. at 5.

[51] Ibid. at 217.

[52] Ibid. at 79.

Thus, according to Verplanck, the very making of a bargain for tobacco under conditions like those in place at the time of the transaction between Laidlaw and Organ involved "an indirect assertion" on the part of Organ, and an "implied confidence" on the part of Laidlaw, that the blockade remained in effect. Organ's suppression of his knowledge that the blockade had been lifted was "therefore dishonest and fraudulent; consequently, the bargain, if the seller objected to its execution, void in conscience."[53] In sum, for Verplanck, Chief Justice Marshall should have invoked the following commonsense moral rule and found for Laidlaw:

> Whenever any advantage is taken in a purchase, or sale, from the suppression of any fact, (not of an opinion or inference,) necessarily and materially affecting the common estimate which fixes the present market value of the thing sold; and in regard whereto, the sale alone conclusively proves, that it was presumed by the losing party, that no advantage would be taken; such advantage is gained by FRAUD.[54]

Verplanck thus attempted to chart a commonsense course between the strict information egalitarianism of Pothier and Cicero before him, and the Darwinian rule of caveat emptor that found its expression in Marshall's *Laidlaw* decision.[55]

While Verplanck offered a commonsense ethical challenge to Marshall's decision and the principle of caveat emptor in general, other scholars have emphasized considerations of market efficiency to justify both. Organ made much of the fact that he rose early in the morning and obtained his information advantage over Laidlaw by "superior diligence and alertness." In a seminal article, Professor Anthony Kronman argued that market efficiency is improved when persons are permitted to trade on information advantages that are deliberately acquired. Kronman explained that, to achieve the most efficient allocation of society's resources, "it is desirable that information which reveals a change in circumstances affecting the relative value of commodities reach the market as quickly as possible."[56] For example, returning to the circumstances surrounding *Laidlaw*, any farmers who planted peanuts instead of tobacco in the expectation that the blockade would persist unwittingly devoted their land to a nonoptimal use. After news of the treaty

---

[53] Ibid. at 124.

[54] Ibid. at 125–26.

[55] As Horowitz explained,

> Verplanck's Essay represents an important stage in the process of adapting contract law to the realities of market economy. Verplanck saw that if value is solely determined by the clash of subjective desire, there can be no objective measure of the fairness of a bargain. Since only "facts" are objective, fairness can never by measured in terms of substantive equality. The law can only assure that each party to a bargain is given "full knowledge of all material facts."

The Transformation of American Law 1780–1860, 182–83.

[56] Anthony T. Kronman, "Mistake, Disclosure, Information, and the Law of Contracts," *Journal of Legal Studies* 7 (1978): 12.

hit the market, these farmers were forced to decide between continuing to devote their land to the less profitable peanut crop and uprooting it and planting tobacco. Kronman pointed out that "[i]n either case, both the individual farmer and society as a whole will be worse off than if he had planted tobacco to begin with."[57] The more quickly valuable information is developed and reaches the market, the more efficient the market becomes.

Kronman observed that valuable information can be acquired either deliberately (e.g., by research) or casually (say, by overhearing it on a bus ride). Persons who deliberately acquire information incur costs that they would not otherwise have incurred. The typical market analyst who deliberately acquires valuable information about traded firms first spends time and money to develop her expertise; she then spends time and money to apply these skills to the task of discovering useful information. It is unlikely the analyst would incur these costs without the promise of some benefit. One way to ensure that people will benefit from deliberately acquired information is to grant them a property right in it. And, as Kronman explained, the "only feasible way of assigning property rights in short-lived market information is to permit those with such information to contract freely without disclosing what they know."[58] Moreover, "since it would enable the seller to appropriate the buyer's information without cost and would eliminate the danger of his being lured unwittingly into a losing contract by one possessing superior knowledge, a disclosure requirement will also reduce the seller's incentive to search."[59]

This is not, however, an economic justification for nondisclosure in all cases. There is no need to incentivize the casual acquisition of information (already acquired at no additional cost to the bearer), and therefore less reason to recognize a property interest in that information for the bearer. Since there are always some costs in terms of disappointed expectations when one party enters into a contract in error, it may be more efficient to require a counterparty who has casually acquired information to the contrary to disclose it and to thereby avoid the error. As Kronman put it, "[a] party who has casually acquired information is, at the time of the transaction, likely to be a better (cheaper) mistake-preventer than the mistaken party with whom he deals – regardless of the fact that both parties initially had equal access to the information in question."[60] Thus, for example, Kronman suggested that the Washington State Supreme Court reached the correct result in *Obde v. Schlemeyer*, when it held that the seller of a home had a duty to disclose knowledge of a latent termite infestation.[61] The Washington court seemed driven by equitable scruple, quoting Professor W. Page Keeton to make the point that the doctrine of caveat emptor belongs to a prior, individualistic era devoted to freedom of contract that

---

[57] Ibid.
[58] Ibid. at 14.
[59] Ibid. at 16.
[60] Ibid.
[61] *Obde v. Schlemeyer*, 56 Wash. 2d 449 (1960).

failed to take morality into account.[62] For Kronman, however, the decision is correct because the seller's information advantage was casually acquired and therefore needed no property right to incentivize its production. The seller is therefore the cheapest mistake preventer. In other words, even if the seller acquired the information of the termite infestation at some cost (say, by paying for a termite inspection), this is a cost the seller would have incurred to protect his home in any event. Requiring him to disclose does not therefore risk a net loss of information to the market.

Thus, for Kronman, the test for whether *Laidlaw* was correctly decided turns on the question of whether Organ's knowledge of the treaty was deliberately or casually acquired. If the information simply fell in Organ's lap by virtue of his partner's happening to have the right brother at the right time, then the case was decided incorrectly because it would turn out that Organ was the cheapest mistake avoider. But if Organ and his associates had spent time and effort developing relationships that finally paid off with information that could be monetized, then there should be no duty to disclose because in that case Laidlaw would be the cheapest mistake avoider. With this in mind, for Kronman, it turns out that a rule permitting nondisclosure of deliberately acquired information "corresponds to the arrangement the parties themselves would have been likely to adopt if they had negotiated an explicit allocation of the risk at the time they entered the contract."[63]

But what if anything should be made of Laidlaw's request for any news that might affect the price of tobacco? Even if one is prepared to accept the economic justification for nondisclosure where information is deliberately acquired, Kronman himself recognized that parties should be free to contract around any proposed default rules and allocate the risks however they see fit.[64] It appears Laidlaw's inquiry was an attempt to do just that. Laidlaw made the case that Organ's silence in the face of this question was itself sufficiently deceptive to constitute grounds for fraud. Professor Randy Barnett has offered a different take.[65] For Barnett, even if we assume Organ's silence in response to Laidlaw's inquiry concerning news that might affect the price of tobacco was misleading, Organ did not breach a duty of good faith by refusing to respond because Laidlaw had no right to ask the question.

Imagine a commodities market (or any market for that matter) in which every trader asked her counterparty whether she was in possession of any information that might affect the future supply or demand of the thing traded. According to Barnett,

---

[62] Ibid. at 452.

[63] Kronman, "Mistake, Disclosure, Information, and the Law of Contracts," 16.

[64] Ibid.

[65] See Randy E. Barnett, "Rational Bargaining Theory and Contract: Default Rules, Hypothetical Consent, the Duty to Disclose, and Fraud," *Harvard Journal of Law and Public Policy* 15 (1992): 783.

legal "entitlement to a truthful answer" to such questions "would virtually eliminate the institution within which both buyer and seller are operating."[66] It would be like asking someone to play poker while showing their cards. Few would play under such conditions, and it would be unfair to ask. Moreover, even if you tried to answer the question honestly and accurately, could you? It is always possible that some information you deem immaterial is precisely the tile your counterparty has been looking for to complete her complex mosaic. It is also possible that information that no one would regard as material at the time of the transaction might be deemed material by a jury years later with the benefit of hindsight.

Professor Saul Levmore has gone so far as to argue that, for reasons of fairness and efficiency, the law should recognize the right to *lie* under such circumstances. Levmore pointed out that demanding a truthful response in these circumstances would always place the questioner in a superior position. Consider the following example. After years of exploration and research a mining company determines there is a strong possibility that a large mineral deposit rests under a farmer's land. When the mining company offers to buy the land, the farmer asks: "Do you have any information about properties or developments in this area of the world such that if I shared your knowledge, I would be likely to raise my sale price by 10 percent or more?"[67] A regime that demands an honest response always places the farmer (and similarly situated buyers or sellers) in a superior position by allowing them to free-ride on the efforts of their counterparty. At the time of contracting, the mining company has only a strong suspicion that the land contains mineral wealth. If the mining company responds to the question honestly, then the farmer will raise the price. If the mining company answers dishonestly, then the contract creates a cost-free option for the farmer. If the mining company is successful, the farmer will assert his claim for fraud and reap the entire benefit of the mining company's exploration and development. If the mining company is unsuccessful, the seller remains silent and the mining company eats all the exploration costs. Not only is such free-riding unfair, it is inefficient because it will discourage mining companies from engaging in socially beneficial exploration. Thus, Levmore suggested that the law should permit a dishonest response where "the misinformation would only cause the misinformed party to behave as he would have without the information, and in which it would be unfair – because of the cost and risk of extortion – to require disclosure of the informed party."[68] Levmore referred to any such misrepresentation as "optimal dishonesty."[69]

---

[66] Ibid. at 799.
[67] Saul Levmore, "Securities and Secrets: Insider Trading and the Law of Contracts," *Virginia Law Review* 68 (1982): 139.
[68] Ibid. at 140.
[69] Ibid.

6.5 AMBIVALENCE PERSISTS AFTER TWO THOUSAND
YEARS OF DEBATE

Just as nearly two thousand years of scholarly debate failed to settle the problem of information asymmetry raised by Cicero's grain merchant, two hundred years of American jurisprudence have not generated consensus concerning the issues at stake in *Laidlaw* or the underlying rationale behind Marshall's decision.[70] Indeed, the contrasting positions of Cicero and Marshall seem to reflect a deep tension in our commonsense attitudes concerning problems of transactions based on information asymmetries that persists to this day. Referencing *Laidlaw*, one commentator opined that if "those facts were given to the normal person, as an abstract question, he would probably say that the buyer's conduct was unethical; on the other hand, if the same individual were given the opportunity the buyer had in *Laidlaw v. Organ*, he would do precisely the same thing."[71] This same ambivalence was borne out in a 1986 *Business Week*/Harris poll concerning insider trading. Amid the media frenzy surrounding Ivan Boesky's arrest, a majority of those polled claimed that insider trading should be illegal, but a larger majority said that they themselves would trade on inside information if the opportunity presented itself.[72]

Cicero and Marshall's conclusory judgments did not themselves offer an analytic framework for addressing the problem of when, if ever, persons should be permitted to profit from information asymmetries in the purchase or sale of something. Nevertheless, the debate they have engendered has certainly helped to frame the issues and to identify the different values and principles in play. Both sides of the debate outlined previously make regular appeals to the commonsense ethical values of good faith, equality, justice, fairness, autonomy, social welfare, the virtue of generosity, and the vice of greed. But at the same time, they recognize that the demands of law cannot be coextensive with the demands of ethics. The law must reflect the value of economic efficiency, and it must be mindful of the practical necessities of trade.

By emphasizing some of these values and de-emphasizing others, jurists and philosophers have offered a number of complementing and competing rules to

---

[70] As one commentator put it, "[n]ot only has the common law been unable in 160 years to resolve the issues raised by Laidlaw v. Organ, but the legal commentators have also been unable to make any progress on the policy concerns, legal arguments, and theoretical foundations of the analysis." Dalley, "From Horse Trading to Insider Trading," 1351.

[71] W. Page Keeton, "Fraud – Concealment and Non-Disclosure," *Texas Law Review* 15 (1936): 32.

[72] "Business Week/Harris Poll: Outsiders Aren't Upset by Insider Trading," *Business Week* (Dec. 8, 1986): 34. Participants were asked, "Suppose you got a tip from a friend that the company he or she works for was going to be purchased for a lot more money than its current stock price. . . . [W]ould you buy stock in that company?" Fifty-five percent answered that they would buy stock in the company, 39% answered that they would not buy the stock, and 6% answered that they were unsure. It is also interesting that though only 55% answered that they would purchase stock based on inside information, 78% answered that other people would trade on inside information. Ibid.

address the problem of when (if ever) information asymmetries may be used to gain a trading advantage. We have seen rules along the spectrum from strict parity of information (Cicero, some Scholastics, Pothier, and others) to strict caveat emptor (Marshall on some readings). Between these extreme positions, we have seen a variety of proposed rules. Some scholars have suggested that nondisclosure be permitted where the parties have equal access to information, sometimes drawing on the nature of the information itself to determine the issue of accessibility (intrinsic or extrinsic, hidden or obvious). Some scholars have looked to the nature of the underlying exchange, permitting nondisclosure where the exchange is objectively equal in value, but requiring disclosure where it is not. Other scholars have sought to strike a balance between commonsense notions of fairness and market realities by requiring disclosure only where information pertains to basic assumptions that inform the market price of the thing exchanged. We have seen scholars look to property rights in information as permitting the owner to disclose or not at her discretion. Drawing on principles of economic efficiency, some would settle the disclosure question by looking at how the information advantage was acquired, finding that casually acquired information must be disclosed, but deliberately acquired information need not be disclosed. And though both Cicero and Marshall agreed that affirmative misrepresentations should never be permitted, we have even seen some scholars prepared to argue that parties should sometimes even be permitted to lie to preserve an information advantage.

Of course, grain and tobacco are commodities. Consequently neither Cicero's merchant nor Organ would qualify as "insider traders" by our contemporary understanding of the term, which presupposes securities trading.[73] Moreover, the parties in these examples did not share the fiduciary or similar relationship of trust and confidence that corporate insiders are sometimes regarded as sharing with their shareholders. Finally, the parties in these examples dealt with one another at arm's length, not through impersonal exchanges. As we have seen, all of these differences have been relevant to the development of insider trading law in the United States and abroad. We have also seen that a perpetual tug of war among all of the values reflected in the debates summarized in this chapter has also informed the adoption, at one time or another, one jurisdiction or another, of virtually every one of the proposed rules discussed previously as the rule for regulating insider trading (from caveat emptor to parity of information). In sum, the development of the law of insider trading (both in the United States and abroad) has reflected the same ambivalence represented in the contrasting opinions of Cicero and Marshall.

*****

---

[73] This is, however, beginning to change in the United States. See, e.g., Andrew Verstein, "Insider Trading in Commodities Markets," *Virginia Law Review* 102 (2016): 447.

The next four chapters will build on the jurisprudential and commonsense ethical ideas introduced here to address the specific problem of insider trading, which is just one subclass of the broader problem of information asymmetries in exchanges. Focused attention will be paid to the problem of insider trading from all of the evaluative standpoints explored in this chapter. What are its economic and moral consequences? Whom does it harm? How does it affect the character of those who engage in it? Any responsible plan for reforming the law of insider trading in the United States must be shaped by our society's honest answers to these questions after disciplined reflection.

7

The Efficient, the Right, the Good, and Legal Reform

The goal of this chapter is twofold. First, this chapter introduces the principal normative values against which the practice of insider trading is to be analyzed and measured in the subsequent chapters: economic efficiency (Chapter 8), moral theories of right and wrong (Chapter 9), and virtue theory (Chapter 10). Economic efficiency is introduced in its neoclassical form as employing rational choice theory to determine the most value-enhancing allocation of society's resources. The more recent behavioralist model for economic analysis of the law is considered as well. Moral theories of right and wrong are then introduced through the two Western liberal approaches of deontology and utilitarianism. These other-regarding theories offer different and sometimes competing accounts of what persons owe one another from the impersonal "moral point of view." Finally, while moral theory focuses on duties owed to others, virtue theory focuses on private pursuits of self-perfection and individual ethical character development. Virtue theory offers substantive practical advice to individuals on how to live the good life.

The second goal of this chapter is to introduce these evaluative perspectives in such a way as to caution against focusing entirely on one to the exclusion of the others while engaged in the project of legal reform. For example, in one of the most often-quoted passages of Henry Manne's seminal book *Insider Trading and the Stock Market*, he lumped together arguments against insider trading that turn on ethical considerations as "it's just not right" propositions.[1] In a footnote, Manne explained that this "expression originated with an anonymous ... law student, who, during a classroom discussion of the subject, stamped her foot and angrily declaimed, 'I don't care; it's just not right.'"[2] For Manne, if repetition of such moral exhortations "were a form of scientific proof, undoubtedly the case against insider trading would long

---

[1] Henry Manne, *Insider Trading and the Stock Market* (New York: The Free Press, 1966): 15.
[2] Ibid. at n. 42.

ago have been proved."[3] Such cynicism concerning ethical justification in the law can be traced back to the early legal realists,[4] but has been particularly pronounced among members of the modern law and economics movement, of which Manne was a founder.

The criticism seemed to be that, by comparison to economic analysis, ethical justification is insufficiently "rigorous" or "scientific" to determine clear and effective legal principles. Indeed, Manne (like many other leaders of the law and economics school) was of the opinion that most, if not all, first-order ethical propositions ultimately rest on economic justifications – that what is right can usually be cashed out in terms of what is efficient. Of course, there are a great many scholars, politicians, and jurists who are convinced that just the opposite is true – that economic analysis has very little to offer the law. For example, some are convinced that economic analysis is built on a false conception of human nature and so should not serve as a model for human institutions. Others point out that the law is (or ought to be) just the institutionalization of our shared conceptions of what is just and fair. So understood, a central aim of the law is to check the heedless pursuit of wealth maximization, and ethical considerations must therefore always trump economic expedience.

It is suggested throughout this chapter that both approaches are wrong, at least to the extent that they attempt to offer a unified theory for analyzing and reforming the law. Economic analysts of law are wrong to suggest that their methods are more rigorous or scientific than moral philosophers' methods, and they are also misguided to claim that ethical claims are meaningful only to the extent that they are reduced to efficiency claims. Ethical philosophers are, however, equally wrong to claim that the economic analysis of law is useless (or even dangerous) because it is based on a false model, or that it is of only ancillary importance because it will always be trumped by considerations of justice and fairness. The approach to legal analysis and reform advocated in this chapter and employed in the remainder of this book is pragmatist. It takes for granted that jurists are better off if they can move beyond the kind of essentialism that suggests one form of legal justification somehow gets it right and should therefore form the basis of a single, unified theory of legal interpretation and reform. Instead, it is suggested that the project of legal reform is best served by striving to achieve a proper balance among all of the values in play.

7.1 RATIONAL CHOICE THEORY AND SOME PROBLEMS

Proponents of the law and economics method tend to analyze legal rules and institutions through the application of microeconomic theory. Microeconomics is

---

[3] Ibid. at 15.
[4] See, e.g., Oliver Wendell Holmes, Jr., "The Path of the Law," *Harvard Law Review* 10 (1897):
     464 ("I often doubt whether it would not be a gain if every word of moral significance could be
     banished from the law altogether.").

"the study of how households and firms make decisions and how they interact in specific markets."[5] There is not, however, just one microeconomic strategy for legal analysis; there are many. The "neoclassical" model, of which Judge Richard Posner is considered by many to be a leading proponent, centers on "the science of rational choice," which begins with the assumption that "human beings [and firms] are rational maximizers of their satisfactions."[6] With this model of practical reason in place, combined with the assumptions that economic agents do not commit errors, sellers are homogeneous, and transaction and information costs are zero, Professor Ronald Coase's theorem[7] is applied to conclude that "resources will instantaneously flow to their highest valued use."[8] Any distribution of goods (or information) under this model will be "efficient" to the extent that "no reallocation would increase their value."[9] Thus, if the economic analysis of the law can be associated with a value, it is that of facilitating something like this efficiency for all markets through legal rules and institutions.

The economic analysis of insider trading law (the focus of Chapter 8) will therefore measure different regimes based on how well they can be expected to facilitate the flow of material nonpublic information to its highest valued use.

7.1.1 *Is Economic Analysis All We Need?*

Judge Posner echoed the view of many proponents of the law and economics movement when he wrote that the "compartmentalization of knowledge – so conspicuous a feature of the modern world – may have condemned [ethical theory] to irrelevance at the level of practice."[10] For Posner, the legal problems facing rich liberal countries in the twenty-first-century West

---

[5]   Economics is traditionally divided into two subfields: microeconomics and macroeconomics. In contrast to microeconomics, macroeconomics focuses on "economywide phenomena," such as "the effects of borrowing by the federal government." N. Gregory Mankiw, *Principles of Microeconomics*, 6th ed. (Mason, OH: South-Western Cengage Learning, 2012): 29.

[6]   Richard A. Posner, *Economic Analysis of the Law*, 9th ed. (New York: Wolters Kluwer, 2014): 3–4.

[7]   Professor N. Gregory Mankiw summarizes that Coase theorem as follows: "if private parties can bargain over the allocation of resources at no cost, then the private market will always solve the problem of externalities and allocate resources efficiently." *Principles of Microeconomics*, 210.

[8]   Joshua D. Wright and Douglas H. Ginsburg, "Behavioral Law and Economics: Its Origins, Fatal Laws, and Implications for Liberty," *Northwestern University Law Review* 106 (2012): 1037.

[9]   Posner, *Economic Analysis of the Law*, 12.

[10]   Richard A. Posner, *Overcoming the Law* (Cambridge, MA: Harvard University Press, 1995): 446. The following critique of rational choice theory expands upon some criticisms first offered in John P. Anderson, "The Final Step to Insider Trading Reform: Answering the 'It's Just Not Right!' Objection," *Journal of Law, Economics & Policy* 12 (2016): 281–83.

present difficult analytical and empirical issues that can no more be understood, let alone resolved, by the intuitions and analytic procedures of persons schooled only in the humanities than problems of high-energy physics or brain surgery can be understood and resolved by the study of the *Tractatus Logico-Philosophicas*.[11]

Posner has been fond of dismissing ethics as a mode of legal justification by claiming that such appeals may "persuade, but not with rational arguments."[12] For Posner, "[a]t its best, moral philosophy, like literature, enriches; it neither proves nor edifies."[13] Good economic analysis of the law, by contrast, is purported to offer firm, rational grounds for its conclusions that are objectively verifiable.[14] Posner has argued that economic analysis "epitomizes the operation in law of the ethic of scientific inquiry, pragmatically understood," and is therefore far better suited than ethical reasoning to the challenges of the age.[15] In sum, economic analysis, which is science, should be privileged over ethical analysis, which reduces to nothing more than "epistemically feeble" exhortation, when analyzing and reforming the law.[16] But just how firm, scientific, and rigorous are the conclusions reached by economic analysts of law?

The rational choice model does not enjoy consensus even among economists. Indeed, it is quite controversial. Professor John Maynard Keynes and Coase, two of the most recognized economists of the twentieth century, were united in their

---

[11] Ibid. at 456. Published in 1921, Ludwig Wittgenstein's *Tractatus* is regarded as one of the most esoteric yet important works of twentieth-century philosophy. The book aims to define the limits of science and metaphysics. It was extremely influential among logical positivists and early philosophers of language. In his later work, Wittgenstein distanced himself from the "dogmatism" of the *Tractatus*. The later Wittgenstein eschewed the *Tractatus's* attempt at logical precision in favor of a pragmatism that regards philosophy as nothing more (or less) than a therapeutic tool that is most useful in "language games" that are divided against themselves, with participants working at cross-purposes. In such cases, philosophy's task is to expose the problem and thereby help to "shew the fly the way out of the fly bottle." Ludgwig Wittgenstein, *Philosophical Investigations*, G. E. M. Anscombe, trans. (New York: Macmillan Publishing, 1953): § 309. With this in mind, Wittgenstein would likely agree with Posner's conclusion that his *Tractatus* is of little use in the language games played by surgeons and physicists as such. He would, however, also be sympathetic to a thesis of this chapter (and this book), which is that there are some dysfunctional language games, of which our current insider trading regime is one, within which the tools of ethical philosophy can be of great practical import by perhaps showing the fly out of the bottle.

[12] Richard A. Posner, *The Problematics of Moral and Legal Theory* (Cambridge, MA: The Belknap Press of Harvard University Press, 1999): ix.

[13] Ibid. at ix.

[14] Other neoclassical economists similarly characterize economics as an objective science:

> Economists try to address their subject with a scientist's objectivity. They approach the study of the economy much the same way as a physicist approaches the study of matter and a biologist approaches the study of life: They devise theories, collect data, and then analyze these data in an attempt to verify or refute their theories.

Mankiw, *Principles of Microeconomics*, 22.

[15] Posner, *The Problematics of Moral and Legal Theory*, 15.

[16] Ibid. at 12.

skepticism of rational choice. According to Coase, the rational choice model is "misleading" in that "there is no reason to suppose that most human beings are engaged in maximizing anything unless it be unhappiness, and even this with incomplete success."[17]

Even those who embrace the rational choice model disagree over its application to legal analysis. Consider, for example, the "policy analysis" and "public choice" schools. While both schools adopt the same assumptions about private choice, they disagree about whether the model should apply to judges and legislators.[18] The policy analysis school assumes that private individuals adopt an economic attitude toward legal rules. In other words, they have self-interested preferences, and they respond to legal sanctions so as to maximize the satisfaction of those preferences. However, it makes very different assumptions concerning the model of choice for public officials. It is assumed that public officials "are conscientious; they faithfully perform their legal obligations."[19] They seek to maximize social welfare, rather than their own private preferences. The public choice school, by contrast, assumes the same self-interested choice model for both private and public officials. On this model, public officials will "only meet their legal obligations if it is in their (self-) interest to do so."[20] Needless to say, these two schools often reach radically different conclusions concerning the economic analysis of law and legal institutions. But it is difficult to imagine an empirical research program that could decide the issue between them.

Another critique of the rational choice model has been developed into a competing theory of the economic analysis of law, "behavioral law and economics."[21] Even the most hard-core proponent of rational choice will admit that people do not always behave rationally. But the neoclassical model accounts for this by concluding that "random deviations from rational behavior will cancel out."[22] Recent studies suggest, however, that some departures from rational choice are not random but systematic, resulting from individuals' cognitive biases.[23] Perhaps the most important cognitive bias for behavioral economists is the "endowment effect." The endowment effect is the cognitive bias of "valuing what we have more than we would value the

---

[17] Ibid. at 23–24, quoting Ronald Coase, *The Firm, the Market, and the Law* (Chicago: The University of Chicago Press, 1988): 4; Coase also referred to the rational choice model as "meaningless." Ronald Coase, "Coase on Posner on Coase," *Journal of Institutional and Theoretical Economics* 149 (1993): 97.

[18] See Lewis A. Kornhauser, "Economic Rationality in the Analysis of Legal Rules and Institutions," in Martin P. Golding and William A. Edmundson (eds.), *Philosophy and Legal Theory* (Hoboken, NJ: Blackwell Publishing, 2004): 69.

[19] Ibid. at 70.

[20] Ibid.

[21] See, e.g., Christine Jolls, Cass R. Sunstein, and Richard Thaler, "A Behavioral Approach to Law and Economics," *Stanford Law Review* 50 (1998): 1471.

[22] Posner, *Economic Analysis of the Law*, 18–19.

[23] See, e.g., Danial Kahneman, *Thinking, Fast and Slow* (New York: Farrar, Straus and Giroux, 2011).

identical thing if it were offered to us."[24] This systematic cognitive bias is particularly devastating to proponents of the rational choice model in that it undermines its application of the Coase theorem.[25] The result is that "market transactions may not lead to an efficient allocation of resources, which in turn has implications for virtually every area of substantive law."[26] Behavioral economists have been quick to exploit such failures in the Coasean bargaining model to challenge neoclassical conclusions across the legal spectrum. Indeed, Professors Cass Sunstein and Richard Thaler have applied behavioral economics to justify what they refer to as "libertarian paternalism," the claim that, in order to account for cognitive bias, private and public institutions should "self-consciously" use default and incentive structures to "steer people's choices in directions that will improve the choosers' own welfare."[27] Though such paternalism is anathema to the typical neoclassical economist of law, it has nevertheless been embraced in contemporary American politics and the legal academy.[28]

Of course, rational choice economists are ready with responses to the behavioral economist. For example, it is argued that behavioral economics ignores self-selection,[29] cognitive bias does not persist in real market settings (as opposed to laboratory settings), and libertarian paternalists fail to account for the social benefits of error in decision-making.[30] In addition, neoclassical economists allege that much of behavioral economics is unsupported by sufficient empirical data and otherwise lacks scientific rigor.[31] Nevertheless, it is alleged that the politics of regulators leads them to irrationally (and unscientifically) buy in to the behavioral economic agenda because it "produces outcomes closest to [their] own preconceptions."[32] And, it is claimed, law professors are worse. For example, neoclassicists point out that, despite behavioral scholars' purported allegiance to "scientific rigor and the pursuit of

---

[24] Posner, *Economic Analysis of the Law*, 18–19 (one might refuse to sell a wristwatch for $100 for which one would not have been willing to pay $90) (citing Elizabeth Hoffman and Matthew L. Spitzer, "Willingness to Pay vs. Willingness to Accept: Legal and Economic Implications," *Washington University Law Quarterly* 71 (1993): 59.

[25] Posner, *Economic Analysis of the Law*, 19.

[26] Wright and Ginsburg, "Behavioral Law and Economics," 1037 (citing Christopher Buccafusco and Chirstopher Sprigman, "Valuing Intellectual Property: An Experiment," *Cornell Law Review* 96 (2010): 13.

[27] Cass R. Sunstein and Richard H. Thaler, "Libertarian Paternalism Is Not an Oxymoron," *University of Chicago Law Review* 70 (2003): 1162.

[28] See Wright and Ginsburg, "Behavioral Law and Economics," 1053–54 (noting that "a recent account in the popular press describes behavioral economics as 'the governing theory' of the Obama Administration's regulatory agenda" and that "[l]egal academics have discovered in the behavioral economics literature a rich supply of empirical findings they can marshal in support of paternalistic regulatory interventions").

[29] See Posner, *Economic Analysis of the Law*, 21.

[30] See Wright and Ginsburg, "Behavioral Law and Economics," 1041–45.

[31] See, e.g., Gregory Klass and Kathryn Zeiler, "Against Endowment Theory; Experimental Economics and Legal Scholarship," *UCLA Law Review* 61 (2013): 2.

[32] See Wright and Ginsburg, "Behavioral Law and Economics," 1045.

objectively verifiable knowledge," pursuit of "the behaviorist policy agenda is only minimally constrained by the norms of scientific inquiry."[33]

Thus, the proponent of rational choice theory persistently levels the same charges against competing schools of economic thought – that they are irrational, unscientific, lacking in rigor – as she does against proponents of ethical theory in the law. But when one realizes that behaviorists could (and do), with equal force, level the same charges against the rational choice theorist, any claim to "objectively verifiable knowledge" on either side falls a bit flat.

7.1.2 *Can the Economic Analysis of Law Be Separated from Ethical Theory?*

Moreover, if one takes seriously Posner's claim that ethical reasoning is decidedly "unscientific," then one has all the more reason to question rational choice's claim to objectivity. This is because there is good reason for believing that the neoclassical economic analysis of law is crucially interrelated with, and perhaps even dependent upon, ethical reasoning and value theory.

Posner has been fond of pointing out that rational choice theory is purely instrumental. It does not set ends; it merely suggests the most efficient means to achieving goals defined by the public political culture.[34] In other words, by "showing how a change in economic policy or arrangements would advance [society] toward a goal, [economists] can make a normative statement without having to defend their fundamental premises."[35] By playing this instrumental role, many economists are convinced that their methods can remain objective or scientific, even while promoting controversial ends. But this is not true.

To begin, instrumental reasoning must always be secondary and therefore subordinate to the ends set before it. As David Hume (a philosopher Posner has cited with approval) famously asserted, "[r]eason is, and ought only to be, the slave of the passions, and can never pretend to any other office than to serve and obey them."[36] For Hume, "reason" would include what Posner has in mind when he articulates rational choice theory, and "passions" would include what Posner would group together under the heading of ethics or morality. If rational choice is the slave to a given society's ethical values, then can the former ever be immune to contamination or influence by the latter?

---

[33] See ibid. at 1047–48.
[34] Posner, *Overcoming the Law*, 16 (noting that "nothing in economics prescribes an individual's goals," but "whatever his ... goals," rational choice theory provides a tool for charting the most efficient path to achieving them).
[35] Posner, *Economic Analysis of the Law*, 16.
[36] David Hume, "Treatise of Human Nature," in Henry D. Aiken (ed.), *Hume's Moral and Political Philosophy* (New York: Hafner Publishing Company, 1948): 25.

For example, many have argued, and some studies have concluded, that simply studying theories that depict people as self-interested leads people to actually become more self-interested.[37] If this is true, then any purported Chinese wall between rational choice theory and the ethical goals to which it is set shows a breach. Consider, if one of a society's principal ethical goals is inculcating or incentivizing pro-social behavior among its citizens, then it may turn out that merely articulating that society's legal rules, institutions, and sanction structures in terms of rational choice theory itself brings about the contrary result. In this way, a society's ethical goals would do more than direct the application of the economic analysis of law; it may force one to revise its key elements – for example, the model of rational choice itself. Of course, the rational choice theorist might simply respond that if publicizing the rational choice model would impede its instrumental success, then it should not be publicized. But then one could hardly present rational choice theory as a theory of legal analysis. Publicity and transparency are typically regarded as key elements of the Western liberal conception of political order.[38]

Moreover, as noted previously, many rational choice theorists are quick to challenge the credibility of behavioral economists and the very concept of libertarian paternalism as driven by their political predispositions, rather than any commitment to discovering the truth of the matter. But, again, if it is the nature of the economic analysis of the law that it plays a purely instrumental role – that it is "slave" to the political goals set before it – can it be a criticism that those ends might have a say in the most effective means to their accomplishment, particularly if (as suggested previously) the nature of the instrumental reasoning applied may help determine its effectiveness?

The interrelatedness of economics and ethical theory also comes to the fore when one considers the concept of "preference" in rational choice theory. In microeconomic theory, preference is a "technical term that refers to a mathematical structure over a domain of 'objects.'"[39] As Professor Lewis A. Kornhauser explained, preference is "a relation R over a domain that is symmetric, complete, and transitive."[40] The relation R can be defined as "at least as good as" or "at least as preferred as."[41]

---

[37] See, e.g., R. T. Gilovich, and D. Regan, "Does Studying Economics Inhibit Cooperation?," *Journal of Economic Perspectives* 7 (1993): 159; Gerald Marwell and Ruth E. Ames, "Economists Free Ride, Does Anyone Else?: Experiments on the Provision of Public Goods, IV," *Journal of Public Economics* 15 (1981): 295.

[38] See, e.g., John Rawls, *Political Liberalism* (New York: Columbia University Press, 1993): 68 ("Publicity ensures, so far as practical measures allow, that citizens are in a position to know and to accept the pervasive influences of the basic structure that shape their conception of themselves, their character and ends ... and that citizens should be in this position is a condition of their realizing their freedom as fully autonomous, politically speaking.").

[39] Kornhauser, "Economic Rationality in the Analysis of Legal Rules and Institutions," 68.

[40] Ibid.

[41] Ibid.

Symmetry means that "for every x in the domain, xRx."[42] Completeness means that "for every x and y in the domain, either xRy or yRx."[43] And, finally, transitivity means that, for any x, y, and z in the domain, if (xRy and yRz) then xRz."[44] For a value pluralist such as Isaiah Berlin, the very idea of, say, completeness, so understood, may be unrealistic.[45] But assume the concept of preference within rational choice theory is not inherently confused; when applying rational choice theory to the analysis of law, how does one interpret the relation "at least as good as" or "at least as preferred as"? Kornhauser explained that preferences in rational choice theory are assumed to be self-interested, but this can mean either (1) a narrow "concern only for the agent's own consumption of goods and services," or it can be interpreted more broadly to mean (2) "any concern of the agent," to include altruistic or other ethical motivations.[46]

Kornhauser has suggested that the formal concept of preference is consistent with both the narrow interpretation and the broad interpretation, and that problems for rational choice theory arise only when they are applied inconsistently.[47] But assume one adopts the broader, "any concern" interpretation of preference that permits moral considerations to influence preference orderings. Application of rational choice theory to the economic analysis of the law requires that a judge or legislator be able to ascertain the all-things-considered self-interest of individuals, but, where the interests of individuals conflict, it must decide conflicts of interest between individuals. If a conflict between two or more individuals turns on their competing moral or religious preferences (for example, concerning the issues of capital punishment, abortion, or same-sex marriage), then how does the rational choice theorist resolve this conflict? To rank outcomes, it would seem the judge or legislator would be forced to rank the moral preferences. How can this be done without making moral judgments? Moreover, once moral preferences are taken into consideration, the practical usefulness of rational choice is called into question. It is at least conceivable that one may be able to identify and weigh individuals' preferences for the consumption of goods and services (under the narrow interpretation of preference), but how can a judge or legislator even begin the project of identifying and weighing individuals' moral preferences by methods that can be regarded as "objective," "rigorous," or "scientific"?

If, alternatively, the rational choice theorist falls back on the narrow interpretation of preference, the theory will lack predictive power in that it will fail to account for

---

[42] Ibid.
[43] Ibid.
[44] Ibid.
[45] See, e.g., Isaiah Berlin, "My Intellectual Path," in Henry Hardy (ed.), *The Power of Ideas* (Princeton, NJ: Princeton University Press, 2000): 12; see also David Wolitz, "Indeterminacy, Value Pluralism, and Tragic Cases," *Buffalo Law Review* 62 (2014): 529.
[46] Kornhauser, "Economic Rationality in the Analysis of Legal Rules and Institutions," 69.
[47] Ibid.

the motivational power of ethical commitment. Even Kornhauser observed that "one must accept that obligation does in fact influence behavior."[48] Consequently, unless the rational choice theorist can offer a reductionist account of ethical obligation (promise-keeping, justice, fairness, etc.) that ultimately cashes this motivation out in terms of pure self-interest (i.e., successfully argue that only incentive structures can determine action), then the theory will be incomplete and presumably fail in its principal objective of predictive accuracy. If the economic analyst of law does offer a reductionist account of ethical obligation in terms of pure self-interest, then the resulting model will fail to account for one of our core intuitions concerning the concept of law – it obligates; it does not merely oblige.[49]

The reductionist rational choice model offers nothing more than a variant of John Austin's imperative theory of law.[50] As Professor H. L. A. Hart explained, the imperative theory offers a simple tripartite structure for law: "command, sanction, and sovereign."[51] But the result is "like that of a gunman saying to his victim, 'Give me your money or your life.' The only difference is that in the case of a legal system the gunman says it to a large number of people who are accustomed to the racket and habitually surrender to it."[52] But, Hart goes on, "[l]aw surely is not the gunman situation writ large, and legal order is surely not to be thus simply identified with compulsion."[53] Hart reminds us that there is a difference between "feeling obliged" and recognizing an "obligation."[54] The gunman situation produces only the former, but the law the latter. Hart makes the point another way that brings the point home cleanly. He distinguishes those who observe rules (but do not accept them) and those who use them as guides to conduct as those who adopt "the 'external' and the 'internal points of view.'"[55] The rational choice theorist who fails to recognize obligation as a source of motivation must regard legal systems from this external point of view. The problem, however, is that viewed from this external standpoint, a legal system is nothing more than the sum of "observable regularities of conduct, predictions, probabilities, and signs."[56] But this is not how we experience law. Those who regard rules only from the external point of view see violations as "merely a basis for the prediction that a hostile reaction will follow ... [but it is not] a reason for hostility."[57]

[48] Ibid.
[49] See H. L. A. Hart, *The Concept of Law*, 2d ed. (New York: Oxford University Press, 1994): 88.
[50] See, e.g., John Austin, *The Province of Jurisprudence Determined*, H.L.A. Hart (ed.) (Indianapolis, IN: Hackett Publishing Company, 1954).
[51] H. L. A. Hart, "Positivism and the Separation of Law and Morals," *Harvard Law Review* 71 (1958): 593.
[52] Ibid.
[53] Ibid.
[54] Hart, *The Concept of Law*, 88.
[55] Ibid. at 89.
[56] Ibid.
[57] Ibid. at 90.

The aim thus far has not been to diminish or discredit rational choice theory or the economic analysis of law. Rather, the aim has been to cast doubt on some economists' pretentions to scientific certainty, and to challenge the claim that ethical claims can always be reduced to efficiency claims. Rational choice, behavioral economics, and economic analysis in general are tools that are (as we shall see in Chapters 8 and 9) sometimes quite useful for identifying legal problems and offering solutions. They are not, however, the only tools, and they are not always the best tools.

7.2 FOOT-STOMPING AND THE LIMITS OF ETHICAL THEORY

The preceding section argued that there is nothing in the nature of economic reasons that grant them some privileged status over ethical reasons in the context of legal analysis and reform. But Professor Manne's foot-stomping student's claim that she does not care what economics has to say about insider trading because "it's just not right" illustrates another error. There are those who would argue that considerations of efficiency are always reducible to prior ethical commitments and therefore the former can never conflict with or challenge the latter. Others have held that conflicts between expedience and morality can arise, but when they do, moral obligations always trump. But the following sections show that ethical theories have their explanatory and normative limits as well, and it would be a mistake to rely on such theories in analyzing and reforming the law of insider trading (or any other problem) to the exclusion of economics and other evaluative tools.

7.3 ENLIGHTENMENT MORAL THEORIES (DEONTOLOGY AND CONSEQUENTIALISM)

Historically, Western liberal jurisprudence has been informed by two competing Enlightenment moral theories: deontology and consequentialism.[58]

7.3.1 *Introduction to Deontology*

The idea that moral principles must take precedence over considerations of prudence or efficiency has been around as long as there has been a belief in some objective moral order, but it finds its most extreme expression in deontological moral theory. As the name suggests,[59] deontology is a duty-based theory. A central premise shared by deontological theories is that there are certain things we as

---

[58] Some of the following summary of deontological and consequentialist moral theories first appeared in John P. Anderson, "Greed, Envy, and the Criminalization of Insider Trading," *Utah Law Review* 2014 (2014): 28–35.

[59] The word "deontology" derives from the Greek words deon (duty) and logos (the science of). Peter Angeles, *Dictionary of Philosophy* (New York: Harper & Row Publishers, Inc. 1981): 60.

moral agents must never do, regardless of the good consequences that may result. This premise is often expressed in the Latin phrase *fiat justitia ruat caelum*, meaning "let justice be done though the heavens fall."[60] The philosopher Immanuel Kant offered the first modern expression of this moral absolutism.[61] He is also the most important deontological theorist. It therefore pays to summarize his position.

According to Kant, if morality does demand that we act in certain ways "though the heavens fall," then its command must be universal and absolute. And, for Kant, to even consider the concept of such a command is to immediately apprehend what it contains. For, as universal, it contains no empirical and therefore contingent conditions (e.g., it cannot be motivated by our desires or caprice). There is "nothing remaining in it but the universality of law as such to which the maxim of the action should conform."[62] Consequently, there can be only one categorical imperative: "Act only according to that maxim by which you can at the same time will that it should become universal law."[63] In other words, one should never act on a reason everyone else could not also act on at the same time without contradiction. This is commonly referred to as the "universal law" formulation of Kant's categorical imperative. The universal law formulation makes explicit the commonsense appeal to fairness that is implicit in the familiar question, "What if everyone were to do that?" If *everyone* could not do it without destroying the good that is sought, then so acting would be to single oneself out as deserving of special treatment without justification.[64]

Kant offered other articulations of the categorical imperative as well. Insofar as persons have the capacity to exercise their practical reason to set their own ends without external influence, each of us is a law unto herself. This recognition yields the second, or "end-in-oneself," formulation of the categorical imperative: "Act so that you treat humanity . . . always as an end and never as a means only."[65] In other words, never act in a way that uses others for purposes they themselves would reject. The end-in-oneself formulation emphasizes that, as rational agents, we all enjoy absolute moral worth or dignity that cannot be purchased in the name of private

---

[60] Paul Edwards (ed.), *The Encyclopedia of Philosophy*, (New York: Macmillian Publishing Co. and the Free Press, 1972): 343.

[61] See generally Immanuel Kant, *The Foundations of the Metaphysics of Morals and What Is Enlightenment?*, 2d ed., Lewis White Beck (trans.) (London: McMillian Publishing Co., 1785, 1990).

[62] Ibid. at 37–38.

[63] Ibid. at 38.

[64] Kant's universal law formulation of the categorical imperative is often identified with the "Golden Rule": do unto others as you would have done unto yourself. This is a mistake. For example, as it is typically articulated, the Golden Rule has no answer to the masochist who wants to torture others. See, e.g., Fred Feldman, "Kantian Ethics," in Louis P. Pojman (ed.), *Ethical Theory: Classical and Contemporary Readings* (Belmont, CA: Wadsworth Publishing, 1989): 266.

[65] Kant, *The Foundations of the Metaphysics of Morals*, 46.

expedience or social exigency. It should be noted that although Kant offered more than one version of the categorical imperative, he claimed they are "fundamentally only so many formulas of the very same law, and each of them united the others in itself."[66] Presumably, the intended advantage of the different articulations was to facilitate apprehension of the moral law.

So how is the categorical imperative applied in practice? Consider one of Kant's own examples. If someone needs to borrow money but does not have the means of repayment, the categorical imperative would preclude her from borrowing money on the promise of repayment. Applying the universal law formulation, if one considers whether the maxim "I will borrow money that I need without the intention to repay it" can be generalized to the form of a law, then it becomes apparent it cannot be so generalized without contradiction. As Kant explains,

> the universality of a law which says that anyone who believes himself to be in need could promise what he pleased with the intention of not fulfilling it would make the promise itself and the end to be accomplished by it impossible; no one would believe what was promised to him but would only laugh at any such assertion as vain pretense.[67]

The universalization of such a maxim into law would involve a contradiction in that the conditions of the promise contained in the maxim would preclude the possibility of such a promise and could not therefore be willed consistently.

This maxim would also violate the end-in-oneself formulation because making a false promise to induce a loan fails to respect the autonomy of the promisee. The obvious end of the promisee in the transaction is to receive repayment and interest, and he would never have agreed to enter into the loan if he knew there would be no repayment or interest. Consequently, to enter into such a loan agreement would be for the promisor to use the promisee, against his will, as a mere means of obtaining the promisor's end.

Kant contrasted the categorical imperative (which is atemporal, necessary, and absolute) with another claim on practical reason, the "hypothetical imperative."[68] Hypothetical imperatives are purely instrumental. They take the form, "if you want x, then do y."[69] This is, of course, precisely the type of imperative used in Judge Posner's rational choice theory. But notice how Kant would turn Posner's cognitive hierarchy on its head. For Kant, it is the moral imperative whose content is certain, necessary, and absolute, while the content of hypothetical imperatives is contingent and conditional. Thus, for Kant, reason will always dictate, a priori, that the moral imperative should prevail when in conflict with a hypothetical imperative.

---

[66] Ibid. at 53.
[67] Ibid. at 39.
[68] Ibid. at 415.
[69] Ibid. at 415–16.

7.3.2 *Introduction to Consequentialism*

Consequentialism is the moral-theoretical foil to deontology. Consequentialism identifies the rightness or wrongness of an act with the goodness or badness of its consequences. The exposition of any consequentialist moral theory comes in two parts: first, the theory must define the good – in other words, it must offer a criterion "for ranking overall states of affairs from best to worst from an impersonal standpoint" (giving equal weight to the interest of every person).[70] Second, once the good is defined, consequentialism holds that right action will simply be a matter of maximizing that good. Thus, for consequentialists, the "good" is morally prior to the "right." Consequentialism is a simple and compelling theory: maximize good and minimize evil. Or, as the philosopher Samuel Scheffler put it, the consequentialist's sole aim is "to make the world as good a place as possible."[71]

There are as many consequentialist moral theories as there are conceptions of the good, but utilitarianism, which defines the good in terms of happiness, is by far the most prominent.[72] When utilitarianism is applied to law, it tests the utility of legal rules and principles (rather than specific acts).[73] The principle of rule utilitarianism can be articulated as follows: "[T]he rightness or wrongness of an action is to be judged by the goodness and badness of the consequences of a rule that everyone should perform the action in like circumstances."[74] Though there are certainly affinities between the economic analysis of law and rule utilitarianism (both are arguably concerned with the maximization of happiness), the former is not grounded in the latter, and the two approaches to law can frequently conflict.[75] When such conflicts occur, the utilitarian will insist that the moral command take

---

[70] Samuel Scheffler (ed.), *Consequentialism and Its Critics* (New York: Oxford University Press, 1988): 1.

[71] Ibid.

[72] Similar to rational choice theory, there are hedonistic and nonhedonistic variants of utilitarianism. The hedonistic variants identify the good with sensual pleasure, while the nonhedonistic versions focus on the satisfaction of preferences. See, e.g., Samuel Scheffler, *The Rejection of Consequentialism: A Philosophical Investigation of the Considerations Underlying Rival Moral Conceptions* (New York: Oxford University Press, 1982): 3 n. 4.

[73] See, e.g., J. J. C. Smart and Bernard Williams, *Utilitarianism: For & Against* (New York: Cambridge University Press, 1963, 2008): 9.

[74] Ibid.

[75] See, e.g., Posner, *Overcoming the Law*, 403 ("the economic approach is neither deducible from nor completely consistent with [utilitarianism]"). Deviations will occur when rules promoting market efficiency fail to maximize social welfare – though rational choice theorists would argue this will rarely occur. See ibid. For example, conflicts will arise where economic and moral conceptions of happiness differ (e.g., preference versus hedonistic, relative versus non-relative) and conceptions of maximization differ (e.g., Pareto efficiency versus the principle of utility). Moreover, recall that utilitarianism is just one form of consequentialism. If the good is defined as something other than happiness (think, e.g., of perfectionist theories of the good), then it is easy to see how these approaches to law may come into conflict. See, e.g., Thomas Hurka, *Perfectionism* (New York: Oxford University Press, 1993): 55–60.

Moral philosophers in the Enlightenment tradition sometimes refer to this impersonal standpoint as the "moral point of view." Though deontologists and consequentialists are convinced that this impersonal standpoint tells us all we need to know about what we can and cannot do to one another, they tend to agree that it tells us almost nothing about the good life, or how to flourish as human beings. Virtue theory, by contrast, focuses exclusively on this substantive ethical question.

Virtue ethics offers a teleological (or goal-directed) normative framework whereby all things (plants, animals, rocks, trees, and associations) exist for some unique good, and the good of that thing is also its telos (goal or purpose). If the good of a knife is to cut well, then a dull knife is out of sync with its telos, and will remain so until taken to the cutler for sharpening. As the philosopher Alasdair MacIntyre put it, the virtue ethicist begins with the recognition that "there is a fundamental contrast between man-as-he-happens-to-be and man-as-he-could-be-if-he-realized-his-essential-nature."[85] The ethical task then becomes that of helping "men to understand how they make the transition from the former state to the latter."[86] Failing to make this transformation leaves persons "frustrated and incomplete."[87]

So understood, virtue ethics is committed to some authoritative account of the essential nature of human beings (the unique human good), and also of how to demonstrate the perfection of that nature in practice (the human purpose or telos). Tracing their classical intellectual roots to Aristotle's *Nichomachean Ethics* and their theistic foundations to St. Thomas Aquinas's *Summa Theologica*, most modern virtue theorists agree that the good life for human beings consists in the exercise of a finite set of well-defined virtues and the avoidance of corresponding vices.[88] Virtues are excellent traits of character (or habits of action), such as courage, temperance, generosity, honesty, justice, and wisdom. Vices, such as greed and envy (both of which play a prominent role in Chapter 10's analysis of insider trading), represent corresponding deficiencies in character. The human telos is realized by the inculcation of virtuous character traits and the promotion of action in accordance therewith.[89]

MacIntyre and the philosopher Bernard Williams criticized Enlightenment moral theories such as deontology and utilitarianism as profoundly misguided.[90]

---

[85] Alasdair MacIntyre, *After Virtue* (South Bend, IN: University of Notre Dame Press, 1981): 52.

[86] Ibid.

[87] Ibid.

[88] See, e.g., Philippa Foot, "Virtues and Vices," in *Virtues and Vices and Other Essays in Moral Philosophy* (Berkeley, CA: University of California Press, 1978): 1 (noting that "it is best when considering the virtues and vices to go back to Aristotle and Aquinas").

[89] See, e.g., Aristotle, *Nichomachean Ethics*, Terence Irwin (trans.) (Indianapolis, IN: Hackett Publishing Co., 1985), Books III-VI.

[90] Bernard Williams, *Ethics and the Limits of Philosophy* (Cambridge, MA: Harvard University Press, 1985): 174 (suggesting that the Enlightenment "morality system" is one we would be "better off without").

For both of these philosophers, ethics took a wrong turn during the Enlighten-ment,[91] and the West needs to right its course by returning to a character-based virtue theory as its dominant ethical framework.

Williams offered a number of reasons why moral theories such as deontology and utilitarianism are problematic,[92] but he was most concerned with their deliberative starting point. As noted previously, the Enlightenment moral project focuses almost exclusively on deriving principles of right and wrong from a standpoint of complete equality and impartiality. The idea is that the standpoint of equality and impartiality generates the only truly objective and purely rational principles of action because it requires that deliberators check at the door all of their contingent personal charac-teristics (desires, projects, relationships, etc.) that may permit them to place their interests over others. But Williams pointed out that Enlightenment moral philoso-phers simply took for granted that insofar as they are rational all humans can and must shed themselves of these "morally irrelevant" personal projects, passions, and concerns in ethical deliberation. Even if it were possible for a human being to deliberate after having shed herself of all the idiosyncratic desires and quirks that make her who she is (a fantastic idea in itself), what reason would she have to deliberate in this way, or to regard this standpoint (as opposed to the infinite number of other deliberative standpoints available to her) as somehow privileged or required? As Williams put it,

> The *I* of reflective practical deliberation is not required to take the result of anyone else's properly conducted deliberation as a datum, nor be committed from the outset to a harmony of everyone else's deliberations – that is to say, to making a rule from the standpoint from equality ... The *I* that stands back in reflection from my desires is still the *I* that has those desires and will, empirically and concretely, act; and it is not, simply by standing back in reflection, converted into a being whose fundamental interest lies in the harmony of all interests. It cannot, just by taking this step, acquire the motivations of justice.[93]

One acquires a genuine commitment to the categorical imperative or the principle of utility not by merely entering the impartial standpoint of equality, but by seeing that one is committed by the rest of one's contingent desires and character traits to let this standpoint of impartiality and equality color the rest of one's practical

[91] For Williams, the wrong turn may have occurred still further back with the "rationalistic metaphysics" of Socrates, Plato, and Aristotle – Williams preferring the ethical tropes offered by the Greek literature of Sophocles and Homer. See generally Bernard Williams, *Shame and Necessity* (Berkeley: University of California Press, 1993).

[92] First, moral theories adopt an "obligation-out, obligation-in" requirement that "only an obliga-tion can beat an obligation." See Williams, *Ethics and the Limits of Philosophy*, 181. Second, morality "misunderstands practical necessity, thinking it peculiar to the ethical." Ibid. at 180. Third, morality "misunderstands ethical practical necessity, thinking it peculiar to obligations." Ibid. at 196. Williams also offered a number of criticisms specific to utilitarianism, most famously that it undermines ethical integrity. See Smart and Williams, *Utilitarianism*, 77–150.

[93] Williams, *Ethics and the Limits of Philosophy*, 69.

deliberation. Some persons' practical commitments are such that once they reach this standpoint of impartiality they are forced by their own lights to stay there when reasoning about what they owe others (e.g., those with a well-developed sense of charity or justice), but others' commitments are not – and rationality alone is powerless to move someone from the latter category to the former.

Setting aside the esoteric problem of whether the moral point of view can issue objective, categorical imperatives, Williams argued that Enlightenment moral theories suffer from other, more significant problems from the standpoint of common sense. For example, the morality system has no resources to explain the phenomenon of supererogation. Some people feel ethically compelled to do more than is strictly required of them by moral law. In being more than what morality requires, supererogatory conduct is not obligatory. Nevertheless, Williams pointed out that "the agent who does such a thing may feel that he must do it, that there is no alternative for him, while at the same time recognizing that it would not be a demand on others."[94] In other words, the morality system cannot account for the very real, yet very idiosyncratic, practical necessity that drives the Mother Teresas of the world. (As we shall see in Chapter 10, the phenomenon of supererogation plays an important explanatory role in accounting for many people's ethical intuitions concerning insider trading.)

MacIntyre offered a similar argument for why Enlightenment moral theories such as deontology and utilitarianism have led to an ethical dead end. Recall MacIntyre's account of virtue ethics as offering a threefold scheme: (1) it offers a conception of "human nature in its untutored state" (man-as-he-happens-to-be); (2) it offers a conception of "human-nature-as-it-could-be-if-it-realized-its-telos"; and (3) it offers a conception of ethical precepts that if followed will move individuals or societies from (1) to (2). According to MacIntyre, each of the three elements of this scheme is intelligible only by reference to the other two.[95] MacIntyre argued that, by issuing their moral commands exclusively from the impartial point of view, Enlightenment moral theories dispense with the notion of a single shared human telos. In doing so, they are left with only (1) a conception of human beings as they are, and (3) a set of rules concerning what they need to do to treat one another equally and impartially. What is missing is (2) – a thick conception of the essential human good (an ideal, substantive conception of the human ideal) that offers a *reason* for treating one another equally and impartially – a telos to work toward as an individual and a society.

Both Williams's and MacIntyre's critiques of the Enlightenment moral theories emphasize the fact that there is much more to our ethical lives than how we treat one another. Our personal pursuits of self-perfection – our striving toward the realization of our ethical, artistic, religious, physical, and intellectual ideals – can

---

[94] Ibid. at 188–89.
[95] MacIntyre, *After Virtue*, 53.

be every bit as practically important to us (and sometimes more important) as the strict moral duties we owe one another. Deontology and consequentialism are formalistic in their practical commands, and offer little if any substantive guidance with respect to these broader practical concerns – indeed, these Enlightenment moral theories may sometimes obstruct and obscure these projects. Virtue theory, by contrast, in offering a comprehensive, thick conception of the human good (comprising the ideal balance of ethical, artistic, and intellectual virtues) is far better equipped to define and arbitrate among these competing values with an eye toward the human ideal, our shared telos.

7.4.1 Some Problems for Virtue Theory and Introduction to Mill's Harm Principle

But whatever the advantages of virtue theory for guiding individuals in their private pursuits of self-perfection, the focus of this book is on the law, and specifically on what ethical theory may have to say about evaluating and reforming the law of insider trading. Virtue theory may have served as an adequate source for law in the West so long as everyone agreed on the essential nature of human beings – as they did, more or less, until the Protestant Reformation. But Enlightenment moral theory, with its relative neutrality concerning comprehensive conceptions of the good life, developed in an attempt to address the new reality of ever-increasing religious, cultural, and ethnic pluralism in the wake of the sixteenth-century Wars of Religion. The old Aristotelean conception of the law as a tool of ethical inculcation and character development[96] then gave way to the Enlightenment conception of the law as authoritative only insofar as it can justify the use of the state's coercive power in terms everyone in a pluralistic society can accept, regardless of their comprehensive conception of human nature and the human good. In sum, after the Wars of Religion, Western liberalism developed based on the agreement that individual pursuits of self-perfection were a private matter, involving beliefs and commitments concerning human well-being upon which reasonable people might disagree. The principal social value or good became the freedom or liberty to pursue these private projects, so long as they did not cross into or interfere with others' peaceful pursuits. Western liberal jurisprudence developed as a means of protecting and enforcing this neutrality – based on the now shared recognition that individual liberty and mutual respect of one another as free and equal citizens are core political values, and most of what we expect of one another under the law.

In the criminal law, this Western liberal neutrality with respect to private pursuits of self-perfection has been preserved by a traditional adherence to the "Harm Principle" first expressed by the British philosopher John Stuart Mill. Under this principle,

---

[96] For Aristotle, the state has one goal: it makes no difference whether one is five years old or seventy; if one has not attained the human good, it will be the responsibility of the state to direct one toward it through habituation. See, e.g., Aristotle, *Nichomachean Ethics*, Book X, 293.

the sole end for which mankind are warranted, individually or collectively, in interfering with the liberty of action of any of their number, is self-protection. That the only purpose for which power can be rightfully exercised over any member of a civilized community, against his will, is to prevent harm to others. His own good, either physical or moral, is not a sufficient warrant. He cannot rightfully be compelled to do or forbear because it will be better for him to do so, because it will make him happier, because, in the opinions of others, to do so would be wise, or even right. These are good reasons for remonstrating with him, or reasoning with him, or persuading him, or entreating him, but not for compelling him, or visiting him with any evil in case he do otherwise. To justify that, the conduct from which it is desired to deter him, must be calculated to produce evil to some one else. The only part of the conduct of any one, for which he is amenable to society, is that which concerns others. In the part which merely concerns himself, his independence is, of right, absolute. Over himself, over his own body and mind, the individual is sovereign.[97]

So understood, the law's limited focus on the question of what we owe to others (and therefore reliance on other-regarding moral theories such as deontology and utilitarianism) is not to diminish or discount concern over individual pursuits of self-perfection (the principal focus of virtue theory), but rather to secure a free space for those projects in an age of reasonable pluralism.

Of course, the application of Mill's Harm Principle has never been perfect in Western liberal democracies. Many moralistic laws concerning purely self-regarding or consensual conduct (sodomy, interracial and same-sex marriage, polygamy, incest, pornography, drug and alcohol use, etc.) have at one time or another been on the books (and some remain).[98] Nevertheless, the vector of Western liberal jurisprudential history trends decisively toward diminishing rather than increasing the law's influence in these areas.[99] It is unlikely, however, that all such moralistic considerations will ever be altogether eliminated from the reach of legal sanctions.

---

[97] John Stuart Mill, "On Liberty," in *Three Essays* (New York: Oxford University Press, 1987): 15.

[98] And some jurists have suggested that at least a few such moralistic laws are helpful, and perhaps even necessary, to maintaining stability in even the most liberal societies. For example, Lord Patrick Devlin challenged the liberalization of Britain's sodomy laws in the 1950s by arguing that laws regulating sexual morality (and sin in general) were essential to maintaining a society's moral structure. For Devlin, without a shared moral structure, a society simply cannot endure: "If men and women try to create a society in which there is no fundamental agreement about good and evil they will fail; if, having based it on common agreement, the argument goes, the society will disintegrate." Patrick Devlin, "The Enforcement of Morals," in David M. Adams (ed.), *Philosophical Problems in the Law*, 4th ed. (Belmont, CA: Wadsworth Publishing, 2005): 205. Devlin concluded that it is therefore "not possible to set theoretical limits to the power of the State to legislate against immorality." Ibid.

[99] See, e.g., Griswold v. Connecticut, 381 U.S. 479 (1965) (state's ban on the use of contraceptives violates right to marital privacy); Loving v. Virginia, 388 U.S. 1 (1967) (Fourteenth Amendment protects freedom to marry someone of another race); Lawrence v. Texas, 539 U.S. 558 (2003) (striking down sodomy laws as violating substantive due process under the Fourteenth Amendment); Obergefell v. Hodges, 576 U.S. __ (2015) (guaranteeing same-sex couples a constitutional right to marry).

Moreover, even liberal societies cannot avoid the question of what kind of citizens their laws and institutions are producing – in the context of education, social programs, and, yes, financial regulation. Concern over the vices of greed and envy persists, and, as shown in Chapter 10, remains relevant to the public debate over the law of insider trading and its reform. Such appeals to virtue theory should, however, always be measured against Mill's Harm Principal, and the liberal jurisprudential commitments to neutrality and toleration.

*****

Imagine implementing a legal regime without considering its economic impact. Then imagine adopting a legal regime by considering only its economic impact, without taking into consideration the ways in which it will affect our rights and duties (what we owe one another) from the impartial moral standpoint of freedom and equality. Finally, imagine implementing or reforming a legal regime without taking into consideration the types of habits it may form in citizens – the kind of people it might create.

One aim of this chapter has been to introduce the evaluative theories that will be employed in the analysis of insider trading in subsequent chapters. A second aim has been to emphasize a point that is perhaps obvious to most, but that often gets lost or obscured: namely that there can be no unified theory of explanation, justification, or reform of the law. The law draws from multiple values latent within the public political culture – values concerning the efficient, the right, and the good. As we look ahead to the daunting task of reforming the insider trading regime in the United States, the most promising approach will be to analyze the practice of insider trading through the lenses of each of these values. And the expectation is that the best insider trading reform program will be the one that strikes the best balance among them.

8

The Economics of Insider Trading

The scholarly debate concerning the economic impact of insider trading on individual traders and the market has been vigorous. This chapter summarizes many of the most important aspects of this debate. It will consider potential economic harms, such as insider trading's impact on counterparties, its effect on investor confidence and market liquidity, and the potential perverse incentives and moral hazards that insider trading might create. Potential economic benefits will also be considered, such as increased price accuracy, real-time access to information, insider trading's market-smoothing effect, and its potential as an efficient form of corporate compensation.[1]

8.1 IMPACT ON COUNTERPARTIES: INVESTORS VERSUS SPECULATORS

Among the early rationales offered by the SEC and commentators in support of the prohibition of insider trading pursuant to Exchange Act Section 10(b) was the protection of the counterparty to a securities trade from economic harm as a result of the insider's information advantage. As the SEC stated in In re Cady, Roberts & Co., "If purchasers on an exchange had available material information known by a selling insider, we may assume that their investment judgment would be affected and their decision whether to buy might accordingly be modified. Consequently, any sales by the insider must await disclosure of the information."[2]

---

[1] Some of the following analysis of the economic impact of insider trading first appeared in John P. Anderson, "Greed, Envy, and the Criminalization of Insider Trading," *Utah Law Review* 2014 (2014): 7–17.

[2] In re Cady Roberts & Co., 40 S.E.C. 907, 914 (1961). See also Morris Mendelson, "The Economics of Insider Trading Reconsidered," *University of Pennsylvania Law Review* 117 (1969): 482 ("Since the information by itself would have caused an increase in the price of the stock, the shareholders who sold their stock to the insiders would have shared the benefits

The idea that any securities trade motivated by material nonpublic information must inevitably injure the counterparty appears uncontroversial at first blush. Absent the informational asymmetry, a counterparty would have certainly demanded either a higher or lower price, depending on whether she is selling or buying. Professor Henry Manne and others, however, have argued persuasively that this proposition is not so straightforward, especially in the context of anonymous exchanges. According to Manne, the relevant question is not what the counterparty to the transaction would do if she enjoyed informational parity, but "whether the person wanting to sell shares for exogenous reasons would behave differently before the information has been disclosed if insiders are or are not allowed to trade on the information."[3] Of course, every participant in the market would prefer complete information, but it makes sense to claim insider trading itself results in an economic harm to the counterparty only if it can be shown that the presence or absence of insider trading in the relevant security would have affected the counterparty's trade in some way.[4] Manne argued that there are both advantages and disadvantages to counterparties to insider trades, depending on whether one is a long-term *investor* or a *speculator*.[5]

Imagine a mining company's stock is selling at $20 a share when it makes a big strike. Upon disclosure, news of the strike will send the firm's stock to $30 a share, but the company keeps the news confidential while it secures mineral leases on adjacent properties. If insiders at the mining company begin trading on this material nonpublic information, the firm's shares will, all things remaining-equal, slowly approach (but not reach) $30 a share.[6] If, however, the firm's insiders do not trade on this information, the firm's shares will, all things remaining equal, instantaneously jump from $20 to $30 at the moment of the announcement.[7] Using this example, the counterparty seller who is an investor will benefit from the insider-created uptrend in price. This is because investors buy stock to hold over the long term. Their decisions to sell are typically driven by timing (for example, their

---

from the price increase with the continuing holders if the insider had not been buying."); William H. Painter, "Manne, Insider Trading and the Stock Market," *George Washington Law Review* 35 (1966): 149 (asserting that the "intelligent long term investor" is "hurt badly" by insider trading because "he is deprived of information obviously relevant to whether he should sell").

[3] Henry G. Manne, "Insider Trading and Property Rights in New Information," *Cato Journal* 4 (1985): 934.

[4] Henry G. Manne, *Insider Trading and the Stock Market* (New York: The Free Press, 1966): 93.

[5] Ibid. at 102. See also David D. Haddock and Jonathan R. Macey, "A Coasian Model of Insider Trading," *Northwestern University Law Review* 80 (1987): 1449.

[6] This is exactly what happened in S.E.C. v. Texas Gulf Sulphur, 401 F.2d 833 (2d Cir. 1968). Texas Gulf Sulphur's shares traded at approximately $18 at the time of the strike in November 1963. The strike was officially announced on April 16 of the following year. Between November and April 16, insider trading pushed the firm's stock price up to around $30 a share. The firm's shares closed at $36 dollars on the day of the announcement.

[7] See, e.g., Stephen Bainbridge, "Insider Trading: An Overview," *Encyclopedia of Law and Economics* (Cheltenham: Edward Elgar Publishing, 2000): § 5650.

retirement, a child going to college, the need for diversification, etc.), not price. Suppose the insider-generated uptick in the mining company's shares pushed the stock's price to $25 a share on the day before the public announcement. If the investor happens to sell the mining company's shares on that day (say because that is the day her daughter's college tuition is due), then she benefits $5 a share by the insiders trading in the other direction. Were it not for the insiders buying, she would be selling on that date at $20 a share. The result is just the opposite for the counterparty who is a speculator. A speculator is one who buys or sells based on price – whether for technical reasons or because, like all "prudent" gamblers, they have predetermined the price at which they will take their profits and run. Suppose, continuing with our example, the insider's counterparty is a speculator who sold shares in the mining company the day before the announcement because the price hit $25 per share and they had pre-committed to sell at that price. That speculator loses $5 per share when the announcement is made the following day.

Thus, assuming there is enough insider-generated volume to materially affect the price of a stock,[8] the insider trader's counterparty wins if she is an investor and loses if she is a speculator. Of course, the realities of today's anonymous exchanges are such that the identity of the counterparty (or counterparties) to any given transaction is virtually unknowable. There would, however, be a significant irony in justifying the prohibition of insider trading strictly on the negative economic impact upon the speculator, particularly under Section 10(b) of the Securities Exchange Act. This is because, as Professor Steve Thel has noted, one of the principal objectives of the Exchange Act in general, and Section 10(b) in particular, was to reign in the excesses of speculators to better protect investors.

In 1909, New York Governor Charles Evans Hughes appointed a committee to, among other things, propose market reforms to address the problem of increases in market speculation. This report, which would later influence the drafters of the Exchange Act, defined speculation as trading based on price and explained that while market speculation may sometimes be legitimate, it often does "an almost incalculable amount of evil. In its nature it is in the same class with gambling upon the racetrack or at the roulette table," but it is far worse because it is practiced "on a vastly larger scale."[9] Indeed, market speculation was often cited among the principal evils causing the market collapse of 1929. Concerned by this, one of Congress's

---

[8] Though *Texas Gulf Sulphur* offers one example of insider trading that seemed to have significantly impacted the price of a stock, Professor Stephen Bainbridge has argued that this is probably the exception rather than the rule. According to Bainbridge, while "derivatively informed trading can affect price it functions slowly and sporadically," and it would only rarely produce the kind of price shift reflected in the fictional mining company scenario laid out in the preceding paragraph. Bainbridge, "Insider Trading," 5650. If insider volume is minimal and the stock's price does not change, then that trading would seem to have no impact on the insider's counterparty whatsoever (investor or speculator).

[9] Steve Thel, "The Original Conception of Section 10(b) of the Securities Exchange Act," *Stanford Law Review* 42 (1990): 398 (quoting the Hughes Committee Report).

principal aims in adopting Section 10(b) of the Exchange Act was to empower the SEC "to regulate any practice that might contribute to speculation in securities."[10] So, since the speculator counterparties to insider traders lose, and investor counterparties to insider traders win, one might expect that the SEC would interpret any ambiguities in Section 10(b) to favor insider trading as a deterrent to speculation and promotion of long-term investment. The story, however, gets more complicated when considering all contemporaneous traders in the stock.

If we expand our focus from the actual counterparty to the insider's transaction to include all investors and speculators trading at the same time as insiders, we discover that any investors trading *with* the insiders will lose. Sticking with the mining company example introduced previously, any investor buying the firm's stock the day before the announcement will buy the stock at $25 when, without the insider-generated uptick in price, she would have paid only $20. (She loses $5 a share.) Similarly, any speculator who trades alongside the insider on the day before the announcement because she was just waiting for the price to hit $25 to buy will win. She will get the benefit of the immediate uptick to $30 after the announcement when, without the insider-generated price increase, she would have remained standing on the sidelines. (She makes $5 a share.)

In sum, to assess whether the actual counterparty to a specific insider trade was made worse off, one would want to know whether the counterparty was an investor or a speculator. But the realities of the modern exchanges are such that the identity of the counterparty (or counterparties) to a transaction is virtually unknowable. More broadly, to determine the net economic impact on all of those trading *against* insiders during a period of insider buying, one would have to know whether the total volume of speculator selling due to the insider-generated price movement was greater than the volume of investors selling irrespective of price. Broader still, to assess the total economic impact on all traders (investors and speculators, whether buying or selling) in shares of the relevant equity during a period of insider trading, one would have to (1) net the volume of speculator buys against speculator sells, (2) net the volume of investor buys against investor sells, and then net the results of (1) and (2). Modern exchanges do not, however, track this information, and it is difficult to imagine how they might.

For these reasons, even those who remain convinced that insider trading has a negative impact on market efficiency tend to agree with Manne and his followers that the "harm to counterparty" argument is a nonstarter.[11] For example,

---

[10] Ibid. at 385.

[11] Professor William Wang has agreed that it is impossible to determine whom the victim of insider trading is in every instance but has nevertheless insisted that all incidents of insider trading harm *someone*, pursuant to his "Law of Conservation of Securities." See, e.g., William K. S. Wang, "Trading on Material Nonpublic Information on Impersonal Stock Markets: Who Is Harmed, and Who Can Sue Whom under SEC Rule 10b–5?," *Southern California Law Review* 54 (1981): 1217. This argument is addressed at length in Chapter 9.

Professor Homer Kripke grudgingly admitted that "[i]n a narrow sense, Manne has been right in saying that insider trading is a victimless crime (at least when done not face to face but anonymously in public markets)."[12] For, "no one knows whether those hurt by insider trading are more numerous than those hurt by trading before inside facts have impacted the market, so that they are price-takers taking a faulty price."[13]

8.2 THE PROBLEM OF ADVERSE SELECTION

As explained in the previous section, there is no quantifiable risk of harm to counterparties from insider trading. There are, however, other ways in which unregulated insider trading might negatively impact securities markets.

One of the principal economic arguments against insider trading rests on the concern that, if insider trading is left unchecked by regulation, then market makers will be forced to increase the spread between their bid and ask prices to protect against "adverse selection" by insiders.[14] The market maker's bid-ask spread (the difference in the prices at which she will buy and sell a given security) represents the "price for immediacy" and a function of "the cost of trading and the liquidity of a market."[15] As Professor Stanislav Dolgopolov has explained, "The essence of the adverse selection model is that because of order imbalances and the difficulty of sustaining a liquid market only with matching, a liquidity provider has to transact with his own inventory and thus bears the risk of consistently buying 'high' from and selling 'low' to insiders."[16] Because market makers cannot distinguish between those who are trading on superior information from those who are not, the concern is that they will be forced to recoup these losses from the general trading public (investors and speculators) by increasing the bid-ask spread.[17] The increased spread therefore operates as a "tax" on traders; investors and speculators are forced to pay a premium to buy and sell stocks regularly traded by insiders.[18] The ripple effect does not end there. An increased bid-ask spread will also decrease a stock's liquidity, which is a function of the transaction costs of trading. And theoretical and empirical evidence suggests that decreased liquidity will in turn increase the issuer's cost of capital

---

[12] Homer Kripke, "Manne's Insider Trading Thesis and Other Failures of Conservative Economics," *Cato Journal* 4 (1985): 953.

[13] Ibid. at 953–54.

[14] See Stanislav Dolgopolov, "Insider Trading and the Bid-Ask Spread: A Critical Evaluation of Adverse Selection in Market Making," *Capital University Law Review* 33 (2004): 104–05.

[15] Ibid. at 89.

[16] Ibid. at 98.

[17] See, e.g., Jonathan R. Macey, *Insider Trading: Economics, Politics, and Policy* (Washington, DC: The AEI Press, 1991): 14.

[18] See Henry Manne, "The Case for Insider Trading," *Wall Street Journal* (March 17, 2003): A.14.

(hampering expansion, research, etc.) and lower the firm's market value.[19] The result is that investors, speculators, and issuers all lose.

But while the problem of adverse selection makes sense in theory, the empirical support is inconclusive. A number of empirical studies have concluded there is likely a correlation between insider trading and increased bid-ask spreads in the United States and abroad.[20] There are, however, also studies showing no correlation.[21] Even if a correlation were confirmed, its significance is also disputed. Surprisingly, market makers themselves have not been among those complaining of an adverse selection problem resulting from insider trading. Indeed a spokesman for the NYSE's Specialists' Association, representing hundreds of Big Board stock specialists, was quoted as saying that "insider trading isn't an issue for its members."[22] Dolgopolov observed that such attitudes "certainly cast doubt on the adverse selection argument's validity. This may be an indication that the magnitude of widening bid-ask spreads is negligible, or that market makers can somehow benefit from observing informed trading."[23] Some have reasoned that insider trading should not matter to market makers because if insiders did not trade, other market participants with superior information (analysts and other market professionals) would simply reap the rewards denied to the insiders.[24] Indeed, Professor Jonathan Macey has argued that, given the choice, investors should prefer to trade with insiders over

---

[19] See Laura Nyantung Beny, "Insider Trading Laws and Stock Markets around the World: An Empirical Contribution to the Theoretical Law and Economics Argument," *Journal of Corporation Law* 32 (2007): 249. See also Dolgopolov, "Insider Trading and the Bid-Ask Spread," 100–01.

[20] See Dolgopolov, "Insider Trading and the Bid-Ask Spread," 144–45. See, e.g., George J. Benston and Robert L. Hagerman, "Determinants of Bid-Asked Spreads in the Over-the-Counter Market," *Journal of Financial Economics* 1 (1974): 362–63 (finding that intense insider trading is positively correlated to an increased bid-ask spread in the over-the-counter market). See also Hans Stoll, "Dealer Inventory Behavior: An Empirical Investigation of Nasdaq Stocks," *Journal of Finance and Quantitative Analysis* 11 (1976): 367 (concluding that the market maker's "losses must be recouped (at the expense of other investors) by setting a wide enough spread"); Dale Morse and Neal Ushman, "The Effect of Information Announcements on the Market Microstructure," *The Accounting Review* 58 (1983): 257 (documenting widening spreads on the days characterized by large price fluctuations and concluding that this could reflect attempts to protect against losses for those enjoying an advantage based on nonpublic information); Uptal Bhattacharya and Hazem Daouk, "The World Price of Insider Trading," *Journal of Finance* 57 (2002): 76 (drawing on the theory of adverse selection to explain a purported correlation between the cost of equity and the enforcement of insider trading regulations in markets around the world).

[21] Dolgopolov, "Insider Trading and the Bid-Ask Spread," 144–45.

[22] Ibid. at 109 (quoting Suzanne McGee, "Where Have the Inside Traders Gone? Options Markets Are Their New Home," *Wall Street Journal* (April 23, 1997): C20).

[23] Ibid.

[24] See Dennis W. Carlton and Daniel R. Fischel, "The Regulation of Insider Trading," *Stanford Law Review* 35 (1983): 880 ("[T]he only effect a ban on insider trading might have is that those with better access to information, such as brokers, would reap some of the gains from inside information. While this may be inefficient because brokers can become informed only at a higher cost, the informed-uninformed trader problem remains.").

market professionals because at least when one trades with insiders, the benefits stay within the firm.[25] According to Macey, when

> market professionals are the next-best information processors, from the shareholder's perspective, a ban on insider trading is the equivalent of a rule requiring insiders to throw money out of a window of the firm's corporate headquarters. The market professionals who happen to be passing by at the time the money flutters down will certainly benefit. But shareholders who have other productive uses for their time have no chance of grabbing any of these funds and inevitably lose.[26]

Moreover, Dolgopolov has pointed out that both "market professionals, who, as frequent traders, could greatly benefit from lower transaction costs, and corporations, which could lower the cost of capital by increasing their shares' liquidity," have virtually ignored the adverse selection problem.[27] This, according to Dolgopolov, has left "the SEC as the only key player in the securities markets that consistently utilize[s] the argument."[28]

8.3 PERVERSE INCENTIVES

Unregulated insider trading may also negatively impact markets due to the perverse incentives it creates for management.[29] First, some have argued that the practice of insider trading will have the net effect of delaying the release of material information to the public.[30] The logic has been that insiders will need time to exploit their information (locate and free up capital, make trades, inform friends or associates, etc.) prior to its publication.[31] There is little doubt that insider traders share this perverse incentive. There is, however, dispute concerning the length of delay that can be expected based on these considerations.

For example, even after a material fact is learned and undisputed within a company, preparation for public disclosure of that information is itself a time-consuming process: drafts of releases must be prepared and then reviewed by management and counsel. One would expect this period to offer insiders ample opportunity to trade on the information without affecting the timing of its release.

---

[25] Macey, *Insider Trading*, 15.
[26] Ibid.
[27] Dolgopolov, "Insider Trading and the Bid-Ask Spread," 109–10.
[28] Ibid. at 110.
[29] Professor Laura Nyantung Beny has noted that "[p]roponents of insider trading regulation emphasize its rent-extraction potential, suggesting that insider trading might simply be an inefficient private benefit of control that accrues to managers and other insiders at agency expense." Beny, "Insider Trading Laws and Stock Markets around the World," 243.
[30] See Mendelson, "The Economics of Insider Trading Reconsidered," 489.
[31] See Roy A. Schotland, "Unsafe at Any Price: A Reply to Manne, Insider Trading and the Stock Market," *Virginia Law Review* 53 (1967): 1448–49.

For, in any event, it can be expected that the time necessary to make the arrangements for market transactions and to inform others will be measured in minutes or hours rather than days. Moreover, insiders will also have every incentive to act quickly to beat other insiders to the punch and minimize the risk that the information will be leaked to the general public and become worthless.[32] More still, insiders will not just be motivated to act quickly, but once they have taken their positions, they will have every incentive to speed up the public release of the pertinent inside information to secure a profit that grows less certain with every passing minute the relevant information is not disclosed. So long as the information is not released, the insider runs the risk that an intervening event will counterbalance information traded on and thereby erode what would otherwise be a certain profit.[33] Finally, given that perfect enforcement of a ban on insider trading cannot be expected, such regulation may have the unintended consequence of itself delaying the release of information. By forcing insiders to conspire and act covertly, such regulation may create its own incentive for insiders to push for a delay in release.[34]

Second, because trading profits can be made on bad news as well as good, insider trading generates a perverse incentive for management to become less concerned with the firm's profitability than with its market volatility.[35] At the extreme, insider trading creates the moral hazard that management may actually attempt to create bad news to profit from it. There are, however, a number of countervailing considerations that may lessen these risks. First, the fear insiders will intentionally create bad news to profit by selling the company's shares short ignores the myriad incentives against such conduct. For example, most insiders in a position to make money on information will want to maintain that position. Producing good news will provide opportunities for trading profits while at the same time securing that insider's place at the firm. By contrast, causing the firm to perform poorly is certain to put an insider's position at the firm at risk.[36] In addition, insiders will rarely be in a position to single-handedly affect the price of the firm's shares. Important firm decisions are almost always made in teams. While it is easy to convince a team to make a good decision for the firm, it will be difficult to convince the team to approve a bad

[32] See Henry G. Manne, "Insider Trading and the Law Professors," *Vanderbilt Law Review* 23 (1970): 553.

[33] See ibid. at 568.

[34] See Harold Demsetz, "Perfect Competition, Regulation, and the Stock Market," in Henry G. Manne (ed.), *Economic Policy and the Regulation of Corporate Securities* (Washington, DC: AEI Publishing, 1969): 14 ("By increasing the cost of using the direct and obvious methods of capturing some of the value of this information, the SEC will encourage insiders to rely in greater degree on the less direct and more time-consuming methods.").

[35] See, e.g., Saul Levmore, "Securities and Secrets: Insider Trading and the Law of Contracts," *Virginia Law Review* 68 (1982): 149.

[36] See Manne, *Insider Trading and the Stock Market*, 150.

decision. Indeed, some have suggested that even if all of the team members set out to collude in bringing the price down to secure trading profits, the benefits of whistle-blowing to any one member (bonus, promotion, etc.) will almost always outweigh any benefits from continuing participation in the scheme.[37]

8.4 IMPACT ON EMPLOYER OR ISSUER IN THE CONTEXT OF MISAPPROPRIATION TRADING

The principal justification for insider trading liability under the misappropriation theory (and arguably under the classical theory) is that material nonpublic information is property, and the unauthorized use of that property for trading deprives the owner of its "right of exclusive use."[38] So understood, trading on misappropriated material nonpublic information is a form of theft. Whether the information is misappropriated directly from the issuer or from some third party, it is virtually certain that such trading (like all theft) imposes costs on the rightful owner. If it did not impose some cost, then there would be no reason for the owner of the information to restrict its use. There would be no need to misappropriate the information in the first place.

Of course, in some cases the only reason a firm might refuse to authorize an individual to trade on its material nonpublic information may be from fear of civil or criminal liability under the existing insider trading enforcement regime. If this is the firm's only reason for withholding assent to trade, then an employee's subsequent trading (or tipping) in defiance of the firm's wishes may still impose costs on the firm (civil or criminal liability, the costs of defending against such liability, or the loss of a good employee due to individual liability), but these are not costs that would justify the regulation of insider trading in the first place. In any event, it goes without saying that firms will often have *real business reasons* for refusing to license employees or others to trade on their material nonpublic information. For example, a planned tender offer or merger may become more expensive or even impracticable due to insider-driven price movement in the target or partner. These are real costs to firms that can be directly attributed to insider trading, and can therefore affect shareholder value. The nature and magnitude of these costs will, of course, vary from firm to firm, and from circumstance to circumstance. They are therefore difficult to quantify other than on a case-by-case basis. It is nevertheless a theoretical certainty that such costs exist.[39]

---

[37] See Carlton and Fischel, "The Regulation of Insider Trading," 873–74.
[38] United States v. O'Hagan, 521 U.S. 642, 654 (1997).
[39] See, e.g., Ian Ayers and Steven Choi, "Internalizing Outsider Trading," *Michigan Law Review* 101 (2002): 313 (noting that insider trading that proceeds with the issuer's consent is presumptively more efficient than outsider trading that proceeds without the traded firm's consent).

8.5 IMPACT ON MARKET CONFIDENCE

The promotion of investor confidence in the securities markets is among the most often-cited policy goals served by the civil and criminal regulation of insider trading. It is also the most difficult to articulate and prove. As the Supreme Court noted in *United States v. O'Hagan*, "Although informational disparity is inevitable in the securities markets, investors likely would hesitate to venture their capital in a market where trading based on misappropriated nonpublic information is unchecked by law."[40] The claim is that investors and speculators will stand on the sideline, refusing to participate because the perceived risks or costs of trading against insiders are too great. In other words, in addition to any inefficiencies directly attributable to the actual practice of insider trading, the decrease in participation resulting from the public's mere perception that insider trading is taking place will itself have the harmful effect of reduced market liquidity and a higher cost of capital.

At least two claims seem implicit in the argument. The first claim is that the general public (or a large portion of it) shares the perception that insider trading is economically harmful or ethically wrong. The second claim is that this perception leads a nontrivial number of potential market participants to stand on the sidelines of markets where insider trading is not regulated, which in turn negatively impacts share liquidity, cost of capital, and shareholder value.

Because the market confidence argument depends crucially on public attitudes and the extent to which attitudes discourage market conduct, it is notoriously difficult to prove or disprove.[41] Few polls have been taken to gauge the public's perception of insider trading, and those that have been taken are inconclusive. For example, a 1986 *Business Week* poll taken in the aftermath of the Ivan Boesky insider trading scandal found that while "Wall Street may be in a tizzy ... Americans don't seem to be particularly upset with the spreading insider trading scandal." The study found that 67 percent of Americans were convinced it is "common" for people on Wall Street to engage in insider trading. And while 66 percent thought insider trading should be illegal, 55 percent said they themselves would trade on an inside tip.[42] A more recent study found a similar ambivalence in popular attitudes. It found that while most people seem "to have strong intuitions that insider trading is wrong, they [are] unable to isolate the victim in one case from the victim in another."[43] The authors concluded that the study's results suggest "that professionals and the lay

[40] *O'Hagan*, 521 U.S. at 658.

[41] Many of the following concerns regarding the market confidence claim first appeared in John P. Anderson, "Insider Trading and the Myth of Market Confidence," *Washington University Journal of Law and Policy* 56 (2018).

[42] "Business Week/Harris Poll: Outsiders Aren't Upset by Insider Trading," *Business Week* (Dec. 8, 1986): 34.

[43] Stuart P. Green and Mathew B. Kugler, "When Is It Wrong to Trade Stocks on the Basis of Non-Public Information? Public Views of the Morality of Insider Trading," *Fordham Urban Law Journal* 39 (2011): 484.

public are united in their confusion over the rationale for prohibiting insider trading."[44] Neither study offers strong support for the Supreme Court's claim that "investors likely would hesitate to venture their capital in a market where [insider trading] is unchecked by law." The studies seem to suggest instead that (1) the majority of people think that insider trading remains prevalent despite being regulated; (2) though most people think it is wrong, they cannot identify the harm; and (3) they would trade on inside information themselves if they had the chance.

Even if it is assumed that the public perceives insider trading to be a risk, does it keep them on the market sideline in nontrivial numbers? The limited empirical evidence that exists on this point is inconclusive. One way to test the theory would be to track the market's reaction to headline-catching insider trading events or enforcement actions. For example, if the market confidence theory holds, one would expect investors to be fleeing the market in droves after *Business Week* ran an April 1985 cover story titled "The Epidemic of Insider Trading: The SEC Is Fighting a Losing Battle to Halt Stock Market Abuses."[45] It turns out, however, that the Dow Jones Industrial Average (DJIA) jumped 27.66 percent in 1985, its largest yearly gain in ten years.[46] Similarly, the market confidence theory would presumably predict a negative market reaction when news broke of Ivan Boesky's insider trading charges in November 1986 – at that point the biggest insider trading case in history. Nevertheless, as one scholar noted, "while the market took a one-day dip, it quickly recovered all of those losses and more, suggesting little concern with Boesky's" tens of millions of dollars in insider trading profits.[47] In fact, shortly after the case went public, the chairman of the SEC "assured Congress that the Boesky revelations had an insignificant effect on the market."[48] This seems to have been true. For almost immediately after news of the Boesky scandal hit, the US stock market began its epic bull run of 1987.

All of this data could, however, be interpreted differently. One might argue, for example, that news of Boesky's arrest brought market participants new confidence that insider trading would be controlled, which in turn initiated the bull market of 1987. In this vein, Preet Bharara, then US Attorney for the Southern District of New York, recently suggested that his office's high-profile prosecutions of insider traders

---

[44] Ibid.

[45] Jeffrey M. Laderman, "The Epidemic of Insider Trading: The SEC Is Fighting a Losing Battle to Halt Stock-Market Abuses," *Business Week* (April 29, 1985): 78–92.

[46] See Bill Sing, "1985 – A Year of Easy Money in Stock Market: Dow Surges to Its Best Annual Gain Since 1975," *Los Angeles Times* (Jan. 2, 1986).

[47] William J. Carney, "Signalling and Causation in Insider Trading," *Catholic University Law Review* 36 (1987): 896. See also Charles C. Cox and Kevin S. Fogarty, "Bases of Insider Trading Law," *Ohio State Law Journal* 49 (1988): 354 (noting that "the highly publicized insider trading prosecutions of 1986, including Dennis Levine and Ivan Boesky cases, although widely interpreted as evidence of pervasive insider trading, seemed to have no substantial long-term impact on investment in securities, which continued to increase").

[48] Carney, "Signalling and Causation in Insider Trading," 896.

in the wake of the 2008 market collapse brought "people back to a level of confidence in the market."[49] But then how does one reconcile this latter interpretation with the fact that the US stock market advanced more than two hundred points on October 5, 2015, the day the US Supreme Court denied certiorari in *Newman v. United States*, thereby letting stand the Second Circuit's decision that prosecutors warned would significantly hamper insider trading enforcement efforts going forward?[50] But regardless of one's spin, it is a problem for the market confidence argument that the data can be interpreted so easily to cut both ways. It invites the conclusion that the market confidence argument is unfalsifiable. An unfalsifiable theory is one that can be proven neither true nor false. Such theories have no predictive power and are therefore of little use.

Another way to test the market confidence theory may be to consider the experiences of other countries after introducing insider trading regulations for the first time. Do those countries' markets show increased liquidity or improved performance after adopting insider trading regulations? The empirical research that has been done in this area offers little evidence that the adoption of insider trading regulations improves market performance.[51] In fact, there are some glaring examples to the contrary. For example, Professor Mark Ramseyer has noted the irony that Japan's initial implementation of its insider trading regime in 1988 was soon followed by a dramatic decrease in market liquidity and a historic collapse in market value.[52] In fact, to this day, the Japanese stock market has failed to return to its 1988 levels. This is not to suggest that the Japanese market collapse was a response to the new insider trading regulations. There were a myriad of causes. The Japanese experience does, however, offer a significant counterexample to anyone suggesting

---

[49] Steve Schaefer, "Wall Street Sheriff Preet Bharara Talks Insider Trading," *Forbes* (Jul. 18, 2012), www.forbes.com/sites/steveschaefer/2012/07/18/wall-street-sheriff-preet-bharara-talks-insider-trading/#4d13add86690.

[50] Prosecutors warned that allowing *Newman* to stand would "raise the bar to prosecuting insider trading," "increase the chances that such conduct will proliferate," and "erod[e] public confidence in the integrity of securities markets." United States of America, Petition for Writ of Certiorari, United States v. Newman (filed July 30, 2015). Equally problematic for the market confidence argument is the fact that the DJIA was down 38.18 points on August 23, 2017, the day that *Newman* was overruled by the Second Circuit's panel decision in United States v. Martoma, 2017 WL 3611518 (2d Cir. 2017).

[51] See, e.g., Bhattacharya and Daouk, "The World Price of Insider Trading," 75 (finding virtually no correlation between the mere adoption of insider trading regulations in other countries and increased market performance – though the study did find improved market conditions after the first insider trading enforcement action in a given country). See also Stephen Bainbridge, *Insider Trading: Law and Policy* (St. Paul, MN: Foundation Press, 2014): 189 (noting that the "empirical case for market liquidity-based theories is further undermined by the well-known observation that highly liquid and efficient stock markets exist in several countries that do not prohibit insider trading or fail to enforce the laws on the books").

[52] See Mark Ramseyer, "Insider Trading Regulation in Japan," in Stephen Bainbridge (ed.), *Research Handbook on Insider Trading* (Northampton, MA: Edward Elgar Publishing, 2013): 348.

that insider trading regulation improves market confidence and therefore market performance. And to simply dismiss this counterexample as driven by alternative causes, once again, exposes the proponent of the market confidence theory to the criticism of unfalsifiability. For what counterexamples could not be dismissed for similar reasons? These and other considerations have driven many to conclude that the hitherto received assumption that insider trading undermines (or should undermine) market confidence may be unfounded.[53]

There is yet another problem for the market confidence argument. Recall that the theory rests on the assumption that the trading public perceives insider trading to be inefficient or morally wrong and that this shared attitude will motivate a nontrivial number of potential traders to stand on the sidelines. But what if this attitude exists though insider trading is *not* in fact inefficient or morally wrong? In this case, the perception of risk (though false) might still affect liquidity, cost of capital, and market value. What would be the appropriate response to such false consciousness? One response would be to regulate insider trading solely to prevent this false consciousness from reducing market participation. But this response would be unwise. It would confront a false consciousness that negatively impacts market performance by reinforcing and perpetuating it. It would also result in the punishment of individuals for conduct that is neither economically harmful nor morally wrong. An alternate response would be to educate the public to correct the false attitude. This takes the far wiser tack of addressing the inefficient attitude by correcting it. Assuming only the latter response would be appropriate, the market confidence argument will provide a sound justification for regulating insider trading only if insider trading is proven to be economically harmful or morally wrong on grounds quite independent of the public's attitudes toward it. The market confidence argument is therefore at best parasitic and of only secondary importance to the more basic economic arguments considered in this chapter and the ethical arguments to be addressed in Chapters 9 and 10.

8.6 POTENTIAL SOCIAL BENEFITS OF INSIDER TRADING

While considering the effects of insider adverse selection to bid-ask spreads, one study observed that the "increase in efficiency [in pricing due to insider trading] may

---

[53] See, e.g., Jeanne L. Schroeder, "Taking Stock: Insider and Outsider Trading by Congress," *William & Mary Business Law Review* 159 (2014): 173 (noting that, if anything, "the meager evidence can be read as an indication [the] widespread suspicion that insider trading often occurs has had little effect on market participation"). See also Cox and Fogarty, "Bases of Insider Trading Law," 353 (noting that the "contention that the existence of insider trading will cause investors to desert the securities markets is doubtful and certainly unproven"); Stephen Bainbridge, "Incorporating State Law Fiduciary Duties into the Federal Insider Trading Prohibition," *Washington and Lee Law Review* 52 (1995): 1242 (arguing that paradoxical public attitudes concerning insider trading have "nothing to do with a loss of confidence in the integrity of the market, but instead arise principally from envy of the insider's greater access to information").

be worth the concomitant decrease in the liquidity of the market."[54] As this point reflects, any study evaluating regulation of conduct based on its potential economic costs must also consider any potential economic benefits. Some of the purported economic advantages of insider trading identified by scholars are summarized here.

8.6.1 *Increased Accuracy of Price, Real-Time Information, and Market-Smoothing Effect*

Most commentators have come to accept that insider trading pushes stock prices in the "correct" direction – to better reflect the company's true value in light of the nonpublic information that directs it.[55] It stands to reason that insiders are in the best position to assess the true value of their company and information affecting its price, and where insider trading is allowed, they can be expected to purchase or sell shares until the market approaches the correct price.[56] Moreover, insider trading allows a company insider's assessments of endogenous information to be reflected in its market price in real time on a daily basis without the costs, risks, and delays associated with formal public releases and filings. Sometimes business reasons preclude disclosure, as they did for Texas Gulf Sulphur when the firm needed the news of its recent strike to remain confidential while it secured additional mining leases. Even when business reasons do not preclude official disclosure, given the scrutiny to which disclosures are subject by analysts and regulators, they are made only rarely (when they cannot be avoided altogether) and usually contain a thoroughly watered-down version of relevant facts. Insider trading, by contrast, allows a stock to reflect insiders' current assessment of uncertain situations on a day-to day basis.[57] It acts as a "replacement for public disclosure of the information, preserving market gains of correct pricing while permitting the corporation to retain the benefits of nondisclosure."[58] The result, some argue, is increased market efficiency. For, as Professor Jonathan Macey explained, "[w]here share prices are inefficient, capital allocation will be irrational: deserving projects will go unfunded in favor of poorly conceived

---

[54] Dolgopolov, "Insider Trading and the Bid-Ask Spread," 175 (quoting Lawrence R. Glosten, "Insider Trading, Liquidity, and the Role of the Monopolist Specialist," *Journal of Business* 62 (1989): 230).

[55] See, e.g., Carlton and Fischel, "The Regulation of Insider Trading," 868 ("If insiders trade, the share price will move closer to what it would have been had the information been disclosed.").

[56] See, e.g., Manne, "Insider Trading and the Law Professors," 569.

[57] See, e.g., Carlton and Fischel, "The Regulation of Insider Trading," 868 ("Through insider trading, a firm can convey information it could not feasibly announce publicly because an announcement would destroy the value of the information, would be too expensive, not believable, or – owing to the uncertainty of the information – would subject the firm to massive damage liability if it turned out ex post to be incorrect.").

[58] Bainbridge, "Insider Trading," § 5650.

ones." According to Macey, this "misallocation of society's resources will lead to unemployment, low productivity, and higher interest rates."[59]

Such real-time reflection of information about a company through its stock price due to insider trading may also benefit the company's own management in its decision-making. For example, insiders often trade on nonpublic information concerning their company's problems (fraud or other issues) that have not yet been brought to the attention of management. A corresponding change in stock price may issue a warning or "red flag" to management to identify and correct the problem before it gets worse. For this reason, some companies set up their own virtual or prediction markets to aid in their decision-making.[60] The idea is that markets can organize and weigh the value of information better than individuals. Moreover, the "lure" of insider trading may also incentivize management to actively seek out material nonpublic information within the firm, rather than sit back and wait "for the bureaucratic pipeline to deliver a memorandum."[61] Indeed, some have argued that the value of insider trading to management in monitoring its company's stock price to predict current issues and future performance may help explain why shareholders and management have rarely sought to restrain insider trading prior to its criminalization.[62]

Finally, the gentle sloping in price resulting from insider trading prior to the release of material nonpublic information mitigates the market-rattling impact of radical price shifts that would otherwise occur upon public release. This has been referred to as the "market-smoothing" effect of insider trading.[63] The resulting "dampening of price fluctuations decreases the likelihood of windfall gains and increases the attractiveness of investing in securities for risk-averse investors."[64] In this way, insider trading may decrease volatility and serve as a stabilizing force that offers long-term benefits to all market participants. Recall that greater market stability was one of the goals of Congress in adopting the Securities Exchange Act of 1934.

8.6.2 *Efficient Compensation*

Another potential economic benefit of insider trading is that it may serve as an attractive form of compensation for company employees that encourages innovation and entrepreneurship at little or no cost to the shareholders. Insider trading's usefulness as a cost-effective mode of compensation persisted as a central component of

[59] Macey, *Insider Trading*, 10.
[60] See Henry G. Manne, "Insider Trading: Hayek, Virtual Markets, and the Dog that Did Not Bark," *Journal of Corporate Law* 31 (2005): 181.
[61] Macey, *Insider Trading*, 37 (quoting Judge Frank Easterbrook).
[62] See Manne, "Insider Trading," 182.
[63] See, e.g., Manne, "Insider Trading and the Law Professors," 574.
[64] Bainbridge, "Insider Trading," § 5650.

Manne's argument for the legalization of insider trading.[65] According to Manne, it is just a matter of "simple economics":

> If any service presently being purchased by the corporation is compensated more highly, more of that service will be offered. Valuable information is an economic good that can be substituted for other media in which the higher compensation can be paid. If the service performed is or can be one which gives access to valuable information, less of other forms of compensation must be paid in order to secure the same amount of the service.[66]

Professors Dennis W. Carlton and Daniel R. Fischel argued insider trading is an efficient form of compensation based on the Coase theorem. They pointed out that the question of whether insider trading is beneficial to a firm can be answered by determining who values the property right to that information more, the firm's managers or the firm's investors. Depending on the answer, the parties will "engage in a value-maximizing exchange by allocating the property right in information to its highest-valuing user."[67] Thus, if the practice of insider trading is inefficient, then both firm insiders and the firm's investors would profit by allocating the property right to inside information to the firm's investors. The fact that firms do not seek (and historically have not sought) to eliminate insider trading other than when already proscribed by law "suggests that the explanation for the absence of such prohibitions is that they are inefficient."[68]

Finally, any objection to insider trading as a form of compensation because it is "secret" or "covert" can be overcome by requiring that corporations announce publicly any policies permitting insider trading. And, in any event, the fundamental premise of this justification of insider trading is that it benefits shareholders and is therefore an arrangement they would, all things being equal, choose for themselves. As Professors Ian Ayers and Stephen Choi explained, "[m]anagers that expect to receive a benefit of $98,000 from their employment due to insider trading will be willing to work at the traded firm for a correspondingly reduced salary."[69] Indeed, recent empirical studies seem to confirm that companies do in fact adjust their executive compensation based on insider trading policies.[70] For example, studies have shown that executive compensation in the United States (where there is strict civil and criminal enforcement of insider trading laws) is much higher than in

---

[65] See, e.g., Henry G. Manne, "Entrepreneurship, Compensation, and the Corporation," *Quarterly Journal of Austrian Economics* 14 (2011): 17–18.

[66] Manne, "Insider Trading and the Law Professors," 579.

[67] Carlton and Fischel, "The Regulation of Insider Trading," 863.

[68] Ibid. at 865.

[69] Ayres and Choi, "Internalizing Outsider Trading," 338.

[70] See, e.g., M. Todd Henderson, "Insider Trading and CEO Pay," *Vanderbilt Law Review* 64 (2011): 509–10.

Germany and Japan where enforcement has historically been lax.[71] And even in the United States, where companies allow their employees to trade the firm's shares through Rule 10b5–1 trading plans, their CEO compensation is on average 20 percent lower.[72] Thus, a number of scholars share the concern that "[a]ny legal prohibitions against insider trading . . . prevent shareholders from reaching mutually beneficial compensation agreements with the managers of their firms."[73]

8.6.3 *Insurance against Accounting Fraud*

Some have argued that, far from creating a moral hazard, in limited circumstances insider trading may offer an effective tool for disincentivizing accounting fraud in publicly traded companies.[74] For example, the personal wealth of CEOs and other senior executives is often tied directly to stock holdings in their company. When these executives acquire inside information they know will negatively affect the price of the stock, they may be forced to choose among the following unhappy alternatives: (1) hold on to their stock and release the information, resulting in personal financial ruin; (2) sell the stock and then release the information, subjecting themselves to disgorgement, fines, and criminal liability for insider trading; or (3) issue fraudulent financials that may buy them time to fix the problem. The third option is often the only one that does not result in immediate ruin for the CEO. This was, for example, the decision faced by Bernard Ebbers of WorldCom. Professor Robert E. Wagner pointed out that if Ebbers could have sold his WorldCom stock prior to announcing the company's earnings misses, his principal incentive for misrepresenting the company's financials would have been eliminated, and perhaps the company might have avoided collapse.[75]

*****

This chapter has considered the economic impact of insider trading by summarizing some of the principal theoretical arguments and empirical research in the area. The results are mixed. Some of the costs of insider trading seem relatively clear (for example, the increased bid-ask spread resulting from adverse selection and the costs of unauthorized trading to the owner of the information). There also seem to be

---

[71] See, e.g., Larry Harris, *Trading & Exchanges: Market Microstructure for Practitioners* (New York: Oxford University Press, 2003): 593.

[72] See Henderson, "Insider Trading and CEO Pay," 505.

[73] Macey, *Insider Trading.*

[74] See Robert E. Wagner, "Gordon Gekko to the Rescue?: Insider Trading as a Tool to Combat Accounting Fraud," *University of Cincinnati Law Review* 79 (2011): 973 (arguing that "one way to help avoid future accounting scandals . . . would be the legalization of 'fraud-inhabiting insider trading'").

[75] See Wagner, "Gordon Gekko to the Rescue?," 976–82. Wagner does not advocate a blanket legalization of insider trading, only legalization of "fraud-inhibiting insider trading" of the type described here.

benefits (for example, price accuracy, market smoothing, and efficient compensation). Weak empirical evidence, however, makes it virtually impossible to quantify the net economic impact of these costs and benefits on counterparties, firms, or the market as a whole.[76] Still, the fact that the economic arguments for or against insider trading are inconclusive does not mean they are not important and useful. At a minimum, this study has helped to identify the relevant stakeholders, and to identify those who are likely to be harmed and those who are likely to benefit from insider trading – even if the relative magnitude of harms and benefits has not been ascertained with any certainty.

In any event, as explained in Chapter 7, some economic harms are just and fair, while some economic benefits (even to society as a whole) may be unjust and unfair. So while the cost-benefit analysis of insider trading is important for purposes of proposing reforms to the current regime in the United States, it cannot be dispositive on its own. Even the most efficient practices may warrant legal proscription if they are unjust or unfair. This has led some scholars to recognize that the "more important argument against insider trading is that it is unfair, either in the sense that it is dishonest or in the sense that it simply does not allow everyone an equal opportunity to profit."[77] The next chapter addresses this question of the moral permissibility of insider trading.

---

[76] See, e.g., Laura E. Hughes, "The Impact of Insider Trading on Stock Market Efficiency: A Critique of the Law and Economics of Insider Trading," *Temple International and Comparative Law Journal* 25 (2009): 505 (noting that the empirical evidence supporting the theoretical economic arguments for and against insider trading is "so limited and weak that any conclusions drawn ... should be regarded with restraint"). See also Cox and Fogarty, "Bases of Insider Trading Law," 357 (noting that "it cannot conclusively be said that the economic benefits outweigh the costs of prohibiting insider trading" because "the comparative costs and benefits have not been quantified").

[77] Cox and Fogarty, "Bases of Insider Trading Law," 353.

9

Is Insider Trading Morally Wrong?

Though the principal criticisms of the current insider trading enforcement regime in the United States have come from economists, its proponents often defend it by appeal to moral considerations of justice and fairness. As SEC staffers once put it, "[m]oral imperatives have driven the development of insider trading law in the United States."[1] Consequently, an honest assessment of the current regime, as well as any suggestions for its reform, will require a clear identification of the moral stakes in play. Is insider trading morally impermissible? If it is impermissible, what makes it so? The answers to these questions will not only help in the determination of whether and under what circumstances insider trading should incur civil or criminal liability; they will also inform the determination of appropriate penalties.[2]

9.1 NECESSITY OF POSITING A NEUTRAL REGIME

To answer the moral question, one must first assume a legal regime that does not prohibit insider trading under either the classical or misappropriation theories. This allows the morality of insider trading to be tested independent of any contingent social expectations or attitudes arising solely from the recognition that it happens to be illegal. For example, a moral evaluation of the conduct of driving one's car on the left-hand side of the road would change dramatically depending on whether the law required people to drive on the right-hand side and set this expectation for other drivers. To drive on the left-hand side when the law requires you to drive on the right needlessly puts other lives at risk. In such cases, the social expectation set by law makes otherwise innocent conduct morally wrong. Presuming an enforcement

---

[1] Thomas C. Newkirk and Melissa A. Robertson, "Insider Trading – A US Perspective" (speech, Cambridge, England, Sept. 19, 1998), US Securities and Exchange Commission.

[2] Much of the following analysis first appeared in John P. Anderson, "Greed, Envy, and the Criminalization of Insider Trading," *Utah Law Review* 2014 (2014): 1.

regime that does not already proscribe insider trading allows us to engage in honest evaluation of this conduct independent of such morally arbitrary considerations. After all, if part of our aim is to determine what moral reasons exist for criminalizing and punishing insider trading, it would be of little help to learn that, like driving on the left-hand side of the road, it is immoral simply because social practices and expectations have been built around its illegality.[3]

The following moral analysis focuses on three types of insider trading that are representative of the universe of conduct legally proscribed under the classical and misappropriation theories of Section 10(b) liability in the United States, but that will be assumed legal for our purposes here:

Issuer-proscribed insider trading: Where an insider trades on material non-public information despite the fact that the insider has promised the issuer – or otherwise undertaken pursuant to company policy (express or implied) – not to trade on such information.

Issuer-licensed insider trading: Where an insider trades on material non-public information with the firm's approval. (It is presumed that (1) the issuer's policy allowing insider trading and (2) any profits earned from such trading are disclosed to the investing public.)

Misappropriation trading: Where an insider or outsider trades on material nonpublic information acquired without the source's knowledge and in violation of a promise (or otherwise-acquired commitment of trust and confidence) to the source of the information.

The remainder of this chapter tests the moral permissibility of each of these three forms of insider trading (as well as the moral consequences of their regulation) from the standpoint of the two principal Western liberal moral theories summarized in Chapter 7, utilitarianism and deontology. The moral lessons learned from this analysis will help to inform and shape the reforms to the current US enforcement regime that will be proposed in Chapter 11.

9.2 UTILITARIAN ANALYSIS OF THE MORAL PERMISSIBILITY OF INSIDER TRADING

Recall from Chapter 7 that utilitarianism identifies the rightness or wrongness of an act by its consequences – whether it optimizes happiness for society as a whole.

---

[3]   Professor Samuel W. Buell makes a similar point when he notes the "odd circularity" of the argument that insider trading is fraudulent because market participants trade on the presumption that the market is free of traders who possess material nonpublic information. This presumption exists only because the law has created it, in which case "the law itself has created the conditions that justify its treatment of insider trading as fraudulent." Samuel W. Buell, "What Is Securities Fraud?," *Duke Law Review* 61 (2011): 563. Though perhaps compelling as an explanation for why insider trading is deceptive once proscribed by law, it offers no moral justification for the adoption of the legal proscription in the first instance.

If the question is whether there are moral grounds for regulating a *type* of conduct (in this case, issuer-proscribed, issuer-licensed, or misappropriation trading), then the utilitarian typically asks if, all things being equal, general compliance with a rule proscribing the relevant conduct would yield as good or better a state of affairs than a rule permitting that conduct. This is the principle of rule utilitarianism.[4] If a rule proscribing the conduct would yield a better state of affairs, then rule utilitarianism demands regulation of the conduct.

In evaluating issuer-proscribed insider trading from the standpoint of rule utilitarianism, one must answer the following question: Would a world in which everyone generally follows the rule not to commit issuer-proscribed insider trading be superior from the standpoint of utility to a world in which there is no such rule and insiders are free to break their promises and make such trades whenever it would benefit them to do so? If the answer is yes, then issuer-proscribed insider trading is morally impermissible on rule utilitarian grounds.

The two principal features of issuer-proscribed insider trading to be analyzed from the rule utilitarian standpoint are (1) the promise-breaking and (2) the utility of the trading itself. Certainly we can anticipate that regular issuer-proscribed insider trading would undermine the practice of promise-making in this corporate context. If such trading became the norm, then no firms would expect their employees to keep their promises not to trade, so the practice of demanding such promises would cease to exist. To measure the impact of this practice falling away, we must consider the interests companies seek to protect and promote via promises not to trade on material nonpublic information. While it is yet to be decided whether companies and their shareholders *always* have an interest in not allowing their employees to insider trade, there are certainly *some* contexts in which promises not to trade will be very important to the company. For example, where the management of a company makes the strategic decision to initiate merger or buyout negotiations with third parties, there is a risk that insider trading will drive up the market price of the issuer and thereby scare off potential suitors. Even more directly, insider trading in advance of a planned share repurchase program competes directly with the firm. Consequently, where such interests are present, and promises not to trade are not honored or cannot be entered into, companies and their shareholders will be harmed. Moreover, regular promise-breaking in this specific context might serve to weaken the socially beneficial practice of promise-making in general.

Turning to the net utility of the trading itself, it pays to revisit some of the conclusions from the economic analysis in Chapter 8. While most are prepared to agree there is no discernible harm to the counterparty, there remains the concern

---

[4] See, e.g., J. J. C. Smart and Bernard Williams, *Utilitarianism For and Against* (New York, NY: Cambridge University Press, 1963, 2008): 9 ("Rule-utilitarianism is the view that the rightness or wrongness of an action is to be judged by the goodness and badness of the consequences of a rule that everyone should perform the action in like circumstances.").

that, where it is understood that insiders are regularly trading on material nonpublic information, market makers are likely to increase the bid-ask spread for stocks – imposing a tax on others who trade in the company's shares, and increasing the cost of capital for the issuer (though, as noted in Chapter 8, the extent of this harm is debated). In addition, since insiders can profit from bad news as well as good, issuer-proscribed insider trading may lead many to succumb to this perverse incentive and create bad news for the firm. Finally, there is a risk that all of these costs associated with issuer-proscribed insider trading will be compounded further by reduced market confidence in the issuer's shares once word of these costs gets around. These potential harms must be netted against the personal benefit of the issuer-proscribed trading to the insider. Of course, the profits enjoyed from insider trading do not represent a net increase in wealth for society as a whole, but they may represent a net increase in *utility*. Insiders will usually dramatically improve their own and their families' lives in one trade, whereas others who trade are unlikely to be made significantly better or worse off when considered together because those who happen to be trading in the direction of the insider will offset the effect of the counterparties. In other words, the insider's trade is likely to have disproportionately high utility by comparison to the combined direct effects on other traders. Finally, there is the potential benefit of increased market accuracy, real-time information to markets and management, and the market smoothing that may result from the general practice of insider trading, as explained in Chapter 8.

Thus, taken together, several harms can be expected from the general practice of issuer-proscribed insider trading: (1) undermining the ability of companies to prevent their insiders from trading where such trading is harmful to the firms' interests, (2) injury to the practice of promise-making in general, and (3) a tax on shareholders and increased cost of capital for firms as a result of an increased bid-ask spread. In terms of benefits, only the disproportionately high utility the insiders will enjoy from their trade by comparison to other traders, the potential for increased market accuracy, real-time information to markets and management, and market smoothing can be expected. Though it is difficult to be exact, it would appear the weight of harms for society resulting from the general practice of issuer-proscribed insider trading (particularly the inability of companies to maintain insider trading discipline where the future of the company depends on it) would be greater than the benefits in terms of net utility. The most compelling evidence of this is, of course, the fact that firms elected to proscribe the trading in the first place. In the laissez-faire regime presupposed here, it must be presumed that in issuing the proscription these firms have already determined that the costs of such trading to the issuer and its shareholders would outweigh any benefits. In sum, based on the information available, rule utilitarian analysis finds issuer-proscribed insider trading to be morally impermissible.

The rule utilitarian analysis of misappropriation trading parallels that of issuer-proscribed insider trading and yields the same result. To begin, each case of issuer-proscribed insider trading will also fit the definition of misappropriation trading, and the rule utilitarian analysis will be the same. But even where misappropriation trading is done by outsiders, the harms outweigh the benefits. To begin, the disutility resulting from the undermined interests of the source of the misappropriated information will, in many cases, be significant. For example, a firm's plan to execute a hostile take-over may be made less advantageous or be entirely undermined by the misappropriation trading in the target by its own employees. Alternatively, the good will of a law firm or financial services firm may be completely undermined by the misappropriation trading of its employees based on the firm's client information; this is entirely independent of the sometimes significant harm that such trading may impose on the client whose information is traded upon. Clients typically have good business reasons for wanting the law firms and financial services firms with which they are dealing to refrain from trading in their shares or on their proprietary information. In addition to the significant direct harm to the source of the information or their clients, add the possible increase in bid-ask spreads and increased cost of capital. Finally, factor the harm such trading may have on the socially beneficial practice of promise-making in general. Taken together these harms likely outweigh the foreseeable utility of the trades to the misappropriators and any increase in market accuracy and smoothing that may result from those trades.

But how would the rule utilitarian evaluate issuer-licensed insider trading? Again, by giving separate treatment to issuer-proscribed and issuer-licensed insider trading, the utilitarian's question seems to answer itself. In terms of harm to the issuer, it can be assumed that in making the determination of whether to license insider trading in any given instance, the issuer will weigh the potential costs against the potential benefits to the firm and its shareholders (including any increase in the bid-ask spread and corresponding effect on cost of capital). If the issuer determines that the costs will outweigh the benefits under the circumstances, then the issuer will not license the trading. But if the issuer licenses the trading, then the firm's own calculus reflects that such trading will result in a net benefit to the firm. Moreover, issuer-licensed insider trading breaks no promises or commitments and therefore does nothing to undermine the socially beneficial practice of promise-making in the corporate context (or in general). As noted in Chapter 8, there will be no discernable direct impact on counterparties as a result of issuer-licensed insider trading. It can also be expected to increase price accuracy and reduce volatility. More still, the disproportionate utility of the trading to the insider weighs in favor of permitting such trading. Finally, to the extent issuer-licensed insider trading would benefit the firm, increase price accuracy, provide real-time information to the markets and management, and have a market-smoothing effect, it should bolster market confidence rather than undermine it. These considerations likely warrant the strong claim that the practice of issuer-licensed insider trading results in a net benefit to society, but at a minimum they entitle the weaker claim that the risk of net harm to society is weaker than the likelihood of a net benefit. Either way, based on the preceding considerations, it must be recognized that issuer-licensed insider trading is morally permissible on rule utilitarian grounds.

9.2.1 *Utilitarian Analysis of Appropriate Sanctions*

For the utilitarian, the wrongness of a type of insider trading does not settle the question of whether acts of that type should be criminalized and subject to government sanction. Sanctions carry inherent disutility. First, there is the obvious disutility of the punishment for the punished, as well as the dependents, friends, and family of the punished. Second, there is the social cost of adjudicating and imposing the punishment. Finally, there are other social considerations such as the general fear of being wrongly punished for the act – which is directly correlated with the weight of the penalty and the specificity with which the crime is defined. Thus, as Jeremy Bentham put it, "all punishment is ... evil."[5] Consequently, the criminalization of a certain type of act will be warranted for the utilitarian only if (1) the general practice of committing such acts will result in net disutility; (2) criminalization and imposing sanctions will prevent such acts (whether by deterrence or incapacitation); (3) the gain in utility from the punishment's preventive effects is greater than the inherent disutility of the sanctions themselves; and (4) the punishment is no more painful than necessary to achieve the result in (3). In short, for the utilitarian, punishment "ought only to be admitted in as far as it promises to exclude some greater evil."[6]

With these principles in mind, since the general practices of issuer-proscribed and misappropriation trading would likely result in a net disutility for society as a whole, these practices are at least candidates for criminalization or civil sanction under utilitarian theory. If such sanctions are to make sense with respect to these types of conduct, however, it must be the case that the punishment will deter, and that the net utility gained by the deterrence will outweigh the disutility of the punishment and the costs of adjudicating and imposing it.

Some argue that the social costs of enforcing and adjudicating insider trading are particularly high because it is difficult to detect and prove.[7] Moreover, despite the severe punishments imposed on those convicted, there is evidence that criminal and civil sanctions against insider trading have had little deterrent effect. For example, the Financial Services Authority in the United Kingdom recently reported that its measure of "market cleanliness," the number of announcements concerning material information preceded by unusual price movements, has remained "between

---

[5] Jeremy Bentham, *An Introduction to the Principles of Morals and Legislation* (Oxford: Oxford University Press, 1879): 170.

[6] Ibid.

[7] See Henry G. Manne, "Insider Trading: Hayek, Virtual Markets, and the Dog that Did Not Bark," *Journal of Corporation Law* 31 (2005): 184 n. 62.

25 and 30 per cent for a decade."[8] A 2014 study suggests the figures in the United States are about the same.[9] In light of these facts, it will be particularly important for utilitarian lawmakers to scrutinize the social costs of the proscribed behavior – asking whether they are clear and significant enough to justify these challenges to enforcement. Whatever the answer, it is important to note that the previous analysis found the disutility associated with both issuer-proscribed and misappropriation trading focused principally on harmful effects of the broken promises or other commitments to the issuer or the source (the rightful owners of the information), and only to a lesser degree on the broader market. With this in mind, we might wonder whether existing state civil and criminal laws against fraud, theft, or conversion would be more efficient enforcement mechanisms from the utilitarian standpoint. The additional costs associated with the extra layer of enforcement at the federal level may not be warranted given the nature of the harmful consequences.

While it is clear that issuer-proscribed and misappropriation trading are at least candidates for criminalization on utilitarian grounds, the preceding analysis indicates that issuer-licensed insider trading is not. It has been shown that utility calculus yields the conclusion that issuer-licensed insider trading results in a net benefit (or is at least utility-neutral) to society. Issuer-licensed insider trading therefore fails to satisfy the first element of the utilitarian test for criminalization or civil sanction. This forces the conclusion that criminalizing issuer-licensed insider trading is morally impermissible on utilitarian grounds.

It could be, however, that this utilitarian analysis is correct as far as it goes, but that utilitarianism just fails to give the correct answer to the moral problem. For example, it may be that what makes insider trading wrong (even issuer-licensed insider trading) is not that it makes society worse off from the standpoint of the utility, but that it is simply unfair – or that it fails to treat people with equal respect as moral agents. Indeed, the principal moral objection to insider trading in the popular and political culture of modern America seems to be that of Henry Manne's student: "consequences be damned; it's just not right!" Or, as Professors Charles Cox and Kevin Fogarty put it,

> What we pay for enforcing public prohibitions against insider trading, for surveillance, litigation, private compliance efforts, as well as what we pay in pricing

---

[8] "Rajaratnam's Guilt and Market Justice," *Financial Times* (May 11, 2011), www.ft.com/intl/cms/s/0/964e92f6-7c01-11e0-9b16-00144feabdc0.html#axzz2oNUnnKau (subscription required).

[9] See Office of Jack Reed, United States Senator for Rhode Island, "Reed & Menendez Introduce Bill to Clearly Define and Ban Unlawful Insider Trading" (March 11, 2015), www.reed.senate.gov/news/releases/reed-and-menendez-introduce-bill-to-clearly-define-and-ban-unlawful-insider-trading. The article cites a 2014 study published by professors at New York University's Stern School of Business and McGill University finding that the public announcement of 25% of public mergers and acquisitions in the United States between 1996 and 2012 were preceded by "trading abnormalities" resulting in an average profit per trader of $1.57 million.

efficiency or other economic costs, are the price we pay for justice. The question is not so much whether insider trading augments or diminishes society's net wealth, but whether it allocates wealth to those fairly entitled to it. However, the form insider trading prohibitions should take depends upon what one's idea of fairness comprises.[10]

The next section explores this question by analyzing insider trading from the standpoint of deontological theories of justice and fairness.

9.3 DEONTOLOGICAL ANALYSIS OF INSIDER TRADING

As explained in Chapter 7, deontology is a duty-based theory. A central premise shared by such theories is that there are certain things we as moral agents must not do, regardless of the good consequences that may result. The following deontological analysis of insider trading begins by considering it from the standpoint of Kant's categorical imperative.

9.3.1 *Kant's Categorical Imperative and Insider Trading*

Recall that issuer-proscribed insider trading occurs when an insider trades on material nonpublic information and the insider has promised (expressly or impliedly) not to trade on such information. It was already shown (in Chapter 7) that the practice of making a false promise is precluded by Kant's categorical imperative under both the universal law and end-in-oneself formulations. Under the universal law formulation, it was shown that the maxim on which this conduct is based cannot be universalized without contradiction because the practice of promise-making could not be sustained if everyone made false promises. This conclusion holds whether the promise is to repay borrowed money (as in Chapter 7's example) or to refrain from trading one's employer's material nonpublic information. In addition, issuer-proscribed insider trading cannot be justified under the end-in-oneself formulation because it necessarily treats the promisee (the company) solely as a means to an end (use of the company's material nonpublic information for trading profits) that the promisee has rejected.[11] Thus, one need look no further than the false promise to identify issuer-proscribed insider trading as morally impermissible under the categorical imperative.

Moreover, insofar as a firm's material nonpublic information is its property, and the issuer-proscribed insider trader denies the issuer of its exclusive use, such trading may also be described as conversion or even theft. The maxim "I will use others'

---

[10] Charles C. Cox and Kevin S. Fogarty, "Bases of Insider Trading Law," *Ohio State Law Journal* 49 (1988): 357.

[11] Though a corporation may not share all of the moral properties of a natural person, the Kantian can grant it derivative end-in-oneself status based on the moral autonomy of its agents and shareholders.

property without their permission whenever I choose" cannot be generalized to the form of universal law without destroying the very concept of property. The maxim results in a contradiction and cannot therefore be willed consistently. The conclusion is the same under the end-in-oneself formulation. By using material nonpublic information against the will of the rightful owner, the issuer-proscribed trader treats the owner as a mere means to the trader's own ends.

As was the case for the utilitarian analysis, there are few morally relevant distinctions between misappropriation trading and issuer-proscribed insider trading from the deontological standpoint of the categorical imperative. In each case, the trading violates a promise or results in the theft or conversion of property. For these reasons, misappropriation trading will violate the categorical imperative for all the same reasons that issuer-proscribed insider trading does, and it is therefore morally impermissible on deontological grounds.

We turn now to issuer-licensed insider trading. Here the issuer has approved the insider's trading on material nonpublic information. Considered first under the universal law formulation, the relevant maxim for action is probably something like the following: "whenever one can profit by trading in one's company's shares based on material nonpublic information and the issuer has licensed such trading, then one will so trade." Could this maxim be made universal law without contradiction? The answer is yes.

Unlike the maxims for making false promises or stealing, there is nothing in the issuer-licensed maxim that, if made law for everyone, would undermine the existence of companies or the markets such that universalization would involve a contradiction. Again, as noted previously, there is the concern that market makers will increase their bid-ask spreads where such conduct is made universal law, but even supposing this worry is warranted, it would not undermine corporations or the markets. Indeed, as has been discussed, when considered in light of other countervailing considerations (such as increased market accuracy, real-time information to markets, decreased volatility, and more efficient corporate compensation), there is little reason to think the universalization of such trading would have a significant impact on companies or the markets at all. It appears, therefore, that issuer-licensed insider trading satisfies the universal law formulation of the categorical imperative. Considering issuer-licensed insider trading under the end-in-oneself formulation can test this conclusion.

At first blush, there appears to be no problem for issuer-licensed insider trading under the end-in-oneself formulation because the counterparty to the trade will always be a willing and voluntary participant. The issuer-licensed trader does not use the open-market counterparty as a mere means to the end of buying the stock at price x because the counterparty has her own reasons for wanting to sell at price x. But there is more to the story: when the issuer-licensed insider buys the stock, he does so knowing the stock is worth more than the sale price based on information the counterparty does not have. One might argue, however, that this must be a possibility the counterparty has considered and a risk she is prepared to take. For, except in the case of a seller who is trading solely to liquidate to cash for exogenous reasons, the counterparty herself is presumably betting that the stock will go down, therefore believing that she has better information than the buyer.[12] As R. Foster Winans (the primary defendant in *Carpenter v. United States*) put it, "The only reason to invest in the market is because you think you know something others don't."[13] Moreover, as noted in Chapter 6, since *Laidlaw v. Organ*, it is a well-settled legal principle in the United States that parties may profit from information advantages acquired by legitimate means.[14] Treating others as ends-in-themselves does not require that each party to an exchange disclose all information asymmetries as proponents of a parity-of-information regime have suggested.[15] A simple parity-of-information model of insider trading regulation may therefore be dismissed on deontological grounds as overbroad. But there is a still-unaddressed moral nuance to the issuer-licensed insider trader's conduct. The issuer-licensed insider trader does more than simply take advantage of information acquired by superior research or skill; he knows the stock is worth more based on information to which *only an insider will have access.*

The fact that the counterparty has no access to the insider's information is where Professor Stuart Green and those who advocate an equal-access model locate the moral wrong in insider trading.[16] According to Green, insider trading is wrong on deontological grounds because it amounts to cheating: an insider cheats the counterparty in a trade where the insider relies on information that, due to the regulatory

---

[12] See, e.g., Basic Inc. v. Levinson, 485 U.S. 224, 256 (1988) (White, J., concurring in part and dissenting in part) (noting that many investors trade precisely because they are of the opinion that the stock price does not reflect the corporation's actual worth); Donald C. Langevoort, "Theories, Assumptions, and Securities Regulation: Market Efficiency Revisited," *University of Pennsylvania Law Review* 140 (1992): 852 n. 6 ("Economists have long wondered about the efficiency paradox – that the existence of a high degree of efficiency depends on a critical mass of persons believing that it is worthwhile to try to beat the market, notwithstanding the model's teachings.").

[13] Jeanne Schroeder, "Taking Stock: Insider and Outsider Trading by Congress," *William & Mary Business Law Review* 5 (2014): 168 (quoting R. Foster Winans, "Thoughts on the Business of Life," Forbes.com).

[14] Laidlaw v. Organ, 15 U.S. 178 (1817).

[15] See, e.g., Alan Strudler and Eric W. Orts, "Moral Principle in the Law of Insider Trading," *Texas Law Review* 78 (1999): 413–19 (arguing that neither the law nor respect for autonomy precludes one from profiting by failure to disclose superior information that was acquired by legitimate means such as research or skill).

[16] See, e.g., Stuart P. Green, *Lying, Cheating, and Stealing: A Moral Theory of White-Collar Crime* (New York: Oxford University Press, 2006): 235–40; Strudler and Orts, "Moral Principle in the Law of Insider Trading," 412 (arguing that any time someone trades on illegitimately acquired material nonpublic information, he cheats his counterparty who does not have equal access to that information).

regime in place, "was not even theoretically accessible to the public."[17] In other words, the wrong of insider trading can be summarized as follows: the insider trader "(1) violates the SEC rule that one must either disclose material non-public information or abstain from trading; and does so (2) with the intent to obtain an advantage over a second party with whom she is in a cooperative, rule-governed relationship."[18] Thus, for Green, cheating occurs when "an advantage is obtained unfairly, through rule-breaking."[19] But, as it stands, this explanation of why insider trading uses the counterparty as a mere means is question begging, at least if what we are interested in is the inherent morality of the trading itself. One is cheating in Green's scenario only if one breaks the law to take advantage of others' compliance with the law. In other words, insider trading meets Green's definition of cheating only if it is first illegal. The obvious problem with this explanation is that we are concerned with determining the morality of different forms of insider trading so that we can intelligently judge whether they should be made illegal in the first place.

As has been explained, the moral analysis of insider trading offered here presumes a legal regime that does not ban any form of insider trading precisely to avoid such question begging. When it is posited that insider trading is not illegal, it is simply not true that it is "theoretically impossible" for the counterparty to have gained the information held by the issuer-licensed trader through legitimate means. She could have sought out a position as an insider in the relevant company or perhaps acquired the information from another insider who was under no promissory obligation not to trade or tip. As Professor Paula J. Dalley has explained, "access can always be purchased in some way; one could, for example, devote one's life to becoming a corporate director and thus have the same legal access to corporate information."[20] Admittedly, these alternatives may not be easy to accomplish, but they could be accomplished if trading on the inside information of this company were important enough to the counterparty. Again, information advantages are often difficult and costly to acquire, and this is one reason why parties are typically allowed to profit from such advantages when the work is done and the costs incurred.[21] So long as there is equal access to the positions, it is reasonable to claim there is equal access to the information.

---

[17] Green, *Lying, Cheating, and Stealing*, 241.
[18] Ibid. at 240.
[19] Ibid. at 241.
[20] Paula J. Dalley, "From Horse Trading to Insider Trading: The Historical Antecedents of the Insider Trading," *William and Mary Law Review* 39 (1998): 1335. See also Frank Easterbrook and Daniel Fischel, "Trading on Inside Information," in Easterbrook and Fischel (eds.), *The Structure of the Corporation* (Cambridge, MA: Harvard University Press, 1991): 241–42 ("If one who is an outsider today could have become a manager by devoting the same time and skill as today's insider did, is access to information equal or unequal?").
[21] See, e.g., Alan Strudler, "Moral Complexity in the Law of Nondisclosure," *UCLA Law Review* 45 (1993): 375 (arguing traders have a right to use information legitimately acquired by their labor to gain a market advantage).

One might continue to object, however, that the issuer-licensed insider is not benefiting from hard work or skill, but rather dumb luck; he happened to be in the right company at the right time. The information advantage is therefore not earned or deserved. Moreover, even if, assuming an equal opportunity employment regime, the counterparty had the same theoretical access to the issuer-licensed insider trader's position in the company (and therefore enjoyed the same theoretical access to the inside information on which he traded), as things turned out in fact, the counterparty had no access to that information at the time of the transaction.[22] There are two responses that prove decisive against this argument.

First, there may be some truth to the claim that the issuer-licensed insider is benefiting from luck, but if the issuer and its shareholders[23] have elected to allow some of their insiders to trade on the company's material nonpublic information (as is the case with all issuer-licensed insider trading), then, as noted previously, they presumably have done so, at least in part, to reward or incentivize work on behalf of the company. So there is a nontrivial sense in which it can be assumed the issuer-licensed insider has earned or deserves this information advantage.

Second, as for the counterparty's lack of access to the issuer-licensed insider's information at the time of the trade, such information asymmetry is common to the markets and not unique to insider trading. Imagine you are a ranch owner and learn from the owners of all of the ranches adjacent to yours that, just yesterday, they entered into contracts to sell the mineral rights to their properties to Big Mining Company for three times the current market value. The next day, Big Mining Company contacts you and offers to buy your mineral rights for three times the current market value. You suspect something is up and refuse to sell. Sure enough, Big Mining comes back and offers you ten times the market value for your mineral rights. You are now convinced that Big Mining has made an important discovery in

---

[22] See, e.g., Kim Lane Scheppele, "'It's Just Not Right': The Ethics of Insider Trading," *Law & Contemporary Problems* 56 (1993): 162 ("The offense lies in the fact that the secret is withheld under conditions in which those with whom the secret-keeper trades cannot discover the information *as easily* . . . as those who have the secret information. . . and that is the problem.") (emphasis added).

[23] As has been noted, it is presumed that the issuer's insider trading policy will be disclosed to the investing public. It is also assumed that the issuers would adopt such a policy only if they could make a case that it will benefit the company (for example, due to one or more of the purported economic benefits identified previously). If shareholders objected to the policy, they would presumably force a change by voting their shares or voting with their feet (i.e., dumping their shares). This tacit consent by shareholders exposes the flaw in the "fraud on the investor" theory advanced by some. For example, Strudler and Orts argue that even issuer-licensed insider trading is immoral on deontological grounds because by "competing with its own investors' rights to the company's profits when using information in which its investors have an interest, the firm or its authorized insiders would steal information that rightly belongs to its investors." Strudler and Orts, "Moral Principle in the Law of Insider Trading," 436. This argument gains no traction where, as in the case of issuer-licensed insider trading, the shareholder has voluntarily traded her right to the information in exchange for the economic benefits to the company (and consequently its share price) advanced by issuer-licensed insider trading.

the area (though Big Mining has not told you this is the case, and there has been no public announcement of a discovery). Before accepting its offer, you immediately leverage all of your assets and buy Big Mining stock. One week later, the discovery is announced and the stock price doubles. This is certainly a case in which the person(s) from whom you purchased the shares on the open market would probably not have sold if they knew what you knew. Moreover, the counterparties to the transaction had absolutely no access to the information on which you traded. This is not the case of a diligent analyst figuring something out by creating a mosaic of publicly available information; even the most dialed-in analyst would not know what Big Mining offered *you* for your mineral rights (or even that an offer had been made).[24] By sheer luck, you received what is by all accounts material nonpublic information through legitimate means and traded on it. Nevertheless, no one would allege that you treated your counterparty as a mere means by this trading. This is, again, because there is no deception. The counterparty trades on the assumption that other market participants may have better information. She does not object to this asymmetry, so long as the superior information was acquired by legitimate means; indeed, as was already noted, the counterparty herself typically assumes she has better information when she makes her own trade. There is no morally relevant difference between the issuer-licensed insider's trade and the one outlined in this paragraph. Market participants usually trade with the *hope* that legitimate information asymmetries exist, not despite the possibility.

Thus, in the hypothetical market assumed here, where insider trading is not illegal, we may presume the counterparty to the issuer-licensed insider trading is (or should be) aware of the possibility that other market participants have significant information advantages acquired without breach of duty or deceit. Such information advantages might be based on superior position (as in the case of the issuer-licensed insider), on superior research or skill (if, for example, one's counterparty happens to be Warren Buffett), on dumb luck (as in the case of the rancher in the previous example), or on a little of all three. The counterparty to the issuer-licensed insider knows all of this and nevertheless sells her shares for her own reasons at the price she wanted to sell them at. The counterparty to the issuer-licensed insider trader is, therefore, not cheated or treated unfairly where we assume such trading is not illegal; she is treated as an "end-in-herself" and not as a mere means. Thus, to the extent that it would preclude issuer-licensed insider trading, the equal-access model for insider trading enforcement can be dismissed as overbroad on deontological grounds. Moreover, insofar as the preceding arguments demonstrate that issuer-licensed insider trading involves no deception, fiduciary-cum-fraud regimes should permit it as well.

---

[24] This example is adapted from one offered by Professor Stephen Bainbridge in *Securities Law: Insider Trading* (New York: Foundation Press, 207): 47–49, 53.

9.3.2 *Fairness and Insider Trading*

The preceding deontological analysis of insider trading allows one to place much that has been alleged concerning the "unfairness" of insider trading in perspective. Kant's categorical imperative offers an explicit theoretical articulation of our commonsense notion of fairness. The philosopher John Rawls offered another.

Rawls gave the conception of justice he defended in his book *A Theory of Justice* the name "justice as fairness." For Rawls, liberal political society is best conceived as a fair system of cooperation among free and equal persons.[25] Rawls claimed his proposed conception of justice is fair because it is the conception members of the relevant society would choose for themselves in an initial choice position of equality, the "original position."[26] The original position generates fair principles by depriving the negotiators of any unearned bargaining advantages turning on the "outcome of natural chance or the contingency of social circumstances."[27] It does this by placing the parties behind a "veil of ignorance." From behind this veil, parties are deprived of any knowledge of their class position, financial status, intelligence, work ethic, and other contingent characteristics.[28] In short, for the purpose of this hypothetical negotiation, they do not know who they will be in the society for which they are choosing the principles of justice. The idea is that whatever principles rational and mutually disinterested parties would choose for themselves in this hypothetical negotiation will be fair because these parties have every incentive to select principles that are to everyone's mutual advantage. "Since all are similarly situated and no one is able to design principles to favor his particular condition, the principles of justice are the result of a fair agreement or bargain."[29]

Rawls's "justice as fairness" is intended to apply only to the basic structure of society (choice of a "political constitution and the main elements of the economic and social system"); it is not intended to apply to private associations or less comprehensive social cooperative arrangements or practices such as a securities market.[30] Nevertheless, applying his familiar concept of the original position to the problem of insider trading is elucidating. If we placed rational, mutually disinterested market participants behind a veil of ignorance that denied them knowledge of their respective roles in the market (for example, as investors, speculators, traders, analysts,

---

[25] John Rawls, *A Theory of Justice* (Cambridge, MA: Harvard University Press, 1971): 11.

[26] Ibid. at 12.

[27] Ibid.

[28] For Rawls, knowledge of these features of the parties' identities would result in an unfair advantage in choosing principles of justice because class, financial status, etc. are undeserved and are therefore morally arbitrary.

[29] Ibid.

[30] Ibid. at 7–8 ("These principles may not work for the rules and practices of private associations or for those of less comprehensive social groups.").

market makers, or firms)[31] and then asked them to choose between systems of market rules that were identical except one allowed issuer-licensed insider trading and the other banned it, which would the parties choose? If we presume along with Rawls that the parties would choose the rule they can expect will be to the mutual advantage of all market participants, then, from what has been said, there is good reason to think the parties would either endorse the system permitting issuer-licensed insider trading or would be entirely indifferent to it.

From the standpoint of Pareto superiority,[32] it has already been noted that there is no reason to think the counterparty to an issuer-licensed trade is made worse off by the transaction. Even if we can consider the possibility that market makers may be forced to increase their bid-ask spreads in light of issuer-licensed insider trading, this does not show that the market makers are worse off. By increasing the spread, they are just passing the increased risk along to other market participants. In light of the likely benefits to the other market participants, such as increased market accuracy, market smoothing, and more efficient corporate compensation, there is no reason to think those other market participants will decrease participation or be made worse off in the end. If they are made better off, then the system permitting issuer-licensed insider trading will result in a Pareto-superior allocation of resources. Thus, given that the market participants behind our veil of ignorance would either select a system of market rules that allows for issuer-licensed insider trading or be indifferent to it, such trading is fair on this account.

9.3.3 *Is Issuer-Licensed Insider Trading Truly Victimless?*

It pays at this juncture to address an important challenge to the claim advanced thus far in this chapter that no one is morally wronged or victimized by issuer-licensed insider trading.[33] In *United States v. O'Hagan*, the Supreme Court relied on a

---

[31] It makes no difference for the purpose of this exercise that market participants often simultaneously play more than one role.

[32] In economic theory, there are several measures of efficiency. Among these are "Pareto optimality" and "Pareto superiority." Jules Coleman, "Efficiency, Utility, and Wealth Maximization," in Avery Wiener Katz (ed.), *Foundations of the Economic Approach to Law* (New Providence, NJ: LexisNexis Matthew Bender Publishing, 2006): 10. As Coleman put it, "Resources are allocated in a Pareto-optimal fashion if and only if any further reallocation of them can enhance the welfare of one person only at the expense of another." Coleman goes on, "An allocation of resources is Pareto superior," on the other hand, "to an alternative allocation if and only if no one is made worse off by the distribution and the welfare of at least one person is improved."

[33] The following discussion draws from arguments first published in John P. Anderson, "What's the Harm in Issuer-Licensed Insider Trading?," *University of Miami Law Review* 69 (2015): 795. This article was published with replies by Professor Wang and Professor Leo Katz. See William K. S. Wang, "The Importance of the Law of Conservation of Securities: A Reply to John P. Anderson's 'What's the Harm in Issuer-Licensed Insider Trading?'," *University of Miami Law Review* 69 (2015): 811; Leo Katz, "The Problem with Consenting to Insider Trading," *University of Miami Law Review* 69 (2015): 827.

frequently cited argument by Professor William K. S. Wang to support the claim that every act of insider trading causes an identifiable harm to someone.[34] The argument proceeds as follows.

If an insider trader purchases shares based on material nonpublic information, then she will have more of the relevant issuer's shares at the time the information is disseminated. Consequently, assuming the number of that issuer's outstanding shares remains constant, someone else must have fewer shares at the time of dissemination. Those who have fewer shares at the time of dissemination were either induced (to sell) or preempted (from buying) by the insider's trading. These individuals were therefore made worse off as a result of the insider's trade. If an insider sells shares on the basis of material nonpublic information, then someone else (the induced buyer or the preempted seller) ends up with more shares at the time of dissemination and is thereby made worse off. "Paraphrasing the law of conservation of mass-energy," Professor Wang has referred to "this phenomenon [as] the [L]aw of [C]onservation of [S]ecurities."[35]

The Law of Conservation of Securities purports to demonstrate that each act of insider trading has specific victims, those who "were either preempted [from acting] or induced [to act] by the insider trading." Professor Wang has admitted that, as a practical matter, the actual identity of these "victims" can almost never be determined, but he has concluded that this does nothing to diminish the fact that they exist.[36]

Thus, at a minimum, Professor Wang has claimed that the Law of Conservation of Securities disposes of the argument that insider trading (like, say, marijuana or sodomy) should not be regulated because it is "victimless."[37] Wang has freely admitted that the mere fact that insider trading has victims does not settle the question of how or whether it should be regulated. Nevertheless, he observed that

---

[34] See United States v. O'Hagan, 521 U.S. 642, 656 (1997). In fact, the Court cites to Barbara Bader Aldave, "Misappropriation: A General Theory of Liability for Trading on Nonpublic Information," *Hofstra Law Review* 13 (1984): 120–21 and n. 107, but the cited language expressly relies on Professor Wang's argument in William K. S. Wang, "Trading on Material Nonpublic Information on Impersonal Stock Markets: Who Is Harmed, and Who Can Sue Whom under SEC Rule 10b–5?," *Southern California Law Review* 54 (1981): 1234–35.

[35] William K.S. Wang, "Stock Market Insider Trading: Victims, Violators and Remedies – Including an Analogy to Fraud in the Sale of a Used Car with a Generic Defect," *Villanova Law Review* 45 (2000): 29.

[36] See William K. S. Wang and Marc I. Steinberg, *Insider Trading*, 3d ed. (New York: Oxford University Press, 2010): § 3.3.7. To identify victims of an insider trading, one would have to compare the universe in which the insider trade was made to the universe in which it was not made. But "it is almost never possible to describe the universe that would have existed had there been no insider trade." Ibid.

[37] Wang, "Stock Market Insider Trading," 28.

"society is more likely to regulate insider trading strictly if," as the Law of Conservation of Securities demonstrates, "it has victims."[38]

Though perhaps compelling at first blush, it turns out that the Law of Conservation of Securities does nothing to answer the question of whether every instance of insider trading has a victim. It proves either too much or too little. To begin, application of the Law of Conservation of Securities finds a harm or victim in *every* profitable market trade in advance of a material disclosure, not just those based on material nonpublic information. Imagine Timmy, a college student, buys a new iPhone and loves it so much that he decides to buy ten shares in Apple Inc. The next day, Apple publicly introduces its much-anticipated iCar. Shares in Apple immediately climb 15 percent on the news. The Law of Conservation of Securities tells us that Timmy's purchase of Apple shares harmed or victimized whoever was induced to sell or preempted from buying as a result of Timmy's trade. But the resulting "harm" or "victimization" has no moral import – it is not wrongful. It simply reflects the trivial truth that *someone* is always made worse off (in this limited sense) as a result of any profitable trade prior to an unanticipated public announcement of material information.

Moreover, it is not just that the Law of Conservation of Securities finds some harm in every profitable trade prior to an unanticipated material disclosure; it identifies the same harm in every profitable trade omission.[39] Continuing with the earlier example, every Apple shareholder at the time of dissemination was, per the Law of Conservation of Securities, the but-for cause of harm to the persons who would have purchased those shareholders' stock had they sold prior to dissemination. Given that there are billions of outstanding shares of Apple, this amounts to a significant number of harms and victims.[40]

Professor Wang seems aware of this odd result, but he has failed to appreciate its significance for his thesis. He observed that "[c]learly, society will not impose liability on traders who unknowingly, fortuitously make advantageous trades prior to public disclosure. Therefore, causing harm under the law of conservation of securities is not sufficient in itself to impose liability."[41] But this acknowledgement misses the point. It is not just that the trivial "harm" identified by the Law of Conservation of Securities is not a sufficient condition for moral censure or legal liability; once it is understood that every profitable securities trade (or omission) in advance of a material disclosure results in the same harm, it becomes clear that this

---

[38] Ibid. at 29.

[39] A logical consequence of the Law of Conservation of Securities's but-for reasoning is that profitable trading omissions (or abstentions) will always make someone worse off by relegating whoever would have been the counterparty to the omitted trade to the sidelines.

[40] Of course, it would likely send the stock price into free fall if all of these Apple shareholders sold their holdings prior to dissemination. This does not, however, diminish the fact that the Law of Conservation of Securities tells us that each such omission makes someone worse off by relegating that person to the sidelines at the time the good news is disclosed.

[41] Ibid. at 36.

law is simply irrelevant when assessing the moral permissibility of – or the moral appropriateness of imposing liability for – insider trading.

It does no good to suggest that the Law of Conservation of Securities identifies the harm but that only knowing or intentional inflictions of the harm are wrongful and therefore worthy of liability. For all unknowing traders (i.e., those who fail to possess material nonpublic information) still trade with a clear intent to inflict precisely the harm identified by the Law of Conservation of Securities on others, which is only to say that they aim to profit by their trades. And to claim that aiming to profit by trading is morally blameworthy is to suggest that all (or virtually all) market participation is wrongful.

In addition, even when an insider knowingly trades on material nonpublic information, the Law of Conservation of Securities only tells us that someone will be made worse off as a result of the trade; it does not tell us who that person or those persons are. The person made worse off could be another insider trader who was preempted. Is the preempted insider "harmed" or "victimized" in any morally interesting sense of these terms? Certainly not. In fact, if we assume arguendo that there is something inherently wrong with insider trading, then we must conclude that this trade actually preempted the other insider from perpetrating a moral wrong. Consequently, even on Professor Wang's own terms, it cannot be said that every act of insider trading victimizes someone.[42]

In light of these considerations, it is misleading to label the preempted or induced traders identified by the Law of Conservation of Securities as "victims" of insider trading. The preempted or induced traders identified by that law are made worse off by all profitable trades or omissions in advance of a material disclosure – regardless of whether they are based on material nonpublic information. Moreover, virtually every time someone trades (or chooses not to trade) on the open market, they intend to inflict precisely this "harm" and create just such "victims." For these and other reasons already offered, the induced or preempted traders identified by the Law of Conservation of Securities are not "victims" within any morally relevant meaning of the term. At the end of the day, Professor Wang's law fails to tell us anything about the moral quality of an act of insider trading. Consequently, the Law of Conservation of Securities does nothing to affect the

---

[42] Professor Wang has responded to this argument by noting that the possibility of another insider being a counterparty to an insider trade is extremely remote because, "[a]ssuming someone is willing to trade on material nonpublic information, as long as she knows that the price remains inaccurate, a price change is unlikely to dissuade her from acting." Wang, "The Importance of the Law of Conservation of Securities," 824. Even so, to the extent insider trading moves a stock price in the direction of accuracy, there will come a point where further insider-induced movement begins to scare off other insiders. Even if this occurs only rarely, its mere possibility is enough to disprove the strong claim that the Law of Conservation of Securities proves that all insider trading has moral victims.

conclusion reached in the previous sections of this chapter that issuer-licensed insider trading is morally permissible.[43]

9.3.4 *Deontology and Market Confidence*

Notice the conclusion that there is nothing fundamentally unjust or unfair about issuer-licensed insider trading (reached by applying both Kant's categorical imperative and the Rawlsian method) also deprives the common "market confidence" argument of any moral support – at least with respect to issuer-licensed insider trading. Recall from Chapter 8 that the market confidence argument leans on the claim that public attitudes concerning the perceived unfairness of even issuer-licensed insider trading might be enough to scare prospective investors and speculators from securities trading and therefore undermine the markets. The preceding deontological analysis suggests that if such attitudes exist, they are unfounded. Of course, the naïve utilitarian might respond that it makes no difference that the attitudes are unfounded. So long as they exist, they support a moral reason for proscribing even issuer-licensed insider trading. But, as noted in Chapter 8, this argument is hardly compelling. The utilitarian has two options for confronting the market inefficiency caused by the false consciousness that issuer-licensed insider trading is harmful. She must choose between (1) correcting the false public perception (presumably at little or no cost in overall utility) and (2) continuing to punish the innocent conduct (which always results in some disutility to those punished and to those who are forced to forgo fruitful opportunities for fear of being punished). The wise utilitarian would choose the first option.

9.3.5 *Deontological Analysis of Appropriate Sanctions*

While utilitarian justifications for punishment are entirely forward-looking (concerned only with the socially useful consequences of punishment), the deontological theory of punishment, retributivism, is entirely backward-looking. For the retributivist, the present justification for punishment turns exclusively on the nature and extent of the past wrongdoing for which the criminal is being punished. Punishment is a matter of ensuring justice both for the criminal and for society. Justice is done to the criminal by imposing the punishment she deserves for the crime (no more and no less). The difficult question for the retributivist, however, is how to determine what punishment will fit the severity of a given crime. The principle of lex talionis, or "an eye for an eye," is often relied upon as a measure

---

[43] Professor Stephen Bainbridge reached a similar conclusion: "To justify a ban on insider trading, you need a basis for asserting that it is inappropriate, undesirable, or immoral for those gains to be reaped by insiders. The law of conservation of securities does not, standing alone, provide such a basis." Stephen Bainbridge, *Insider Trading Law and Policy* (St. Paul, MN: Foundation Press, 2014): 198.

of proportionality, though it has obvious limitations if applied literally. Beyond justice for the criminal, retributivism also seeks justice for society as a whole. For the retributivist, society is a cooperative enterprise to achieve order (among other things). The criminal takes an unfair advantage of this order. Consequently, the criminal owes a moral debt to society that must be repaid, and it is society's moral responsibility to demand repayment as much as it is the criminal's to offer it.[44] In short, for the retributivist, punishment is about righting wrongs by returning the moral scales to a balance for both the criminal and society. This balance is effected through punishment that is neither more nor less severe than the offending conduct warrants.

We have seen that both issuer-proscribed insider trading and misappropriation trading are immoral from the deontological perspective. At a minimum, a wrong can be traced to the breach of promise between the trader and the rightful owner or steward of the information. Either the insider broke her promise not to trade in the company's stock based on material nonpublic information, or the misappropriator deceived the source into giving access to material nonpublic information and then traded on it against the source's will.

Once it is settled that a wrong was done, the retributivist's next concern is determining a punishment that is neither more nor less severe than the crime. Disgorgement and some proportionate fine would seem in order. Indeed, depending on the circumstances, the lie, deception, or theft might even warrant incarceration, but the retributivist must be careful to maintain proportionality with the wrong. Lying, deceiving, and stealing can be harmful, but recall that the preceding analysis was unable to pin down a clear harm to either the counterparty or the market as a whole. Thus, the magnitude of the wrong must be measured in relation to the importance of the promise to the issuer (in the case of the issuer-proscribed insider trader) or the source (in the case of the misappropriator). Such analysis must be done on a case-by-case basis, but in light of the measurable economic and moral consequences identified in this chapter and the last, it would be difficult to justify the sentences in excess of twenty years that are now being sought by prosecutors. As Professor James Cox asked, "where are the bodies, where is the blood?"[45] Given the nature of the impact and the wrong, it rings false to claim that issuer-proscribed insider trading and misappropriation trading are wrongs of the same magnitude as murder and rape.

---

[44] For this reason, Kant famously argued that even if we knew our society would end tomorrow, we would have a duty today to march out "the last murderer remaining" in prison and execute him. Immanuel Kant, *The Metaphysics of Morals*, Mary Gregor (ed. & trans.) (Cambridge: Cambridge University Press, 1996): 106.

[45] See Jonathan Stempel, "Rajaratnam Sentencing May Be a Fight to the Death," Reuters (Aug. 10, 2011), www.reuters.com/article/2011/08/10us-galleon-rajaratnam-insidertrading-idUSTR E7795MV20110810.

With respect to issuer-licensed insider trading, of course, there is absolutely no retributivist justification for punishment. Such trading results in no wrong, so there is no moral imbalance to correct.

*****

The conclusion that issuer-licensed insider trading is morally permissible from the standpoints of both utilitarianism and deontology – which are the two dominant moral theories in Western liberal jurisprudence – will no doubt be controversial for many, particularly in light of the fact that such trading remains subject to criminal liability in the United States and most of the world over. Further exploration is warranted. Perhaps there are alternative ethical justifications for the criminalization of even issuer-licensed insider trading. If no alternative justification is available, then, at a minimum, the criminalization of this morally innocent conduct should be explained or accounted for. The next chapter considers virtue theory as a possible justification or explanation for the criminalization of even issuer-licensed insider trading.

10

Greed, Envy, and Insider Trading

Chapter 7 argued that normative conceptions of the efficient, the right, and the good are all important tools in evaluating existing legal regimes, and in advocating for their reform. One way or another, the law gives expression to society's commitments to each of these values, and any proposed legal reform would be lacking if it were to ignore one of these values entirely in favor of the others. Chapter 8 outlined the principal economic efficiencies and inefficiencies of insider trading. Chapter 9 then evaluated insider trading under the two leading Western liberal conceptions of right and duty – utilitarianism and deontology. This analysis yielded the conclusion that while issuer-proscribed insider trading and misappropriation trading are inefficient and morally impermissible, issuer-licensed insider trading is neither. Such arguments seem to deprive those who would legally proscribe even issuer-licensed insider trading of any reason-based justification in terms of market efficiency, social welfare, fraudulent deception, justice, or fairness. But moral conceptions of duty and right do not exhaust the ethical landscape. It remains to consider insider trading from the standpoint of the good life and individual character formation. What type of habits might insider trading form in citizens? What kind of people might it create?

Many journalists, politicians, and judges object to insider trading as a manifestation of the vice of greed. As Professors Charles Cox and Kevin Fogarty put it, "[t]he wave of major insider trading prosecutions has been taken by many as a symptom of cancerous greed on Wall Street."[1] Professor Stephen Bainbridge quoted a California state court's dictum that insider trading is "a manifestation of undue greed among the already well-to-do, worthy of legislative intervention if for no other reason than to send a message of censure on behalf of the American people."[2] And a Manhattan

---

[1] Charles C. Cox and Kevin S. Fogarty, "Bases of Insider Trading Law," *Ohio State Law Journal* 49 (1988): 353.

[2] Stephen Bainbridge, *Insider Trading: Law and Policy* (St. Paul, MN: Foundation Press, 2014): 192 (quoting Friese v. Superior Court, 36 Cal. Rptr. 3d 558, 556 (Cal. App. 2005)).

US Attorney announced that "[g]reed is at work" when the feds unveiled the Galleon Group insider trading case in 2007, celebrating it as "the biggest insider trading bust" since the 1980s.[3] As Professor Donald Langevoort put it, insider trading regulation may perform an expressive as well as a retributive or deterrent function, reflecting "the belief that insider trading is a manifestation of greed on the part of the privileged."[4] Perhaps even issuer-licensed insider trading should be legally proscribed, if for no other reason than as a means of policing the vice of greed.[5]

10.1 GREED IS NOT GOOD, BUT IT SHOULDN'T BE CRIMINAL

"Greed is all right, by the way. I want you to know that. I think greed is healthy. You can be greedy and still feel good about yourself."[6] Ivan Boesky spoke these words in a 1986 commencement address for UC Berkeley's Haas School of Business. He would surrender to federal authorities on charges of insider trading and other securities law violations just a few short months later. The fictional Gordon Gekko paraphrased Boesky's remarks when he proclaimed that "Greed . . . is good" in Oliver Stone's motion-picture exposé on insider trading, *Wall Street*.[7] Boesky, Gekko, and their brazen insider trading have become iconic of the 1980s, "The Greed Decade."[8] They were, of course, wrong. Greed is, by definition, not good.

Aristotle explained that greed is the vicious contrary of the virtue of generosity. Generosity is the "mean concerned with the giving and taking of wealth."[9] The generous person is one who will "both give and spend the right amount for the right purposes . . . and do this with pleasure."[10] He does not honor wealth for its own sake, but nevertheless acquires it "for the sake of giving."[11] By contrast, the greedy are "shameful love[rs] of gain" who "go to excess in taking, by taking anything from any source."[12] In their pursuit of wealth for its own sake, they are prepared to go to "great efforts and put up with reproaches."[13]

---

[3] Charles Gasparino, *Circle of Friends* (New York: Harper Collins, 2013): 104.
[4] Donald C. Langevoort, "Fine Distinctions in the Contemporary Law of Insider Trading," *Columbia Business Law Review* 2103 (2013): 440.
[5] Much of the following analysis of virtue theory and insider trading first appeared in John P. Anderson, "Greed, Envy and the Criminalization of Insider Trading, *Utah Law Review* 2014 (2014): 43–53; John P. Anderson, "The Final Step to Insider Trading Reform: Answering the 'It's Just Not Right!' Objection," *Journal of Law, Economics & Policy* 12 (2016): 272–75.
[6] James Stewart, *Den of Thieves* (New York: Simon & Schuster Paperbacks, 1991, 2010): 261.
[7] 20th Century Fox (1987).
[8] Stewart, *Den of Thieves*, 20.
[9] Aristotle, *The Nichomachean Ethics*, Terence Irwin (trans.) (Indianapolis, IN: Hackett Publishing Company, 1985): 89.
[10] Ibid.
[11] Ibid.
[12] Ibid. at 92.
[13] Ibid. at 93.

There is no question that the facts of many insider trading cases reflect the grasping smallness of character Aristotle describes. Consider the following passage describing Michael Milken's trading in James Stewart's *Den of Thieves*:

> For Milken, the transaction was just another trade, and the more one could squeeze out of the person on the other side of the trade, the better. For years to come, his colleagues on the trading desk would watch in amazement at the pleasure, even glee, that Milken displayed when he squeezed an extra fraction of a point out of an unwitting trader.[14]

But while acts of greed are always harmful to the actor's character, they need not be harmful to others. In fact, greedy acts will typically directly harm others only when they are also unjust or unfair. We have, however, already considered and rejected the argument that issuer-licensed insider trading is unjust or unfair in Chapter 9. So, if issuer-licensed insider trading is regarded as unethical because it reflects the character flaw of greed, then it is a completely self-regarding wrong. In other words, it harms no one and nothing but the character of the person who engages in it.

There are at least three points to be made here. First, though insider trading may sometimes be motivated by greed, it is not necessarily so. Jean Valjean stole a loaf of bread to feed his starving family in Victor Hugo's classic *Les Miserables*. Similarly, the generous insider trader may seek gain to help a family member to go to college, to pay for a friend's medical treatment, or to engage in some other form of philanthropy. For example, Rajat Gupta, an ex-Goldman Sachs director who was convicted of insider trading as part of the Galleon Group sting, offered evidence of his extensive philanthropy at the sentencing phase of his trial.[15] Gupta is said to have raised millions in support of the global fight against malaria, AIDS, and tuberculosis.[16] Raj Rajaratnam, who received the longest sentence in history for his insider trading as the head of Galleon, also had a reputation for being "extremely generous." According to one employee, Rajaratnam is said to have remarked "This country has been good to me" as he wrote a $500,000 check to the New York City Fire Department after the terrorist attacks in 2001.[17] Of course, these are just illustrative anecdotes, and one swallow does not make a summer. Nevertheless, it can be said with some certainty that any legal prohibition of issuer-licensed insider trading (or any form of insider trading for that matter) as a means of preventing greed would be over-inclusive in its reach.

---

[14] Stewart, *Den of Thieves*, 56.

[15] See Peter Lattman, "Push for Leniency as an Ex-Goldman Director Faces Sentencing," *New York Times* (Oct. 17, 2012), https://mobile.nytimes.com/blogs/dealbook/2012/10/17/in-sentencing-memos-two-views-of-gupta/?_r=0&referer=. Indeed, Gupta submitted more than 400 letters in defense of his kind and generous character, including one from Kofi Annan, former secretary-general of the United Nations.

[16] See Gasparino, *Circle of Friends*, 196.

[17] Ibid. at 115.

Second, even if a good argument could be made that permitting issuer-licensed insider trading will tempt citizens to the vice of greed, this has been historically regarded in the West as insufficient justification for its criminalization. Such justification is paternalistic and moralistic in nature. It would place issuer-licensed insider trading into the same class as now-disfavored (indeed unconstitutional in the United States) moralistic laws against sodomy, adultery, and same-sex marriage. As explained in Chapter 7, such laws violate the long-standing tenet of Anglo-American justice and jurisprudence expressed in John Stuart Mill's Harm Principle: "[T]he only purpose for which power can be rightfully exercised over any member of a civilized community, against his will, is to prevent harm to others. *His own good, either physical or moral, is not a sufficient warrant.*"[18]

Finally, even if moral contempt for greed were relied upon to justify the criminalization of issuer-licensed insider trading in the United States, the current state of the law would be woefully under-inclusive in its reach. Aside from the many other ways in which the vice of greed may be exercised legally in our society, as was shown in Chapter 4, there are a number of circumstances where persons are free to trade on material nonpublic information without violating insider trading laws (e.g., where the material nonpublic information is acquired by eavesdropping or dumb luck, where the tipper does not benefit but the tippee does, where the misappropriator announces an intent to trade to the source, or where the misappropriator abstains from buying or selling based on material nonpublic information).

10.2 A SOCIOPSYCHOLOGICAL EXPLANATION

If current attitudes about issuer-licensed insider trading and its criminalization cannot be justified on grounds of immorality or moralism, then it still remains for them to be explained, perhaps as the result of some sociopsychological phenomenon. Professors Dan Kahan and Eric Posner have offered one account of how a harmless form of insider trading might come to be criminalized in a society and later perceived to be morally wrong by its citizens.[19]

According to Kahan and Posner, insider trades, like sodomy and abortion, are "examples of behavior that are at different times and places considered morally culpable or not."[20] Kahan and Posner offered a hypothetical sequence of events to explain how these changes in attitudes may come about. Imagine a society in which the general public considers insider trading harmless. Then imagine that insider

---

[18] John Stuart Mill, "On Liberty," in *Three Essays* (New York: Oxford University Press, 1987): 15 (emphasis added).

[19] The following summary of Professor Kahan and Posner's arguments first appeared in Anderson, "Greed, Envy, and the Criminalization of Insider Trading," 50–51.

[20] Dan M. Kahan and Eric Posner, "Shaming White Collar Criminals: A Proposal for Reform of the Federal Sentencing Guidelines," *Journal of Law and Economics* 42 (1999): 376.

trading is identified in that society with some unfortunate event such as a stock market crash: "No one knows whether the insider trading caused the crash, but some entrepreneur – maybe a government official – seizes the moment, blames the stock market crash on the insider traders, and starts prosecuting insider traders by exploiting some vague law."[21] Whether or not everyone buys into this rhetoric at first, some, "maybe those who never engaged in insider trading because they never had the chance," might pile on.[22] If a critical mass jumps on this bandwagon, a new equilibrium is established in which those who might profitably trade on insider information refuse to do so (even if they see nothing wrong with it), both to remain law abiding and to avoid the reputational damage that comes with criminal liability. The result is that eventually "only bad types" (those who don't care about being law abiding or about their reputation) engage in insider trading.[23] This empirical fact then further reinforces the behavior: people will refrain from insider trading for the additional reason that they do not want to be mistaken for a bad type.

Ultimately, to avoid cognitive dissonance (i.e., engaging in action inconsistent with one's beliefs), those who originally believed there was nothing wrong with insider trading will actually revise their beliefs about the morality of such trading to cohere with the reputational and criminal consequences they impose on others for such behavior. They "convince themselves, through a psychological process that is not well understood, that not only do bad people engage in insider trading but that insider trading is morally wrong."[24] This account offered by Kahan and Posner is particularly helpful in that it offers a clear sociopsychological explanation of the paradoxical attitudes that empirical studies have shown are in fact held by the public with respect to insider trading. As noted in previous chapters, a 1986 *Business Week/ Harris* poll found that while 66 percent of Americans polled thought insider trading should be illegal, 55 percent said they themselves would trade on an inside tip.[25] A much more recent study, taken more than thirty years later, showed that "[a]lthough subjects seemed to have strong intuitions that insider trading is wrong, they were unable to isolate the victim in one case from the victim of another."[26] This result is consistent with Kahan and Posner's thesis that people may subsequently revise their moral beliefs concerning insider trading to bring them in line with their society's criminal enforcement practices – even if there is no reasoned moral basis for this revision.

---

[21] Ibid. at 377.

[22] Ibid.

[23] Ibid. at 378.

[24] Ibid.

[25] "Business Week/Harris Poll: Outsiders Aren't Upset by Insider Trading," *Business Week* (Dec. 8, 1985): 34.

[26] See Stuart P. Green and Matthew B. Klugler, "When Is It Wrong to Trade Stocks on the Basis of Non-Public Information? Public Views of the Morality of Insider Trading," *Fordham Urban Law Journal* 39 (2011): 484.

10.3 ENVY AND INSIDER TRADING

Even if Kahan and Posner's thesis begins to offer a plausible explanation of how even issuer-proscribed insider trading came to be criminalized and then falsely regarded by many as immoral in our society, an important element seems to be missing from the story. Recall that social attitudes regarding insider trading in the Kahan and Posner hypothetical did not begin to change until enough people jumped on the prosecutor's bandwagon to reach a tipping point. Given that the hypothetical presumes a starting point at which insider trading is generally regarded as harmless, more must be said about the motivations of the prosecutor and those who initially side with him. Kahan and Posner suggested that many would be motivated to side with the prosecutor by the desire to "reveal, by contrast, the purity of their own behavior."[27] In other words, the prosecutor offers them an opportunity to signal to others that they are free of all responsibility for the social problem and at the same time gain a reputational advantage by helping to "out" those who were responsible. The motivation to find scapegoats in the wake of a painful event like a market crash or economic downturn can, of course, be powerful,[28] but for our purposes, we still need an explanation of why *issuer-licensed insider traders* would make for promising targets. Contempt for the greed displayed by some insider traders, as discussed previously, offers one possible motivation. Another possible motivation may be envy.

The philosopher John Rawls defined envy as "the propensity to view with hostility the greater good of others even though their being more fortunate than we are does not detract from our advantages." According to Rawls, we "envy a person whose situation is superior to ours ... [when] we are willing to deprive them of their greater benefits even if it is necessary to give up something ourselves."[29]

The tremendous wealth that is often gained with little risk by insider traders cannot be ignored as a possible source of public envy. The average citizen is often struck by the immense compensation that Wall Street executives receive. But the reaction is typically more like the reaction to a professional athlete's salary: people may wonder how anyone could be worth that much, but they are not envious because they know that they could never do what those executives can do – nor would they want the stress and time commitments such jobs entail. The insider trader, however, is different. The average citizen *could* do what the insider trader does. It does not take any particular skill to trade on material nonpublic information. This is where the envy comes in – envy at the good fortune of risk-free trading for

---

[27] Kahan and Posner, "Shaming White Collar Criminals," 377.

[28] Indeed, some have suggested that the prosecution of Raj Rajaratnam and other Galleon Group traders was the Justice Department's attempt to create a "scapegoat ... for the much bigger and yet to be prosecuted crimes of the financial crisis" of 2008. Gasparino, *Circle of Friends*, 253.

[29] John Rawls, A *Theory of Justice* (Cambridge, MA: Harvard University Press, 1971): 532.

those who already enjoy tremendous wealth. US Attorney Preet Bharara seemed to give expression to (or bait) precisely this sentiment when he described his mission against insider traders:

> Disturbingly, many of the people who are going to such lengths to obtain inside information for a trading advantage are already among the most advantaged, privileged, and wealthy insiders in modern finance. But for them, material non-public information is akin to a performance-enhancing drug that provides the illegal "edge" to outpace their rivals and make even more money.[30]

As Bainbridge put it, absent evidence of investor injury, any anger the public feels "over insider trading ... has nothing to do with a loss of confidence in the integrity of the market, but instead arises principally from envy of the insider's greater access to information."[31] Or as Professors Cox and Fogarty explained, the prohibition against insider trading "is not so much an antifraud rule as a law against easy money."[32] Professor Donald Langevoort also noted that the criminalization of insider trading sometimes "smacks ... of envy ... directed at the privileges of class and wealth," reflecting the attitude that insiders "should be content with their paychecks and not overreach for profits."[33]

Envy must be distinguished from resentment. According to Rawls, "resentment is a moral feeling. If we resent our having less than others, it must be because we think that their being better off is the result of unjust institutions, or wrongful conduct on their part." Envy, by contrast, cannot be justified by appeal to moral principle. To explain envy, "[i]t is sufficient to say that the better situation of others catches our attention. We are downcast by their good fortune and no longer value as highly what we have; and this sense of hurt and loss arouses our rancor and hostility."[34]

If the arguments offered in Chapter 9 are credited, the criminalization of issuer-licensed insider trading cannot be explained as an expression of public resentment unless such resentment is misplaced or deluded. Issuer-licensed insider trading harms no one and violates no other-regarding principles of justice or morality. Consequently, if contempt for the profits earned by issuer-licensed insider trading explains the public support for its criminalization, then the contempt itself can be explained only as envy.

---

[30] See Gasparino, *Circle of Friends*, 223.

[31] Stephen Bainbridge, "Incorporating State Law Fiduciary Duties into the Federal Insider Trading Prohibition," *Washington & Lee Law Review* 52 (1995): 1242.

[32] Cox and Fogarty, "Bases of Insider Trading Law," 360.

[33] Donald Langevoort, "Fraud and Insider Trading in American Securities Regulation: Its Scope and Philosophy in a Global Marketplace," *Hastings International & Comparative Law Review* 16 (1993): 182. See also Jeanne L. Schroeder, "Envy and Outsider Trading: The Case of Martha Stewart," *Cardozo Law Review* 26 (2005): 2023 (public attitudes concerning insider traders are often driven by envy of those who receive an "easy buck").

[34] Rawls, *A Theory of Justice*, 533.

If envy does factor as an explanation for the criminalization of issuer-licensed insider trading, then this is concerning for two reasons. First, envy is generally regarded as one of the worst vices. This is because the perverse goal of envy is the destruction of what is good solely to see another deprived of it.[35] In fact, Aristotle described envy as a perfect or "unconditional" vice because it cannot admit of moderation. According to Aristotle, envy's name alone (like "murder") implies badness.[36] Kant described envy as the vice of "hatred for human beings."[37] And as Professor Jeanne L. Schroeder put it, envy is "second only to pride in its potentially corruptive effect on the soul. As etymology reveals, envy – *invidia* – is the most invidious sin."[38] Thus, to the extent envy explains our harsh criminal and civil sanctions against issuer-licensed insider traders, the sanctions do not recognize a vice in the traders, but rather give expression to our society's own vicious tendencies.

There is yet further cause for concern if envy serves as a motivation for the criminalization of insider trading. Rawls has argued that the prevalence of envy in a society risks economic and political instability. For not only are the envious prepared to do things that make both themselves and the objects of their envy worse off, "if only the discrepancy between them is sufficiently reduced," but when the objects of envy realize they have been targeted, "they may become jealous of their better circumstances and anxious to take precautions against the hostile acts to which [others'] envy makes [them] prone."[39] The objects of envy may, for example, take measures to further diminish the position of those who are envious to lessen their threat, and the result is increased social instability and diminished positions for all. Envy is therefore not just harmful to the envious person's character; it is collectively destructive. Indeed, it has been argued that some of the worst social horrors in the modern world (racism, anti-Semitism, and terrorism) have been planted with the seed of envy.[40]

10.4 FROM COMMON SENSE AND POSITIVE LAW TO CRITICAL ETHICAL UNDERSTANDING: RECONCILING CICERO AND MARSHALL

Recall from Chapter 6 the commonsense ethical tension over the problem of information asymmetries reflected in Cicero's grain merchant example and Chief Justice Marshall's decision in *Laidlaw v. Organ*. In both examples, one party profited from an information asymmetry that was not acquired through any deception, but which nevertheless could not be overcome by the counterparty through publicly

---

[35] See Schroeder, "Envy and Outsider Trading," 2031.
[36] Aristotle, *The Nichomachean Ethics*, 45.
[37] Immanuel Kant, *The Metaphysics of Morals*, Mary Gregor (ed. & trans.) (Cambridge: Cambridge University Press, 1996): 206.
[38] Schroeder, "Envy and Outsider Trading," 2031.
[39] Rawls, *A Theory of Justice*, 532.
[40] See Schroeder, "Envy and Outsider Trading," 2031.

available means at the time of the transaction. The commonsense tension was reflected in the recognition that though most agree there is *something* ethically concerning in profiting from such asymmetries (Cicero's point), many would make the trade themselves, or would at least be uncomfortable demanding disclosure in such cases as a matter of law (Chief Justice Marshall's conclusion). Conclusions from this chapter and Chapters 8 and 9 now allow for a critical ethical understanding of this problem and permit some resolution as to how it should be addressed by positive law – in general, and in the context of issuer-licensed insider trading.

The commonsense ethical tension over the problem of non-deceptive information asymmetries in exchanges can be resolved by considering it in light of the distinction between moral duty and ethical supererogation. Consider the Biblical parable of the Good Samaritan. In it, a traveler is assaulted by thieves, stripped of his possessions, and left to die by the side of the road. A number of people pass the poor traveler, take note of his pitiful condition, but continue on their journeys without offering aid. Finally, a certain Samaritan comes along and shows compassion for the victim. He treats the victim's wounds, puts him on his own mule, and takes him to an inn for the night. Then, needing to continue on his journey, the Samaritan pays the innkeeper in advance to take care of the victim until he is fully recovered.

The ethical concept of supererogation was introduced in Chapter 7. A supererogatory act is one that goes beyond the demands of moral duty. Supererogation distinguishes the Good Samaritan's conduct from that of everyone else in the story. We praise the Good Samaritan because, in going far out of his way to provide aid to the victim in need, he displayed a superior ethical character and virtue. While we recognize that those who fall short of the Good Samaritan's example have room for ethical improvement, we nevertheless are not prepared to recognize an absolute duty to always behave as the Good Samaritan would. Morality does not demand that everyone behave as saints. This distinction is important: it represents the boundary between the categorical moral demands of justice and fairness on the one hand, and our private pursuits of ethical self-perfection on the other.

There is a reason why we distinguish the notion of duty from supererogation in ethics. It makes sense to say we have done our duty. But supererogation will always ask more of us. There is always more we can do to improve our characters, to become better people by our own lights. The task of self-perfection is never complete, and, moreover, perfection means different things to different people – particularly in a pluralistic liberal society. It therefore makes no sense to recognize supererogatory conduct as anything more than aspirational, both ethically and under the law.

Emphasizing this divide between moral duty and supererogation in the context of information asymmetries allows us to reconcile Cicero and Chief Justice Marshall. The rule in *Laidlaw* recognizes that Organ violated no moral duty (did no injustice) in failing to disclose his information advantage. Disclosure may have been charitable or kind, but, as Marshall recognized, it would be unwise for the law to enforce such ethical perfectionism. Recall, however, that Cicero wrote *De Officiis* to offer guidance for his son on how to be the best among men – not as a legal treatise. It should come as no surprise then that Cicero would expect his son to aspire to do more than what is minimally required. He would rather his son earn a reputation for generosity than be wealthy. Though the grain dealer would commit no injustice by failing to disclose (and his conduct should not, therefore, be illegal), he would display a generous character if he *did* disclose. There is room for both Chief Justice Marshall and Cicero to be correct.

All of the aforementioned is instructive in the context of insider trading. It is expected that the conclusion that issuer-licensed insider trading does not violate a moral duty will meet some resistance from the standpoint of common sense. Many will continue to complain that "it just seems wrong!" Considering issuer-licensed insider trading alongside *Laidlaw's* Organ and Cicero's grain dealer helps to flesh out a possible source of this commonsense objection. Just as there is room for Chief Justice Marshall to find Organ violated no duty and at the same time for Cicero to find fault in the character of the grain dealer, there is also room for one to find the conduct of the issuer-licensed insider trader violates no moral duty and should not be punished by the law, but that it *may* (in some cases, though certainly not in all) nevertheless betray an ethically flawed character – one lacking in generosity, or perhaps even reflecting the vice of greed.[41]

*****

So where does this leave us as we look ahead to proposed reforms to the current insider trading regime in the United States? It seems the strict parity-of-information model demands too much to the extent that it would preclude even issuer-licensed insider trading. Utility, justice, and fairness do not demand that market participants conduct themselves as saints – always placing the interests of others before their own, and that is precisely what parity of information demands. Similarly, even equal access demands too much, at least to the extent that it demands more than equal access to employment opportunity. For those who enjoy privileged access to information upon which their firms allow them to trade do no harm or injustice to counterparties or the broader market by so trading. Only those who trade contrary

---

[41] Professor Marc I. Steinberg made a similar point concerning insider trading and the "aggressive" demands of Jewish law. Steinberg explained that "Exodus 23:7 not only prohibits lying but also mandates that an individual 'distance himself from falsehood' … Deuteronomy 16:20 directs that 'Justice, Justice you shall pursue,' suggesting that 'the Torah is mandating a particular aggressiveness in performing this commandment.'" From this Steinberg concluded that "allowing those persons who are selectively privy to material inside information (regardless of how and from what sources such information was obtained) to financially benefit at the expense of uninformed traders … [may be] contrary to Jewish Law." Marc I. Steinberg, "Insider Trading Regulation – A Comparative Analysis," *International Law* 37 (2003): 168. Steinberg's conclusion is consistent with the distinction made here between the minimal requirements of justice and the virtue and ethical praise associated with supererogation.

to an express or implied commitment to the owner of material nonpublic information, either issuer-proscribed insider traders or misappropriation traders, violate a moral duty – whether defined pursuant to the principle of utility, the categorical imperative, or other principles of fairness. Again, this is consistent with Chief Justice Marshall's decision in *Laidlaw*, that absent some deception or other wrongful conduct, market participants are free to profit from information asymmetries.

As explained in Chapter 7, the other-regarding demands of moral theories such as utilitarianism and deontology, though certainly important, are neither necessary nor sufficient for legal justification. At the margins, economic and other normative considerations such as those expressed in virtue theory can inform and sometimes determine the legal question. In this case, the economic conclusions of Chapter 8 inform and reinforce the conclusion from Chapter 9 that issuer-licensed insider trading neither harms nor wrongs. And though this chapter suggests that the vice of greed is sometimes reflected in issuer-licensed insider trading, it need not be. Moreover, while good character formation is an important value to weigh in determining how we use the law to shape our institutions, to the extent we value liberty, Mill has taught us that we must be careful in how we use the criminal law to address such concerns. Finally, and perhaps most importantly, if the criminalization of issuer-licensed insider trading is motivated by the vice of envy, we may be purporting to stamp out one character flaw (greed) while giving expression to another that is more invidious and socially dangerous.

With the critical ethical analysis of the practice of insider trading complete, the tools for constructing informed and focused guidelines for reforming the positive law of insider trading in the United States are now in place.

PART III

Reform

11

The Path Forward

An Outline for Reform

Chapter 4 identified a number of problems with the current insider trading enforcement regime in the United States that render it unjust, incoherent, and irrational. Its injustice was identified in three principal concerns. First, the absence of any clear definition of insider trading by statute or rule leaves the current regime to suffer from significant ambiguity in its elements. One result of this ambiguity is that, like most common law crimes, it violates the time-honored principle of legality, providing insufficient notice of criminal wrongdoing. Second, in addition to providing insufficient notice, ambiguity in the law permits vast discretion in enforcement for prosecutors and regulators. Such discretion, in turn, invites abuse – for example, the prosecution of insiders for the political or personal reasons of the prosecutor. Third, and perhaps most importantly, Chapters 8, 9, and 10 have demonstrated that by criminalizing even issuer-licensed insider trading, the current regime commits the gross injustice of punishing economically harmless and morally innocent conduct.

In addition to showing that the current insider trading enforcement regime is unjust, Chapter 4 showed that it is also incoherent. Insider trading jurisprudence in the United States reflects a tension between the SEC's preferred equal-access model and the fraud-based model mandated by Section 10(b) and the US Supreme Court. These two models are often mutually exclusive in rationale and application. This has resulted in a schizophrenic regime that is either under- or over-inclusive, depending on the lens through which it is viewed. Judged by the equal-access model, the current US enforcement regime is under-inclusive by permitting trading based on material nonpublic information acquired by eavesdropping, when the tipper fails to benefit, when the tippee announces the intent to trade, when insiders refrain from selling or buying, and when insiders make strategic use of 10b5–1(c) trading plans. Viewed through the lens of fraud, the current regime is over-inclusive to the extent that recent SEC rules have seemingly done away with the element of scienter and, most importantly, to the extent that the law criminalizes issuer-licensed insider trading, which involves no deception.

Finally, Chapter 4 explained that the current insider trading enforcement regime in the United States is irrational. To begin, without a clear definition of what the law proscribes, regulators demand the impossible when they require issuers to design and implement effective insider trading compliance programs. This problem of uncertainty is then compounded by the threat of heavy civil and criminal sanctions for violations. Placed between this rock and hard place, issuers tend to adopt over-broad insider trading compliance programs, which come at a heavy price in terms of corporate culture, cost of compensation, share liquidity, and cost of capital. Since all of these costs are passed along to the shareholders, insider trading enforcement under the current regime achieves the opposite of its intended goal of protecting average investors. This is the paradox of insider trading compliance under the current US regime. But the irrationality does not stop there. Chapter 4 pointed out another absurdity in the current enforcement regime, namely that most theories of derivative corporate criminal liability for insider trading in the United States are designed to punish the victim of the crime (the employer or the shareholder) for the crime itself.

The goal of this chapter is to outline a plan for reforming the insider trading enforcement regime in the United States that draws upon the global lessons of Chapter 5, and the economic and ethical lessons of Chapters 6 through 10, to address each of the defects just identified. But before new guidelines for reform are offered, it pays to consider some pros and cons of recent legislative reform efforts.

11.1 SOME RECENTLY PROPOSED REFORMS

As explained in Chapter 3, the Second Circuit's 2014 decision in *United States v. Newman* represented a significant setback to the SEC's slow push through rule-making and enforcement actions toward a de facto equal-access (and perhaps even parity-of-information) insider trading enforcement regime.[1] Recall that the *Newman* court held that a fact finder is not permitted to infer a tipper personally benefited by gifting confidential information to a trading relative or friend absent "proof of a meaningfully close personal relationship" between the tipper and tippee "that generates an exchange that is objective, consequential, and represents at least a potential gain of a pecuniary or similarly valuable nature."[2] This test was far more difficult to satisfy than the government's preferred test, which would permit the inference of a personal benefit from any gift of confidential information from an insider for a non-corporate purpose. When combined with the *Newman* Court's added insistence that the government also prove a tippee's knowledge that this personal benefit test was satisfied, the Second Circuit's decision made it exponentially more difficult for the SEC and prosecutors to establish remote tippee liability.

---

[1] United States v. Newman, 773 F.3d 438, 452 (2014).
[2] *Newman*, 773 F.3d at 452.

And after the Supreme Court's narrow holding in *Salman v. United States*, much (though certainly not all) of *Newman's* rigor remained intact.[3]

It was noted in Chapter 3 that the SEC, prosecutors, and many scholars expressed concern that the Second Circuit's *Newman* decision opened a concerning loophole for insider trading resulting from gratuitous tipping, and some scholars scrambled to identify new theories of liability from within the existing regulatory framework that would capture such conduct. Members of Congress took action as well. Three new insider trading bills were introduced (one in the Senate and two in the House of Representatives) in the weeks and months following the *Newman* decision. All of the bills would eliminate the "personal benefit" requirement for tippee liability, and all would bring greater clarity and certainty to the law of insider trading by finally offering a statutory definition of the offense. Though each of these three bills would arguably expand insider trading liability from the current understanding of its scope, some would expand it more than others. All of these bills are, however, defective in light of the conclusions drawn in previous chapters of this book.

The Senate bill, titled the Stop Illegal Insider Trading Act, offers the most extreme overhaul of the current US regime by outlining what amounts to a parity-of-information model along the lines of that found in Europe and Australia.[4] Under the bill, sponsored by Senators Jack Reed and Bob Menendez, Section 10 of the Exchange Act would be amended to make it illegal to "purchase, sell, or cause the purchase or sale of any security on the basis of material information that the person knows or has reason to know is not publicly available."[5] As Senator Reed's office explained, the bill offers a "clear and simple, bright-line rule: if a person trades a security on the basis of material information that he or she knows or has reason to

---

[3]   Salman v. United States, 137 S.Ct 420 (2016). The *Salman* Court reaffirmed the personal benefit test and did not overturn the *Newman* Court's requirement that the government prove the tippee's knowledge of the personal benefit. Moreover, the Court was very careful to limit its decision to the facts of *Salman*, where the tipper was the brother of, and had a "close relationship" with, the tippee. 137 S.Ct. at 424. The Court noted that these facts were within the "heartland of *Dirks's* rule concerning gifts" of confidential information to trading relatives, and left open the question of whether proof of a tangible benefit may be required where a gratuitous tip is made to a remote relative or to a mere acquaintance (as was the case in *Newman*). Ibid. at 429. Without question, *Salman* established that the "tangible benefit" test is not a necessary condition for tipper-tippee liability in all cases, but it left the door open for courts to decide that it is necessary in *some*. As noted in previous chapters, however, on August 23, 2017, a split Second Circuit panel reversed *Newman's* holding that tippers personally benefit from their gifts of material nonpublic information only when they share a "meaningfully close personal relationship" with the tippee. See United States v. Martoma, 2017 WL 3611518 (2d Cir. 2017). That decision was pending en banc review before the Second Circuit, and potentially Supreme Court review, at the time this book went to press.

[4]   See Chapter 5.

[5]   Senate Bill S.702 – 114th Congress (2015–2016).

know is not publicly available, then he or she has engaged in unlawful insider trading."[6] The bill addresses tipper-tippee liability by making it illegal to "knowingly or recklessly communicate material information that the person knows or has reason to know is not publicly available to any other person under circumstances in which it is reasonably foreseeable that such communication is likely to result" in trading.[7] Though the bill is admirable in its simplicity, it suffers from a number of defects.

First, in offering a parity-of-information regime, the Reed-Menendez bill is over-inclusive in its reach. Chapter 9 concluded that issuer-licensed insider trading is economically harmless and morally permissible. Consequently, any civil enforcement or criminal law that punishes such conduct would be unjust and inefficient. Second, by imposing liability where the trader merely "has reason to know" of the nonpublic nature of her information, the bill appears to impose criminal liability for mere negligent conduct. Though criminal negligence is by no means a novel concept, insofar as it lacks mens rea, it is usually reserved for particularly dangerous or socially costly behavior (e.g., negligent homicide or negligent endangerment of a child). Even economically costly and morally culpable forms of insider trading (e.g., issuer-proscribed and misappropriation trading) probably do not rise to this level. Third, despite its simplicity, by failing to define what information is "material" and what information is "not publicly available," the Reed-Menendez bill will no doubt generate a great deal of uncertainty as to its scope. As Professor Peter Henning noted, it is unclear whether "volume of stock orders obtained by high-frequency traders or even intentions of a particularly influential investor – think Warren E. Buffet" would count as "not publicly available" under the proposed bill.[8] Such uncertainty would allow the problem of lack of notice to persist, and it would continue to wreak havoc on compliance regimes. Finally, the Reed-Menendez bill does nothing to solve the problem identified in Chapter 4 that, under the current regime, the principal victims of insider trading (corporations and, by extension, their shareholders) may be subject to derivative criminal liability for crimes perpetrated against them by their employees.

Representative Stephen Lynch introduced the Ban Insider Trading Act of 2015 in February 2015. Unlike the parity-of-information model offered by Senators Reed and Menendez, the Lynch bill looks to maintain aspects of the existing fraud-based model while improving its clarity and expanding its scope. The bill would proscribe the purchase or sale of any security "based on information that the person knows or, considering factors including financial sophistication, knowledge of and experience

---

[6] Office of Senator Jack Reed, "Reed & Menendez Introduce Bill to Clearly Define and Ban Unlawful Insider Trading" (March 11, 2015), www.reed.senate.gov/news/releases/reed-and-menendez-introduce-bill-to-clearly-define-and-ban-unlawful-insider-trading.

[7] Senate Bill S.702 – 114th Congress (2015–2016).

[8] Peter J. Henning, "Court Strikes on Insider Trading, and Congress Lobs Back," *New York Times* (March 16, 2015), www.nytimes.com/2015/03/17/business/dealbook/court-strikes-on-insider-trading-and-congress-lobs-back.html?mcubz=0.

in financial matters, position in a company, and amount of assets under management, should know is material information and inside information."[9] The bill then defines "inside information" as any information that is "nonpublic" and obtained "illegally," "directly or indirectly from an issuer with an expectation of confidentiality or that such information will only be used for a legitimate business purpose," or "in violation of a fiduciary duty." To address tipper liability the bill holds anyone liable who

> intentionally discloses without a legitimate business purpose to another person information that the discloser knows or, considering factors including financial sophistication, knowledge of and experience in financial matters, position in a company, and amount of assets under management, should know is material information and inside information.[10]

The bill also expressly provides that an insider trading action does not require "a personal benefit to any party."[11]

Liability under the Lynch bill preserves the current regime's requirement that there be a breach of duty to incur insider trading liability, though it clearly broadens the scope of this duty to include all information obtained "illegally" or in breach of an expectation of confidentiality, and by expressly dispensing with the need to prove a personal benefit. By requiring that the trading breach a duty, it is not as broad in its reach as is the Reed-Menendez Senate bill. Nevertheless, it would almost certainly be interpreted to criminalize issuer-licensed insider trading, and therefore its scope would still extend beyond what justice permits. Moreover, though the Lynch bill makes it clear that its reasonable person test will take into account the "financial sophistication" of the trader, it nevertheless stands ready to impose criminal liability for negligent conduct, and to that extent it suffers the same moral responsibility concern raised by the Senate bill. The Lynch bill offers a definition of "material information" as "information that relates, directly or indirectly, to an issuer or a security, and that, if it were made public, would likely have a significant effect on the price of a security."[12] While some statutory definition is better than none at all, this new "significant effect" test is unlikely to bring greater clarity than the current common law tests outlined in Chapter 3. The Lynch bill does not offer any definition of when information is "nonpublic," when it is obtained "illegally," or what constitutes a "fiduciary duty," "an expectation of confidentiality," or "a legitimate business purpose." Like the Reed-Menendez bill, the Lynch bill also fails to address the potential paradox of derivative corporate criminal liability for the victim of the crime.

---

[9] House Bill H.R. 1173 – 114th Congress (2015–2016).
[10] Ibid.
[11] Ibid.
[12] Ibid.

Representative Jim Himes introduced the Insider Trading Prohibition Act in March 2015.[13] The bill provides that

> [i]t shall be unlawful for any person, directly or indirectly, to purchase, sell, or enter into, or cause the purchase or sale of or entry into, any security, security-based swap, or security-based swap agreement, if such person knows, or recklessly disregards, that such information has been obtained wrongfully, or that such purchase, sale, or entry would constitute a wrongful use of such information.[14]

The bill also prohibits anyone whose own trading would be prohibited under the preceding language from "wrongfully" communicating "material, nonpublic information" relating to the security to "any other person" if the other person then trades on that information or communicates it to another person who trades.[15] The bill explains that trading while in possession of material nonpublic information (or communicating such information) is only "wrongful" if it was

> obtained by, or its communication or use would constitute, directly or indirectly –
>
> (A) theft, bribery, misrepresentation, or espionage (through electronic or other means);
> (B) a violation of any Federal law protecting computer data or the intellectual property or privacy of computer users; or
> (C) conversion, misappropriation, or other unauthorized and deceptive taking of such information, or a breach of any fiduciary duty or any other personal or other relationship of trust and confidence.[16]

The Himes bill also lays out the knowledge requirement in admirable detail, providing that

> [i]t shall not be necessary that the person trading while in possession of such information [as proscribed by the preceding], or making the communication [as proscribed by the preceding], know the specific means by which the information was obtained or communicated, or whether any personal benefit was paid or promised by or to any person in the chain of communication, so long as the person trading while in possession of such information or making the communication, as the case may be, was aware, or recklessly disregarded that such information was wrongfully obtained or communicated.[17]

Finally, the Himes bill places explicit restrictions on derivative liability for insider trading, providing that "no person shall be liable under this section solely by reason of the fact that such person controls or employs a person who has violated this

[13] House Bill H.R. 1625 – 114th Congress (2015–2016).
[14] Ibid.
[15] Ibid.
[16] Ibid.
[17] Ibid.

section, if such controlling person or employer did not participate in, profit from, or directly or indirectly induce" the proscribed trading or communication.[18]

Of the post-*Newman* insider trading bills, the Himes bill comes closest to the conclusions of this book. Its focus on only trading based on information "wrongfully" obtained (with an explicit and exhaustive list of what conduct counts as wrongful) at least purports to ensure that the proscribed conduct captures only morally impermissible acts. It implicitly recognizes a firm's material nonpublic information as its (or its shareholders') property and then looks to proscribe all and only trading on that information by those who wrongfully acquire or use it. Its limitation on derivative liability appears designed to address the current law's absurdity in holding corporate victims liable for the crimes against them. By including computer hacking and outright theft among the wrongful means of acquiring information, the Himes bill also fills an awkward gap in the current fraud-based regime. Finally, by avoiding the "or should have known" language in the knowledge requirement, the Himes bill also avoids the problem of criminal liability for negligent conduct. Despite these virtues, the Himes bill nevertheless falls short in a number of respects.

To begin, by only proscribing wrongful conduct, the bill could be interpreted to permit issuer-licensed insider trading. Without expressly exempting issuer-licensed trading, however, the bill would almost certainly be interpreted by the SEC, prosecutors, and the courts as criminalizing such conduct – most likely as a breach of fiduciary duty or other "personal or other relationship of trust and confidence." Moreover, by failing to define such terms as "material," "nonpublic," and what counts as a fiduciary, "personal or other relationship of trust and confidence," the bill would leave much of the vagueness that pervades the current enforcement regime in place, at great economic and moral cost. More still, though it excludes negligent liability, it expressly recognizes criminal liability for reckless (or unintentional) conduct. Despite these flaws, there is much to admire in the Himes bill, and some of its advances will be modeled in the guidelines for reform that follow.

11.2 ADOPT A WRONGFUL USE THEORY OF LIABILITY

The goal of the remaining sections of this chapter is to offer general guidelines for reform that, if followed, would do much to correct the injustice, incoherence, and irrationality of the current insider trading enforcement regime in the United States. Though these guidelines are presented as a comprehensive reform program, they need not be implemented as such. Each proposed reform – even if taken in isolation – would improve upon the current regime. Taken together, however, it is suggested that the law would approach a complete fix.

---

[18] Ibid.

The first step in this direction is to suggest a coherent theory of liability that proscribes only economically harmful and morally impermissible conduct as identified by previous chapters. Recall from Chapters 8 and 9 that when insider trading results in economic or moral harm, it is almost always suffered by the originating source of the information, which is usually (though not always) the issuer of the traded stock (and by extension its shareholders). The Supreme Court was correct to recognize in *United States v. O'Hagan* that the ultimate source of the information is typically its owner, who, all things being equal, has a right to its exclusive use.[19] When such information is taken and used by some third party without the owner's tacit or express consent, the owner is wronged. This wrong may be committed by fraud (the sole focus of the current regime), but it might also be done by outright theft, conversion, bribery, espionage, or computer hacking. An insider trading law that imposed liability for all and only such conduct would capture all the economically and morally harmful insider trading identified in Chapters 8 and 9 – namely issuer-proscribed and misappropriation trading – while leaving economically and morally harmless issuer-licensed insider trading free of liability. Such reform would also fill the awkward gap in the current regime that proscribes trading on the basis of information obtained by fraud, but not by more straightforward wrongful conduct such as outright theft. This theory of insider trading liability would therefore, if properly executed in clear and well-defined statutes and rules, remedy much, if not all, of the injustice, incoherence, and irrationality of the existing regime.

In sum, the law should be reformed to expressly recognize material nonpublic information as property with respect to which the firm, as the originator and owner of the information, has a right to exclusive use. Any use of that information against the will of the owner (whether by fraudulent deception, conversion, theft, bribery, espionage, or computer hacking) for the purpose of trading or tipping on the basis of that information is morally wrong and economically harmful (for reasons identified in Chapters 8 and 9) and should therefore be prohibited by law. To avoid the vagueness that plagues the current US insider trading regime, this proposed reform should be made manifest in a clearly defined statute, which should include some important provisos and definitions to bring justice and certainty to its enforcement.

---

[19] United States v. O'Hagan, 521 U.S. 642, 654 (1997) ("A company's confidential information . . . qualifies as property to which the company has a right of exclusive use."). See also Stephen Bainbridge, *Insider Trading Law and Policy* (St. Paul, MN: Foundation Press, 2014): 204–05 (citing Diamond v. Oreamuno, 248 N.E. 2d 910 (N.Y. 1969) for the proposition that the US insider trading enforcement regime rests on "an implicit assumption that as between the firm and its agents, all confidential information about the firm is an asset of the corporation"). Professor Bainbridge has also argued compellingly that assigning the property right to "agent-produced information to the firm maximizes the social incentives for the production of valuable new information." See ibid. at 204.

11.3 EXPRESSLY AUTHORIZE ISSUER-LICENSED INSIDER TRADING

With the general proscription of the wrongful use of material nonpublic information to trade in place, one important proviso or clarification must be made explicit by statute or rule: the express authorization of issuer-licensed insider trading. There is no single solution to the dysfunction that pervades the existing US insider trading enforcement regime, but expressly legalizing issuer-licensed trading would dramatically improve clarity, coherence, and rationality in the law. An express safe harbor should permit issuers, at their discretion, to allow their employees to trade the firm's shares based on material nonpublic information so long as the following conditions are satisfied:[20]

(1) **The insider must submit a written plan to the issuer that details the proposed trade(s).** The law should require that the written plan identify the type of trade (buy, sell, etc.), the number of shares to be traded, and the approximate date and time the trade is expected to take place. Firms should be required to maintain these records for reporting (discussed later) and to aid in any investigation of, or litigation over, trading that does not comply with the plan. Beyond these requirements, firms may choose to demand more extensive disclosures from insiders who propose to trade. For example, a firm might require that any proposed trading plan explain the material nonpublic information upon which it is based, and perhaps even how it was acquired, as a means of facilitating intra-firm information dissemination.

(2) **The firm must authorize the trading plan.** It should be up to the firm that owns the information to assign the responsibility of authorizing these trading plans, whether it be a compliance officer, general counsel, the CEO, the board of directors, or someone else. Whomever it is, they should be prepared to offer a legitimate business purpose for the authorization. In some cases, the purpose may be to reward the entrepreneurial success of an employee, as Henry Manne envisioned. In other cases, it may be to shield from the risk of liability an employee who possesses material nonpublic information but wishes to trade for another reason (for example, to diversify her portfolio, to pay for a child's college, etc.).

---

[20] This reform was first proposed in John P. Anderson, "Anticipating a Sea Change for Insider Trading Law: From Trading Plan Crisis to Rational Reform," *Utah Law Review* 2015 (2015): 380–81; see also John P. Anderson, "Solving the Paradox of Insider Trading Compliance," *Temple Law Review* 88 (2016): 308; John P. Anderson, "The Final Step to Insider Trading Reform: Answering the 'It's Just Not Right!' Objection," *Journal of Law, Economics and Policy* 12 (2017): 265.

(3) **The firm must have previously disclosed to the investing public that it will permit its employees to trade on the firm's material nonpublic information through these plans when it is in the interest of the firm to do so.** The law should require that this disclosure be made through a separate SEC filing that is easily accessible to the investing public. This ex ante disclosure need only announce that the issuer reserves the right to license trading on its material nonpublic information pursuant to trading plans filed with the firm when it is in the interest of the firm to do so. Such an announcement is sufficient to put the investing public on notice of the potential for issuer-licensed insider trading in the firm's shares and defuse any charge of deception.[21] Once the disclosure is made, investors are left free to avoid the stock or reprice it. A more demanding ex ante disclosure requirement should be avoided at the risk of generating more confusion than clarity. For example, announcing in advance that a specific plan was issued, the identity of the trader, or even the volume of the trade may lead to speculation and volatility in the stock. But since the actual basis for the trade would not be disclosed (for this would defeat the point), any such speculation would be uninformed and dangerous. Our disclosure regime is designed to avoid such rampant speculation, not to promote it. Moreover, what if a plan were announced and then later cancelled after the market had reacted? Disappointed speculators would no doubt cry foul.[22] It may be that some of these concerns explain why the SEC has resisted disclosure requirements for Rule 10b5–1 trading plans.[23]

(4) **The firm must disclose ex post all trading profits resulting from the execution of these plans.** Although firms should not be required to disclose individual trading plans ex ante, profits derived from these plans must be disclosed ex post in the firm's financials so that the market can factor this as compensation paid by the firm. This disclosure will also allow the market to adjust the price (or bid-ask spread) of the issuer's shares as necessary based on the volume of issuer-licensed trading in the stock.[24]

---

[21] See, e.g., Saikrishna Prakash, "Our Dysfunctional Insider Trading Regime," *Columbia Law Review* 99 (1999): 1515–20 (arguing that disclosure of general intent to allow trading on the firm's material nonpublic information avoids deception).

[22] See, e.g., Allan Horwich, "The Origin, Application, Validity, and Potential Misuse of Rule 10b5–1," *Business Lawyer* 62 (2007): 921 (noting the possible undesirable effects of requiring detailed advance disclosure of 10b5–1 trading plans).

[23] See Anderson, "Anticipating a Sea Change for Insider Trading Law," 372–74 (a disclosure requiring disclosure of 10b5–1 trading plans was proposed by the SEC in 2002 and was dropped).

[24] See, e.g., M. Todd Henderson, "Insider Trading and CEO Pay," *Vanderbilt Law Review* 64 (2011): 550–51 (suggesting an ex post disclosure of issuer-licensed insider trading for similar reasons).

There is nothing novel about issuer-licensed trading plans. As noted in Chapter 3, the SEC introduced Rule 10b5–1 trading plans as an affirmative defense to insider trading liability in 2000. Enforcement regimes in other countries have also made use of trading plans as safe harbors from insider trading liability.[25] Of course, no enforcement regime has expressly recognized a safe harbor for issuer-licensed trading on material nonpublic information through trading plans, as is proposed here. Nevertheless, issuer-licensed insider trading through plans following the guidelines outlined in this chapter would arguably be permissible under some existing regimes. For example, the Supreme Court has made it clear that Section 10(b) insider trading liability requires some proof of fraudulent deception on the part of a trader.[26] But it was shown in Chapter 9 that issuer-licensed insider trading involves no such deception. This realization has led a number of scholars (including this author) to suggest that issuer-licensed insider trading is permissible even under the current Section 10(b) insider trading regime.[27] Given, however, that the SEC would almost certainly challenge any such interpretation – and at least some lower courts would back it – no firm would (or should) take the risk of testing the theory absent clear guidance from the SEC. This is why an express safe harbor for issuer-licensed insider trading is so important to the reform program outlined here.

Finally, it is important to emphasize that this proposed safe harbor is only for issuer-licensed insider trading pursuant to trading plans that comply with the expressed guidelines. The proposed safe harbor would therefore not affect the current regulation of issuer-proscribed insider trading (classical insider trading where the insider trades based on material nonpublic information despite the fact that the issuer has proscribed such trading), nor would it affect the current regulation of trading under the misappropriation theory. As explained in Chapters 8 and 9, such trading is economically harmful, morally wrong, and should continue to be proscribed along with the other wrongful forms of trading outlined in the previous section.

So how would authorizing issuer-licensed insider trading improve matters? The reform does not solve the problem of vagueness in the legal elements of the insider trading. (This problem is addressed in the next section.) It does, however, bring relative certainty to a large, perhaps the largest, class of potential insider traders, namely issuers and the corporate insiders whom they employ. Issuers who are concerned about the risk of civil and criminal exposure for their trading and the trading of their employees could take refuge in the safe harbor offered by the reform.

---

[25] For example, as noted in Chapter 5, India's 2015 regulation tempers its broad equal-access enforcement regime by offering issuer-licensed trading plans as an affirmative defense to insider trading liability.

[26] See, e.g., Chiarella v. United States, 445 U.S. 222, 225 (1980).

[27] See Anderson, "Anticipating a Sea Change for Insider Trading Law," 385–86. See also Henderson, "Insider Trading and CEO Pay," 505; Prakash, "Our Dysfunctional Insider Trading Regime," 1515–20.

With the proper disclosures in place, they could be certain that any authorized trades in the firm's shares would not run afoul of the insider trading enforcement regime. Corporate insiders themselves would enjoy the same certainty with any authorized trade, regardless of whether they possess material nonpublic information. In addition, this increased certainty for issuers and insiders would decrease the risk of abuse of regulatory and prosecutorial discretion.

Notice that this reform would also resolve the paradox of insider trading compliance for issuers. With the trading plan safe harbor in place, firms would no longer feel compelled to preclude otherwise harmless trades for fear they might incur civil or criminal penalties. A firm's business judgment, not fear of regulatory scrutiny, would determine trading decisions and the liquidity of employee shares. If a firm rejects an insider's trading request and the employee trades anyway, then any insider trading enforcement action by regulators would be consistent with the firm's interests. In short, the proposed reform would significantly reduce the heavy costs of insider trading compliance for issuers under the current regime, and it would improve the alignment of issuer and regulator interests.

11.4 DEFINE ELEMENTS BY STATUTE OR RULE

Expressly authorizing issuer-licensed insider trading within a codified wrongful use regime would help to bring certainty to the law of insider trading, but it would not solve the problem of vagueness. As explained in Chapter 3, simply codifying terms such as "material," "nonpublic," "on the basis of," etc. would still leave significant ambiguity as to their meanings. Some definition of these elements by statute or rule is needed to provide notice to traders and to constrain discretion in prosecution. The US regime may have something to learn from the recent global experience in this context. As noted in Chapter 5, a number of countries have experimented with offering more clearly defined insider trading elements, some even allowing the issuers to define those elements for themselves.

11.4.1 *Materiality*

Materiality is a relative concept and cannot therefore be defined by statute with the precision necessary to offer absolute ex ante certainty to traders. Even assigning an objective percentage point (say, information that moves a stock's price 5 percent) would not give advance notice to traders because it would remain difficult, if not impossible, to determine the price effect of such information in advance. It may even be difficult to determine ex post because price movements may have multiple causes (both market- and firm-specific). The most promising tack is therefore to combine a general definition with an exclusive list of types of information that will be deemed material if they satisfy that definition. So, for example, following the European lead, "materiality" might be effectively defined as "information that is of a type identified in statutory subsection [x] and which relates, directly or indirectly, to an issuer or a security, and that, if made public, would likely have a significant effect on the price of a security." Statutory subsection [x] could then offer an exclusive list of types of information that may be material. Borrowing from the Chinese model, this list might include earnings information, any plan to distribute dividends, any changes in equity structure, any acts by senior management exposing the company to liability, or plans to be acquired.[28] Whatever its content, this list of types of potentially material information should be exhaustive, so that it can provide relative notice and certainty to market participants. But, following the Russian model, the list should also include an issuer-specific category that would grant the issuer the opportunity to identify additional types of potential material information by publicly filing them in advance. For example, product sales data may be material to a manufacturer, but not to a bank. If so, the manufacturer would file it as a type of potentially material information, but the bank would not.

In sum, on this model, a person who trades on information that, though wrongfully acquired and nonpublic, is not of a type identified on the exhaustive list (including the issuer's supplement) cannot be prosecuted for insider trading. A person who trades on the basis of wrongfully acquired information that falls within a statutorily defined category, but that would be unlikely to have "a significant effect" on the price of the stock, also could not be prosecuted for insider trading. Only one who wrongfully trades on nonpublic information that is likely to have a significant effect on the stock price when released *and* that is of a type identified by the statute or issuer supplement may be liable for insider trading on this model.

This hybrid approach to materiality cabins the unavoidably vague "significant effect" (or some similar) test with a precise and exhaustive list of types of potentially material information. In doing so, it maintains flexibility for prosecutors and regulators within the identified categories, while the categories themselves provide some certainty and notice to traders. Adding the issuer-specific category also grants power to the issuer – the owner of the information, and the principal victim of any potential insider trading – to supplement the statutory list as needed to protect the firm and its shareholders.

---

[28] The list could also be modeled upon the guidance offered by the SEC concerning compliance with Regulation Fair Disclosure:

> (1) earnings information; (2) mergers, acquisitions, tender offers, joint ventures, or changes in assets; (3) new products or discoveries, or developments regarding costumers or suppliers (e.g., the acquisition or loss of a contract); (4) changes in control or in management; (5) change in auditors or auditor notification that the issuer may no longer rely on an auditor's audit report; (6) events regarding the issuer's securities – e.g., defaults on senior securities, calls of securities for redemption, repurchase plans, stock splits or changes in dividends, changes to the rights of security holders, public or private sales of additional securities; and (7) bankruptcies or receiverships.

See Selective Disclosure and Insider Trading, Exchange Act Release No. 43,154, 65 Fed. Reg. 51,716, 51,721 (Aug. 24, 2000).

11.4.2 *Nonpublic*

As noted in Chapter 3, the current common law tests for determining when information is nonpublic for purposes of insider trading liability are the "dissemination
and absorption" test and the "efficient capital market hypothesis" test. Neither one of
these vague standards provides adequate certainty or notice to traders ex ante. The
most promising approach to reforming this element of insider trading law would be
to follow Japan in adopting a bright-line rule. Under the Japanese rule, information
is public twelve hours after its disclosure to at least two media outlets.[29] Whether
the disclosure needs to be to two (as opposed to one) media outlet is debatable.
Disclosure to one media source may be sufficient in this digital age of immediacy
and viral dissemination through electronic means. There is also no reason to assume
that the disclosure must be to a media outlet; any number of other sources may work
just as well (e.g., the issuer's Facebook, Instagram, or Twitter account, the issuer's
website or LISTSERV, a webcast conference, or an SEC filing). The key to
ensuring adequate notice to traders will be to adopt the bright-line approach of
offering an exhaustive list of forms of acceptable disclosure. There is always the
risk that information might be made public through some other channel, or that
dissemination through one of the identified channels would not lead to full dissemination. The certainty and notice associated with an exhaustive list of modes
of dissemination and a clear time frame are, however, well worth these risks. In
addition, as with the materiality element proposed previously, the exhaustive list
of acceptable modes of dissemination should include an issuer-specific category
whereby issuers may identify modes of dissemination that make the most business
sense for the firm. The twelve-hour rule should, however, remain uniform to ensure
certainty and to prevent gaming. Under the guidelines proposed here, issuers will
always be free to license trading through a properly executed trading plan if they
would prefer that some individuals be permitted to safely trade sooner.

11.4.3 *On the Basis Of*

Recall from Chapter 2 that the Supreme Court has consistently held that Section
10(b) insider trading liability requires inter alia that one trade "on the basis of"
material nonpublic information.[30] But interpreting "on the basis of" literally to
require some causal connection between the information and the trading creates
difficulties for enforcement. It is easy for individuals charged with Section 10(b)
insider trading to fabricate alternate, innocent explanations for their trading while in

---

[29] See J. Mark Ramseyer, "Insider Trading Regulation in Japan," in Stephen Bainbridge (ed.),
Research Handbook on Insider Trading (Northampton, MA: Edward Elgar Publishing, Inc.,
2013): 357.
[30] See, e.g., *United States v. O'Hagan*, 521 U.S. 642, 652–53 (1997).

possession of material nonpublic information. For example, they might claim that they did not trade on the basis of the material nonpublic information but rather to diversify their portfolio holdings, or to pay for their child's college tuition, or to make a down payment on a new home. Concerned that such explanations are easy to fabricate but difficult to disprove, the SEC and prosecutors began taking the position that the "on the basis of" element could be satisfied by trading while in knowing possession of material nonpublic information. When federal courts started rejecting the knowing possession test as exceeding the authority of Section 10(b), the SEC rushed to adopt Rule 10b5–1(b), which expressly defines trading "on the basis of" inside information as trading while "aware" of material nonpublic information.[31]

Chapter 3 raised concerns that Rule 10b5–1(b)'s definition of trading "on the basis of" material nonpublic information as trading while "aware" of such information risks chilling legitimate trading by insiders who would like to make an innocent trade but who, because of their position at the firm, can rarely if ever be certain that they are not "aware" of material nonpublic information. The term "on the basis of" just means "a cause of" or "providing the foundation for." It therefore defies everyday use to suggest that one trades "on the basis of" material nonpublic information when one's sole motivation for selling shares is, say, to pay for an emergency heart surgery. Any such interpretation is a perversion of the English language and therefore raises notice concerns. But more importantly, even if the awareness test currently employed by the SEC were expressly avowed by the Supreme Court as an element of Section 10(b) insider trading liability, it would still be unjust to impose criminal liability for such conduct because it is not economically harmful or morally wrongful. An issuer or other source is simply not wrongfully deprived of the exclusive use of its material nonpublic information if there is no trading on the basis of that information. In such a circumstance, the material nonpublic information had nothing to do with the trade – and the trading itself was completely innocent.

The law should therefore make it clear that civil and criminal liability for trading on the basis of material nonpublic information requires that the material nonpublic information must have a "but-for" causal relationship to that trading. Such a requirement would not undermine the task of prosecutors. After all, as noted in Chapter 3, part of the justification for the knowing possession test in the first place was the SEC's claim that knowing possession of material nonpublic information while trading itself offers significant circumstantial evidence of a causal connection between the information and the trading. Such circumstantial evidence will still be placed before the fact finder, and jurors are free to dismiss alternative explanations for the trading as mere pretexts or fabrications. This is precisely the juror's task. What possible justification could there be for forcing a juror to convict an insider for trading that the juror is convinced had nothing to do with the possession of

---

[31] 17 C.F.R. § 240.10b5–1(b) (2016).

material nonpublic information? Proof of mens rea is a standard requirement in criminal law, and there is no good reason for making insider trading an exception to its application.

11.4.4 *Violations of Trust and Confidence*

Most of the means of wrongful acquisition and use identified in the theory of liability proposed here (e.g., theft, bribery, espionage, computer hacking, and conversion) have relatively clear common law or statutory definitions – and this clarity is not expected to be diminished by adding them to the definition of insider trading. Only information whose use involves fraudulent deception requires explication here, and this only because the common law of fraud in the context of insider trading has been so muddled by the incoherent approaches of the courts and SEC in recent decades.

By including fraudulent deception as one of the forms of wrongful use of material nonpublic information that could incur liability under the reform outlined here, it is expected that much of the current common law understanding of when a duty to disclose or abstain would arise (as summarized in Chapter 2) will be preserved. Nevertheless, as explained in Chapter 3, there are some ambiguities that should be addressed expressly by statute or rule.

First, it should be expressly stated by statute or rule that the duty to disclose or abstain (licensing the attribution of fraud by omission) arises only for those who owe the owner of the information (the issuer, the shareholder, or some other source) a "*fiduciary or similar* duty of trust *and* confidence." This is the sensible language used by the Supreme Court to identify the relationship that will give rise to the duty to disclose in the context of insider trading. As noted in Chapter 2, this language was, however, disregarded by SEC Rule 10b5–2, which instead defines the requisite relationship as simply one of "trust or confidence." Rule 10b5–2 dropped the "fiduciary or similar" language that the Second Circuit had previously identified as necessary to keep the relation from losing "method and predictability."[32] It also changed the conjunctive "and" to the disjunctive "or" in "trust *or* confidence," which opened the door to insider trading liability for mere breaches of confidence – effectively severing the law from its roots in fraud (see Chapter 3). The law should be reformed to expressly foreclose these expansive interpretations.

Second, as explained in Chapter 3, there has been much uncertainty over the need for proof of a personal benefit to the tipper in the context of tipper-tippee liability for insider trading since the Second Circuit's 2014 decision in *Newman*. It was noted previously that some recently proposed legislation would expressly remove the personal benefit test as an element of tipper-tippee liability. Eliminating the personal benefit test under the fraudulent nondisclosure theory would, however,

---

[32] United States v. Chestman, 947 F.2d 551, 567 (1991).

sever the liability from its moral justification. As the Supreme Court has consistently maintained, if there is no personal benefit to the tipper, then there is no breach of fiduciary or similar duty of trust and confidence. The controversy should instead be settled by codifying the definition of "personal benefit" found in *Dirks* and recently affirmed in *Salman*. It should be made explicit that tipper-tippee liability in cases where material nonpublic information is acquired by fraudulent deception requires objective proof of a personal benefit to the tipper.[33] Such proof may be obvious and direct (such as an exchange of cash for information), or it may be more subtle and indirect (such as proof of a reputational benefit, or sharing with a family member or friend whose relationship with the insider or misappropriator is so close that the tip resembles trading by the tipper and a subsequent gift). However worded, the codification should make it clear that the personal benefit test requires proof of an objective benefit to the tipper, and not (as the SEC and prosecutors have at times suggested) mere proof of a gift of information for a non-corporate purpose. Of course, under the reform program proposed here, fraudulent deception is only one of several modes of wrongful use that might serve as a predicate for insider trading liability. One need not prove a personal benefit if, say, theft or computer hacking is the means of acquiring material nonpublic information – only if fraudulent nondisclosure provides the basis for the liability.

Third, it was also noted in Chapter 3 that the personal benefit test under the current fraud model has been plagued by ambiguity concerning the "daisy-chain" problem. Again, the law in the United States is clear that tipper liability requires a personal benefit to the original tipper, but it has yet to settle the question of whether the original tipper must also personally benefit from every subsequent tip in the daisy chain to maintain derivative liability for remote tippees. Settling this problem has recently become more important as prosecutors focus increasingly on more remote tipper-tippee relationships. Since the theory of liability that informs the outline for reform here is wrongful trading that denies the material nonpublic information's rightful owner its exclusive use, it makes sense to require only proof of personal benefit to the original tipper from the original tip. The tainted source is enough to support derivative liability for downstream tippers and tippees who profit from the original wrongdoing and compound its harmful effects – assuming they share the requisite mental state, which is the subject of the next section.

11.4.5 *Mental State*

The recognition that greater certainty in the law will improve its justice, coherence, and rationality is a central theme of the reform program proposed in this chapter. The law of insider trading in the United States is fraught with ambiguity on the question of the mental state required for liability. As explained in Chapter 3, absent

---

[33] Dirks v. S.E.C., 463 U.S. 646, 664 (1983).

clear statutory guidance, courts, regulators, and scholars have applied a myriad of mental state requirements to insider trading liability: "knows or should know," "intentional," "willful," "willful blindness," "conscious avoidance," "recklessness," "general understanding," etc. And to make matters worse, courts have sometimes applied different mental state requirements to different elements of insider trading. Any reform to the law should offer a clear statutory definition of the requisite mental state.

Insider trading liability should require proof of knowledge for each element. Following the Model Penal Code, the statute should define "knowing" conduct for purposes of insider trading liability as being "aware" of the relevant "nature" or "attendant circumstances" of one's actions, or being "practically certain" of the result of one's actions.[34] The definition should also recognize along with the Model Penal Code and the US Supreme Court that "willfully blind" conduct is equivalent to knowing conduct. To be willfully blind, one must (1) "subjectively believe that there is a high probability that a fact exists" and (2) "take deliberate actions to avoid learning of the fact."[35] Mere reckless conduct (where one "merely knows of a substantial and unjustified risk of ... wrongdoing") or negligent conduct (where one "should have known of a similar risk but, in fact, did not") should not be sufficient to satisfy any element of criminal liability for insider trading.[36]

The knowledge requirement is enough to ensure that even remote tippers and tippees are complicit in wrongdoing because they know the material nonpublic information they are passing along or trading upon was wrongfully acquired and therefore their conduct wrongfully deprives the rightful owners of their exclusive use. This will be true whether the information was acquired as the result of a theft, a computer hack, or a breach of fiduciary duty. Knowledge that goods are stolen provides the moral warrant for holding a fencer liable, and similarly knowledge that information was wrongfully acquired provides the warrant to hold the remote tipper and tippee liable.

In addition to capturing only morally culpable traders, as noted in Chapter 3, clearly articulating the knowledge standard should remedy the chilling effect current ambiguity over the requisite mental state requirement has had on market professionals who regularly receive market information that is several levels removed from its original source. In some cases, the type and specificity of information alone may be enough to put one on notice of the *risk* that the original source of the information was a wrongdoer. Though knowledge of such risk would not (without affirmative steps to avoid knowing more) satisfy the willful blindness test recommended here, it may satisfy the test for recklessness. Uncertainty as to the applicable mental state under the current regime has almost certainly had a chilling effect on

---

[34] Model Penal Code § 2.02(2)(a)-(d).
[35] Global-Tech Appliances, Inc. v. SEB S.A., 563 U.S. 754, 769 (2011).
[36] Ibid. at 770.

otherwise legitimate trading subject to such "risks." Adopting the knowledge requirement remedies this concern entirely, but leaves exposed to liability those who
actively take steps to avoid learning that information was wrongfully acquired.

11.5 CORPORATE CRIMINAL LIABILITY

A clear statutory constraint should be placed on the scope of derivative corporate
criminal liability for insider trading. Chapter 4 explained that derivative corporate
criminal liability under the current regime is irrational and absurdly overbroad in
that it threatens the corporate victim of insider trading (the person from whom the
material nonpublic information is wrongfully acquired) with criminal liability for
the crime perpetrated against it. To avoid this absurdity, derivative criminal liability
for insider trading under the wrongful use regime proposed here must be expressly
limited. One approach would be to modify the language first proposed in the
2015 Himes bill (noted previously) as follows:

> No person shall be liable under this section solely by reason of the fact that such
> person controls or employs a person who has violated this section, if such control-
> ling person or employer did not participate in, profit from, or directly or indirectly
> induce the acts constituting the violation of this section. *And under no circum-
> stances may derivative liability under this section be imposed upon a controlling
> person or employer who is the owner of the material nonpublic information that was
> traded upon.*

Though the first sentence should be sufficient to avoid the absurdity of holding the
corporate victim liable for the crime, the lived experience of corporate criminal
liability under the *New York Central & H.R.R. Co. v. United States* test (as summarized in Chapter 4) suggests that the second sentence is necessary to eliminate
the risk of creative interpretation by enterprising regulators and prosecutors to gain
unfair leverage over employers.[37] This language would protect ABC Corporation
(and by extension its shareholders) from liability for the issuer-proscribed insider
trading of its employees in ABC shares. It would also protect XYZ Newspaper from
the misappropriation trading of one of its reporters who trades ahead of a forthcoming story. But the proposed language would leave hedge funds and other finance
companies exposed to derivative corporate criminal liability for the trading of their
employees based on information that is wrongfully acquired from a third party and
traded upon for the mutual benefit of the traders and their employers.

11.6 LOOSE ENDS AND LINGERING QUESTIONS

Taking stock, this chapter has recommended a number of reforms to the current
insider trading enforcement regime in the United States. These reforms include

---

[37] *New York Central & H.R.R. Co. v. United States*, 212 U.S. 481 (1909).

(1) codifying and expanding the scope of liability from the current fraud-based regime to a broader wrongful use model; (2) expressly codifying a safe harbor for issuer-licensed insider trading, so long as it is done pursuant to trading plans that meet certain requirements; (3) codifying clear definitions of the principal elements of the crime of insider trading; and (4) codifying clear limits on the scope of derivative insider trading liability to protect victim firms from being held liable for the insider trading crimes perpetrated against them. It has been argued that these reforms would dramatically improve the current regime in terms of justice, efficiency, coherence, and rationality. There are, of course, a number of lingering questions, loose ends, and potential objections raised by these proposed reforms. Some of these are addressed in the remaining sections.

11.6.1 Federal Enforcement

This book has found much to criticize in the current federal insider trading enforcement regime in the United States. In light of these criticisms, it is fair to ask whether federal enforcement of insider trading is necessary at all. Where enforcement is needed, perhaps it could be left to individual firms or to state-law enforcement. Professor Stephen Bainbridge and others have, however, offered a number of compelling reasons why federal enforcement of insider trading remains necessary. First, individual firms could never hope to identify insider trading over anonymous exchanges without the police powers of the government.[38] Second, the SEC has a comparative advantage over individual firms and even state-law enforcement in detecting insider trading violations through its national computer monitoring of stock transactions, and from "reporting of unusual activity by self-regulatory organizations and/or market professionals."[39] Third, securities markets are now international. Extraterritorial investigations and enforcement actions pertaining to cross-border insider trading violations will be most effective when ordered at the federal level.[40] Thus, while the US insider trading regime should be reformed pursuant to the guidelines outlined in this chapter, its enforcement should continue to be led by the federal government.

11.6.2 Civil Liability

The weight of the evidence presented in the preceding chapters supports the view that vagueness and incoherence in the current insider trading regime warrant reform in both the criminal and civil contexts. And for this reason the recommended approach is to maximize notice and certainty by applying the previously described

---

[38] Bainbridge, *Insider Trading Law and Policy*, 206.
[39] Ibid.
[40] Ibid. at 207.

reforms uniformly to criminal and civil liability. The aforementioned statutory reforms should therefore be applied more or less uniformly to SEC enforcement actions, private rights of action, and criminal actions.

An anticipated objection to this approach is that these reforms will weaken the SEC's enforcement powers and undermine the deterrent effects of civil actions upon illicit insider trading. For, despite the fact that switching to the proposed wrongful use regime would expand the scope of insider trading liability, the codification of the elements with clear definitions (including proof of use and knowledge) will otherwise make insider trading actions more difficult for the SEC and private citizens to prove. Indeed, it was noted in previous chapters that the SEC and others have consistently resisted efforts to bring greater clarity to the law of insider trading out of the somewhat paradoxical concern that greater clarity in the law will decrease flexibility in its enforcement. This book has, however, argued that the uncertainty such flexibility in enforcement creates for issuers and market participants acting in good faith (the intended beneficiaries of our securities regulations) risks real economic harm and injustice that far outweigh the potential benefits of deterring potential bad actors through ease of enforcement. Moreover, the increased flexibility for issuers to define the class of potentially liable insider traders (through discretion in executing issuer-licensed trading plans) and to define the elements of liability (such as what counts as "material" and "nonpublic") will remove much of the regulatory burden of civil insider trading enforcement from the SEC and place it on the issuers themselves.

Nevertheless, SEC enforcement and private rights of action have a crucial role to play in protecting market participants from wrongful trading based on material nonpublic information, particularly in light of private parties' limited means of identifying when wrongful trading has occurred. And legislators may become convinced that greater flexibility for regulators is needed for civil actions to fulfill their role in the insider trading enforcement ecosystem. If so, then a compromise regime may be effected whereby criminal liability and civil liability are defined separately. To maximize clarity, this bifurcated regime should, of course, share the same wrongful use theory of liability, but it may demand a lesser threshold of proof for certain of the elements. For example, civil liability may require only possession of material nonpublic information while trading (by contrast to the criminal requirement of a causal connection between the information and the trade). Or civil liability might require only a reckless or negligent mental state to some elements (by contrast to the requirement of knowledge for criminal liability).[41] At a minimum,

---

[41] Professor Miriam Baer has suggested that a balance between the need for certainty in the law of insider trading and the need for flexibility in enforcement could be achieved by codifying a tiered approach to criminal liability. Under this approach, the crime of insider trading might be broken into three tiers corresponding to the trader's culpability. For example, the crime of Aggravated Insider Trading might be reserved for "serial violators or ringleaders ... such as Raj Rajaratnam," while a misdemeanor of Reckless Trading "could attach to those remote traders

any differences between criminal and civil liability should be codified, and every effort should be made to ensure that the language of the criminal and civil statutes conforms in all other respects to maximize certainty in the law.

11.6.3 *Effect on Existing Statutes, Rules, and Precedents*

It remains to address the question of how the guidelines for reform outlined in this chapter would affect existing statutes, rules, and precedents. It was noted in Chapter 2 that Section 16 is the only original provision of the Securities Exchange Act that expressly addresses insider trading. It was also explained that Section 16 is extremely limited in scope. Its application is limited to only high-level "directors," "officers," and "principal stockholders" as defined by the statute.[42] The statute imposes reporting and trading requirements on these insiders. Section 16(a) requires that these insiders report any holdings or transactions in their company's shares, and Section 16(b) precludes these insiders from enjoying any short-swing profits from trading in their firm's shares, requiring that any profits from a purchase and sale (or sale and purchase) of the firm's shares that occurs within a period of less than six months inure to and are recoverable by the issuer regardless of whether the trading was based on material nonpublic information. Finally, Section 16(c) precludes the insiders defined by the statute from selling the firm's shares short.

Section 16 is admirable for its clarity, and it would continue to play a useful role in checking issuer-proscribed insider trading by high-level insiders in firms that do not opt to implement an issuer-licensed trading plan policy. The role of Section 16(b)–(c)'s trading restrictions would, however, become more complex when applied to firms that adopt issuer-licensed trading plan policies. In such firms, an insider wishing to trade in the firm's shares must first file a trading plan that has been approved pursuant to the firm's policy. If the firm approves the trade in the sound exercise of business judgment (even if it is a short trade), then where is the harm or wrong?[43] Of course, even firms that adopt issuer-licensed trading plans may wish to recognize the Section 16(b)–(c) trading restrictions as a pre-commitment strategy, guarding against the potential moral hazard that high-level insiders will be

---

who ignored a substantial and unjustifiable risk" that they were trading on wrongfully acquired material nonpublic information. Miriam Baer, "Insider Trading's Legality Problem," *Yale Law Journal Forum* 127 (2017): 129. While such a codified regime would be an improvement over the current common law regime, for reasons already stated, I am convinced that even misdemeanor criminal liability for insider trading should not be predicated upon a reckless or negligent mental state. I agree with Professor Baer that the innovation of a tiered system may be workable in the criminal context, but at least as far as mental state is concerned, there should be only two tiers – criminal (requiring knowledge) and civil (which may require only recklessness or negligence).

[42] 15 U.S.C. § 78p.
[43] Admittedly, it is hard to imagine a circumstance in which sound business judgment might warrant licensing a trading plan that shorts the firm's shares.

tempted to abuse trading plans for self-serving purposes. Thus, Section 16(b)–(c) should remain on the books as a default restriction that firms adopting issuer-licensed trading plan policies may choose to opt out of with the appropriate ex ante disclosures.

As explained in Chapter 2, Exchange Act Rule 14e-3 was adopted pursuant to Exchange Act Section 14(e) to preclude all trading based on material nonpublic information in the context of tender offers.[44] The rule proscribes any trading based on "material information that relates to a tender offer by another person which information he knows or has reason to know is nonpublic and was acquired, directly or indirectly, from that person or the issuer of the securities" being targeted by the offer.[45] As with Section 16, Rule 14e-3 may continue to play a useful (though perhaps redundant) role under the reformed insider trading enforcement regime proposed here. Assuming that it is modified to incorporate definitions of "material" and "nonpublic" that comply with the guidelines proposed in this chapter, Rule 14e-3 may continue to be an effective prophylactic against wrongful trading in the context of tender offers. That said, trading on material nonpublic information concerning tender offers would not be wrongful if licensed by the firms involved. Consequently, it would not offend the reform guidelines proposed here to retain Rule 14e-3 tender offer trading restrictions as a default rule that firms who have adopted issuer-licensed trading plan policies have the option of publicly opting out of.[46]

Of course, Exchange Act Section 10(b)'s application to the criminal and civil enforcement of insider trading would be entirely superseded by the codification of the reforms proposed here. Since Section 10(b) makes no express reference to insider trading, this will not require significant revision to the statute itself. It would be enough to simply amend Section 10 to expressly state something like, "This section shall not apply to insider trading, the definition and requirements pertaining to which are addressed elsewhere in this title." Other statutory provisions historically enlisted in insider trading enforcement actions, such as the general fraud provision of the Sarbanes-Oxley Act of 2002[47] and Securities Act Section 17(a),[48] should also be amended with similar language.

With Section 10(b) superseded, all SEC rulemaking pertaining to insider trading pursuant to that section (specifically SEC Rules 10b5–1 and 10b5–2) would also be invalidated. Of course, the SEC should retain rulemaking authority pursuant to the newly codified insider trading laws, but the more explicit language recommended in

---

[44] 17 C.F.R. 240.14e–3.

[45] Tender Offers, Exchange Act Release No. 17,120 (Sept. 4, 1980), 1980 WL 20869 at *1.

[46] Professors Ian Ayres and Stephen Choi similarly suggested that Rule 14e-3 might be retained as a default rule that may be opted out of by parties to a tender offer in a liberalized insider trading regime that permits issuer-licensed insider trading. See Ian Ayres and Stephen Choi, "Internalizing Outsider Trading," *Michigan Law Review* 101 (2002): 356.

[47] 18 U.S.C. § 1348.

[48] 15 U.S.C. § 77q(a).

the guidelines for reform outlined in this chapter will provide clearer boundaries to that authority than have heretofore existed.

What about Regulation FD? Recall from Chapters 2 and 3 that Regulation FD requires that whenever an issuer (or certain defined persons acting on its behalf) discloses material nonpublic information concerning the firm or its shares to market professionals or those who are likely to trade the firm's shares, it must simultaneously disclose that information to the investing public.[49] To begin, the SEC has made it clear from its adoption that Regulation FD is not an insider trading rule; it is an issuer disclosure requirement adopted pursuant to Sections 13(a) and 15(d) of the Exchange Act, and Section 30 of the Investment Company Act of 1940.[50] Indeed, as explained in Chapter 3, the SEC took great pains in the language of the rule to expressly preclude the violation of Regulation FD from serving as a predicate for insider trading liability. For example, Rule 101(c) of Regulation FD expressly excludes tipping "in breach of a duty of trust or confidence to the issuer" from the regulation's coverage.[51] Moreover, Rule 102 provides that no "failure to make a public disclosure required solely by [Regulation FD] shall be deemed to be a violation of Rule 10b–5."[52] That said, it is not expected that Regulation FD would come into conflict with the reforms proposed in this chapter, except on very rare occasions. The most obvious tension would come from the safe harbor for issuer-licensed trading plans. But even there, most such trading plans will no doubt be issued to insiders, so Regulation FD (which regulates only external disclosures by issuers) would not be impacted by these plans. On occasion, issuers may choose to issue trading plans to outsiders (which would be permitted by the proposed safe harbor so long as the appropriate ex ante and ex post disclosures are made).[53] This tension could be addressed quite easily by either expressly providing that the issuer-licensed trading plan safe harbor applies to liability for Regulation FD violations, or amending Regulation FD itself to recognize the safe harbor.

Finally, there remains the question of whether and to what extent prior judicial precedent should continue to apply to an insider trading regime that is reformed pursuant to the guidelines proposed in this chapter. As with any body of the common law that is superseded by statute, the courts should look to prior insider trading precedent as providing persuasive, but not dispositive, authority in the

---

[49] 17 C.F.R. § 243.100 (2011).

[50] In its issuing release, the SEC expressly stated that Regulation FD "is not an antifraud rule," and it does not create any new duties under Section 10(b) or any of the other "antifraud provisions of the federal securities laws or in private rights of action." Selective Disclosure and Insider Trading: Final Rule, 65 Fed. Reg. 51,716 (Aug. 24, 2000).

[51] 17 C.F.R. § 243.101(c) (2011).

[52] 17 C.F.R. § 243.102 (2011).

[53] Recall from Chapter 2 that one of the principal justifications advanced by Justice Powell in defense of the personal benefit test in *Dirks* was that it would preserve a space for legitimate selective disclosures to further the issuer's interests and speed information to the market. See *Dirks*, 463 U.S. at 658 (expressing concern that too broad a restriction on selective disclosure could inhibit analysts in their useful role of "ferret[ing] out and analyz[ing] information"). The safe harbor for issuer-licensed insider trading would restore this space.

interpretation of the new statute. Where, for example, fraud forms the basis of the wrongful use of material nonpublic information by a trader under the new statute, it is expected that the courts will continue to look to the past fifty years of insider trading case law for guidance where consistent with the spirit and language of the new statute. At the same time, the promulgation of a superseding statute will also free the courts of the shackles of stare decisis, offering the welcome opportunity to sweep aside some of the mangled logic of the past.

*****

The guidelines for reform proposed in this chapter do not address every concern raised in Part I of this book, nor do they anticipate every conceivable ripple effect their adoption might have upon the broader legal landscape. This is intentional. Too detailed a proposal is apt to lose focus and punch; it would risk making the perfect the enemy of the good. Moreover, though it is recommended that the proposed changes be adopted as one comprehensive statutory reform package, adopting any one of the proposed reforms, even piecemeal, would improve the current system in terms of justice and rationality.

Some may object to the guidelines for reform proposed here for no other reason than that, after fifty years of insider trading enforcement under the current regime, it would simply be too costly for regulators and market participants to change course now. There is, however, little force to this path-dependence argument. It is expected that the proposed reforms would be adopted as statutory amendments to the Securities Exchange Act, and the SEC would therefore retain authority for the civil enforcement of insider trading. Adding theft, conversion, computer hacking, and espionage to fraud as wrongful bases for insider trading liability would not require significant retrofitting within the SEC or compliance departments. Indeed, as explained in Part I, the SEC has repeatedly attempted to expand the scope of insider trading liability through the common law and rulemaking to incorporate just such conduct. In this respect, the proposed reform would improve certainty for all parties by removing a source of long-standing frustration for the SEC. Most of the other proposed reforms would simply bring improved statutory clarity to currently recognized elements of insider trading liability.

Of course, it is anticipated that the main obstacle to complete implementation of the reforms proposed in this chapter will be the political and cultural unpalatability of liberalizing the regime to permit issuer-licensed insider trading. This obstacle, though real, is not insurmountable. Part II of this book has demonstrated that such resistance results from a false consciousness that has been perpetuated by the fact that the moral and economic bases for our insider trading enforcement regime are typically assumed and rarely justified. This is an error that can and must be corrected through open and honest public discourse. The aim of this book has been to lay the historical, comparative, and theoretical foundations for such discussion.

Index